The Making of a Lynching Culture

The Making
of a Lynching Culture

Violence and Vigilantism
in Central Texas, 1836–1916

WILLIAM D. CARRIGAN

University of Illinois Press
URBANA AND CHICAGO

First Illinois paperback, 2006
© 2004 by the Board of Trustees
of the University of Illinois
All rights reserved
Manufactured in the United States of America
1 2 3 4 5 C P 5 4 3 2 1

∞ This book is printed on acid-free paper.

The Library of Congress cataloged the cloth edition
as follows:
Carrigan, William D., 1970–
The making of a lynching culture : violence and vigilantism
in central Texas, 1836–1916 / William D. Carrigan.
p.   cm.
Includes bibliographical references (p.) and index.
ISBN 0-252-02951-8 (cloth: alk. paper)
1. Mobs—Texas—History—19th century. 2. Mobs—Texas—
History—20th century. 3. Vigilance committees—Texas—History—
19th century. 4. Vigilance committees—Texas—History—
20th century. 5. Lynching—Texas—History—19th century.
6. Lynching—Texas—History—20th century.
I. Title.
HV6481.T4C37   2004
303.6'2—dc22   2004007217

PAPERBACK ISBN 978-0-252-07430-1

Lynching becomes chronic and contagious. Boys grow to manhood with the idea, ingrained in them that lynch law is right and proper, and worthy of applause, and they follow the example set them by their fathers.

—J. N. Bennett
    Editor, *Waco Weekly News*
    24 February 1893

Contents

Acknowledgments   *ix*

Introduction   *1*

1. "Texas Shall Be . . . Americanized": Mob Violence in the Conquest
   of Mexican Texas   *17*

2. "Necessity Knows No Law": Mob Violence in the Conquest
   of Central Texas's Native Americans   *31*

3. "Slavery with a Will": Slave Resistance and the Origins
   of the Panic of 1860   *48*

4. "Hung Sure as Hell": White-on-White Mob Violence in Central
   Texas   *81*

5. "No Justice in It": Racial Violence and Reconstruction   *112*

6. "A New Crime": The Changing Character of Mob Violence
   in the Late Nineteenth Century   *132*

7. "A Damnable Outrage": Mob Violence in Twentieth-Century
   Central Texas   *162*

Epilogue   *189*

Notes   *209*

Appendix A: Victims of Mob Violence in Central Texas,
1860–1922   *275*

Appendix B: Unconfirmed Cases of Mob Violence
in Central Texas, 1835–1922   *289*

Appendix C: Terms, Sources, and Methods   *295*

Index   *301*

Acknowledgments

During the decade that I spent researching and writing this book I benefited greatly from the help of others. Archivists and librarians graciously helped me access the scattered primary sources upon which this study is erected, and I thank the staffs of the Texas Collection at Baylor University, the McLennan County Archives in Waco, the Center for American History at the University of Texas at Austin, the Texas State Library and Archives in Austin, the Special Collections of Tuskegee University, the Manuscript Division of the Library of Congress, National Archives 1, in Washington, D.C., the Bancroft Library at the University of California, the Huntington Library in San Marino, California, the South Caroliniana Library of the University of South Carolina, the Special Collections of the University of Mississippi, the Southern Historical Collection at the University of North Carolina, the Woodruff Library Archives of Emory University, and the Special Collections Library of Duke University.

Several individual archivists and librarians have gone far beyond the bounds of professional courtesy in helping with this project: Ellen Brown, Kent Keeth, Kathleen Schwartz, and Donaly E. Brice. The Inter-Library Loan Offices of Emory University and Rowan University have been essential for the completion of this book. I am particularly grateful to Cynthia Mullens and Joyce McCaughey, who, with patience and understanding, were instrumental in helping me acquire sources. I have also enjoyed the help of a wonderful research assistant. Janice Barrow, now a graduate of Rowan University and a Ph.D. student at the University of Delaware, helped me go through reel upon reel of central Texas court records, proofread and checked earlier versions of the manuscript, entered data into the computer, and generally proved invaluable.

Richard Wentworth, Laurie Matheson, and Mary Giles at the University of Illinois Press have been supportive and encouraging from the very beginning of this project. Their comments and those of anonymous readers greatly strengthened this work.

I have received generous financial support, first as a graduate student and now as an assistant professor, and Rowan University has awarded me with alternate load course reductions to complete research since 1999. I have also received financial support from the Texas State Historical Association, the University of Texas at Austin, the Huntington Library, and the Clements Center for Southwest Studies at Southern Methodist University. James Allen graciously agreed to reproduce one of the images from his collection of lynching photographs at no cost. His bravery in forcing America to gaze upon its violent past has been an inspiration to me.

Margery Ganz and Jim Gillam, colleagues from when I taught at Spelman College, provided constant support and encouragement, and the wonderful and engaging students at Spelman influenced my thinking on race and gender in profound ways. Colleagues and the undergraduates at Rowan University have been equally important. I am especially grateful to Edward Wang, chair of the Department of History, and Denise Williams, the department's administrative assistant, for support and guidance.

Many people have read all or part of this book in manuscript form. The comments of two readers for the University of Illinois Press greatly improved the text, and I thank them. I also thank the following individuals who made valuable comments about the project: Alexander Auerbach, Edward Ayers, Michael Bellesiles, Michael Belknap, Leslie Brown, W. Fitzhugh Brundage, Derek Buckaloo, David Carter, Randolph B. Campbell, Thomas Charlton, Barry Crouch, Chris Curtis, Leroy Davis, Matthew Davis, Bobby Donaldson, Crystal Feimster, Neil Foley, Elizabeth Fox-Genovese, Aaron Frith, Raymond Gavins, Eugene Genovese, Ronald J. Grele, Barry Hankins, Leslie Harris, James Heinzen, E. Brooks Holifield, Andrew Kaye, Charles H. Martin, Patrick Mbajekwe, Helen McLure, Gregg L. Michel, T. Michael Parrish, Matthew Payne, David Preston, Nicolas W. Proctor, Steve Reich, James Roark, Armstead Robinson, Hyman Rubin, Douglas Sackman, Rebecca Sharpless, Kris Shepard, Michael Simoncelli, James SoRelle, Michael Stark, James Tuten, Christopher Waldrep, Katherine Walters, and David Weber. Over a number of conversations, including one that roused him from bed early on a Saturday morning, Derek Buckaloo helped me with the title. I would like to thank Cary D. Wintz for notifying me of several errors in the cloth edition that have been corrected in this edition. Finally, no single scholar has helped me shape my thinking about race and violence more than Clive Webb of the University of Sussex, and I thank him for sharing his insights and advice in conversations too numerous to count.

One of the most rewarding aspects of studying Texas history has been the frequent need to return to the state where I grew up and where most of my family lives. My mother, father, grandmother, and brother have never ceased to support me on the many paths this project has taken me. I also thank the following men and women for graciously allowing me to interview them about race relations in central Texas: the Rev. James Howard Berry, Dillie B. Black, A. M. Booker, Kneeland H. Clemons, Mary Denkins, Marvin C. Griffin, Sedalia Harris, Rev. Eric Hooker, George and Cleo McGrue, Ida J. Scott, Willie Long Smith and Clemmie Holloway Long, Richard Stark, Lovie Taylor, Hayward Weaver, Curtis L. Wilburn, and Margaret Wilson.

More than any of those listed so far, three people are responsible for this book. George C. Wright, who taught my section of the introductory survey of American history, provoked me to change my major from mechanical engineering to history. Wright soon agreed to direct my senior thesis on race relations in central Texas, and then he convinced me to pursue history at the graduate level. He continues to be a font of advice. Dan T. Carter was a model dissertation adviser. He encouraged my interest in central Texas and this project from my arrival in Atlanta, even when I was not quite clear on what I wanted to do. He has continued as a mentor in the years since graduation and was particularly important in guiding me to the University of Illinois Press. And it is impossible to express my debt to my wife, Emily Blanck, who suggested that I join her in taking George Wright's class and has listened to me ramble on about the history of central Texas on more occasions than should be tolerated by any human being. She has always been my greatest supporter, and I do not know how I would have persevered though such a long process without her help and love. I hope to repay her in kind over the next fifty or so years.

In 2002, as this project entered its final stages, I witnessed the birth of our first child, a beautiful daughter named Julia Katherine. Julia has not only changed everything in my life but also increased my hope that the future will be a more tolerant and less violent place.

The Making of a Lynching Culture

Introduction

Until the burning of the Branch Davidian compound outside Waco on 19 April 1993, the most infamous day in the history of central Texas was 15 May 1916. That was the day an estimated crowd of fifteen thousand witnessed the lynching of an eighteen-year-old black farm worker named Jesse Washington. Washington was the chief suspect in the 8 May murder of Lucy Fryer, who had been killed in Robinson, a farming community outside Waco in McLennan County. Fearing mob violence, Sheriff Samuel Fleming first spirited Washington to the city of Hillsboro (approximately thirty miles to the north) and later to Dallas. There, Washington confessed to killing Lucy Fryer, and authorities hastily set the trial for 15 May in Waco. In court, prosecutors rested their case on the discovery of the murder weapon on the Fryer farm and Washington's confession. The defense made no effort on their client's behalf and asked Washington if he had anything to say to the jury. Just four minutes after the jury retired the foreman delivered the verdict of guilty and assessed a penalty of death by execution.[1]

As officials prepared to remove Washington, an unidentified white man shouted, "Get the Nigger," and members of the crowd seized and dragged Washington from the McLennan County Courthouse. He was beaten and stabbed as the mob proceeded to the bridge that spans the Brazos River. The crowd changed directions, however, when its leaders heard of a fire intended for burning Washington at city hall. Bricks and shovels continued to pelt Washington, and his body soon became covered in blood. Then one of his ears was cut off and he was castrated. As the fire grew, Washington tried unsuccessfully to get away. The mob threw a chain over a tree and pulled him off the ground. When Jesse Washington tried to grab the chain above his head, his fingers were severed, leaving him to slap at his noose. He was then lowered into the fire several times and then raised so the crowd, now numbering in the thousands, could see his remains. "A mighty shout rose in the air" each time.[2] Eventually, a man on horseback tied a rope to the body, pulled the corpse around City Hall Plaza, and paraded it through the main streets of Waco. It was finally dragged to the town of Robinson, put in a sack, and hung for public display in front of a blacksmith's shop.[3]

The lynching of Jesse Washington has become a defining moment in the history of racial violence in the United States. The shocking brutality of his murder—detailed in contemporary newspaper coverage and powerfully captured in photographs—has endured as a symbol of the era of segregation. Washington's long-drawn-out execution by a combination of stoning, cutting, dismemberment, hanging, and burning underscored the virulent racism behind mob law. His killers were not evenhanded dispensers of justice. They were violent, brutal sadists who took pleasure in torturing another human being. What is most compelling about the lynching of Jesse Washington, however, may not be the racial killing itself. Unfortunately, such murders have been a common occurrence in American history and persist even into the present. What draws a historian to Jesse Washington are the throngs who attended and then celebrated his death.

Jesse Washington's was not the only lynching that drew thousands of spectators, but no other lynch mob was so vividly photographed as that in Waco on 15 May. Fred Gildersleeve's images, later turned into a widely sold set of postcards, reveal that thousands watched and cheered the work of the mob leaders. The photographs show that Washington was not lynched under the cover of night or by a band of masked men. Rather, he died a few minutes before noon in the center of town, and the mob then posed for pictures with the corpse.[4] They wore no masks. Their identities were well known. A single investigator from the National Association for the Advancement of Colored People was able to come up with the individuals' names in mere days. Most central Texans, nevertheless, failed to call for punishment of the mob's leaders.

The size of the mob and the failure to arrest its leaders suggests that Jesse Washington's murder cannot be dismissed as the work of a few bloodthirsty men. The lynching deserves scholarly attention not because it was a singularly infamous event in the history of mob violence but because members of the mob, and residents of the community who tolerated the lynching, represent a deeply disturbing part of American culture in the early twentieth century. This study seeks to explain not how a fiendish mob lynched one man but how a culture of violence that nourished lynching formed and endured for so long among ordinary people.

*
* *

This book, then, is not a history of the lynching of Jesse Washington. It is not even a history of lynching in central Texas. It is a book about violence. It is a book that explores the question of why Americans in the nineteenth and early twentieth centuries tolerated such a high degree of extralegal violence in their communities. I will focus on events such as the murder of Jesse Washington, which participants labeled "lynchings," and on other informal and extralegal citizen actions that neither participants nor historians have traditionally identified as lynchings. My goal is not to catalog and enumerate every act of mob violence that occurred in central Texas (an impossible task) but to understand how and why central Texans came to embrace mob action as a legitimate means of maintaining social order. This study examines when, where, and how central Texans drew the line between maintaining order through legal means and violently securing justice through extralegal methods.

My intention is to contribute to the literature on lynching and mob violence in the United States in two ways. First, I will employ a new approach to study of the topic. Most work in the field falls into two groups: the case study of a single episode and the statewide survey. By contrast, I will discuss a region within a state—central Texas—in order to be able to research local sources deeply while exploring extralegal violence over time. Other monographs on lynching tend to concentrate on the period between 1880 and 1930. By contrast, this study traces mob violence over eight decades, beginning with the independence of Texas in 1836 and continuing until the lynching of Jesse Washington in 1916. Thus, I will explore not only many of the traditional explanations of lynching—the roles of the frontier and local and state officials, economic tension, political conflict, and black resistance—but also acts of violence that many studies of lynching ignore, particularly citizen violence against Native Americans and vigilante executions of Anglo-Americans.

My second purpose is to focus on an underappreciated explanation for the persistence and power of mob violence in American history: historical memory. Although memory is not the only cause of mob violence in the region, the connective tissue that linked and shaped central Texas's violence was the region's historical memory of vigilantism, lynching, and murder.

Jesse Washington's charred corpse, Waco, Texas, 15 May 1916.

(LC-USZ62–35740 in Library of Congress, Prints and Photographs Divison, Visual Materials from the NAACP Records)

Below: The crowd's reaction to the event.

(Photo by Gildersleeve; LC-USZ62–38917 in Library of Congress, Prints and Photographs Division, Visual Materials from the NAACP Records)

As many as fifteen thousand witnessed Washington's lynching.

(LC-USZ62–36635 in Library of Congress, Prints and Photographs Division,
Visual Materials from the NAACP Records)

Below: Spectators watch as a chain or rope is secured in
preparation for the lynching.

(LC-USZ62–102807 in Library of Congress, Prints and Photographs Division,
Visual Materials from the NAACP Records)

In shaping the memories of those who committed certain acts of violence as community heroes and defenders of justice, central Texans created, justified, and long preserved a robust culture of violence.

Before proceeding to a discussion of how this book supports these claims, some key terms and decisions need to be defined and explained. Central Texas, like any discrete community, is not a mirror of America. There are, however, good reasons for a case study of violence in the region. Central Texas, as defined by historical geographer D. W. Meinig, extends south of the present-day city of Dallas, then to a southwestern corner at San Antonio, and to a southeastern corner in Houston. Its western border follows along the line where the Texas prairies meet the Great Plains, and the eastern border corresponds roughly to the Trinity River. This study concentrates on the heart of this region, the area that begins with the Falls of the Brazos and stretches northward along the river's banks to the beginning of the Texas Plains. Although county boundaries did not exist in central Texas in 1836, the region roughly corresponds to the seven present-day counties of Bell, Bosque, Coryell, Falls, Hill, Limestone, and McLennan.[5]

The region, sometimes referred to as the Upper Brazos River valley, was the farthest place west that cotton agriculture was profitable before the Civil War. Central Texas can thus be said to lie on the edge of the South and the brim of the West. This study attempts to bridge southern and western history—two fields that have concentrated most extensively on the history of violence in American life. Central Texas lends itself to such cross-field comparisons not only because it lies geographically on the border between South and West but also because it played host during the nineteenth and early twentieth centuries to a complicated struggle for power between a diversity of historical actors not often found in the same locale. In particular, the region found itself contested by a slaveholding and mercantile elite, small landholders, poor farmers, African Americans, Native Americans, and Mexicans. Many people came together in the cultural borderlands of central Texas. It is unfortunate but hardly surprising that they did not always come in peace.[6]

The types of struggles that emerged—bloody battles against local Indians, imperial struggles with other nations for political sovereignty, periods of outlaw activity, episodes of vicious labor strife, and acts of racial violence—did not differ from the range of conflicts found in most other American communities at one time or another. Indeed, central Texas is an important laboratory for studying violence precisely because it does not differ from many other regions in the United States.

At the same time, however, the region offers unique advantages for historical investigation. The diverse forms of conflict that have punctuated

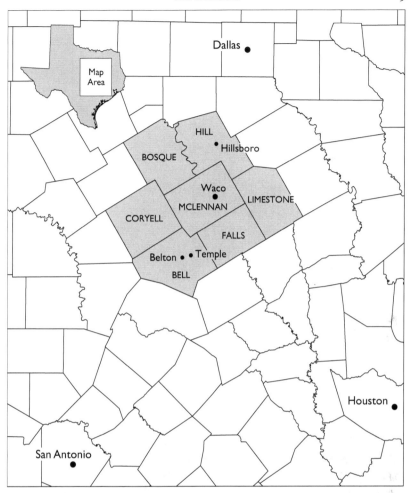

Counties and Principal Towns in Central Texas

American history occurred in central Texas over a relatively short period. The racial and social conflict that stretched over centuries in places like Virginia was collapsed into eight decades in central Texas. Between 1836 and 1916 the region weathered violence and conflict along a hyper-accelerated timeline.

Waco, the most important city in central Texas, receives significant attention in the pages that follow. Understanding even the events of 15 May 1916, however, requires that the scope of inquiry be broadened beyond Waco to include regional and national contexts. Many members of the mob that killed Jesse Washington hailed not from Waco but from a nearby farming commu-

nity. In justifying their actions the mob embraced and molded doctrines of racial supremacy that flourished throughout the American South and the United
States.

Throughout this work I will use several terms to refer to the region's extralegal violence. Central Texans themselves never agreed upon a single word
to describe their region's community-sanctioned violence. They referred to
those who committed acts of mob violence as vigilantes, outlaws, whitecappers, and lynchers. They used phrases such as "men taking the law into their
own hands" or "men were a law onto themselves." Some central Texans used
even more colorful and creative phrases. One pioneer described hanged men
as having been "ventilated."[7] Another central Texas resident described the
extralegal execution of a "hoss" or "critter" thief as an act of "naturaliza-
tion." The longtime resident admitted, however, that he had never actually
seen "a rustler in the act of being naturalized."[8]

As Christopher Waldrep has noted, lynching cannot be precisely defined.
Its history is the history of rhetoric. Community residents molded and shaped
several different words, lynching among them, to justify acts of violence. I understand lynching as a summary execution committed by a self-appointed
group without regard for established legal procedures. Although that understanding helped guide my research and the writing of this book, I understand
that the word's meaning was not always the same for the people I studied. Especially during the nineteenth century, they were more likely to understand
lynching as an extralegal killing broadly supported by the community.

Despite the difficulties of definition, I will employ the word *lynching* and
attempt, at times, to summarize data on mob violence in central Texas. There
are several reasons for doing this. First, historical actors and participants used
the word to describe their actions and the activities of others. The word itself was powerful and reverberated throughout central Texas history. Second, although the words they used changed over time, central Texans distinguished acts of mob violence from simple murders. It is possible, with
careful attention to sources, to study the act of mob violence itself even
though the words used to describe it change. And, finally, phrases such as
"extralegal crowd killing" or "community-sanctioned murder by multiple
individuals" are too awkward to use consistently.[9]

*   *   *

One of the central premises, theoretical approaches, and analytical positions
of this volume is that historical memory—the ways in which individuals, social groups, and communities shape recollections to suit present needs—is
critical for understanding the ebb and flow of mob violence. The questions

of how, why, and what people remember are central to historical inquiry. As David Thelen has argued, the "challenge of history is to recover the past and introduce it to the present. It is the same challenge that confronts memory."[10]

Scholars are becoming increasingly aware that remembering is a creative process and both subjective and collective.[11] Memory is always at work, interacting with the present, forging visions of the past, and preparing models of action for the future. Individuals construct their own memories, but they do so in reference to other people and in a social context. It is this social quality of memory that offers unique opportunities to investigate the past. Through the shaping of memory, people decide what events they think are important, reveal their beliefs and feelings, and mold their attitudes about past and future.[12]

Despite the centrality of memory to historical experience, historians are only just beginning to realize the importance of historical memory in shaping perceptions of the past and the course of events themselves. This study attempts to chart the influence of historical memory in shaping one community over an eighty-year period.[13] I do not, however, deny the importance of actual historical events. Real people burned, killed, and maimed other people, and such events mattered. George Santayana was right when he said that history is always written wrong. It is impossible to recapture the "true" past. Handicapped by an incomplete documentary record and the weakness of human language for capturing the texture of life, historians can only reconstruct shady, blurry images of subjects. Yet we are wrong if we conclude that historians should act as if there is no connection between recollections and (to use the words famously attributed to Leopold von Ranke) "what actually happened."[14]

The starting point for this study is that one cannot truly understand how historical memory works in a given community without detailed knowledge of that community's specific history. The most powerful historical memories, especially before the twentieth century, were intensely local. The continuous creation, revision, and transformation of memory is shaped by specific events from a community's past, by the needs and dictates of that community's present, and by the national and regional discourses in which local communities participate. Even when communities share the same basic collective memory, local communities invariably tie the general memory to a specific episode or individual from their own past. For example, white Southerners throughout the Confederacy crafted memories of "carpetbaggers" ravaging their region after the Civil War, but each community illustrated and passed on the memory by connecting condemnation of carpetbaggers to particular persons from their communities and personal experiences. Beginning in the nineteenth century and accelerating in the twentieth, the rise of mass culture and com-

munication ensured that national and regional events played a proportionately greater role in shaping historical memory. Mass culture, however, has
not completely displaced local history and personal experience, even to the
present.

A number of noted historians have examined the influence of memory
on violence in the United States, especially in the American South, but have
tended to focus upon what I call "cultural memory" rather than local memory. They have sought the origins of southern violence in deeply seated cultural traditions inherited from the Celtic origins of the region's settlers. Although I do not dispute that British folkways influenced southerners, I do not
find such explanations completely satisfactory. Vigilantism and lynching varied tremendously from place to place and time to time, even in regions dominated by the same ethnic and cultural groups. Mob violence in the South was
too episodic to be explained by such timeless cultural characteristics. Local
memory, constantly shaped and reshaped by specific events and the actions
of particular individuals, better explains the chaotic history of extralegal violence in the United States.[15]

* * *

The seven chapters that follow argue that memories crafted around four key
historical developments were particularly critical in shaping central Texas's attitudes toward extralegal justice. The first factor is the frontier experience. Frederick Jackson Turner argued in 1893 that the frontier was especially important
in shaping American character and institutions. Although subsequent historians have found many, if not all, of Turner's specific conclusions to be flawed, he
was not wrong in asserting the important place of the frontier in American life.
Before they ever crossed into Texas, settlers—Mexican and American, black and
white, men and women, future mob leaders and future mob victims—were
deeply shaped by stories, myths, and tales about the frontier. Not surprisingly,
frontier rhetoric in the mid-nineteenth century focused on the dangers posed
by Texas's Native Americans and by outlaws taking advantage of the state's still-
developing legal system. Subsequent encounters challenged and reshaped those
notions but did not alter the basic importance of the frontier for people who
lived in central Texas. In forming ideas about the necessity of vigilantism and
extralegal violence, generation after generation relied heavily on notions and
memories of life on the frontier.

Racial slavery is a second factor of significant importance in the history
of mob violence in central Texas. Slavery was, in my opinion, the most important institution that the region's nineteenth-century settlers imported. It
structured the economy and the political system. It led to a high level of day-

to-day violence between the enslaved and those who would control them. It undermined the formal legal system by informally handling the investigation, judgment, and sentencing of many crimes. It gave a structure to the mob by creating the slave patrol. It gave rise to a strange historical consciousness that simultaneously downplayed black resistance to white mastery while embracing a paranoid fear of "outside agitators" and antislavery whites. Such thinking led the proslavery majority to exercise repressive measures, even to the level of murder, against the antislavery minority. Emancipation heightened rather than diminished the fear and violence that slavery wrought. What central Texans feared, remembered, and thought about slavery and their slaves deeply shaped the region's culture of violence for decades before, during, and after the Civil War.

The third factor shaping the history of lynching in central Texas is resistance by racial, ethnic, and political minorities. From the first arrival of white settlers in the region, central Texas was a contested place. Mexicans, Native Americans, African slaves, and dissident whites clashed with the Anglo majority over the future of the prairies. Those battles loomed large in the region's historical consciousness and contributed to the rise of central Texas's culture of vigilantism and lynching. By the late nineteenth century, historical memory in the region portrayed early settlers as heroic men and women who acted outside the law when necessary to combat the threats of "civilized" society's enemies. That glorification of extralegal violence rippled throughout society and helped justify mob law during the late nineteenth and early twentieth centuries.

The fourth and final factor may be the most important. Throughout the history of central Texas, mob violence rose and fell according to the degree to which constituted authorities, especially the courts, condemned or tolerated it. Mobs frequently defended their actions by invoking the claim of popular sovereignty and the right of the people to govern themselves. At times, the will of the majority became so hardened to the legal system that opposition from law officers and court officials would have made no difference. At other times, however, no clear consensus for mob violence existed. In those cases, the attitudes of local authorities—police, district attorneys, judges, and jurors—mattered.

The actions, decisions, and statements of local officials toward acts of mob violence were critical in sustaining central Texas's culture of violence. Throughout most of the eight decades of this study, local authorities tolerated mob violence because the region's whites remembered extralegal violence as a just and necessary part of their history. In other words, local memories and attitudes influenced the operations of the legal system and courts. The subsequent action (and inaction) of the courts provided an informal sign of community approval and thus colored how acts of mob violence would be remembered, strengthening the culture of violence that had influenced the court's actions in the first place. The courts thus shaped and were shaped by central Texas's culture of violence.

Local memories of extralegal violence were powerful in central Texas. They encompassed rebellion against "despotic" Mexico, battles against "savage" Native Americans, repression of "carpetbagging" whites, and control of "beast-like" emancipated African Americans. Such memories sustained a culture of violence for eight decades but were never so powerful that they completely determined events and outcomes. Memory and community opinion, for example, greatly influenced central Texas's courts but did not necessarily control every officer, judge, and juror in the region. Courts, when led by brave judges willing to risk community outrage, could curb mob violence. Specific episodes and specific individuals shaped the history of mob violence in central Texas, none more so than the lynching of Jesse Washington.

After the nationally condemned lynching of Washington in 1916, local leaders reconsidered their support and tolerance for mob action. Washington's brutal murder embarrassed the civic-minded leaders of the region. In the years that followed, successful campaigns by civil rights groups such as the National Association for the Advancement of Colored People successfully painted lynching as a brutal crime of a backward and "uncivilized" people. Over the next several decades, white central Texans not only abandoned public lynching spectacles but also made a conscious effort to strike lynching from the region's historical memory. African Americans, however, did not and could not forget the history of violence.

This book's chapters are arranged both chronologically and thematically. The first three survey the antebellum roots of mob violence: the birth of Texas in bloody revolution with Mexico, a tradition of conflict with Native Americans, and tensions caused by slavery. These chapters focus not only on the initial creation and diffusion of the historical memories that fueled central Texas's culture of violence but also on historical events themselves. Some understanding of events is necessary to understand subsequent developments in central Texas's historical memory. The chapters emphasize the importance of rhetoric and language in shaping events and actions, both present and future.

The next four chapters examine lynching and vigilantism after the outbreak of the Civil War, focusing first on those vigilantes that targeted whites, then concentrating extensively on the lynching of blacks, and finally considering the relationship between newly arriving Mexican immigrants and mob violence in central Texas. Taken together, the chapters argue that the origins of mob violence are complex and not easily summarized by sociological theory.[16]

A deep understanding of historical context at the national, regional, and local level is paramount for comprehending the history of lynching. In particular, mob violence is best understood by tracing how national and regional discussions of race and lynching impact local people and fuse with historical experiences and memory.

1. "Texas shall be . . . Americanized": Mob Violence in the Conquest of Mexican Texas

In 1837 Mexico's secretary of war, José María Tornel y Mendívil, wrote an account of the conflict between the American settlers of Texas and the Mexican government. Tornel argued that Texan colonists "followed no law except their whim" and cited an incident in which Anglo Texans, "as a result of their hatred of the Mexican nation," had assassinated six Mexican settlers. Texans, Tornel concluded, would only have remained united with Mexico if the government had disregarded "all their crimes."[1]

Tornel's version of events was, of course, not incorporated into the historical memory of most Americans. Instead, the English-speaking residents of Texas and the Americans who cheered Texas independence remembered the conflict with Mexico as a struggle against an oppressive enemy seeking to crush the democratic and constitutional rights that had been promised to the early colonists. The influential *United States Magazine and Democratic Review* defended the War for Texas Independence by observing that the "independence of Texas was complete and absolute. It was an independence, not only in fact but of right." Mexico had "deceived" Texans and sought to have them "enslaved" under a dictatorial government. Such editorials helped justify the annexation of Texas and the U.S.–Mexican war that soon followed, and they also created a powerful set of memories celebrating the use of violence against Mexico and Mexicans.[2]

No period of Texas history shaped subsequent historical memory in the state more than that from 1821 to 1848, an era encompassing American colonization, the War for Texas Independence, the years of the Texas republic, and the U.S.–Mexican War. A survey of this era is useful for two reasons. First, it is impossible to understand historical memory in central Texas without some understanding of the experiences that would later become so ingrained in Texas myth and memory. Second, events in Texas during the 1830s and 1840s shaped more than the attitudes of those living in Texas. The tales told about the Anglo-Texas frontier, real and imagined, traveled across the Red River to those who lived in earlier settled parts of the United States and molded the way they perceived Texas. Thousands of American immigrants arrived in Texas by the 1850s, and they had preconceived notions about the dangers of life there. They feared the state's Mexican and Indian population and came prepared to defend themselves and their families with violence.

* * *

For the first two centuries of European contact with the New World, Spanish monarchs ruled one of the richest, most powerful empires in the world. A slow decline in that empire began, however, during the seventeenth century.[3] Sapped of its energy and resources, and less flexible in responding to local conditions, Spain's control over its northern provinces in America waned at the end of the eighteenth century. In 1821 Mexico declared independence. Whether due to violence or flight, Texas lost a third of its population during the struggle.[4] The independence of Mexico initiated sweeping changes for Texas. Mexico lifted old trade barriers, legalizing the flourishing contraband trade between Texas and the United States.[5]

Although the introduction of free trade helped expand the economy of the northern Mexican frontier, liberalization of immigration policies paved the way for an even greater transformation of Texas. Before independence, the crown strictly controlled immigration, and, as a result, much of New Spain's northern frontier had yet to be settled in the early nineteenth century. Insightful leaders had long warned the crown about the nonsettlement of Texas. In 1819 the tottering Spanish government departed from traditional policy and gave permission to Moses Austin to settle three hundred American families on the Lower Brazos River. In 1823 the new Mexican state approved the grant, which had by then fallen to Austin's son, Stephen. In fact, Stephen F. Austin settled the three hundred families in late 1821. The growth of Austin's colony to more than two thousand people during the next three years convinced Mexican leaders of the experiment's success. In 1824 the Mexican congress passed a new colonization law that provided cheap landownership and tax shelters for immigrants to Texas. Others soon followed Austin's lead and secured similar grants to colonize Texas. Under the generous terms the Mexican government provided, immigrant farmers and ranchers had six years to pay for grants of up to 4,065 acres. By 1830 at least seven thousand Americans were living in Texas, as opposed to three thousand Spanish-speaking residents.[6]

The immigration of thousands of Americans to Texas launched more than a simple demographic transformation. It altered the very character of Texas society. Most Anglo immigrants spoke English, could not converse in Spanish, and knew little of the languages of the Texas Indians. Moreover, whereas most Mexican citizens embraced Catholicism, the majority of incoming settlers hailed from Protestant backgrounds. Just as significant, the new residents often lived apart from their longer-settled neighbors. Americans located their settlements along the river valleys of south central Texas and along the Gulf Coast. Such a geographical location was a natural outgrowth of another fundamental difference between immigrants and the older Spanish-speaking communities—agricultural economy. Some engaged in stock raising, as in the Tejano culture of south Texas, but most migrated to the fertile lands of Texas to engage in staple crop agriculture.

The most important change that American immigration brought to Texas may have been the establishment of slavery, an institution with a long history in other parts of Spanish America. Although slave traders delivered more than one and a half million enslaved Africans to Spanish possessions in the New World between 1492 and 1870, few had been settled in Texas by the early nineteenth century. In 1785, for example, a census listed only forty-three slaves out of a Texas population of nearly three thousand. As the American population increased in Texas during the nineteenth century, however, so, too, did the number of slaves. Georgian Jared E. Groce, for example, settled his family and ninety slaves on a plantation in the Lower Brazos River valley in January 1822. Like Groce, most American immigrants came from the southern United States, where the "peculiar institution" had become an important part of the regional economy. Many settlers believed that successful cultivation of plantation agriculture, especially where land was readily available, required use of forced labor. In the fall of 1825 a census of Austin's colony found 443 bondsmen, almost a quarter of the total population.[7]

The success of slavery in Texas only increased the hunger for Texas land. Americans, especially white southerners, followed the colonization of Texas with great interest. Many believed that the economic health and future of slavery depended on westward expansion. As one South Carolinian wrote in 1830, "I pray that by hook or by crook Texas will belong to the United States."[8]

Almost from the beginning, tensions between American settlers of Texas and the Mexican government began to mount. Colonists believed that the legal maneuvering of the new Mexican republic threatened the type of life they had come to build in Texas.[9] Although many aspects of Mexican rule irritated the Anglo Texans, their most enduring frustration centered on the future of slavery.

That future was in doubt throughout the period of American colonization in Mexican Texas.[10] In deliberations over a new state constitution in 1826, the congress of the state of Coahuila and Texas considered the prohibition of slavery there. Anglos were so worried that, as Stephen F. Austin wrote, more "than one half of these people are awaiting the decision of Congress in regard to their slaves, as they intend to leave the country if their emancipation is decreed."[11]

Although a compromise between the state government and American colonists was reached, federal threats to the institution resurfaced in 1829, and in the fall of that year the president of Mexico issued a proclamation emancipating slaves everywhere in the republic. Although a December decree exempted Texas from emancipation, the intervening confusion reminded Anglos that local control over slavery was tenuous. On 6 April 1830, a federal pronouncement brought those fears home by calling for strict enforcement of laws prohibiting the introduction of slaves into Mexico. Two years later the state of Coahuila and Texas partially closed an indentured servitude loophole by limiting labor contracts to ten years. Yet slavery continued to grow in Texas. By 1834 a conservative estimate placed the slave population there at two thousand out of a total population just over twenty thousand. Slavery, however, rested on an insecure foundation. Anglo slaveholders relied upon the fact that the Mexican government had no effective enforcement agency short of the army.[12]

In 1834 Mexico's new leader, General Santa Anna, began to centralize power in the federal government. Such actions did not immediately affect Texas. To be sure, any reining in of local power frustrated American colonists, but many settlers hoped that Texas's position on the northern frontier would continue to shield them from the reach of the central government. After all, Anglos already flagrantly violated Mexican laws against immigration, slavery, and trade. Colonists could tolerate continued changes in government policy as long as the new policies had little practical impact on their part of the Mexican world.[13]

In 1835, however, the Mexican government signaled an end to the era of Texas's salutary neglect, and local authorities became less tolerant of Anglo violations of Mexican policy.[14] As they began to realize the seriousness of Santa Anna's commitment to centralization, Anglo Texans rallied to the independence movement. In June 1835 a small group of armed radicals led by William Travis marched on Anáhuac and forced the surrender of a tiny Mexican military garrison. Although many moderate Anglos continued to hope for peace, Anglo colonists refused to turn over the treasonous band to authorities. Anglo support for the Mexican government had all but disappeared.

Travis's attack may have ruffled some Anglo feathers, but the event revealed the chasm that had developed between Mexico and the Anglo Texans. In August the longtime moderate Stephen F. Austin, recently released from a Mexican prison, broke with the "peace party" and proclaimed that "Texas shall be effectually, and fully, Americanized. Texas must be a slave country. It is no longer a matter of doubt."[15] On 8 September, Austin warned Mexican authorities that Anglo Texans would not suffer further restrictions on their autonomy and that the "inevitable consequence of sending an armed force to this country would be war."[16] In December it was declared at a public meeting in Austin that Americans and Mexicans were two different people, and Mexican leaders were criticized for attempting to end slavery and "free the negroes."[17]

At this point, however, Santa Anna refused to brook the continued attacks of colonists such as Travis and the brazen snubbing of Mexican authority. He brought his army northward in early autumn. Colonists greeted the arrival with gunfire, and neither side backed down over the next several months. On 3 October the Mexican congress dissolved the state legislatures, brought state governors directly under presidential control, and closed the final door on any hope for Texas autonomy under Mexico. Meanwhile, Texas colonists formed extralegal committees of correspondence (a tradition borrowed from their American Revolutionary ancestors) and issued statements of grievances.[18] On 2 March 1836, a group of rebels, predominantly Anglo Texans joined by some Mexican Texans, took the next step and officially declared independence. Four days later the Mexican army stormed the Alamo. After weeks of retreat, Sam Houston took charge of the Texas army, winning a stunning victory over the surprised Mexican force at San Jacinto on 21 April 1836. The victorious rebels forced Santa Anna to sign a treaty acknowledging Texas's independence north of the Rio Grande.[19]

Slavery, it is true, was not the only reason for the War for Texas Independence. The marriage of Catholic, Spanish-speaking Mexican rulers and Protestant, English-speaking American colonists was doomed from the beginning. Nevertheless, slavery's role in the divorce was critical. The importance of slavery can be seen clearly in the actions Texans took to form their new government. Section 9 of the General Provisions of the new constitution made the place of slavery in the Texas republic quite clear. "All persons of color who were slaves for life previous to their emigration to Texas," the section begins, "and who are now held in bondage, shall remain in the like state of servitude."[20] Although that passage secured the slave property already resident in Texas, framers of the Texas constitution sought to ensure the future security of slavery as well. They declared that "Congess shall pass no laws to prohibit emigrants from bringing their slaves into the republic with them, and holding them by the same tenure by which such slaves were held in the United States."[21]

Having protected slavery, the framers moved to protect white supremacy by placing severe limitations on Texas's free black population. "Nor," section 9 continues "shall congress have power to emancipate slaves; nor shall any slave holder be allowed to emancipate his or her slave or slaves without the consent of congress, unless he or she shall send his or her slave or slaves without the limits of the republic." Lawmakers then focused on free blacks already resident in Texas, stating that "No free person of African descent, either in whole or in part, shall be permitted to reside permanently in the republic, without the consent of congress."[22]

Despite the success of the Texas War for Independence and the establishment of a constitution that protected slavery, the settlers of Texas found themselves unable to turn the region into a quiet farmers' haven. For centuries mobile Plains Indians had blocked Spanish settlement and expansion in Texas, and they continued to be an elusive foe whose carefully planned raids often ended with easy escape. One of the greatest stumbling blocks to a more effective Indian "defense" was the financial instability of the new Texas government. The young nation's treasury was remarkably low, and whatever meager funds did exist for military operations had to be further divided between demands for protection from Indians and the need to defend the Republic of Texas from its former mother country. The Mexican government never recognized Texas an independent state and never hid the desire to reacquire its lost province. When in 1842 Mexico briefly recaptured parts of south Texas, including San Antonio, the Republic of Texas found itself forced to defend its southern border from Mexico and its western and northern borders from Indians.[23]

Facing so many difficulties, it is hardly surprising that Anglo Texans looked eastward for help. Most who lived in Texas during the republic had been born and raised in the United States of America. Since 1836, most of these men and women wanted Texas to join the nation of their birth. Emerging sectional differences between the North and the South, however, cooled the enthusiasm of America's leaders for annexing a slave state the size of Texas. Yet by December of 1844 those who supported expansionism had gained enough power to push through a joint resolution annexing Texas to the Union. A few months later Texas enthusiastically and officially joined the United States.[24]

The annexation fulfilled the dreams of many of the state's settlers. As one early settler recalled, "A new era had commenced."[25] In particular, many Anglo Texans welcomed the U.S. Army into the region. With the help of the federal army, Texans were certain they could finally end their conflict with Mexico and the Indians. As one Texan recalled the mood at the time of annexation, "We felt something like the children of Israel probably did, when Jehovah flung the Red sea betwixt them and their foes."[26]

President James K. Polk's expansionist plans had long been fixed on northern Mexico, and when a diplomatic solution did not seem likely he threatened a military conflict and convinced Congress to issue a declaration of war in 1846. Although officials in the Spanish period had recognized the Nueces River as Texas's southern border, Polk decided to test Mexico's resolve by claiming the Rio Grande as the border. When he sent U.S. troops south of the Nueces, they were attacked as invaders by the Mexican army. Polk seized the opportunity to deplore that "American blood had been shed on American soil."[27]

In the formation of the army for the invasion of Mexico, six thousand Anglo Texans eagerly enlisted. Even central Texas, dangerously close to the Indian frontier, produced a large number of volunteers. Mounted volunteers from the Lone Star State—calling themselves the Texas Rangers—won a reputation for valor from their American comrades and compiled a record of brutality according to the Mexican people, who labeled them "Los Diablos Tejanos." The Mexican government collapsed during the invasion. The United States emerged from the Mexican war in 1848, having secured Texas independence and acquiring much of the territory located in the present-day states of New Mexico, Arizona, California, Nevada, Utah, Colorado, and Wyoming.[28]

The impact of the successful War for Texas Independence and the U.S.–Mexican War on historical memory was significant. Anglo Texans, for example, were proud of their revolt against Mexico, which they characterized as the "Texas Revolution" in order to draw parallels with 1776. Like their revolutionary forebears, the people of Texas invoked the right of rebellion against a corrupt government. As early as 1832 colonists formed themselves into extralegal citizens' committees to resist Mexican authorities. William Travis and his men became heroes for their extralegal attack on the Mexican government's garrison at Anáhuac in 1835, and the martyrs of the Alamo were seen as volunteers dedicated to the cause of justice and right no matter the consequences. The surprising victory of a ragtag army of volunteers over a better-trained Mexican army, combined with vicious racist stereotyping of Mexican soldiers, reinforced notions about Anglo racial supremacy that persisted for decades.

The most powerful historical legacy of the revolution and the republic, however, was probably the creation of the first iteration of the Texas Rangers. The establishment of the Rangers in 1835 gave institutional form to the ad-hoc neighborhood groups of men who were already defending settlements against attacks from Native Americans. The early Texas Rangers were not a permanent frontier defense force but rather ordinary frontier farmers and stock-raisers who banded together in times of need. Yet the reputation of Texas Rangers as courageous, resourceful heroes of the frontier evolved rapidly. In 1846 one newspaper editor famously wrote that a "Texas Ranger can ride like a Mexican, trail like an Indian, shoot like a Tennessean, and fight like a very devil."[29] Well into the twentieth century Texas Rangers were famous for enforcing their own brand of justice and ignoring formal legal procedures. In doing so, they were loved and worshipped by Anglo Texans.[30]

* * *

Much changed in Texas between 1821 and 1848. In a little over a quarter of a century a demographic, political, and economic revolution had been accomplished. Texas had been a sparsely populated, economically marginal frontier region on Spain's northern frontier. It was, after 1848, a destination of choice for thousands of immigrants from the United States and Europe. The new Texas economy revolved around the world's most important product: cotton. And Texas existed not as a northern province of Spain's New World empire but on the western edge of a young and expanding United States. All these changes would matter greatly in the years ahead. Yet the period also produced a range of less obvious, but no less significant, cultural and social transformations that help explain the origins of Texan attitudes toward extralegal violence.

Migrants to Texas, of course, did not arrive shorn of experiences gained earlier in life. Despite the diversity of their backgrounds, they arrived with clear notions about the utility of vigilantism.[31] Most Texas immigrants came from the American South, a region long noted for its predisposition to violence and extralegal justice. White southerners since at least the late eighteenth century had been organizing themselves outside the law to protest the judicial system's perceived failures. They also served on slave patrols, quasi-legal bodies that meted out justice to wayward African Americans directly and without mediation of trial or jury.[32] Although only a smattering of nineteenth-century Texans grew up in the North, historians have noted that the region also had a history of self-appointed citizen committees that took the law into their own hands.[33] Some Texas pioneers were on their way east when they arrived in the Lone Star State, having spent time in the California goldfields where mob violence, vigilance committees, and lynching flourished.[34]

Although mob violence was part of the experience of most American communities in one way or another, Texas increasingly came to be seen during the nineteenth century as a frontier region inhabited by quick-thinking men capable of taking justice into their own hands. Stories about Texas circulated from neighbor to neighbor; were exchanged through the nation's mail; and were read in newspapers, magazines, travel accounts, and literary works. In 1836 David Edward, a visitor, observed that Texans "were accustomed to the appearance of fugitives from justice" and that the citizenry themselves punished crime "whether by assisting the demands of justice, emanating from the lawful authorities . . . or of supporting it in their own."[35]

One of the most common stories focused on those who had suddenly left their old homes for Texas, often to escape their pasts. Historian Frank Owsley wrote that "going from old communities into the new country was, to many a migrant, like passing through a doorway, which closed behind him and through which he returned no more."[36] Immigrants sometimes carved "G.T.T." (gone to Texas) on their houses before departing, and soon the acronym was widely used to describe those who suddenly abandoned their homes for parts unknown. The stories told about these former neighbors often speculated on the individual's familial difficulties, criminal past, or financial indebtedness. In 1857 Frederick Law Olmsted noted that "G.T.T. (gone to Texas) was the slang appendage" given "to every man's name who had disappeared before the discovery of some rascality."[37] If lynchings occurred in Texas with greater frequency than elsewhere, so the thinking went, that was to be expected among so many characters of questionable social value.[38]

Contemporary literature also played a role in shaping Texas's image as a lawless frontier populated by "natural" men not bound by the limitations of "civilization." As traditional defenses of vigilantism fell from favor in earlier-established states, novelists recast their stories and set them in Texas. For example, an 1848 novel published in New York contains one of the most routinely justified killings in popular literature—a brother kills the man who has deviously seduced his sister. What distinguishes the account, however, is the justification of the brother's actions. He acted so decisively because his time in Texas helped rid him of "unnatural requisitions" and enabled him to act upon those "conscious instincts of honor, justice, and right, which are common to all mankind."[39]

Another way to explore how outsiders perceived Texas is to examine recently arrived Texans' correspondence with relatives and former neighbors. In these journals and letters authors work hard to dispel an image of Texas as a dangerous place filled with outlaws and criminals, governed only by vigilantes and mob law. In 1858, for example, Emma Elliot wrote to a friend in South Carolina that her worries of the "wilds of Texas" were misplaced and, she added, "I assure you I never had an idea I would ever like Texas as well as I do."[40] A diarist visiting Texas in 1846 from Mississippi found fault with the popular image of Texans, who, he wrote, had been unfairly "derided and slandered called cut throats robers."[41] These writers hoped to convince others that Texas was a "civilized" place, but the fact that they worried over its misperception reveals much more about how Texas was viewed in earlier-settled states.

Sometimes, of course, letter writers confirmed outside perceptions of Texas as a place set apart. In 1845 one recently arrived settler wrote that those born in Texas were different from those born elsewhere. The "unsettled state of the country," he contended, had given Texans a range of experiences not possessed by others.[42] The diarist from Mississippi who disagreed with the image of Texans as outlaws wrote that a Texan would pursue an enemy "until his blood pays the forfeit of his insult."[43] Olmsted proclaimed that early Texas held "a more reckless and vicious crew" than any before assembled. He concluded that justice "descended into the body of Judge Lynch, sleeping when he slept, and when he woke hewing down right and left for exercise and pastime."[44]

Conditions in Texas after the Texas Revolution were thus especially ripe for the creation of a culture of violence and vigilantism. Settlers entering the region arrived believing that Texas was rife with dangerous characters. They found those already settled in the region to be firm believers in the right of revolution and of the people to take the law into their own hands. Finally, they found ready-made institutions, the Texas Rangers and other companies of Indian fighters, practicing and demonstrating the art of "rough justice."

* * *

Many of the same sources that painted Texas as a frontier region overrun with outlaws and in need of vigilante justice also contributed to the racist stereotyping of Mexicans. Few Americans had actual experience with Mexicans before the settlement of Texas, but between the beginnings of Stephen F. Austin's colony in 1821 and the gold rush of the 1850s they came into direct contact with Mexicans as never before. Unfortunately, the encounters were not ideal for breaking down old stereotypes. Instead, the violent conflicts that emerged between Americans and Mexicans highlighted cultural differences and amplified racial prejudice.

Whites from the United States, of course, already had a long history with racism. Discrimination against Africans and Native Americans was hundreds of years old by 1848, and most whites in the United States inherited negative images of Spaniards from the so-called Black Legend popular among the English.[45] The Texas Revolution, however, did much to enhance American racism. Leaders of the Texas revolt emphasized that the war was a cultural battle between Mexico and Anglo America. One settler had written to the provisional government requesting protection against the "glittering spears and ruthless sword of the descendants of Cortes, and his modern Goths and Vandals."[46] At a meeting in San Felipe de Austin in 1835 it was asserted that contact between Anglo Americans and Mexicans had hardened preexisting prejudices and led Americans to conclude that the "two peoples cannot mingle together."[47]

Such feelings only increased once the fighting began. In an effort to recruit volunteers for the struggle for Texas independence, a poster issued in New Orleans in 1836 called upon Anglo men to save "the wives and daughters of Texas . . . from the brutality of Mexican soldiers."[48] Such rhetoric was not that unusual in wartime societies. Few leaders rally their troops with precise explanations of the underlying political and economic ramifications of defeat or victory. Indeed, Anglo Texans were borrowing from an old tradition when they translated their struggle over local autonomy and slavery into a defense of Anglo-Texan masculinity and a cultural attack on Mexico and Mexicans.

Although war with Mexico shaped the attitudes of Texas settlers in the 1830s and 1840s, events in Texas also had great impact on those elsewhere in the United States. Texas's population grew rapidly after annexation, and most new settlers had conceptions of Mexicans based on speeches, addresses, newspaper stories, memoirs, and other information they had read or heard before coming to the Southwest.

The debate over annexation and the U.S.–Mexican war provoked much discussion of Mexicans in the eastern United States. One of the most influential voices during this critical period was John O'Sullivan, editor of the *United States Magazine and Democratic Review* and defender of the War for Texas Independence. Historians traditionally attribute O'Sullivan with having popularized the phrase *manifest destiny.* He understood that northern worries over admitting another slave state had long blocked Texas from joining the Union, and he and the writers at the *Democratic Review* hit upon a novel way of defusing this objection. The addition of Texas, they wrote, would "tend to facilitate and hasten the disappearance of slavery from all the northern tier of the present Slave States." Moreover, the great demand for labor in the fresh cotton fields of Texas would draw African slaves westward, allowing gradual emancipation in the Upper South. Furthermore, it would be good to move the African population closer to the "Spanish-Indian-American populations of Mexico, Central America and South America," because those people of "mixed and confused blood" were a worthy "receptacle" for slaves once the nation had decided on emancipation.[49] The *Democratic Review* thus painted the Mexican population of Texas as a "colored" race more in common with Native Americans and Africans than with Anglo Americans and Europeans.

Derogatory comments toward Mexicans seemed to be one of the few unifying themes of the fierce debate over the future of Mexico. In 1848 John C. Calhoun of South Carolina argued against the annexation of additional territory from Mexico by suggesting that the population of Mexico was either "Indian" or "of mixed tribes." He warned that the "greatest misfortunes of

Spanish America are to be traced to the fatal error of placing these colored races on an equality with the white race."[50]

Although such vitriol certainly shaped the way nineteenth-century Americans thought about Mexicans, political speeches and magazine stories were not the only sources of information on Texas for settlers pondering a move. Beginning in the 1820s and continuing throughout the nineteenth century, Anglo American and European visitors to Mexico and the Southwest published accounts of their journeys. Invariably, such accounts contained harsh descriptions of the Mexicans encountered.[51] The accounts became more virulent as America expanded westward.[52] During the 1850s thousands of Americans came into contact and conflict with Mexicans because of the California gold rush, and the published diaries and letters that flowed eastward from the gold mines stigmatized Mexicans as untrustworthy, degenerate criminals.[53]

By the time settlers began to enter central Texas in large numbers, Anglo attitudes toward Mexicans were already hardened. Most, settlers were convinced, were not to be trusted. One historian of the Southwest aptly summarized that view when he wrote that early settlers "made little effort to hide their feelings of racial superiority" and considered Mexicans "as placid, illiterate, and superstitious."[54] Such attitudes did not remain static but fluctuated and evolved as white settlers and Mexicans interacted. Nevertheless, the early impressions influenced Anglo-Mexican interactions in Texas for decades to come. In 1894 an observer of Texas race relations noted, "It is difficult to convince these people that a Mexican is a human being. He seems to be the Texan's natural enemy."[55]

The racist stereotyping of Mexicans affected the history of central Texas. Mexican families had been among the earliest settlers of the region. Although it is exceedingly difficult to determine exactly how many lived in the Upper Brazos River valley before the Texas Revolution, land had been deeded to seven Mexican families between 1834 and 1835.[56] A local historian of present-day Falls County listed some thirteen Mexican men among the earliest pioneers of the region.[57] What became of these settlers is unclear. By 1850 and 1860 few if any remained. Many of these individuals, like all central Texas settlers, probably abandoned their homes before the advance of the Mexican army during the Texas War for Independence. From what evidence survives, it appears that most Anglos returned but most Mexicans did not. To what extent that choice was voluntary is unrecorded.

Some Anglo Texans feared the return of Mexicans into Texas. Lawmaker F. J. Harris sought to block their immigration, especially those Mexicans who had some Native American ancestry. "I fear not the Castilian race," he said, "but I fear those who, though they speak the Spanish language, are but the descendants of that degraded and despised race which Cortez conquered."[58] Both the Mexicans who remained in Texas and those who arrived after the War for Texas Independence faced significant discrimination and violence in Texas. The *Texas State Gazette* in Austin described Mexicans as "half-negro, half-Indian greasers."[59] A Brownsville newspaper noted that Mexicans "are unquestionably more exposed to wrong" and suggested that "Americans have at times committed offenses which . . . have been overlooked, but which, if committed by Mexicans would have been severely punished."[60] In 1854 a vigilance committee formed in Austin and threatened violence against all "transient Mexicans" who refused to leave in ten days. The committee also promised to enforce a ban on employing Mexican workers.[61] The Austin vigilantes forced approximately twenty Mexican families to abandon central Texas.[62] Two years later, vigilantes expelled all Mexicans from Colorado County.[63]

Mexicans had more to fear than being chased from their native land. Anglo mobs executed Mexicans for a variety of offenses before the Civil War. In 1850 a small mob in Brownsville whipped and then killed Juan Chapa Guerra for theft. Later, authorities learned that the mob had misidentified their victim. The man the mob sought was named Juan Chapa Garcia.[64] In 1857 a band of Anglos murdered a Mexican for killing a cow.[65] When Frederick Law Olmsted visited Texas during the mid-1850s he noted that a San Antonio mob had hanged a Mexican for horse theft.[66]

At times individual acts of lynching were dwarfed by more systematic assassinations of Mexicans. Anglos in south Texas erupted in anger in 1857 over the success of a number of Mexican freight-runners who transported goods from the Mexican border to San Antonio. During the summer of that year an unknown number of Anglos banded together, donned masks, and set about intercepting and killing the Mexican cartmen. An estimated seventy-five were killed before diplomatic pressure from Mexico finally provoked U.S. officials and the governor of Texas to act.[67]

The motives behind the killing of individual Mexicans were complex. Mob leaders, for example, frequently accused them of criminal actions and unfair economic practices. Although mobs killed few Mexicans strictly because of their ethnic background, the mobs were animated by racism. Such prejudice was hardly surprising. The historical memory of most Anglo Texans viewed Mexicans through the lens of the Alamo, Goliad, and the U.S.–Mexican War.

Surviving records say little about what happened to the early Mexican settlers of central Texas. By 1850, in any event, very few remained. According to that year's manuscript census records, only four individuals in the two sprawling counties then encompassing the Upper Brazos River valley were born in Mexico. None headed a household. Three were listed as working for the U.S. Army (one as a servant and the other two as muleteers), and the fourth was listed as thirteen-year-old boy living in the household of Daniel Hollis.[68] Luis Sanchez, a translator for the Anglos and the Indians of the Texas frontier, was one of the last remaining Mexicans in the region. In 1844 he noted his solitary existence at a meeting of Anglo and Indian leaders in central Texas, describing himself as "a Mexican in the midst of you, like a lone tree in the prairie."[69]

* * *

Many who moved to central Texas during the years before the Civil War came from communities and regions that tolerated mob violence. They surely would have been prepared to embrace vigilantism to secure their vision of central Texas, even had they no particular preconceptions of Texas. In the years before 1860, however, writings about Texas had reinforced American attitudes toward the necessity of extralegal justice. In particular, diaries, memoirs, journals, speeches, and addresses often portrayed the Southwest as a place of danger and enhanced preexisting prejudices against Mexicans. Furthermore, the history of Texas colonization, the War for Texas Independence, and the U.S.–Mexican War painted Texans as a people particularly proud of (and disposed to) extralegal action. Not surprisingly, Mexicans found themselves victims of Texas mobs. The exodus of Mexican settlers from central Texas, however, did little to diminish central Texas's culture of violence. The very success of Anglo violence against Mexico and Mexicans reinforced and strengthened the region's commitment to extralegal violence. As the years passed, those who fought against Mexico achieved mythic status in the region's historical memory. Central Texans lavished praise on those early pioneers who did not wait for the arrival of formal legal structures to shape the course of Texas history.[70]

2. "Necessity Knows No Law": Mob Violence in the Conquest of Central Texas's Native Americans

During the early 1850s five white men from central Texas decided to pursue a band of Indians whom they thought had stolen horses and killed livestock belonging to the Wilkerson family. The group elected a leader, prepared rations, and began tracking the alleged horse thieves. Although the trail split at one point the men eventually came across six Indians seated around a campfire. They charged the Indians, shooting without warning; five escaped, but the sixth was killed. According to one account the Indian begged for his life before one of the Anglos shot him dead. After returning, one participant remembered that they "celebrated" the "death of the red man" in the "usual way in frontier settlements." In celebrating their "victory" and later composing their version of the "battle," the men demonstrated how much value central Texans placed on the act of killing Indians and on the memories of such violence. Nineteenth-century central Texans bestowed social prestige on Indian killers, and establishing such an identity was valuable to central Texans. Those who killed Indians were seen as natural leaders, brave men who had risked great danger to do their part in the settlement of the Texas frontier. Given such benefits, it was not surprising that a fight erupted over the memory of "Wilkerson's Valley Raid." When it came time to write a "history" of the encounter, several participants claimed to have been the one who actually killed the Indian.[1]

"The first lynchings in this country," wrote sociologist W. D. Weatherford in 1916, "were perpetrated on Indians."[2] Few scholars of lynching, however, have followed Weatherford in tracing the chain of mob violence back to Anglo encounters with Native Americans.[3] From a certain perspective that is understandable and justifiable, conflicts between Europeans and Native Americans often resembled warfare. Without a shared legal system between the two people the concept of extralegal violence falls apart. Neither side defined the killings that resulted from these conflicts as "lynchings." Anglo men who killed Indians were usually seen as "Indian fighters" and rarely as vigilantes. Yet Indian fighting, both in its daily operation and in its mythic justifications, deeply shaped central Texas attitudes toward extralegal mob action.

The violence that early Anglo settlers of central Texas committed reinforced and strengthened the region's culture of vigilantism and lynching in three ways. First, the spontaneous ways in which early bands of "volunteer Indian fighters" organized themselves provided a model for the structure of later mobs. Second, the rhetoric of Anglo-Indian violence influenced vigilantes and defenders of extralegal violence in the late nineteenth and early twentieth centuries. The region's early settlers were establishing patterns that would persist for eighty years when they transformed the national discourse of expansion and "manifest destiny" into daily justifications of Anglo violence. Third, the success of the use of force against Native Americans colored the perception of those who committed acts of violence in later years. During the late nineteenth and early twentieth centuries, central Texans routinely celebrated the contributions of the region's Indian fighters. They elected them to political office, lauded them in newspaper articles and local histories, read and praised their memoirs, invited them to speak to civic groups and at local festivals, and commemorated their deeds with historical markers. Such acts of celebration, and the memories they sustained, defended not only the killing that was central to the Anglo-Indian conflict but also extralegal violence in general.

* * *

By the time Anglo Americans entered central Texas, Native Americans had been living there for at least twelve thousand years. Indeed, the lands surrounding the Brazos and Trinity river valleys were something of a cultural crossroads. From the north, the southernmost subtribes of the Wichitas—Wacos, Tawakonis, Kichais, Taovayas, and Wichita proper—were already familiar with the region. The Wichitas were a loosely allied confederation of prairie Indians whose domain stretched from the Arkansas River valley of present-day Kansas to the Upper Brazos River valley of central Texas. They lived in villages for most of the year, planting and raising crops, but they hunted buffalo during the winter. Wichitas were not alone in central Texas. Nomadic hunters known as the Tonkawas criss-crossed the prairies and valleys and were the frequent enemies of Wichita subtribes. Two other Indian nations also had an impact on central Texas during the early nineteenth century. The domain of the agricultural Caddos of east Texas extended as far west as central Texas, and the Comanches counted central Texas as the eastern border of their range.

By the time Americans began settling in the lower river valleys of Texas, the population and strength of the majority of the Texas Indians—small to begin with—had been greatly reduced by three hundred years of contact with Europeans. During the eighteenth century the horticultural Caddo confederacy suffered from outbreaks of disease, and the decline of Spain coupled with the rise of the United States to undermine their ability to negotiate their borderlands position with the New World empires of Spain, France, and England. In 1820 the men, women, and children of the Wichita subtribes numbered between 1,200 and 1,400, a drastic reduction from 1773, when these same tribes could muster a thousand warriors and probably numbered more than five thousand. Time wore even more heavily on the Tonkawas, who had reached the point of near collapse when Anglo colonists encountered them. Only the Comanches, "the Lords of the Southern Plains," stood at full strength when American immigrants first entered Texas.[4]

Conflict erupted in 1821 when Karankawas, a small Gulf Coast tribe, attacked one of the first boatloads of Stephen F. Austin's colonists. For the next six years the Anglos and the Karankawas battled until the Karankawas—defeated badly on the field of battle and their numbers cut in half—finally signed a treaty recognizing the hegemony of the white settlers. Tonkawas also roamed throughout the area of Austin's colony, and during the early 1820s settlers rounded them up and attempted to expel them from the region. The Lipan Apache, allies of the Tonkawas, interceded, however, and the Tonkawas drifted back to the colonies over the next few years.[5]

In 1823 colonists had their first contact with Wacos when a group camped near the settlements after completing a raid against the Tonkawas. If they were to strike again, Austin worried, "the only alternative [would] be an expedition to destroy their village."[6] For the next several years American colonists considered a war against the Wacos and their allies the Tawakonis, and in 1826 Austin called on the militiamen of his young colony to join an expedition to destroy the Waco Indian village. He implored the men "to protect your own homes, your own property, to shield your wives and children from the arrows of a savage and merciless enemy." They had, Austin declared, no choice in the matter because their foes had driven them "to the necessity of taking up arms in self defence."[7] Austin also contacted the recently arrived Cherokees and asked them to assist in attacking the Wacos; three hundred agreed, but the Mexican government suspended the expedition.[8]

Although the Indians of central Texas had not been eliminated, encroaching white and black settlers began moving into the region anyway. As early as

1826 the Mexican government granted Benjamin Milam the right to settle the land above Austin's colony. Weary of Indian attacks, pioneers moved slowly up the banks of the Brazos River, and nearly a decade passed before the first white settlers came to the Upper Brazos valley. In 1834 and 1835 Sterling Robertson established the capital of the new colony on the Falls of the Brazos River, and by the time of the Texas War for Independence that village was home to three or four hundred people. Records indicate that land had been deeded to 256 individuals.[9]

Early Anglo settlers did not arrive alone in the rush for the fertile farmland of central Texas. At least a few brought slaves along with them. By "September of 1834 or sooner," the wife of one early settler recalled, her husband and his slaves were "already there" and had begun building houses at the Falls of the Brazos for "his white and black families to live in."[10] Another who arrived in the young colony and planned to locate his homestead above the Falls wrote to his wife on 3 January 1836 and noted that "all the negroes are well—Moses & Aggy are both delighted with the country."[11]

Indians of the Texas prairie, although reduced in strength and increasingly outnumbered, refused to concede the fertile land of the Upper Brazos River valley to these invaders. The Wacos and Tawakonis resisted by raiding the settlements and attacking anyone who ventured into their territory. A group of surveyors inspecting central Texas for future settlements was attacked in 1833. The Indians killed one of the men, but the others escaped. In 1834 a Mexican official reported that Waco and Tawakoni Indians were the most frequent raiders of Texas settlements.[12]

Despite such attacks, white settlers moved farther up the Brazos River in 1835, closer to the Waco Indian village. "Quite a number of people around this time were killed around Fort Marlin by the Indians," who "also robbed the settlement of an immense amount of property and did all they could to break it up," historian J. W. Wilbarger noted. "For some reason," he concluded, "the Indians fought harder to retain the [Upper] Brazos country than any other portion of the state."[13]

Whether or not Wilbarger was right about the relative resistance of Texas Indians, it is clear that the fierce defense of central Texas stymied the Anglo advance. Yet the War for Texas Independence probably did more to devastate early American settlements than the Indians. With the approach of Santa Anna's army, almost all the region's initial settlers abandoned their newly built homes near the Falls of the Brazos River. "The houses were burned," noted one local historian "and the fields grew up in brush and weeds."[14] John Love, a former slave, recalled that "dey breaks up de settlement an' de most of dem leave, some go to other places in Texas an' others go back to Tennessee whar dey cum's from."[15]

The region remained bereft of whites and blacks for only a short time, however. John Marlin was among the first Anglo settlers to return to the Falls of the Brazos River after the War for Texas Independence. Unlike most other returning Texas pioneers, he and the other central Texans chose not to go back to the homes and farms carved out the previous year. Marlin was cognizant of the continuing danger of Indian attacks from the west and decided to abandon the dangerously exposed earlier village site on the west bank of the Brazos.[16] The new commitment to practicality even extended to nomenclature. In sharp contrast to Viesca, the more formal name of its predecessor, the reconstituted frontier community became known as Bucksnort.[17]

Early Anglo pioneers and their slaves came to Texas for a variety of reasons. Some fled from bleak and tragic lives in their home states in the hope of a new start, certain that life could not be much worse on the Texas frontier. In August 1836, South Carolinian Louis T. Wigfall declared in a letter to a friend the reasons for wanting to move to Texas: "You and I are differently situated— you have a father & sisters to feel for your loss—I am, I may almost say, alone in the world, the last of my family." Wigfall had concluded that "life or death are equally of little importance." His more successful friend, he noted, could not fathom his plan because "you have wealth & talents & a contented disposition. You have the certainty of succeeding in life. Why should you go to Texas?" For Wigfall, Texas offered the possibility of success and the certainty of change. "The dice are now in the box. I have shaken them & I hope soon to throw them. Death is on one side and fortune on the other. As to the result, I am almost indifferent."[18]

Early central Texas was dotted with taverns, brothels, and gambling houses, and many men were, like Wigfall, lured to the frontier by dreams of a new life. The adventure of pioneering, the absence of law enforcement, and a rough life free of the trappings of more settled life appealed to many east of the Mississippi. When a legal system finally did emerge, juries and court officials spent a significant amount of time indicting and trying such men. Before the Civil War, juries in McLennan County alone indicted 127 individuals for crimes against the moral order, such as gaming, gambling, illegally selling liquor, and "keeping a disorderly house." Likewise, violent crimes against persons were frequent in central Texas. McLennan County juries indicted sixty men for assault, attempted murder, and murder before the Civil War.[19]

It would be a mistake, however, to assume that all central Texans were violent gamblers who shared Wigfall's desperation and disregard for life. Many came to Texas not for the dangers of an unsettled land but for the simple economic opportunities the new republic offered. Perhaps they had read David B. Edward's *The History of Texas; or, the Emigrant's, Farmer's, and Politician's Guide to the Character, Climate, Soil, and Production of that Country*, first published in 1836. Edward observed that Texas possessed "exuberant fecundity" that was "excelled by no other country I have ever known."[20] Those prospective immigrants unable to obtain a copy of Edward's book may have been influenced by its reviews in a number of southern magazines. The *Southern Literary Messenger*, for example, printed an excerpt, praised the objectives of the author, and declared that the work gave a "flattering little picture of Texian comfort and abundance."[21]

Shapley P. Ross and his family came to Texas two years after the publication of Edward's guide. Upon arrival in 1838, Ross recalled, "We were filled with awe and admiration as we gazed on the far distant horizon . . . I wondered how soon these fruitful plains would attract others; there was so much good land to provide homes for thousands from the old states who could aid in redeeming it from the savages; such fields of wealth to be cultivated and stocked and I hoped I should live to see it all come true."[22] Not only would Shapley Ross live to see the white man invade central Texas, but he and his sons would also play leading roles in that conquest.[23]

* * *

Violence between the American settlers and Indians of the Texas prairie was nearly constant from the 1830s to the 1870s. Many, if not most, Americans who participated in attacks on Indians were ordinary settlers and "volunteer Indian fighters." To be sure, Texas Rangers and eventually the regular soldiers of the U.S. Army played an important role in the conquest of central Texas, but the frontlines of the Anglo-Indian conflict were staffed by small bands of farmers. These temporary and unpaid Indian fighters provided their own equipment, from horses to guns. As volunteers, they made their own decisions about patrols and the pursuit of Indians. They formed into companies as needed, and the personnel of any region's group of Indian fighters shifted constantly. In Bell County these men were known by several names, including the Independent Blues, the Bell County Minute Men, the Bell County Rovers, and Texas Mounted Rangers from Bell County.[24] The character of many bands of Indian fighters paralleled the organization and structure of vigilante mobs. In the years that followed, central Texans interested in orchestrating mob violence against whites, blacks, and Mexicans could justify their actions as essentially similar to the work of the revered Indian fighters.

Although the farmers of central Texas were willing to respond when necessary, they hoped for the creation of a full-time paramilitary force of Indian fighters. In 1835 settlers pleaded with the newly formed government of the Republic of Texas that "[t]he defenceless situation of our oppressed country calls for your prompt attention and speedy relief."[25] And in November of that same year the fledgling national government authorized a complement of fifty-six men. These men, the Texas Rangers, were to patrol the territory surrounding the Upper Brazos River.

The Indians of central Texas took note of the changes taking place in the region. They witnessed the seemingly unending flow of new white settlers. Even more significant, they were pressured by the influx of new Native Americans, such as the Cherokee, from the east. As the winter buffalo hunt of 1835 approached, the Wacos and Tawakonis finally gave in, deserted their village near present-day Waco with its great natural spring and fertile soil, and relocated farther up the Brazos River.[26]

Relocation did not mean the Wacos had conceded central Texas to American settlers. Throughout the period of the republic Indian attacks severely limited Anglo and African settlement in the region. In 1836 an Indian agent in Texas wrote that "the Comanches, Whacos, Tawaccanoes, Cadoes, Pawnees, and others, have already concentrated on the Trinity, and have been at war with the Americans since the settlement of the country."[27] George Bonnell reported in 1840 that pioneers living around the Falls of the Brazos had "suffered much annoyance from Indians."[28] During the fall of 1843, Central Texas resident and Indian fighter Jackson Puckett recalled that "the Indians, Comanches and Kioways, had refused to allow the whites to occupy that portion of the country [Hill County], claiming it as a hunting ground." Puckett maintained that pioneers who acquired land in central Texas failed to move to the region because "the danger of the country from hostile Indians was such that actual occupation of homesteads was impossible so many of the settlers sought new homes where there was protection."[29]

For those who braved the central Texas frontier in spite of its dangers, Indian raids greatly frustrated attempts at farming and ranching. John Love remembered the "Waco's an' other tribes dat kept robbin' dey cattle an' horses."[30] On occasion, however, young Indian warriors issued a more radical statement than simple theft. In 1836, for example, they murdered everyone in Laughlin McLennan's family settlement on Pond Creek in central Texas except for two young boys whom they carried off into captivity.[31] In 1839 three members of James Marlin's family were likewise killed by Indians.[32]

In responding to such attacks some leaders looked for alternatives to violence. Sam Houston, the republic's first president, pledged in 1836 that his government would "abstain from aggression, establish commerce with the different tribes, . . . [and] maintain even-handed justice with them."[33] Houston's peace policy, however, did not sit well with many Texans. The majority of Anglo Texans felt no remorse in pursuing a brutal policy of Indian removal and extermination, and a more aggressive President, Mirabeau B.

Lamar, succeeded Houston in 1838. Lamar increased the size of the Texas army and ordered it to remove Indians from their villages in east and central Texas.[34]

Such state-sanctioned violence was, however, far from the most common form of conflict between whites and Indians in central Texas. Many unauthorized bands of local Anglo settlers organized to attack Indians, and there is no doubt that they saw violent response as just. During the late 1830s John Marlin and a band of central Texans trailed a group of Indians, bested them in the ensuing battle, and forced them to agree to relinquish their land claims.[35]

Such success was not easily duplicated. In 1831 a group of some forty Americans left Austin's colony for central Texas in pursuit of the Tawakoni Indians, trailing them, a Mexican official reported, "in order to do them all the harm they could."[36] Much to their disappointment, the official reported two weeks later that the Anglos had been unable to find the Tawakonis.[37] In 1833 a settler named Martin Wells concocted a plan to lure Indians into an ambush only to have his scheme thwarted by a loss of the settlers' horses to the Indians.[38]

Like lynch mobs fifty years later, posses pursuing Indians desperately wanted to find their enemies and exact vengeance. Such emotions did not always lead to exacting investigations into the guilt or innocence of Indians they happened to encounter. One example of the desperate actions sometimes endorsed by Indian fighters emerged in a battle between whites and Tawakonis in present-day Limestone County. In July 1835 a group of eighteen whites attempted to surprise the Tawakonis and massacre them at their village. Much to the attackers' displeasure, however, a dog alerted the Indians. During the ensuing battle the Tawakonis killed one Anglo, badly wounded three others, and forced the Anglos to retreat. After gaining reinforcements the whites returned, only to find the village abandoned. Not giving up, they trailed the Indians for more than a hundred miles. When they suddenly came upon a small camp of them, they opened fire, killing three and capturing six others. A nearby, and larger, encampment of Tawakonis heard the gunfire and fled. The Anglos, already deep into Indian country, decided to return to the settlements with their captives. While camping on the Brazos River on the return trip, a Tawakoni mother—fearing captivity—killed her daughter and attempted to take her own life. As she lay bleeding, one of the Anglos finished the job by decapitating her. What could drive a mother to take the life of her own child? The subsequent actions of these Anglos sheds some light on the mother's actions. "Having procured some smallpox virus," recalled Indian fighter John Jenkins many years later.[39]

Even with such deadly tactics as germ warfare, settlers of central Texas had a difficult time defeating the prairie Indians. They needed the help of the state, but war with the Indians was not a wise course of action for the young republic. After the Texas Revolution, the Lone Star Republic was deeply in debt and could not muster the financial resources necessary for a more active policy of Indian removal. Some Texas leaders, such as Houston, hoped to resolve the disputes with the Indians through diplomacy, and in 1838 three years of negotiations finally led to a peace treaty being signed between some Indians of the Texas prairies and Indian agents of the Republic of Texas. The Texas legislature, however, never ratified the treaty, and a number of Texas Indians refused to be bound by its terms.[40]

Talks began again when voters returned Sam Houston to the presidency. In 1843 and 1844 Texas Indians and officials of the Republic of Texas met several times at the Indian council grounds in central Texas to discuss terms of peace. Negotiations culminated with a talk in October 1844 between the republic and most of the region's Indian leaders, and the treaty that resulted succeeded in bringing together most Texas Indians and led to a decline in hostilities for a time. President Sam Houston agreed that the republic would cease all military expeditions, establish trading posts among the Indians, and allow Comanches to hunt south of the old San Saba Mission. The Indians agreed to cease their attacks on white settlers.[41]

As long as new Anglo settlers continued to desire Indian land, however, treaties would never last. Jackson Puckett believed that "evil white men violated the Treaties" and spurred on "retaliation by the Indians."[42] Based on observations made during his trip through Texas from December 1845 to April 1847, Ferdinand Roemer predicted that Indians there would "be driven from their homes and eventually be exterminated." Roemer noted that whites had already taken the best Indian land and foresaw that the "white, greedy conqueror" would soon take remaining hunting grounds as well.[43]

Although Roemer clearly believed that injustice prevailed in Anglo actions toward Indians, the vast majority of white Texans held no such reservations. On 12 October 1837 the Texas republic's Standing Committee on Indian Affairs issued a report on the legitimacy of Indian claims to the lands of Texas. The committee ruled an earlier treaty between Sam Houston and the Indians invalid and declared that upon the "most mature consideration" and the "most assiduous inquiry" that Indians of Texas did not have "a vested right of any kind" to the land there beyond "the *Prima Facia* right of Occupancy."[44]

The committee found several reasons for denying Indians any land in Texas. First, many had migrated to Texas from other parts of the country and could not claim Texas soil as their ancestral land. Second, some tribes that had lived in Texas for a long period of time were the responsibility of Mexico and had forfeited their rights when Mexico forfeited theirs on the field of battle. And, third, the remaining Indians in Texas could not claim land there because they were either too mobile and nomadic to claim any specific territory or so "fiendish" that they were unworthy of any rights whatsoever.[45]

In addition to legally stripping them of any rights to their land in Texas, the Anglo vision of Indians as brutal murderers, rapists, and kidnappers helped enlist local volunteers for Indian fighting. Accounts of life in Texas frequently justified preemptive Anglo violence against Indians by conjuring up an image of them as a threat to central Texas's family life. A "man with a heart-endearing wife, and a family of beloved children" should be careful, warned one account, because of reports in which "not only the houses have been rifled, but the inmates subjected to savage brutality, in the absence of their husbands, brothers, or hired protectors."[46]

In 1837 the Committee on Indian Affairs noted that Indians posed a grave threat to the home life of pioneers. Indians, warned the committee, "carry off children and females as prisoners . . . [who] are forced to subserve the purposes that any beings other than *fiends* would blush to think of."[47] Most young white men found they had little difficulty in killing Indians, who, they were told, threatened to attack their homes, kidnap their children, and rape their wives.

Such appeals combined with a strong, underlying confidence in the "manifest destiny" of Anglo-Saxon racial progress. "What," the editor of a Waco newspaper asked rhetorically in 1878, "shall the country do with its Indian population?" His answer? "It is a question of manifest destiny, in which one race is bound to annihilate another."[48] Central Texans had been following such a plan for nearly fifty years.

* * *

Such rhetoric often overwhelmed diplomatic and political attempts to reduce tensions on the frontier. Although Texas Indians signed a new treaty with the federal government after the state's annexation by the United States, Indians noticed that nothing checked the expansion of whites into central and north-western Texas. Furthermore, the new settlers had begun to kill the buffalo in greater numbers. Indians hoped the federal government would be strong enough to enforce its treaties and prevent Texans from expanding their holdings. "For a long time a great many people have been passing through my country; they kill all the game, and burn the country, and trouble me very much," declared a Comanche leader at mid-century. "I believe that our white brothers do not wish to run a line between us, because they wish to settle in this country. I object to any more settlements. I want this country to hunt in."[49]

Anglo Texans looked forward to annexation for different reasons. They welcomed the aid of the U.S. Army in protecting settlements from Texas Indians. Although the war with Mexico delayed the arrival of federal troops, by 1849 the government had erected a system of forts along the Texas frontier, fulfilling the long-held dreams of many Texas leaders. The federal army claimed that its mission was to defend white and Indian from one another. The Anglo Texans believed, however, that the federal government's mission was to make central Texas a safer place for white immigrants. For their part, Indian leaders thought the military did little to protect them from settlers. "You told me that troops were placed for our protection as well as the whites," a Comanche leader pointed out, "that I know is not so."[50] The army was caught in the middle. The region's Native Americans did not trust the government, and many central Texas settlers believed the army was not doing enough to end the "Indian problem."[51]

Central Texas's anger with the federal government grew quickly. Residents charged that the military fort system was ineffective. In 1854, protesting conditions on the frontier, they petitioned the governor of Texas that the "military forces of the General Government" were "too far out, to render timely and efficient aid when most needed." Seventy-eight residents signed the document.[52]

Early settlers also argued that the federal government's policies were unsuited to warfare against Indians. In particular, they decried the extension of due process to Native Americans. As one early settler recalled, "Unfortunately the Department officers at Washington hold the idea that Indians should be tried in civil courts for outrages committed." He defended Indian fighters who acted outside the law by noting that "savages in war paint descending on a surprised and peaceful settlement could not be well identified by a frightened survivor of their raid when later he saw them under control and in entirely different surroundings."[53]

The growing frustration with the federal government's Indian policies climaxed during the late 1850s. Bosque County citizens submitted a petition to the governor in 1857, seeking aid against "the marauding savages that infest our frontier." They wrote that the "regular troops placed here for the purpose of protecting the frontier afford us not protection."[54] In 1858 one veteran of the frontier concluded that "the Federal Government has failed to protect us."[55] Such comments were echoed in newspapers and in meetings held throughout central Texas in 1858 and 1859.[56]

The great source of tension between central Texans and the government was the Brazos Indian reservation, which the Texas State Legislature and the U.S. government agreed to set up in 1854. Over the next two years several Texas

Indian tribes agreed to live on the reservation, including the Wacos. Although most Indian attacks were probably committed by the Comanches and other Indians who refused to live on the reservation, central Texas farmers blamed the raids on Brazos reservation Indians almost from the beginning. In 1857 the *Belton Independent* noted that "Indians in the Reserve are in our humble opinion at the foot of it, if not the actor in these villanies—and the best that can be done with them is to exterminate them."[57]

Anger and frustration boiled and finally exploded on 27 December 1858, when Anglo settlers descended upon a band of Indians in north central Texas. As it turned out, they were peaceful Caddos and Anadarkos from the reservation and possessed passes from government officials allowing them to hunt off the reservation. This mattered little to these settlers who hoped to remove all Indians from Texas. Finding many of the Indians asleep, the Anglos charged and opened fire. When the smoke from the settlers' guns cleared and the "battle" was over, seven Native Americans were dead. Of the seven killed, three were women. One Anglo was killed, although some speculate that his friends shot him in the confusion.[58]

The brutal attack so angered government officials that they issued orders to arrest the settlers involved. Bringing the men to trial was difficult, however, because of great resistance from the vast majority of white citizens in central Texas and their elected civil officials. George Erath advised the governor that the attack on the Indians was "excusable" because settlers were not "able to distinguish different tribes."[59] Edward Gurley wrote that deputized officials refused to execute arrest warrants against the men who attacked the Indians. They were, he warned, armed and would not be arrested unless overwhelmed by force. If they could be arrested, he worried that any trial would be interrupted by violence on behalf of the accused.[60] Not surprisingly, the settlers who murdered these Indians did not come to trial.

Emboldened by defying the government, central Texas settlers now turned on the Brazos Indian reservation itself. Beginning in April, hundreds of central Texans organized for the purpose of destroying the reservation. Fully aware that they planned to commit extralegal violence, some 250 armed men marched under the banner "Necessity Knows No Law." Their intention was to "fall upon" the reservation's Indians and the white government officials there and "kill them indiscriminately." Federal troops defended the agency and ordered the vigilantes to leave the reservation, which they did—but not before killing and scalping an eighty-year-old Waco. The murder prompted reservation Indians to attack the Anglos as they left. In the investigation and negotiations that followed the attack, no one arrested members of the mob or its leaders. In fact, the mob's action was instrumental in prompting the government to remove the reservation's Indians from Texas and relocate them in Oklahoma.[61]

Even after the Native Americans had been relocated, members of the mob continued to hunt the agency officials who had prevented the Indians' massacre. Leaders of the vigilantes offered a reward for the scalp of Robert Neighbors, the U.S. superintendent of Indian affairs in Texas, and on 14 September 1859, a man named Edward Cornett assassinated Neighbors in Young County, Texas. Stories circulated that the assassin had been provoked into a state of rage by the abduction of his wife by Neighbors's Indian friends. Evidence, however, suggests that Indians did not abduct Mrs. Cornett. In fact, she did not go missing until after the assassination, and even then she was likely visiting friends or relatives. It is not surprising that Neighbors's murder would be tied to a story involving the kidnapping of someone's wife by Indians. For generations, central Texans had considered such reasoning to be a legitimate justification for extralegal killing.[62]

The removal of the Brazos reservation Indians has long been recognized as a great turning point in Anglo-Indian relations in Texas. Although warriors occasionally raided settlements during the 1860s and 1870s, the Indians of the Texas prairie now had no safe haven anywhere in the state. The assault on the reservation was also an important moment in the history of Texas mob violence. Central Texans no doubt drew several lessons from the episode. First, they learned that there was widespread support, at least in certain situations, for extralegal violence in the region. Hundreds participated directly in the march on the reservation, and thousands throughout central Texas sympathized with the mob's demands and actions. Second, local authorities—even under pressure from the state and federal government—were not likely to arrest, much less convict, participants in acts of vigilantism. Third, mob violence was an effective instrument of change. Although no one had proved that reservation Indians constituted a legitimate threat to settlements, the mob's actions of 1859 influenced the government to close the reservation. A few weeks of direct and illegal citizen intervention accomplished more than years of peaceful and legal protest.

* * *

The removal of reservation Indians in 1859 did not end conflict between whites and Native Americans in central Texas. Over the next fifteen years, bands of Indians from the Plains periodically swept into the region and raided it, exciting tensions and provoking posses to renewed action. Yet 1859 is a critical dividing line in the history of mob violence in central Texas. In the years that followed, other developments—sectional tensions over slavery, the Civil War, and Reconstruction—quickly surpassed conflict with Indians in importance. The legacy of the region's early violence, however, lived on. The subsequent history of mob violence in central Texas subtly reflected its roots in the Anglo-Indian struggle for the prairie.

Violence between whites and Indians in central Texas reinforced and molded mob violence in the region in three ways. First, it provided the form of the mob itself. In the years to follow, central Texans showed themselves quite comfortable with spontaneously organizing into posses and vigilance committees. The easy creation of such groups, and their implicit claim to legitimacy not to mention actual membership and leaders, rested on the region's thirty-year history of volunteer Indian fighters.

Second, central Texans justified their actions against Native Americans in ways that foreshadowed future defenses of mob violence. Early settlers did not emphasize the underlying cause of the Anglo-Indian conflict: land. Instead, they shrouded the economic and political origins of the conflict by emphasizing racial and cultural differences. The early central Texans did more, however, than invoke the long-standing tradition of Anglo-Saxon racism; they cast their enemies as a threat to the region's white women and children. Native Americans were declared to be not only racially and culturally inferior to whites but also a threat to masculine honor. Husbands, fathers, brothers, and sons faced an immoral foe bent on raping, kidnapping, and assaulting wives, daughters, sisters, and mothers. All these justifications for mob violence—whether the slighting of economic motives or an emphasis on masculine honor—would reappear during the late nineteenth century as white mobs turned their attention to the region's African Americans.

Third, and most important, a successful "defense" of settlements from Indians provided central Texans with heroes and stories that reinforced the legitimacy of mob violence for future generations. The actions of early central Texan settlers themselves were important not only because such actions had great impact on later patterns of mob violence but also because the early violence became the foundation for the region's myths, legends, memories, and exaggerations of violence.

* * *

Texans memorialized the deeds of their Indian-fighting heroes in writing. In 1880 one-time central Texan John Henry Brown published *Indian Wars and Pioneers of Texas,* a compendium of heroic Anglos in struggle against savage Indians. The "dedicatory preface" reads: "When a good action is performed we feel that it should be remembered forever." The volume was well regarded at the time of publication and considered worthy of republication in 1978.[63]

In 1889 J. W. Wilbarger published one of the most enduring accounts of the conflict between Anglos and Texas Indians, and it is apparent from the title where Wilbarger's sympathies resided: *Indian Depredations in Texas: Reliable Accounts of Battles, Wars, Adventures, Forays, Murders, Massacres, etc., etc., Together with Biographical Sketches of Many of the Most Noted Indian Fighters and Frontiersmen of Texas.*[64] County and town histories also praised the region's Indian fighters. In 1951 *Western Falls County, Texas,* written by Lillian St. Romain, expressed the widely held view that "leniency toward savages had no place in the practical world of the frontier where hardships were plentiful enough without constant Indian troubles."[65]

In addition to these overviews, central Texans also learned about the region's early settlers and Indian fighters from memoirs, biographies, and newspaper profiles. *A Texas Ranger and Frontiersman: The Days of Buck Barry in Texas* was first published in 1932. The deeds of Bosque County's James Buckner ("Buck") Barry were soon lauded from Southwest to the Northeast. The *Houston Gargoyle* wrote that Barry was one of the "he-men who fought the battles of the wilderness," the *New York Times* called him "very much of a man," and the *New York Herald Tribune* referred to Barry as "absolutely fearless." The *Boston Evening Transcript* praised his "uncommon knowledge of human nature and Indian character."[66]

Barry's memoir was hardly unique. John Holland Jenkins wrote of fighting Indians and about frontier life in *Recollections of Early Texas;* George Barnard Erath's memories came to print in *The Memoirs of Major George B. Erath;* and Elizabeth Ross Clarke, Shapley Ross's granddaughter, compiled "YA-A-H-H-OO: The Life and Adventures of Captain Shapley P. Ross and a Biographical Sketch of Lawrence Sullivan Ross."[67] In addition to book-length memoirs, newspapers would frequently print short accounts of early Texas history. Frank Collier, for example, entitled his series of newspaper articles about the deeds of pioneers "Frontier Sketches."[68]

Such works praised central Texans for resourceful acts of self-defense, but the writers also justified the pioneers' aggressive actions by invoking race and the rhetoric of manifest destiny. Clarke, for example, justified the displacement of Indians, whom she described as "inveterate gamblers" with "an aversion to labor."[69] A central Texas newspaper wrote that "Texas, lying as she does upon the extreme verge of the Anglo-Saxon civilization in the Western World, is the advance picket of the progress and ideas of this sturdy race."[70]

Local histories, memoirs, and newspaper stories were important in the formation of the historical memory of violence in central Texas, but they always worked in conjunction with even more accessible modes of shaping public opinion and collective memory. Central Texans honored the region's early Indian fighters through oral tradition, local folklore, and the creation of historical markers and museums.

Mrs. William Price, interviewed during the 1930s by the Works Progress Administration, reflected on the passing down of stories from generation to generation. She noted that "folklore handed down to us children in the days of our childhood makes the history and the legends of what happened and how they lived as real as if I had lived" there and then. Price, who moved to Texas in 1849, recalled the fear early settlers had of "hostile Indians" and "Mexicans" but admitted, "I do not remember any attacks on my people by either one."[71] Belle Little also recalled that some of "my earliest memories are of continual fear of the Indians."[72] Interviews with central Texans from this period, whether conducted with white pioneers or former slaves, routinely identified the names and deeds of the region's early Indian fighters.[73]

Central Texas's civic leaders were not satisfied with honoring the region's pioneers through oral tradition alone. They named towns, counties, and streets after the men, and they erected historical markers. James Buckner Barry's marker, for example, praises his efforts for preventing "Indian attacks." The marker for Alison Nelson, a leader of the assault on the Brazos reservation, proudly identifies Nelson as an "Indian fighter." A marker at the site of John Marlin's home in Falls County notes that at the site of the marker in 1839 four heroic settlers held off an assault by seventy Indians, killing seven and sustaining only one man wounded. In Bell County a historical marker was placed at Bird Creek Battlefield, which was named "in honor of Captain John Bird who lost his life here May 26, 1839." The marker's text concludes, "With only 34 Texas Rangers he met 240 Indians at this point, and routed them."[74] Markers have been placed throughout central Texas at sites of early forts, which, information on them indicates, were built for "protection from the Indians" or to guard against "hostile Indians."[75]

Central Texans also honored the region's early settlers by developing exhibits for local festivals and, eventually, museums. Now, the most impressive repository of artifacts and memories of Texas's early Indian fighters is the Texas Ranger Hall of Fame and Museum located in Waco. The museum, however, was not built until 1968. During the early twentieth century the history of early central Texas was remembered at Waco's Texas Cotton Palace, which hosted annual festivals. On such occasions the few remaining Waco Indians living in Oklahoma would sometimes be returned to the one-time site of their village to be viewed by passing crowds. The historical marker erected to remember the Cotton Palace refers to these and other Indian exhibits as a "warpath" of sideshows.[76]

Central Texans—through writing, passing down folklore, and creating public markers and exhibits—lavished praise on the violent acts of the region's early settlers. Such praise alone, however, cannot explain the continued strength of the area's culture of violence. Other communities in the United States, those in the American South and even in Texas, honored the violence of their ancestors without the levels of murder and killing seen in central Texas. Moreover, central Texas settlers did not necessarily thirst for violence and killing. Most of the early ones, people like Shapley Ross, did not go to Texas to fight the Indians but to become successful farmers, cultivate the "fruitful plains," and live on the "good land." They hoped to provide first and foremost for themselves and their families, and they also hoped to become rich from the fertile prairie soil. Conflict with Indians made doing so difficult, but after the collapse of the Brazos reservation in 1859 central Texas seemed safe for farming.

Immigrants now arrived in even larger numbers. Some raised livestock, but most probably planned to grow that most important of southern crops, cotton. Quite a few brought African slaves with them to aid them in that endeavor. One African who found himself in Texas was John Love. During the 1930s he recalled how life in the late 1850s had improved and changed for early settlers. Love remembered that "de people wuz gittin along fine. De Indians wuz not as troublesome out in de West, where dey had been so bad ter kill de settlers, de folks wuz er plantin dey patches which dey wuz gradually turnin into big plantations."[77]

Such a portrait, however, belied the tensions brewing beneath the surface of the master-slave relationship. With the conquest of Mexico and the Indians of the Texas prairie nearly complete, settlers might have believed that their need to resort to frequent acts of violence would decline. Little did they understand the extent to which the introduction of slavery would require continuation of the region's history of violence.

3. "Slavery with a Will": Slave Resistance and the Origins of the Panic of 1860

During the summer of 1860 vigilance committees across Texas executed an unknown number of men, both black and white, for allegedly conspiring to incite a series of slave rebellions. Eyewitness accounts confirm the killing of thirty men during the "Panic of 1860," although the number was in all likelihood closer to a hundred. The death toll and the geographical range of the vigilante movement mark this episode as the most important slave panic since Nat Turner's insurrection in 1831.[1]

Historians who have studied what contemporaries labeled the "Texas Troubles" have convincingly demonstrated that the mob violence of 1860 was motivated far more by a sense of fear than by any actual plot concocted by white abolitionists or the enslaved. Not as well explained is the reason that such a panic should have developed in Texas. John Brown's 1859 raid on the armory at Harpers Ferry is often suggested as a major spur to the violence of 1860. Yet Brown's raid occurred in Virginia, about as far away from Texas as possible in the South. What made Texas and not some other southern state the scene of this outbreak of vigilantism?[2]

A number of factors—the sparsely settled condition of the state, a recent history of conflicts with both Mexicans and Native Americans, and a pervasive perception that Texans were especially tolerant of vigilantism—contributed to creating a robust tradition of extralegal action in the years leading up to 1860. In order to understand the fear that gripped white Texans in the summer of 1860, however, additional factors must be considered.

First, the role of slave resistance, a primary contributory factor in the growth of extralegal violence, must be explored. Historians, however, have been skeptical about the role of the enslaved in the plot of 1860, and evidence for an actual plot against slavery in 1860 is, in truth, thin. The spark for the panic was a series of fires in north central Texas. Vigilantes alleged arson, but spontaneous fires ignited by extreme heat and newly introduced phosphorous matches seem more plausible. Confessions from enslaved witnesses were no doubt obtained through whipping and other forms of torture. Some degree of uncertainty will always persist, but it seems likely that no coordinated plan of action existed.[3]

Yet the absence of evidence linking the enslaved and the Panic of 1860 does not mean that black Texans did not resist slavery. Indeed, it is clear that they harbored bitter resentment toward bondage. For decades before 1860, slaves in Texas resisted the institution in almost every possible manner. That history of resistance—which exceeded similar contemporary resistance by slaves in earlier-settled parts of the South—did not go unnoticed by Texas slaveholders and must be considered at least an important backdrop, if not an essential element, of the Panic of 1860.

A closely related second factor was the rhetorical response that emerged to the resistance, a rhetoric that shaped the region's mob violence and prepared whites for the Texas Troubles. Resistance by slaves in central Texas exacerbated the daily level of violence already present in master-slave relations and required episodic extralegal action from whites to maintain control. Instead of using violence as something necessary to put down the willful flight of servants, however, Anglos chose to cast their actions in the light of self-defense. More specifically, they did not justify violence as necessary to intimidate and undermine the actual, everyday resistance of their slaves. Such justification would have undermined the institution in the eyes of outsiders by revealing that most slaves were not content with bondage. Instead, whites justified extralegal actions by claiming that malcontent interlopers, primarily Mexicans and Northern abolitionists, periodically misled the region's slaves into attempting to plot revolts. A general paucity of evidence, and the fact that such revolts failed to occur, did not interfere with this rhetorical creation.

Results were spectacular. First, blaming outsiders obscured the actual cause of violence: everyday slave resistance. Second, emphasizing the danger of slave rebellions (over the actual primary form of resistance, flight) provoked fear throughout the general white community—slaveholder and nonslaveholder alike. Third, calling for emergency action as a means of self-defense led to widespread participation and linked mob violence against slaves and abolitionists to local patterns of violence against Native Americans.

* * *

Black slaves accompanied white settlers into central Texas from the very beginning of American settlement. Determining exactly how many slaves resided in central Texas during the early years is difficult. The entire Upper Brazos River valley was but one part of what became the two sprawling counties of Milam and Robertson. In 1840 Milam County stretched westward from the Brazos River to the edge of the Plains, and few Anglo or African settlers lived there. Most of those who did probably lived well below the Falls of the Brazos for fear of Indian attacks. Robertson County stretched from the west bank of the Trinity River to the east bank of the Brazos. Both counties extended great distances north and south. Robertson County likely contained almost all the Anglo and African settlers in the Upper Brazos River valley. County-level data for 1840 reveal that 47 (17 percent) of some 271 tax-paying residents of Robertson County owned approximately 284 slaves. The average holding was six slaves per master, and the largest consisted of forty-five African men, women, and children. Although these numbers are certainly imprecise, they indicate that both slaveowners and slaves were far from uncommon, even during this early stage of central Texas history.[4]

After Texas's annexation by the United States, a massive wave of American migrants flocked there. "From 1840 to 1860, and particularly from 1850 to 1860, the 'Texas fever' developed almost into a delirium," observed historian Lewis Cecil Gray. Newspapers throughout the South resounded with "accounts of the wonderful fertility of Texas land, the salubrity of the climate, and the enormous fortunes to be made in planting cotton."[5] In 1850 the population of the state was 212,592, but a decade of growth later Texas boasted 604,215 men, women, and children.[6]

Central Texas received many of these settlers. More than 90 percent of the migrants came from southern states, and the vast majority engaged in agriculture, primarily cotton production and subsistence farming.[7] By 1860 McLennan and Falls counties alone produced 4,359 bales of ginned cotton. Although the Upper Brazos River valley became home to a substantial number of yeomen farmers and cattle ranchers who had few or no slaves, by 1860 many incoming families brought perpetual servants with them. On the eve of the Civil War, slaves accounted for a third of the valley's population.[8]

Central Texas during the mid-nineteenth century was a world torn in three directions by four different cultures.[9] From the east came white and black settlers of the young and expanding United States. To the north and the west, Native Americans roamed the Texas plains and prairies. And in the south, Mexico's outposts and settlements continued to dot the landscape. To be sure, the success of Texas's independence limited the reach of Mexico in central Texas, and the ongoing struggle against Indians reduced their power in the region as well. Nevertheless, these groups remained embroiled in a host of bloody conflicts until the coming of the Civil War.

An analysis of central Texas during the middle of the nineteenth century alters scholarly understanding of runaway slaves in the United States.[10] During the conflicts that ensued on the little-populated but multicultural Texas prairie, thousands of slaves took the opportunity to escape to freedom. Although masters had often contained the scope of the power struggle between masters and slaves in earlier-settled regions of the South, the Texas prairie offered opportunities that heightened contention. As slaves sought to escape authority and slaveholders strove to reestablish control, both combatants revealed much about the peculiar nature of their society—its fluidity and complexity, its tensions and conflicts, and its foundation in fear and violence.[11]

"One thing is certain," wrote a Texas newspaperman in the 1850s, "unless something be done to arrest the escape of slaves, this class of property will become valueless in Western Texas. . . . As yet, but few of those escaping have been caught."[12] Another observer remarked, "Texans were more or less used to losing their slaves, who would often run away."[13] In March 1860 the near-escape of two recently arrived bondsmen from South Carolina prompted the *Corpus Christi Ranchero* to warn Texas planters to watch their slaves "a little closer." The runaways, the newspaper noted fearfully, had almost reached the Mexican border despite being largely unfamiliar with local geography. The editor concluded that fellow slaves had conspired with the two black newcomers and helped them navigate the southern branch of the Underground Railroad.[14] Such comments cannot be dismissed as the opinions of naturally exaggerating Texans or the panic-stricken cries of paranoid slaveholders. Texas did indeed witness an exodus of African slaves. Their resistance helps shed light on the Slave Panic of 1860 as well as on daily battles for power between masters and slaves.

Most masters, of course, were well acquainted with a certain amount of slave resistance. Masters on many southern plantations recognized the broken hoes, stolen chickens, and verbal sparring for the resistance to authority that they represented. Unlike their Caribbean and Brazilian contemporaries, however, slaveholders in the United States had little experience with direct assaults on the slave system. The most serious form of resistance masters were likely to encounter was flight. But many slaveholders, especially those in the Lower South, assured themselves that their slaves, even if they left temporarily, would soon return to the fold and that they had largely contained resistance within an acceptable range. As one historian remarked of the difficulties runaways encountered, "The quarter had no mansions, but the swamp offered no comfortable beds. The plantation diet was not sumptuous, but rabbits were hard to catch."[15] Slaves might hide in the woods and escape work for a couple of days, but they were unlikely to engage in resistance serious enough to undermine the system of slavery itself.

As black and white settlers entered Texas, slaveholders had no reason to think that their control over their slaves was especially fragile.[16] Some masters even hoped the move would curtail resistance. Frederick Law Olmsted recalled meeting a slaveholder in the mid-1850s who believed he "could break [his slave] of running away [to Illinois] by bringing him down to this new country." But the move to Texas only changed the direction of the slave's flight. "I expect he's making for Mexico, now," the slaveholder admitted.[17]

The move to Texas paved the way for resistance because it often disrupted slave family life. A number of slaves arrived in Texas via the interstate slave trade.[18] But even for those who had come with their masters, the move meant leaving relatives and friends. It is possible to grasp the move's impact by comparing the experiences of slaves in central Texas with those who lived throughout the South. In *Slavery Remembered,* historian Paul Escott examined thousands of slave narratives collected throughout the South by the Works Progress Administration during the 1930s. He found that a little over one in five former slaves reported some kind of family disruption during slavery. When Escott's statistical model is applied strictly to the narratives of slaves who lived in central Texas, however, three out of four slaves there reported such separations.[19]

Slaves considered being torn from their old environments, separating mothers and children, husbands and wives, to be a violation of the master-slave relationship. Henry Caufield reported that "Steve [his slave] is tolerable well satisfied [but he] would be very well, if there were more Negroes [because] he gets lonesome at times." Five months later Caufield remarked, "Steve is in good health [and] does not say anything but [he] is not very well satisfied with Texas."[20] Incensed at being forced from their homes, the slaves grew bitter on the journey to Texas.

At first they could not act on their anger and resentment. They depended on white masters for food, and the move was itself frightening and disconcerting. One former bondsman recalled that Indians "wuz roaming everywhar, An' hit made us uneasy, for de safety of our Hair."[21] Another former slave remembered being too "scairt in de strange country an' strange folks to run away from de ones us knowed."[22] Although they detested bondage, slaves thought twice about leaving their masters and fellow slaves for Indian territory, which often seemed dangerous and foreboding.

This initial reluctance, however, faded quickly after arrival.[23] Apprehension of the new country lessened with increased familiarity. Wild game proved plentiful, undercutting the slaves' dependence on masters for food. Once they learned the contours of the new country they realized that it possessed unique opportunities for resistance to slavery.[24] In a rich but thinly settled land peopled with Native Americans and bordered by a free country, blacks had a much better chance to escape the peculiar institution. They often struck out across Texas, and in a very short time the prairie allowed them a chance to free themselves from the carefully constructed master-slave relationship they had been forced to reluctantly accept in their old states.

Mexico's stance on slavery had long proven a thorn in the side of Texas slaveholders. Indeed, fears over the security of slavery played an important role in the coming of the War for Texas Independence. Yet as many historians have pointed out, Mexican actions before 1836 had not unduly disrupted the development of bondage in Texas. Ironically, a revolution fought in part to secure slavery from Mexican interference provided far more opportunities for slave resistance than had ever existed under Mexican rule.

As Santa Anna's army marched northward, Anglos feared that the Mexican army might liberate their slaves—or even worse, entice them to rebel. During the summer of 1835 it was reported that the commander of a Mexican war schooner had sailed into Galveston Bay, intending to "take all the negro slaves in the country that he could get in his possession, and offer them their liberty after one year's service."[25] An open letter to the Texas public warned that one of the goals of the impending invasion of Texas was the "emancipation of her slaves."[26] In separate letters, Benjamin Milam and Horatio Allsberry declared that the official policy of the Mexican army was far worse—it was intended to "get the slaves to revolt" and "let them loose upon their families."[27] According to William Parker, Sam Houston had ordered the retreat of the colonists and the Texas army across Texas "to prevent the negroes from joining the enemy in small parties."[28]

In reality, the policy of the Mexican army toward African slaves was far from coordinated. On 16 February 1836 the army's commander-in-chief queried the secretary of war on army policy toward Texan slaves. "There is a considerable number of slaves in Texas," observed Santa Anna, "who according to our laws should be free." Although he offered no concrete plan for their liberation, he asked, "Shall we permit these wretches to moan in chains any longer in a country whose kind laws protect the liberty of man without distinction of cast [*sic*] or color?"[29] Despite such enlightened concern, no evidence exists that the Mexican army actively pursued a policy of liberating blacks during the Texas Revolution.

Although the Mexican army's actions toward slavery did not live up to fears voiced by anxious Anglos, Texas slaves raised concerns by taking matters into their own hands. As Mexican soldiers attempted to ford the Colorado River on 10 April 1836, "several natives, a mulatto woman, two Negro women and several Negro men" appeared to help them cross.[30] Such episodes were repeated again and again, even after the Mexican army was defeated and had begun to retreat.[31] Although the total number of slaves that sought refuge with the Mexican army is unknown, their numbers were sufficient enough that Anglo Texans made their return part of the battlefield agreement signed by Santa Anna and also the subsequent Treaty of Velasco.[32]

Even after Anglo Texans had thrown off Mexican rule and expelled its army, the new republic's southern neighbor continued to pose a danger to the institution of slavery. "The proximity of Texas to the Mexican border," noted a Texas historian, "made the escape of slaves a rather frequent occurrence."[33] Fugitive slaves who escaped to Mexico entered a free nation, freer than the American North that was burdened with the Fugitive Slave Act. Relations among Mexico, Texas, and the United States remained strained throughout the antebellum period, complicating diplomatic attempts to solve the fugitive problem. As late as 1854 the U.S. minister to Mexico, James Gadsen, complained that the Mexican government was issuing "Cartas de Seguridad" with passports that allowed fugitive slaves an easy escape into the interior of Mexico. Gadsen "strongly admonished" Mexico that such actions encouraged slave flight and warned of "the increasing evil of Slaves thus encouraged to abscond from Texas."[34] Such protests had little practical impact, and Mexico, as a result, became a haven for runaway slaves. One newspaper reported that the land across the Rio Grande had "long been regarded by the Texas slave as his El Dorado for accumulation, his utopia for political rights, and his Paradise for happiness."[35]

"Seen anything of a runaway nigger over there, anywhar?" a Texan asked of Frederick Law Olmsted in 1854. A fugitive slave had fled his master for the border of Mexico, Olmsted reported, and the Texan claimed the slave had been out "nigh two weeks." The runaway "liked to have killed the judge" who owned him, and he cut his young master "right bad." After trailing the fugitive for days, the master said, "We caught him once, but he got away from us again. . . . We shot at him three times with rifles, but he'd got too far off, but we must have shaved him close." Although they eventually lost the slave, "we run him close, though, I tell you. Run him out of his coat, and his boots, and a pistol he'd got. But 'twas getting dark, and he got in them bayous, and kept swimming from one side to the other." They stayed after him for ten days, but, as the master observed, "If he's got across that river, he'd get to the Mexicans in two days, and there he'd be safe. The Mexicans'd take care of him."[36]

Despite such concerted efforts to recapture fleeing slaves, escape into Mexico became a recurring theme for Texans during the 1850s. "Something should be done," one newspaper proclaimed in 1855, "to put a stop to the escape of negroes into Mexico. If the General Government cannot protect us, we should protect ourselves."[37] Although no precise figures for the numbers of runaways can be given, it surely was in the thousands. One source claimed in 1851 that an estimated three thousand escaped slaves lived in Mexico. Olmsted noted three years later that "runaways were constantly arriving" at Piedras Negras on the Mexican side of the Rio Grande, and a Texas Ranger claimed that four thousand fugitive slaves lived in northern Mexico in 1855.[38] As late as 1858 and 1860 Texas newspapers reported instances of Mexicans aiding runaways attempting to escape south of the border.[39]

Although slaves in southern Texas were nearer the Mexican border, runaways came from as far away as Arkansas and Louisiana for a chance at freedom. The sheriff of McLennan County reported the capture of a runaway slave from Louisiana in January 1861.[40] Former slaves from the region remembered others who fled to Mexico. "My grandfather run 'way an' went down to Mexico," recalled one.[41] "De Mexicans," said a former slave in Falls County, "would try to git dem [rebellious slaves] ter run away an stay across de border wid dem an some ob dem did."[42] George Glasker, a former slave who lived on the Brazos River in McLennan County, recalled that "de Mexicans down on de border would git de slaves to run away befo' the Civil War cum."[43]

One of the most unusual aspects of slave flight in Texas was the fact that groups and not just individuals attempted to reach Mexico, and hundreds succeeded. Flight for Mexico often involved larger groups and more sophisticated planning than more typical slave escapes in other parts of the South. In 1837, for example, a group of runaways reached Mexico after a violent encounter with a sheriff. They had killed him and concealed his body so well that it was not found for five years.[44] On 27 December 1844 a group of twenty-five slaves—mounted on stolen horses and armed—fled Bastrop for the border. A little over a week later Anglos caught seventeen of them, but authorities believed that the remaining eight had made good their escape.[45] In 1845 six fugitives from the Waco area fled for Mexico. In what was no doubt an effort to start new lives across the border, they took a herd of twenty-five horses with them.[46]

Most slaves in Texas considered flight across the Rio Grande, not rebellion, to be their best way to escape bondage, and Texas slaveholders and their allies spent considerable time and energy attempting to recapture them. On occasion the problem of fugitive slaves became so great that slaveholders employed professional slave catchers and "blood hounds to track the run-a-way slaves." According to Burke Simpson, a former slave from central Texas, "I kin hear in my memory how dey would go thro' de country a yelpin' as dey chase de niggers thro' de bottom."[47]

Slaveholders also sought to catch runaways by offering large rewards to Indians for their return. In 1845 George Barnard's trading post in the Upper

Brazos River valley paid $300 to a number of Cherokees "for the apprehension and delivery of the runaway negroes." Barnard noted that they were "taken up about fifteen miles west of the head of the Guadalupe river, making their way to the Spanish country."[48]

Once slave catchers had recaptured the fugitives, however, there was still the problem of what to do with them. When two slaves who fled from Austin were recaptured in 1840, for example, their owner whipped them.[49] Yet slave narratives and other testimonies indicate that the use of the lash often led to further slave flight. "I was afraid to chastize them," another slaveholder declared, "as we were right on the line where they could cross over into Mexico and be free."[50] J. D. B Stillman, a physician from New York who traveled through Texas in 1855, confirmed the possibility of recaptured slaves returning to Mexico. Near the border he encountered a group of slave catchers and their recently captured quarry. The slave had escaped to Mexico, was recaptured, escaped again, was recaptured yet again, escaped a third time, and was finally recaptured still again.[51]

Ample evidence exists that slaveholders in the Texas interior readily used the whip, but some recognized the ineffectiveness of such increased punishment alone to douse dreams of freedom. In the case of the slaves who fled Austin in 1840, a friend of their owner suggested a different course of action, "Would it not be prudent for you to sell black John in the lower country instead of bringing him up here where the Mexicans and renegade whites may again encourage him to run away?"[52] Only by selling and removing his slave from the Texas prairie could the Anglo quiet the rebellious behavior of "black John."

Slave catchers did not have an easy time recapturing fugitives in Texas. Not only did runaways have the benefits of a sparsely settled landscape, but they also often took advantage of a relatively plentiful number of horses and guns along the border. Noah Smithwick observed firsthand the dangers of confronting fugitive slaves. One night he noticed an unfamiliar campfire near his home on the Colorado River. After discovering that the trespassers were runaways, he decided to perform his duty as a citizen and attempt to recapture them. He, six friends, and a pack of bloodhounds descended on the two black men at dawn the following morning. The group was in for a shock, however, because the runaways possessed a gun. When one slave shot a hound it "put a serious aspect upon the affair; we had not counted on armed resistance." Showing determination (and realizing that his party had several guns and a half-dozen dogs to the single rifle of the slave), Smithwick did not give up. "We intercepted them and demanded an unconditional surrender," he recalled, but the only reply given was "the presentation of a rifle in the hands of a powerful black fellow." After a bloody exchange of fire "the negroes had gotten the best of the fight and were off." Smithwick and his party, wisely, retired. "Several days later the fugitives were heard from over on Sandy," Smithwick wrote, "where they held up Jim Hamilton and made him give them directions for reaching Mexico." Smithwick added that "one or two" other parties had attempted to capture the two runaways but also failed. Reflecting on the humbling experience, Smithwick noted of his opponent that morning: "Single-handed—his companion being unarmed—he had whipped six white men, all armed, and as many fierce dogs."[53] Although the occurrence was unusual, slaveholders certainly believed they were all too common.

Fugitive slaves bound for the free border of Mexico angered Texas slaveholders, but hostile Native Americans posed a deadlier threat. Many Indians of Texas refused to peacefully acquiesce to the cultural annihilation that white and black settlement entailed. Taking to the warpath, they routinely raided and harassed settlers. Many of the first families to settle in the Upper Brazos River valley during the antebellum period suffered a fatality at the hands of Indian raiders.[54]

In their attacks on southern society Native Americans often failed to distinguish white from black. For them, it was easy to associate the coming of blacks with the coming of whites. Anglos and Africans lived and worked together. They often fought the Indians together.[55] In time, fugitive slaves might convince Indians that they were not the willing allies of whites, but runaway slaves did not always get such time.[56] Similarly, it was easy for black slaves to see Indians, as their white masters did, as threats to their well-being. Reports of slaves killed by Native Americans appeared during the 1830s, 1840s, and 1850s.[57] When assailed by Indians, enslaved Texans showed no hesitancy in responding in kind.[58]

Not all Indians in Texas proved hostile to settlers, white or black, and there were former slaves who remembered positive relations with friendly Native Americans. Amos Clark hunted with them in central Texas.[59] Anderson Jones remembered that "dey wuz de East Texas Indians mostly, an' most of dem wuz friendly Indians. . . . My gran-mammy being a Choctaw Indian could talk to some of dem."[60] Slaves learned to distinguish among the various groups of Native Americans in Texas. Although they rightly feared and avoided those who were more hostile, they embraced relationships with more amicable neighbors.

Occasionally, slaves did more than establish a friendly relationship with Indians. Fugitives in several instances joined and lived with Native Americans. As one former slave recalled, "De Brazos bottom wuz a good place for de run-a-way slaves to hide an' sometimes dey would cum from way down in Texas an' live up in de Tehuacana an' de Brazos bottom wid de Indians."[61] Evidence of blacks who were peacefully acclimated to Indian life can be found at least as early as 1834. Two years before the Texas revolt against Mexican rule, a party of whites encountered an escaped slave living with the Tawehash Indians in northeastern Texas. He had been initially captured by the Comanches, but perhaps because they had little experience with Africans they gave him to their Tawehash allies. The fugitive told the whites that the Indians "had treated him well [and] had given him corn mellons Buffaloe meat &c to eat." The Anglos noticed that "he appeared very well satisfied with his situation" because the Indians required "of him nothing but to graze their horses."[62] After some interrogation the slave admitted that "he had his own horse & Indian equipment & was much better contented there than at home."[63]

Although this black-Indian union was broken up when the Anglo party surely restored the slave to his master, more enduring examples of black adoption into Indian societies can be found. Four years later, for example, Anglos encountered a black man acting as a translator for a party of Cherokees.[64] In 1840 an Anglo in Red River county reported that "negros have been seen with the Hostile Indians and Mexicans on our frontier."[65] In August 1848 the "Annual Report of the Commissioner of Indian Affairs" noted that "a fine looking gentleman of color, somewhat inclined to be bowlegged, also very dark . . . says his name is Abraham, and belongs to John Ecleson on the Brazos, near Nashville" was in camp with a band of Wacos and other Indians of the Texas prairie.[66]

So successful were some fugitives in adapting to Indian society that they were able in time to establish families and attain positions of leadership in their new culture. In 1837 a group of Indians and a black man ("a large Negro who was looked upon with great respect by the tribe and seemed to hold undisputed dominion with the chief himself") appeared in Houston and shocked the racial sensibilities of resident Anglos.[67] Sophia Bereall's father was an Indian chief and her mother an escaped slave. Had she been born in white society, her mother's status would have meant Bereall's enslavement. But Bereall was born in Indian society; she married an Indian and did not enter white society until after the Civil War.[68] In 1852 Anglos discovered another black woman who had been absorbed into Comanche society and given birth to four children of Indian and African ancestry.[69] Despite a common current of hostility between Indians and blacks, a number of fugitive slaves managed to cross the cultural divide and start a new life among Native Americans.[70]

In some instances fugitive slaves did more than trade white society for Indian; on rare occasions they used their connections with Native Americans to wreck havoc. Individual slaves sometimes committed acts of violence be-

fore fleeing to the Texas interior and what they hoped were their Indian allies. Edward Jenkins was reportedly killed by "a half-Negro, half-Indian slave
of Moses Rousseau" who "was never again heard from in civilized circles, it
was supposed that he joined the Indians or was killed by them."[71]
   The inability to bring such criminals to justice angered slaveholders, but
more fearsome combinations of Indians and blacks haunted Anglo Texans.
On 1 August 1841 a party of blacks and Indians attacked a family of white settlers in Fannin County. The settlers repulsed their assailants, killing "a big
burly negro."[72] Although such attacks were infrequent, the threat of black and
Indian unions prompted concern among Anglo Texans.
   Relations between blacks and Indians on the Texas prairie differed considerably from both black-white and white-Indian interactions.[73] The Indians undoubtedly provided an alternative to enslavement under Anglo masters for a small number of blacks. Throughout Indian Territory, however,
many blacks who lived among the Indians were enslaved. Even so, they often
found their lives preferable to life among Anglos. One observer suggested
that Indians who held blacks as slaves treated them differently than did
whites. "These new disciples of civilization have learned from the whites to
keep Negro slaves for house and field labour," wrote a traveler to Oklahoma,
"but these slaves receive from the Indian masters more Christian treatment
than among the Christian whites."[74]
   The evidence for increased slave resistance, at least as presented so far, has
come largely from central Texas. Subsequent research may reveal that other
parts of Texas also played host to high levels of slave flight, but it is certain
that several characteristics of late-antebellum central Texas greatly enhanced
the ability of that region's enslaved men and women to resist their bondage.
   The physical environment of the Upper Brazos River valley itself was an
important factor in encouraging slave flight in the area. Before undertaking the long trip to Mexico or allying with Texas's nomadic Indians, central
Texas's slaves had to first elude the determined pursuit of local slave catchers, and the region's wooded hills, forested river bottoms, plentiful game,
and abundant wild plants proved advantageous in doing so. Indeed, George
Barnard's records concerning the recapture of runaways indicate that fugitive slaves recognized the environmental benefits of central Texas before
white settlers reached the area. Willis Easter recalled that the river bottoms
of the Upper Brazos River valley "wuz good hidin' places on er count ob de
caves an' woods in de hills."[75]
   The Upper Brazos River valley, however, was not the sole reason for central Texas's high rate of slave resistance. Many other areas in Texas and in the
U.S. South possessed environmental advantages but had lower rates of slave

flight. In fact, the terrain of some of those areas was no doubt superior to central Texas for eluding pursuit. That was not, however, by itself sufficient to bring about high levels of slave flight.

Low population density was another factor that set central Texas apart from other regions in the slaveholding South. Central Texas, located on the ninety-eighth meridian, was the farthest region west that plantation agriculture could be profitable during the antebellum period. Although settlers had long known that the fertile Upper Brazos River valley could produce large amounts of cotton, readily available land closer to the Atlantic and Gulf coasts and difficulties with hostile Indians limited growth in the region. As late as 1850 the entire region above the Falls of the Brazos River— some three hundred thousand square miles—held fewer than nine thousand people.[76] At a time when the population density of the entire slaveholding South was more than ten residents per square mile, the prairie of central Texas held fewer than one person for every three square miles. Although thousands of Anglo immigrants arrived with thousands of slaves, the population density of the Upper Brazos River valley had reached only 4.11 residents per square mile by 1860 and still lagged far behind that found in other slaveholding states. Even when compared to other slaveholding areas in Texas, central Texas maintains a significantly lower population density (tables 1 and 2).

The low population densities of central Texas significantly benefited fugitive slaves. Chances of eluding white patrols greatly increased in places where immense distances separated the farms of a few free citizens. All slaveowners depended on the use of power and violence to maintain appropriate discipline, prevent rebellions, and deter flight. Other than on their plantations,

Table 1. Population Densities of Selected
Slaveholding Regions in Texas, 1860

Region of Texas	Number of Residents per Square Mile
Upper Brazos River valley	4.11
South-central Texas	5.48
Middle Brazos River valley	7.39
Lower Brazos River valley	9.08
Northeast Texas	10.47

Sources: Mary G. Ramos, ed., 1996–97 Texas Almanac and State Industrial Guide (Dallas: Dallas Morning News, 1995); U.S Bureau of the Census, Population of the United States in 1860 Compiled from the Original Returns of the Eighth Census (Washington: Government Printing Office, 1864).

Table 2. Population Densities of Selected Slaveholding
States, 1860

State	Number of Residents per Square Mile
Alabama	18.65
Arkansas	8.19
Florida	2.40
Georgia	17.95
Kentucky	28.60
Louisiana	14.92
Mississippi	16.59
Missouri	16.96
North Carolina	18.85
South Carolina	22.62
Tennessee	26.33
Texas (includes unsettled western Texas)	2.26
Virginia	24.56
Regional average	12.92

Sources: Mary G. Ramos, ed., *1996–97 Texas Almanac and State Industrial Guide* (Dallas: Dallas Morning News, 1995); U.S. Bureau of the Census, *Population of the United States in 1860 Compiled from the Original Returns of the Eighth Census* (Washington: Government Printing Office, 1864).

Note: Virginia's total square mileage includes the square miles listed for Virginia and West Virginia.

the reach of central Texas slaveholders' power was greatly limited. Unlike slaveowners in older, more settled slave states, they could not rely, at least initially, on institutions of local government or even an abundance of neighbors in the quest to recapture escaped slaves.

Thus, enslaved central Texans possessed several advantages for resisting slavery over slaves in earlier-settled states. Low population density and being located between Mexico, the U.S. South, and Indians who lived in the West spurred attempted flight. Texas slaveowners, it is clear, were deeply concerned, and they, like their slaves, adapted to the conditions of Texas. Some adjusted their rules of plantation management to the new environment. Others looked to the state and legal action as a means of limiting slave resistance. A number, however, lurched toward violence, vigilantism, and the Panic of 1860.

*   *   *

Many who owned slaves in central Texas attempted to follow the patterns and methods that had served them successfully in earlier-settled parts of the South. Violence and the threat of violence were staples of plantation life. Churchill Jones, an Alabama planter who relocated to the Falls of the Brazos, provided his overseer in Texas with detailed instructions for plantation management. "I am afraid," he wrote, "you have have got the negroes to like you and not fear you." Based on his experiences in Alabama, Jones noted that this would not do because "they must know when you speak they have to obey, and to do this you have to stand square up to them and show yourself master. You cannot coax a negro to do his duty. You have to force him, and if they only like you and not fear you they will soon hate you and get tired of you." But, Jones continued, if you can "make them fear you and like you both you can do anything you want with them."[77]

Scores followed Jones's method and attempted to increase whippings and other forms of punishment—but with mixed results. Bob Maynard, a former slave born in Falls County, recalled that "sometimes the slaves would run off and the Patroller would catch 'em and have 'em whipped." The patrols would place a recaptured fugitive in a wooden stock, "strap him down, take off his clothes and give him 25 to 50 licks."[78] Maynard's account was by no means unusual. Paul Escott reports that thirty-two of every one hundred slave narratives studied in his *Slavery Remembered* reported cruel treatment, but forty-two of every one hundred central Texas slaves remembered such incidents of persecution.[79] Violence, cruelty, and physical punishment seem to have been more common there than elsewhere in the South, and increased resistance to white authority seems a plausible explanation.

Whipping and increased brutality, however, proved only partially effective in curtailing resistance. The primary reason for the limited effectiveness of violence as a deterrent to slave flight was the conducive environment of the Upper Brazos River valley. As former slave Calvin Kennard told his interviewer, "I 'member de furst time my ole mistress got atter me to whup me, I runned off an' stayed four or five days."[80] Slaves could live in central Texas's wooded hills and forested river bottoms and find temporary respite from bondage. "De Brazos bottom wuz a good place for de run-a-way slaves," recalled George Glasker, and "mos every one of de plantations had some who wuz always runnin' away."[81]

Although similar patterns of resistance developed throughout the Old South, slaves in central Texas held more leverage by virtue of their enhanced opportunities to resist.[82] Comparisons of slave resistance are always difficult, but central Texas slave narratives suggest that resistance occurred more frequently in the Upper Brazos River valley than in the South in general. Thirty of fifty former slaves in central Texas (60 percent) reported some incidents of resistance, nearly twice the rate that Paul Escott found in his study of the slave South—826 acts of resistance in 2,358 narratives (35.03 percent). Central Texas bondspeople, it appears, resisted more often than slaves across the entire South.[83]

Whipping and a simple policy of increased violence and cruelty, then, brought immediate obedience in the short term while encouraging slave flight in the long term. Such conclusions are confirmed by the slave narratives. One slave recalled that "when my father wuz whipped he would run away and hide in the river bottom. I seen them bring him several times. If dey whipped when dey brought him in, he would run away ag'in."[84] Increased punishment by slaveholders often only strengthened the commitment of slaves to resist bondage, exacerbating their problems. The continued resistance of central Texas's slaves did not please their masters. Realizing that a successful plantation depended on a stable workforce, wise slaveholders also realized that they could not rely on coercion alone.

Fortunately, an alternative model for slave control had been employed in the Old South for some time. Beginning in the 1820s and 1830s, important changes in southern society began to encourage development of a system of slave control that historians call "paternalism." After the U.S. Congress banned the slave trade in 1808, planters began to realize that the future of the slaveholding South depended on the reproductive capacity of those slaves already in the United States and began to pay more attention to the health and physical needs of their bondsmen and bondswomen in order to increase life expectancy. In what Willie Lee Rose called the "domestication of slavery," planters began to curb the worst abuses of bondage; at the same time, the abolitionist attack on slavery began in earnest.

The need to conserve their investment in human property and defend their institutions drove slaveholders to construct an ideological defense of slavery. Where they once might have characterized their institution as a "necessary evil," planters increasingly argued that human bondage was preferable to many other forms of social organization. In support, slaveholders claimed that slavery was an age-old institution, prevalent in history and supported by scripture. Superior to the modern free labor system that abandoned the poor, slavery was an organic system of mutual responsibility and duty that bound the strong and the weak together. Most important, the new defense of slavery squared with white racism, the original and ultimate justification of African slavery. As a bulwark against Northern criticism, as a successful system of plantation management, and as an important means for rationalizing the ownership of human beings, paternalism spread quickly in the slaveholding South.[85]

Texas slaveholders, like their counterparts elsewhere, attempted to inculcate a paternalist ethos on their plantations by laying out complex sets of customs, rules, and reciprocal obligations between masters and slaves.[86] For just that purpose Charles William Tait, a Brazos River plantation owner, kept an extensive list of twenty-nine "General" and "Particular" rules. "A regular and systematic plan of operation is greatly promotive of easy government," ar-

gued Tait. "Have all matters therefore, as far as possible reduced to a system."
In this spirit, Tait sought to reduce plantation management to a system. The
first General Rule sought to ensure that enforcement of the rules would pro-
ceed rationally: "Never punish a negro when in a passion. No one is capable
of properly regulating the punishment of an offence when angry." Tait's second General Rule, not to "require of a negro what is unreasonable," suggests
that wise masters paid careful attention to the reactions of slaves. Furthermore, Tait meant his rules to be understood by slaves as well as slaveholders.
When a slave did require punishment, for example, Tait's rules prescribed that
the master "let him know for what offence he is punished."[87]

Many paternalistic slaveholders used the practice and allocation of med-
icine to reinforce their role as caretaker. In several letters Churchill Jones encouraged his overseers to pay attention to the cleanliness and health of his
slaves.[88] One former slave recalled that "Marse Jones doctored us an' got de
w'ite doctor dat dey had when we was sick."[89] Like slaveholders across the
Old South, however, Jones continued to dispense punishment, but he limited the ability to punish to encourage acceptance of his authority. Another
former slave, Ned Broadus, remembered whippings as being commonplace
on Jones's plantation, but "Ole man Jones had a rule nobody could never cut
de hide off no nigger wukkin' fer him, no matter what he done wrong."[90]

Many slaveholders of central Texas were familiar with such a system because they had lived in other Southern states. In the Upper Brazos River valley, however, they were forced to confront the fact that slaves in central Texas
possessed more power to resist bondage than slaves elsewhere. Although
some owners sought to curb resistance through harsher and more frequent
punishment, many increasingly came to realize that they would have to make
concessions. They learned, and slave narratives confirm, that punishment
led to flight. Many central Texas masters sought a more effective means of
personally controlling their slave population and found they could better reduce resistance by giving into certain demands rather than by increasing
punishment. After Allen V. Manning arrived in central Texas, he remembered, his master "seem like he changed a lot since we left Mississippi, and
seem like he paid more attention to us and looked after us better."[91] Henry
Childers remarked that his master had fewer problems than others in central Texas because he "wuz a good Master an' [therefore] his slaves wuz not
always a runnin' away like [s]ome did."[92]

Travelers who visited Texas remarked that slaves there possessed intolerable levels of rights and freedoms. One white woman reported that she had
heard that, in Texas, "the negroes are as much respected as the whites and go
on their fine horses."[93] In central Texas, many masters employed their slaves

to handle stock. One former slave recalled that "some ob de slaves wuz trained ter be good cowboys as dey call de ones dat ter cattle on de range." Limestone County slave Giles Cotton operated independent of an overseer and "was allowed to own a wagon and a team of mules."[94]

The ability to ride horses, however, was limited neither to work duties nor to an elite group of slaves on each plantation. Henry Masters allowed some of his slaves to ride for recreational purposes. After being apprised that two had been out riding all night, "He jes' laff and laff," saying, "'Sam an' Moor allus git time to git ter de fiel.'" Even though the Masters furnished them with passes, Sam and Moore enjoyed out-running slave patrols, antics that led "our neighbors" to "all call dem Marster's free niggers."[95]

With twenty-three slaves in 1860, E. C. Zollicoffer was the fourth-largest slaveowner in Hill County. None of his slaves worked as field hands but rather tended to stock on horseback.[96] Former slave Tobe Zollicoffer had been trained to herd cattle. Riding Jim, his favorite cutting horse, and roaming throughout the Texas hills, he possessed rights and privileges realized by few slaves in the Deep South. "The Zollicofer slaves," he recalled, "were only whipped when they didn't obey orders and then not very hard like some white owners did."[97] Although E. C. Zollicoffer might have been a truly benevolent owner, it seems more likely that both master and slave compromised. Zollicoffer may have realized that the intense control necessary for gang labor would have meant constant battle with his bondsmen and women. In allowing them more independence and freedom than found on most plantations, Zollicoffer succeeded in minimizing such conflict.

A less common but more surprising facet of slave life on the edge of Anglo settlement was the preponderance of slaves allowed to carry firearms on a daily basis. Slaveowner Moses Johnson "had allowed [his slave, Brit Johnson] the *enlarged liberty which belongs to the frontier,* often relying upon his strong arm to help defend the family and neighborhood from the raids of hostile Indians."[98] In 1838 a slave named Tom—wielding a gun and an axe—protected his mistress from the threatened attack of Tonkawa Indians.[99] In 1839 a Fannin County slave named Smith successfully defended himself from attack by Indians because his master had armed him with a gun and a knife.[100] Armistead, the enslaved servant of Wacoan Shapley Ross, drove off an Indian attack with a rifle given to him by his master.[101] On one level the threat of Indian attack made arming one's slaves in Texas quite logical, yet Texas lawmakers passed codes limiting such behavior because of the difficulties of dealing with armed fugitive slaves. Likewise, central Texas courts prosecuted those who allowed slaves to carry firearms, and only the dangers of the most remote parts of Texas overcame slaveholders' fears of doing so.

The existence of greater privileges for Texas slaves does not, however, necessarily indicate that paternalism was a stronger or a more important part of slave life in that state.[102] The extent and effects of paternalism are difficult to estimate because a number of former slaves refused to speak with anyone about slavery. The WPA slave narrative interviewers do not mention interviews that failed, yet some former slaves refused to speak about their experiences. According to a group of white women who eventually collected fifteen interviews with former slaves in Waco, "There were about eight or ten more Negro men and women, whom we knew to be ex-slaves, but upon approaching them they were not willing to give us any information. Some told us that the times had been so terrible that they did not even want to tell their own children, much less to us, as it would only stir up old memories in their minds, and cause hatred on both sides."[103] Moreover, some white interviewers probably did not follow through on some interviews because they did not hear what they wanted to hear. According to former slave Wesley Burrell, "A white lady was here de other night wanted to know 'bout slavery time an' when I started to tell her she said she didn't want to hear dat stuff."[104] Such a bias in the collection of the slave narratives undercuts the extent to which they can be used to gauge the extent of paternalism.

If paternalism represented one strategy of undermining slave resistance, it is certain that slaveholders did not rely on it entirely. They also embraced another significant strategy: strengthening the legal system and community resources for punishing slave resistance. Encouraging white immigration to central Texas was critical to that strategy.

The growth of the white population was certainly a factor in diminishing opportunities for slave runaways. In 1844 George Barnard had been one of the first whites to settle in the Upper Brazos River valley. In the five years following the 1845 annexation, Texas's population increased by 40 percent, from approximately 120,000 whites and 30,000 slaves to 154,431 free people and 58,161 slaves. During the 1850s the population continued to explode, and by 1860 the Upper Brazos River valley had grown from one permanent Anglo settler (Barnard) and a handful of runaway slaves to 10,409 whites and 5,054 blacks. The flood of white and black settlers had greatly changed the character of the valley. Not only were more and more white people available to pursue runaways, but the population increase also eliminated the large game that made life on the run easier.[105]

The changing fate of George Barnard and the city of Waco epitomized the shifting conditions of central Texas. In 1849 Barnard decided to move his Indian trading post further northwest to a location more convenient to his Native American customers. Seeing that he could profit from the incoming white and black population, Barnard set up a second trading post in the just-established city of Waco.[106] Established in 1849, Waco became one of the symbols of the growing stability of central Texas. Although its population remained small in the decade preceding the Civil War, the city on the Brazos was the political and religious center of the Upper Brazos River valley. Waco became a meeting ground for local whites. On the steps of the courthouse, in their houses of worship, and along the aisles of the trade stores, local planters and farmers learned of the Indians, heard of runaway slaves, and debated ways to solve these problems. Within a few years the talk began to take the form of action.[107]

During the 1850s, slaveholders began to limit, through legal action, routes to freedom for the region's slaves.[108] Anglos in east Waco constructed a whipping post and an auction block to loom as physical symbols of their desire to crack down on slave resistance.[109] Moreover, Waco began construction of the city's first jail in June 1855, in part to have a place to deposit recaptured slaves.[110] Before the jail was built, central Texas's facilities for detaining fugitives had been barely adequate, and, in truth, the wooden jail likely held more resemblance to a barn.

James Buckner Barry, sheriff of Bosque County, recorded numerous difficulties with runaway slaves. On 24 June 1855 he imprisoned one named Peter, who soon escaped. A local man named William Lockhart, however, recaptured him. Peter's misfortune did not deter him from continuing to test the strength of his jail. Late one night Barry awoke, "alarmed about 12 or 1 oclock of a Negro named Peter set fire to the jail and was about to burn up in it." Barry doused the fire and had the rebellious arsonist "whipped severely."[111] The resistance of fugitives such as Peter convinced central Texas's slaveholders that their tax dollars were well-spent on a more reliable jail in Waco.

Over the next two years, central Texas's slaveholders took an even more important step. In 1856 the commissioner's Court of Falls County authorized "a company of Patroll [*sic*]" and directed it to cover "all the territory west of the Brazos River in this county."[112] In January 1857 the city council of Waco approved measures to check the runaway slave problem. No doubt based on other experiences in slaveholding communities, Wacoans authorized funding for two patrols of four persons, one for each side of the city. The men, who patrolled from nine in the evening until daylight, received $5 every week. The council instructed them to "suffer any negro to pass unmolested who shall have a special pass" but to jail all others. Before imprisoning the escaped slaves, however, the patrols frequently subjected fugitives to "a penalty of thirty-nine stripes."[113] The master of each slave confined to jail would be fined $1.[114] A year and a half later the council went even further in attempts to close avenues for possible rebellion by prohibiting "the master of any slave to permit such slave to hire his time, or to hire him to any other slave or free person of color."[115] Because only one free family of color resided in McLennan County, it seems likely that the council meant to do all it could to block avenues of escape for slaves.

Constructing a permanent jail and establishing slave patrols coincided with a rise in local court prosecutions involving the enslaved. During the 1850s central Texas courts began to try slaves for certain crimes, although punishment for most remained on the plantation because slaveholders almost always trusted their own judgment over that of even a friendly and sympathetic court. On some occasions, however, they depended on the legal system to maintain order, deter certain types of activity, and enforce the law of slavery. That was especially the case when free persons conspired with slaves to commit an illegal activity. Slavery could not have long existed without the legal power to punish these individuals.

Beginning shortly after independence, the Texas legislature began to specify a special code of laws regulating slaves. A wide range of crimes involving slaves and free persons of color were carefully enumerated (tables 3, 4, and 5).

The slave code of Texas became more detailed and complex as slaveholders' influence expanded. Between 1850 and 1860 their numbers in the Texas legislature rose from 38.8 to 54.3 percent. At the same time, the number of

Table 3. Selected Laws of Texas Regulating Slaves

Crime	Penalty
Insurrection "or any attempt to excite it"	Death
Poisoning or attempting to poison	Death
Committing a rape "or attempting it on any free white female"	Death
Assaulting "a free white person, with intent to kill, or with a weapon likely to produce death"	Death
Maiming a free white person	Death
Arson	Death
Murder	Death
Using "insulting or abusive language to, or threaten any free white person"	"stripes not exceeding one hundred nor less than twenty-five."
Carrying a gun without written permission of owner or overseer	Confiscation of property

Source: H. P. N. Gammel, *The Laws of Texas, 1822–1897* (Austin: Gammel Book Co., 1898), 1:1385–86, 2:346.

Table 4. Selected Texas Laws Regulating Free Persons of Color

Crime	Penalty
Insurrection "or any attempt to excite it"	Death
Poisoning or attempting to poison	Death
Commiting a rape "or attempting it on any free white female"	Death
Assaulting "a free white person, with intent to kill, or with a weapon likely to produce death"	Death
Maiming a free white person	Death
Arson	Death
Murder	Death
Using "insulting or abusive language to, or threaten any free white person"	"Stripes not exceeding one hundred nor less than twenty-five."
Emigrating to Texas	Removal from Texas or enslavement
Harboring or concealing a fugitive slave	Fine (not more than $500) and imprisonment (1–6 months)

Source: H. P. N. Gammel, *The Laws of Texas, 1822–1897* (Austin: Gammel Book Co., 1898), 1:1385–86; 2:345–46, 2:650.

seats held by the richest—planters who owned at least twenty slaves—jumped from a mere five in 1850 to twenty-five ten years later.[116]

The slave code theoretically brought slaves into courtrooms for a wide variety of crimes. In early central Texas, however, relatively few appeared in court. The criminal court minute books of McLennan, Falls, and Bosque counties contain no record that a slave was even indicted for a crime until the spring of 1858, when the District Court of McLennan County indicted "Simon, a slave of Thomas Alexander" for burglary. In September he was brought to Waco for trial, found guilty, and sentenced to be lashed with a whip 150 times.[117] A year later a court in Falls County indicted "Fed, a Slave" for attempted murder. Fed's case, however, never came to trial.[118] These cases were very unusual.[119] Most central Texas owners, it is clear, avoided the courtroom by punishing their slaves within the confines of the plantation and household.

Free persons who engaged in illegal activities with slaves, however, posed a different concern altogether. Two white men, for example, were indicted on 24 September 1857 for "conspiracy to steal negroes." With the prices of enslaved labor so high in Texas, such a conspiracy demanded stern action. Nevertheless, they seem to have escaped central Texas; their case never came to trial.[120]

Table 5. Selected Laws of Texas Regulating Interaction among Free
White Persons, Slaves, and Free Persons of Color

Crime	Penalty
Bringing, importing, inducing, aiding, or assisting in the emigration of any free person of color into Texas	Fine ($1,000–$10,000)
Selling "ardent spirits or intoxicating liquors" to slave without written permission of owner or overseer	Fine ($20–$200)
Buying "cotton, corn, meat or other valuable produce or article whatever" from slave without written permission of owner or overseer	Fine ($20–$200 plus value of property sold)
Unreasonable or cruel treatment or abuse of slave	Fine ($200–$2000)
Murder of slave	Death (punished as in other cases of murder)
Harboring or concealing a fugitive slave	Fine (not more than $500) and imprisonment (1–6 months)
Stealing or enticing "away any slave out of or from the possession of the owner"	Death
Conspiring with a slave to rebel or make insurrection	Death
Making a slave "discontented with his state of slavery"	Imprisonment (5–15 years)

Source: H. P. N. Gammel, *The Laws of Texas, 1822–1897* (Austin: Gammel Book Co., 1898) 1:187; 2:345–46, 2:650; 3:1061, 1511.

The courts were also essential in regulating day-to-day interaction between the free and the unfree. During the late 1850s, central Texas courts indicted white men for unlawfully trading with slaves, specifically targeting those who sold liquor.[121] Although local authorities may have tolerated some degree of trading between slaves and free persons, courts took other cases more seriously. In 1856 and 1857 the court of Falls County indicted, tried, and convicted John Long and Labor Dodson for allowing their slaves to carry firearms in violation of the law. Both men were fined $25, a significant amount because it exceeded many other fines awarded during the 1850s.[122]

The courts also sometimes prosecuted masters whose cruel treatment of their slaves threatened to further weaken the international perception of slavery. Most central Texans, like most Southerners, understood that the institution of slavery was under moral attack from an international abolitionist movement. Texans heard abolitionist critiques of their state in particular throughout the antebellum era. International attention to slaveholding in Texas was perhaps greatest during the debate over annexation. During a tour of Ireland and England in 1845 and 1846, Frederick Douglass described white Texans as "a set of swindlers" and repeatedly attacked them for allowing human bondage after "Mexico came forward and nobly abolished slavery."[123]

In defending the institution against these attacks, slaveholders often argued that masters who abused slaves were not only in the minority but also punished by the legal system when they overstepped the bounds of Christian decency. One such case did emerge in central Texas. In 1858 the district court of McLennan County indicted Alexander McGehey for "cruel and unreasonable abuse of Samuel, a slave." The courts, nevertheless, had a hard time convicting a white man for beating a black man. Whether due to a problem with the earlier indictment or to two separate incidents of abuse, McGehey was indicted in the spring and then again in the fall. In 1859 the venue of his trial was changed from McLennan to Hill County, and then, in 1862, the case was transferred back to McLennan County, where it disappears from the record books. Despite a spirited effort the courts were unable to convict McGehey; his case is the exception that proves the rule. Central Texas's slaveholders were allowed to punish their own slaves in whatever manner they saw fit and with very little interference from constituted legal authority.[124]

The court system was not the means by which most whites disciplined their slaves and curbed resistance. On 18 November 1858 the *Southern Democrat,* published in Waco, admitted that the laws regulating slaves and free persons were rarely enforced, although enforcement of existing laws was about to tighten. Readers were urged to adjust to the court's new resolve. In particular, the *Democrat* noted that the Penal Code of 1856 prohibited a wide range of interactions between free persons and slaves and singled out Article 918, which prohibited masters from allowing slaves to hire their time.[125]

The *Democrat* was right about the court's actions and the direction it would take. Before that time, central Texas courts had indicted only a few free persons for illegal interaction with slaves. In the three years preceding the Civil War, however, the number of individuals charged with violating the proper relationship between free and enslaved increased significantly. Unlawful trading was the most common charge; some illegally sold or gave liquor to bondsmen. Courts also cracked down on mixed-race relationships. In Falls County, the court indicted a Mexican man, it appears, for having illicit sexual relations with a black woman, and the McLennan County District Court indicted an Anglo man for "fornication with a negro."[126]

Most slaveholders did not depend upon the increased resolve of the local courts to successfully deter slave resistance. They believed that even a combination of the strategies explored so far—increased physical punishment, greater efforts at paternalism, and reliance upon the local court system—were, at best, partially effective. Many central Texans emphasized vigilantism and extralegal action as an additional means of checking slave insurgency.

One frequent extralegal action involved crossing the Mexican border to re-capture runaways. In May 1850, for example, a central Texas man named McIntere, tired of the problem and the government's inability to control the escape of slaves, crossed with some accomplices and, after a violent encounter with local residents, forcibly recovered a fugitive.[127] The state of Texas some-times encouraged these actions, which the Mexican government, naturally, deemed illegal. In September 1851 Gov. P. H. Bell appointed Warren Adams to recover runaways among a band of Seminoles that had fled Oklahoma for Mexico. Adams, a notorious and successful slave hunter, managed to steal two blacks from the Mexican colonies, including the famous black Seminole leader Juan Caballo (John Horse). Caballo's Native American ally Coacoochee (Wild Cat) paid a ransom and arranged for the release of his black friends.[128]

Coacoochee's and Juan Caballo's colonies in Mexico greatly angered slave-holders, who expected them to lure runaways from plantations in Texas, Arkansas, and Louisiana. Indeed, the colonies almost certainly contained fugitives. In 1855, and after several years of diplomatic and political failure to halt the escape of slaves, Anglo Texans decided to make a covert strike across the Mexican border and recapture their human property. Using the excuse that they were trailing marauding Indians, an expedition led by Texas Ranger captain James Callahan crossed the border but retreated after clashing with the Seminoles and plundering their village.[129]

Although the expedition recaptured no fugitive slaves, Callahan's raid was probably partially responsible for the decline in successful flight to Mexico during the late 1850s. The raid sent a message to Mexican officials and to po-tential fugitives that Texans would respond with force in recovering their property.[130] Mexican officials, cognizant of the Callahan raid, became less in-terested in harboring fugitives and irritating militant Texans. Moreover, and perhaps more important, the United States was now wary of embarrassing border problems and began stationing more troops at the border to make slave flight more difficult.[131]

Texas lawmakers were not finished with encouraging individuals to cross into Mexico and recapture fugitive slaves. In 1858 the legislature passed "An Act to Encourage the Reclamation of Slaves Escaping beyond the Slave Ter-ritories of the United States." The law provided that taxpayers would pro-vide slave hunters with one-third the value of any slave they could bring to Travis County, provided the slave had escaped beyond the slave territories of the United States.[132] The extraordinary law stimulated ambitious and brave individuals, and although it in theory applied to a number of different parts of North America it seems likely that escaped slaves in Mexico were its object. A report by the Mexican government confirmed that a number of Americans illegally crossed the border before the Civil War to recapture fugitive slaves.[133]

Texas slaveholders often found it difficult to accept that their supposedly devoted servants had taken advantage of conditions in Texas to escape bondage. Many had even selected their loyalest slaves to accompany them to Texas.[134] How could these most trusted bondsmen and women turn their backs on them? Furthermore, it was difficult to admit that enslaved Texans so frequently attempted escape because doing so made individual slaveholders appear weak and unable to maintain mastery over their slaves—something unacceptable to men who valued personal honor.[135] Moreover, increased resistance was a result of the greater opportunities that conditions in the state provided. This explanation, although nearer the truth, was politically unacceptable. In an era of sectional conflict over slavery, such an admission would have revealed slaves as thoroughly discontent with enslavement and undermined a pillar of the Southern defense of slavery. Given these alternatives, most slaveholders chose a third option: blaming "outside agitators" for their troubles.

Mexicans in particular drew blame for the increased rebelliousness of Texas slaves. One historian reported that Anglos charged Mexicans in Texas with "exercising a mischievous influence among the slaves."[136] Another noted that concerned Anglo Texans held public meetings in Austin, Gonzáles, and other places advising other planters not to employ Mexican laborers because they "thought a portion of the Mexican population in Western Texas aided" the escape of slaves.[137] In 1854 Frederick Law Olmsted remarked that Mexicans in Texas "are regarded by slaveholders with great contempt and suspicion, for their intimacy with slaves."[138]

In 1857 Anglos in Limestone County claimed to have discovered a plot between ten or twelve slaves and a group of Mexicans who had promised freedom in Mexico if the slaves would run away with them.[139] In 1856 and 1857, due to the alleged connection between Mexicans and slave resistance, three Texas counties—Colorado, Matagorda, and Bastrop—took the extreme action of expelling all Mexicans.[140] As late as 1858 the *San Antonio Herald* announced that Anglos had uncovered and thwarted a Mexican plot to help runaway slaves in Gonzáles.[141]

There is not much evidence (beyond white hysteria) for significant Mexican intervention in master-slave relations. Texas slaveholders blamed Mexicans for slave resistance because it was rhetorically useful to do so. Not only did it mask the rebelliousness and discontent of their slaves, but it also, conveniently, painted slaveholders and whites as victims. This rhetorical strategy was not new. Accounts of the War for Texas Independence emphasized the aggressive Mexican army and the massacres at the Alamo and Goliad—not the provocative actions of Anglo Texans that prompted the invasion. The defeat and removal of Native Americans was also portrayed in terms of self-defense. Narratives portrayed the conflict as one in which white families defended themselves from marauding Indians instead of one in which Anglos moved in and occupied Indian land.

Blaming Mexicans for encouraging flight was not the only way that Texas slaveholders portrayed themselves as being under attack. They suggested that outside agitators did more than urge flight—they encouraged slave revolts. The danger of a bloody revolt helped slaveholders justify the extralegal action and acts of terror they needed to limit slave resistance, and it encouraged unity among the region's white settlers.

One of the first instances justifying vigilantism as necessary to put down a slave rebellion came during the War for Texas Independence. On 17 October 1835 B. J. White wrote to Stephen F. Austin that he had "found much confusion" in the Lower Brazos River valley and now possessed "unpleasant news to communicate." White's bad news was that "the negroes on Brazos [river] made an attempt to rise." The rebels had decided exactly what parts of the property they gained in the rebellion would belong to each former slave. They planned to continue to raise cotton and ship it through New Orleans but intended to reverse positions with their masters and have white men serve them. This radical plan was no spontaneous revolt of a few discontented slaves, White reported, but "near 100" had participated in the rebellion. Fortunately, he concluded, the revolt was quickly put down. Slaveholders apparently forfeited some of their valuable property in order to issue a warning to potential insurgents. They had "many [of the rebels] whipd nearly to death some hung etc."[142]

As with many slave uprisings, evidence for this revolt remains far from conclusive, and no accounts survive from its enslaved participants. Perhaps a serious plot was developed in 1835. We will never know. We do know, however, that slaves during the War for Texas Independence were fleeing to join the Mexican army. We can also imagine that the extralegal execution of several was intended to dampen the spirits of potential fugitives as well as potential rebels.

Less than a year later, Texans were still concerned about the rebelliousness of their slaves and worried that they were being encouraged by Native Americans and Mexicans. "The Negroes high upon the Trinity have manifested a disposition to become troublesome and in some instances daring" wrote Col. Thomas Morgan on 24 March 1836. Although they had not yet taken direct action, he believed they were seeking an alliance with the Coushatta Indians and preparing to come south to "murder the inhabitants and join the Mexicans."[143]

Fears of slave rebellions receded after the War for Texas Independence but resurfaced during the late 1850s as the sectional crisis accelerated.[144] During that time, vigilante organizations, safety committees, and other groups of armed volunteers, which were already commonplace in Texas, became more active and visible. Concern with threats to slavery began to rival concern with Native Americans after the discovery of several insurrectionary plots in 1856. The *State Gazette* urged Texas communities to rely on vigilantism to meet the dangers that abolitionists and rebellious slaves posed. "We are advocates of law and order," the editors wrote, "but we believe that there are times like these, when the popular vengeance may be meted out."[145]

On 9 September 1856 John H. Robson, H. A. Tatum, and J. H. Hicks of Colorado County sent a letter to a variety of newspapers in Texas under the heading "Contemplated Servile Rising in Texas." The letter of the vigilance committee does not say how they learned of the plot but that their "suspicions were aroused" during the last week of August. The slaveholders of this mid-Brazos county formed a vigilance committee "to ferret out the whole matter." They had uncovered "a well-organized and systematized plan for the murder of our white population, with the exception of the young ladies, who were to be taken captives, and made the wives of the diabolical murderers of their parents and friends." The rebellion was set to begin late at night on 6 September, when slaves, in groups ranging from two to ten, were to go to nearly every house in the county, kill the white men, plunder their homes, take "their horses and arms," and fight their way to a "free state" (thought to be Mexico by the vigilance committee). The committee also believed that two hundred slaves were involved in the conspiracy, and they punished all the rebels with whippings so severe that two died from the lash. Three of the insurrection's leaders were hanged. According to the vigilance committee, the entire Mexican population of Colorado County "was implicated," and "they were arrested, and ordered to leave the county within five days, and never again to return, under the penalty of death."[146] The *True Issue* of LaGrange reported on 5 September that the Colorado County slaves "had organized into companies of various sizes, had adopted secret signs and passwords, sworn never to divulge the plot under penalty of death, and had elected captains and subordinate officers to command the respective companies."[147]

The Colorado County plot was not the only one uncovered in 1856. Over the last three months of the year, authorities claimed to have discovered plans for three additional slave revolts in Texas. In October in Lavaca County, a white man was given a hundred lashes after confessing to his role in a plot set for 31 October in which local slaves would rebel, kill their masters if necessary, and flee to Mexico. A month later a slave allegedly betrayed the plans of his enslaved comrades in DeWitt, Lavaca, and Victoria counties. Apparently, the slaves had already taken the first step in their plot—killing all dogs in the neighborhood—before their revolt was ended. Later in November a Texas and a Louisiana newspaper reported a vague plot between slaves in east Texas and Louisiana.[148]

Evidence for these plots is quite limited, and escalating white fear rather than increased black rebelliousness may have been the prime catalyst for the reports.[149] On 17 January the *Galveston News* admitted that some evidence for the recent plots was "very unsatisfactory" but argued nonetheless that never had "there been a time in our recollection when so many insurrections, or attempts at insurrection, have transpired in rapid succession as during the past six months." The *Cherokee County Texas Enquirer* proclaimed that "Servile insurrections seem to be the order of the day in this State."[150]

Whatever the actual extent of slave participation in these plots, it is clear that Texans from 1856 until the outbreak of the Civil War embraced vigilantism and extralegal action as the primary means of preventing slave resistance and encouraging white unity in the emerging sectional crisis. Special committees of safety met across the state to prevent slave insurrections and root out suspected abolitionists. One white man who fled Texas because of vigilantism wrote that men born in the North were approached and questioned about their views on slavery. Declaring support for it where it existed was not satisfactory. Before the Panic of 1860, the usual pattern was for a mob to whip a suspect and order him to leave the state. If the suspect failed to do so in a few days, the mob would lynch him.[151]

The number of free persons and slaves that central Texas vigilance committees investigated and punished is not known. The committee that in 1857 discovered a plot between ten or twelve slaves and a group of Mexicans in Limestone County did not leave records describing the punishments they inflicted on alleged conspirators. Presumably, the committee was debating hanging when the Mexicans escaped from jail—and wisely did not return to learn the result of the deliberations.[152]

Although vigilantes in Limestone County did not mete out final justice in that case, such periodic bursts of vigilante organizing helped foster a tradition of extralegal action and prepared central Texans for the summer of 1860. During the panic that year, central Texas was one of the regions supposedly in danger from an abolitionist-provoked slave rebellion. Committees of safety arose throughout the region. Yet relatively little is known about what these committees actually did. Central Texans were especially careful to be silent about vigilante actions.

One of the few records from central Texas to survive the Panic of 1860 was a petition to the legislature signed at a meeting called in McLennan County to debate the dangers facing slavery. Richard Coke, a native of Virginia who had moved to Waco in the early 1850s and was an attorney, was the first man to sign. He was joined by 140 others, among them the most prominent leaders of the community. Although not dated, the petition almost certainly is from the summer of 1860. It begins by declaring the institution of slavery to be "all-important to the interests and well-being of the state." Petitioners then enumerate the dangers facing slavery. First, they worried, "free and unlicensed circulation" of antislavery newspapers was "corrupting the minds of the people." Second, "emissaries of Northern associations" who were "laboring to destroy slavery" had instigated among certain slaves the desire to desert their masters or plan a "conspiracy and insurrection." The petitioners concluded that these "infamous and dangerous" abolitionists were "safe from prosecution and conviction" and urged the creation of new laws in response to the crisis.[153] The mass meeting that produced this petition was, of course, only one part of a greater mobilization against perceived threats to slavery. Other actions that took place as a result of this mobilization, however, remain largely unknown.

After the crisis of the summer had passed, William H. Parsons, the staunchly pro-secessionist editor of the *Southwest,* wrote a defense of Texas vigilance committees. Responding to the criticism that evidence for an actual slave rebellion was less than convincing, Parsons noted that every "committee of public safety has startling facts in its possession." The decision to not make such evidence available to the general public, he continued, was a boon both for the public good and the committee's search for conspirators. With the crisis passed, Parsons observed that there is no "necessity for further concealment." He then provided great detail on a plot to overthrow slavery in central Texas. Six abolitionists—mounted and well-armed—had approached groups of local slaves on two separate occasions, urging them to pursue the dream of freedom by cooperating with them. They asked "how the business part of Waco lay" and detailed a plan to rise up in insurrection, burning and killing from Waco to Austin.[154]

Parsons was one of the forty men who participated in the committee of safety, a body he said was composed of citizens of "the highest standing." Parsons claimed that the committee obtained information voluntarily from a slave informant. Furthermore, he assured readers that the description of the chief abolitionist in Waco was the same as the description provided of the ringleader in Dallas, two hundred miles away. Other aspects of the plan, such as timing, purpose, and means, were too coincidental to be anything less than a wide-ranging abolitionist plot. The subsequent actions of the committee of safety, Parsons concluded, were justified because of the veracity of the abolitionist threat. Despite the great lengths to which Parsons went to defend the committee of safety, he never mentioned specific punishments or actions it took.[155] Even less is known about other central Texas vigilance committees. All that is known of Bell County's 1860 vigilantes, for example, is that the county court "organized a strong patrol to protect its citizens from incendiarism."[156]

It is clear from what little evidence that does survive, however, that central Texans lynched several suspected abolitionists in 1860. One lynching that does appear in the contemporary record is the hanging of an enslaved boy in Georgetown for allegedly setting fire to a stable.[157] Vague reports of other executions exist as well. James Buckner Barry noted in his diary that there was "some excitement" about the hanging of abolitionists "without law" in central Texas.[158] Some killings from 1860 do not appear in the historical records until after the Civil War. "There have been no Union men killed here [in Bosque County] since the Rebellion that I know of," wrote Freedmen's Bureau agent Philip Howard in 1866, "but several a short time before."[159]

Clearly, historians will never know how many alleged abolitionists and suspected slave rebels died at the hands of central Texas mobs during the Panic of 1860. What does seem fairly certain is that the violence unleashed by white Texans surpassed the actual threat to the institution of slavery. Some who were involved were seemingly seized with a sense of fear that was out of all proportion to the dangers they faced. One Texan wrote to the *New Orleans Times Picayune,* declaring that Texas's "Vigilant Committees have determined to order no one to leave, but to hang every man who puts his feet on Texas soil, avowing the 'doctrines' of the Free Soil party." Such actions were justified because "the young women and little girls were to be saved to become the wives or concubines of these fiends of hell." The dangers were so great, he concluded, that "we will hang every man who does not live above suspicion" and that "it is better for us to hang ninety-nine innocent (suspicious) men that to let one guilty one pass."[160]

Another letter writer from Texas confirmed the spirit of the times by noting that the "wildest excitement prevails throughout the north-western, north-eastern, and central portions of Texas, in consequence of Abolition incendiarism." Women and children, he lamented, had been chased from their homes or driven to insanity because of the plots. Half of all citizens were on patrol, but he worried that lynch mobs had so far only been able to hang or burn ten whites and sixty-five blacks. The "school boys have become so excited by the sport of hanging Abolitionists that the schools are completely deserted." Moreover, companies would travel as much as a hundred miles on horseback "to participate in a single session of Judge Lynch's Court."[161]

* * *

The Panic of 1860 was an important moment in the history of the Upper Brazos River valley, and fear generated that summer strengthened secessionists' hands and allowed them to paint a bleak portrait of life under Abraham Lincoln and a Republican administration. The intense sectional tension that existed in 1859 and 1860 is critical to understanding the origins of the Texas Troubles. Likewise, it is important to remember that Texas—embroiled in conflicts with both Mexico and hostile Native Americans—contained a society that had a robust tradition of vigilantism well before the summer of 1860. Any explanation of the panic must rest on those two factors.

To that foundation, however, should be added something about the slaves themselves. The best scholarship on the panic minimizes the role the enslaved played. Because evidence for a plot of any type in 1860 is regarded as being so weak, scholars have concluded that African Americans played no role in the origins of the panic. Yet slaves in Texas had their own history, and it was one of flight, resistance, and even rebellion.

Frederick Olmsted, one of the most widely cited observers of the antebellum South, traveled extensively throughout the region during the 1850s, and on 3 June 1854, the *New York Daily Times* printed a report he had written. Olmsted claimed that "the facilities for escape of negroes from slavery are greater than anywhere else in the South."[162] Although he only spent a few months in Texas, Olmsted had concluded that bondage in the Southwest differed from slavery in other parts of the South. Three years later he wrote the phrase "Slavery with a Will" for his book-length account of his trip to Texas. "Elsewhere at the South, slavery had seemed to be accepted generally, as a natural, hereditary, established state of things," Olmsted concluded, but "in Texas, the state of war in which slavery arises, seems to continue in undertone to the present."[163]

It is easy to exaggerate the significance of this resistance to slavery. Even in central Texas, many freedmen pointed out, most slaves did not succeed in their escape attempts. Most never attempted to escape. Despite the relative vigor of resistance in Texas, the institution of slavery itself was never seriously threatened. It remained politically safe and economically profitable throughout the antebellum period. The central Texas frontier weakened old bonds of the master-slave relationship but left slaveholders enough power to fashion new chains.

To recognize that slave resistance in Texas did not seriously undermine the institution does not mean that the enslaved's actions had no impact on Texas society. What seems clear from the surviving evidence is that Texans, regardless of the actual threat to slavery, worried greatly about the actions of their slaves. Although fear over possible slave insurrections flourished throughout the South, no state can compete with Texas in the late 1850s and early 1860s for bloody overreaction. Slaveholders there perceived themselves as being under constant danger from rebellious slaves, Mexicans, hostile Native Americans, and Northern abolitionist "sojourners." When Frederick Olmsted wrote that Texas slaveholders were in a "state of war" with their slaves, that conclusion was based primarily on what he observed of whites in Texas. They worked themselves into a frenzy by reading sensationalist newspaper stories, participating in hastily called and emotional meetings, agreeing to mass expulsions of suspected abolitionists, listening to rumors, and believing what were clearly fabrications.

Why were Texans so apt to believe such stories and lapse into this state of panic? First, conditions of antebellum Texas allowed slaves slightly more opportunity for resistance and flight than they had elsewhere in the South. Slaveholders perceived and understood this increased rebelliousness as a threat to their authority and to the institution of slavery and embraced legal and extralegal methods to limit the resistance. Second, slaveholders, to camouflage the discontent of their slave population and justify the vigilantism they found necessary, created narratives of docile slaves whom mischievous outsiders provoked into gangs of bloody, deluded slave rebels. This exaggerated rhetoric found a ready audience among the whites of Texas, who knew firsthand how frustrated many were with bondage. The result was an escalating reliance upon vigilantism that peaked tragically during the Panic of 1860.

4. "Hung Sure as Hell": White-on-White Mob Violence in Central Texas

In the spring of 1868 a mob of vigilantes murdered seven white men in central Texas. Members of the mob justified their actions by claiming that the victims had committed horse theft. A government agent from McLennan County who investigated the murders, however, reported that the men were killed because they were "Union men." He further alleged that the mob contained members of the Ku Klux Klan and that the attack was part of a larger campaign in which Northern-born Unionists in the area were "hunted down with hounds and murdered."[1]

Compared to the attention devoted to white-on-black lynching, white-on-white mob violence has drawn relatively little attention from historians since the 1980s.[2] Throughout the United States, however, white mobs often targeted other whites for extralegal execution. In the seven central Texas counties at the heart of this study, mobs murdered at least sixty-seven Anglos between 1860 and 1921.[3] Such numbers are significant and demand explanation. Mob violence against whites in central Texas followed a quite different trajectory than did mob violence against blacks in the region.

Vigilantes in central Texas murdered whites for several reasons, the first of which was being accused of serious crime. Mob leaders routinely justified their actions as necessary because the region's slow and ineffectual court system could not speedily punish the alleged outlaws. Such reasoning, directly or indirectly, justified many acts of vigilantism in central Texas. Yet as the case of the murdered Unionists in 1868 reveals, the mob's alleged justifications did not always accurately indicate its true underlying motives. A second motive for white-on-white mob violence involved political conflict. Mobs executed whites who resisted the will, especially the political will, of the white majority. Resistance to the pro-secessionist, pro-Confederate, and later pro-Democrat white majority provoked frequent acts of mob violence during the 1860s and 1870s. Local authorities and officers of county courts were particularly important in stoking the mob spirit during the era of Reconstruction. By failing to punish those who attacked white Unionists and Republicans they encouraged acts of violence and murder. Finally, vigilantes organized because the act of "lynching," especially by the late nineteenth century, had been enshrined in historical memory as a civic virtue. Vigilantes were leaders of the community, heroes who did what had to be done for the greater good. Young men welcomed the opportunity to follow in their forefathers' footsteps and prove their bravery.

*　*　*

Central Texas mobs justified their actions as necessary in a frontier society beset by outlaws and rogues. Vigilantes often described the region as one that required men to take matters into their own hands because "law enforcement was still in its infancy."[4] It is true that most white victims of mob violence usually aroused the wrath of the community by committing a specific crime. It is also true that some central Texas counties did not have a functioning court until the 1850s. Nevertheless, this simple portrait of central Texas obscures as much as it reveals. Relatively few whites suffered lynching in the first quarter-century of Anglo settlement in central Texas. The region was rife with extralegal violence from its earliest days, but vigilantes and citizen posses focused almost solely on Native Americans. The first documented case of white-on-white mob violence in central Texas did not occur until 1860, a quarter-century after whites settled in the area.

The circumstances and the justification for this important turn of events are worth examining closely. Between June and September 1860 central Texans hanged three white men. The first to be executed was remembered only as Covington, an alleged horse thief. He was captured by a mob of some fifteen men after being trailed to Meridian in Bosque County. "He was hung," recalled local rancher and Indian fighter James Buckner Barry, "after being given the opportunity for confessions and a last speech."[5] Covington's partner, Tucker, was captured in Arkansas and returned to central Texas in early August. The vigilance committee initially decided to turn Tucker over to the civil authorities, but after he had spent ten days in jail it was decided to take him back from the legally constituted authorities. "Over one hundred men were present and there was no voice of dissent raised at the quiet execution which justice and conditions demanded."[6] The third white victim of mob violence in 1860 was named John Garner. Unlike Covington and Tucker, Garner's crime was participating in the murder of two white families in Jack County. He was hanged from a live oak limb near Waco by a mob that included Barry and "several others."[7]

Why did central Texans in 1860 decide that these three white men deserved a form of punishment previously reserved, at least in central Texas, for Indians, Mexicans, and rebellious slaves? The answer lies in the one connection that Barry believed Covington, Tucker, and Garner all shared—acting like Indians. Barry and many members of the mob that hanged the three had just returned from killing four Indian horse thieves. At home, they found themselves facing white men who—in their opinion—had taken on the worst habits of Indians. Barry underlined the uneasiness by distinguishing Covington and Tucker from Indians, referring to them as "white horse thieves." If the existence of Covington and Tucker collapsed central Texans' simple racial dichotomy of bad Indians and good Anglos, John Garner exploded those racial lines altogether. Garner had not just imitated Indian ways, but he had also joined an Indian tribe and helped kill whites. If white men ever deserved to be lynched, central Texans must have reasoned, it was surely these three men who had become "white Indians" in their behavior and values.[8]

Apparently, the message of deterrence intended to be conveyed by the lynchings of Covington, Tucker, and Garner did not make much of an impression. Six years later reports continued to surface that "reckless bad white men [are] associated with the indians in stealing and killing."[9] Such vague rumors were backed up by specific reports. The district attorney of the Eleventh Judicial District, for example, reported to Gov. J. W. Throckmorton in December 1866 that "a young white man" and "an Indian or half-indian" had killed two white men, cutting their throats "from ear to ear." Their heads "were hacked all over, their hands hid and the bodies taken into the bushes & laid on their faces, that the blood settling in their faces, recognition might be difficult."[10]

The blurring of the line between white desperadoes and Indians had become nearly complete. "The Indians and [white] hors[e] thieves broke in to our Country at its desperat[e] state," wrote William Baker to his mother. "They kill women and children, car[r]y off same, drive horse and cattle out by thousands."[11] The differentiating category of "whiteness" that separated Anglos from Indians in early central Texas had to be revised when Anglos began to be lynched. To be sure, the category *white* remained important, but what it meant and what it bestowed were fluid, dependent upon a number of factors beyond complexion. After 1860 being white certainly no longer protected one from lynching in central Texas.[12]

Although the first lynchings in central Texas reveal that the motives of lynch

mobs were complex and not easily reduced to the pure desire to punish criminals, they also suggest the importance mob members placed in charging victims with specific crimes. From 1860 to 1890 mobs charged whites with horse
or cattle theft more than any other crime. Twenty-two of the sixty-seven
whites lynched died because they were alleged to have committed one of those
crimes. As one central Texan remembered, it "was not uncommon for cattle
thieves to be hung when caught" because stealing "was the greatest crime."[13]
In 1862 a mob hanged two men for horse theft in McLennan County.[14] Frustrations grew even stronger after the Civil War. In 1866 a correspondent from
Bell County reported to the *Galveston Daily News* that a man named Park had
been recently hanged. He also warned that others were "in danger of sharing the same fate" because horse thieves "attract a large part of the people's
attention here."[15]

The years of the Civil War and Reconstruction were inundated with white-
on-white mob violence, but the most infamous central Texas lynching involving white victims occurred in Belton in 1874. On 25 May a mob estimated
to number between three and five hundred men surrounded the Bell County
jail. They came because the local sheriff and his deputies had recently arrested ten suspected criminals, nine horse thieves and a murderer. News of
the arrests was warmly received throughout central Texas. Many men, angry
from suffering property loss or worse during the previous several years, decided to travel to Belton. At some point twenty to fifty members of the mob,
including "some of the best citizens of Belton," decided to lynch the alleged
criminals, although the jailer did his best to prevent that from happening
and hid the cell keys. Undeterred, the mob stuck their rifles and revolvers
through the cell bars and opened fire, riddling the inmates with bullets. The
only man to escape death was a prisoner who had fallen ill and been removed
from the main cell. The next day the bodies were thrown outside the jail,
where they remained "on exhibition to curious eyes" for several hours. Late
in the afternoon the corpses were piled on a wagon, hauled to the cemetery,
and buried. The lynching of nine men by one mob represents one of the most
deadly lynchings in the history of the United States.[16]

The frustrations and anger that fueled this lynching had been building for
years. In the decade following the conclusion of the Civil War, central Texas
experienced great turmoil. The rocky political situation and the thinly settled nature of the region combined to make it a common destination and
refuge for criminals. "Under the reconstruction period," recalled Emma Falconer, "thieves were numerous and bold and found a secure retreat in the
thickets and timber of the Brazos bottom."[17] Given the pre-war experience
of many with extralegal justice, it is not surprising that a number of vigilante

organizations arose. John Robertson of Marlin remembered that after the Civil War "there were Vigilant societies who took the law into their hands for the citizens' protection."[18] Another central Texan recalled that the law was "so often delayed and not enforced" that criminals had "to be dealt with without recourse to a trial by jury."[19]

After theft of livestock, the most common crime for which mobs lynched in central Texas was murder. Twenty of the sixty-seven Anglo victims of mob violence died because they were charged with murder or a combination of murder and another crime. In 1861 a posse of men from several central Texas counties joined together and hanged three men for committing both murder and cattle theft.[20] The Belton mob of 1874 was determined to execute the horse thieves lodged in the county jail but did not hesitate to shoot the one not charged with horse theft because he was accused of murdering his wife.[21]

Although securing justice and revenge for murder and horse theft were important for central Texas vigilantes, men were executed for numerous other crimes as well, including fence cutting, robbery, arson, and rape. In 1876 a white man known only as Dickson fled Bosque County after offending a white woman. Although newspaper coverage of the crime was vague, the event clearly angered those who pursued Dickson. Two men, Markaberry and Mayfield, trailed him until they caught him on the banks of the Brazos River. Instead of returning with Dickson for prosecution, they tortured and then murdered him. They cut his legs so he could not escape and then sliced off various parts of his body. After additional hacking, they tore pieces from his flesh. Finally, they hanged Dickson to a tree on the verge of a cliff. Returning to Bosque County, they reported that the prisoner had escaped.[22] The sadistic murder was an exception; although sexual crimes greatly angered local citizens, Anglos in central Texas were rarely lynched for committing them.[23]

The Dickson murder also reveals the blurry line that sometimes separates mob violence from murder. Some would judge the killing to be a murder and not a lynching because it received limited public support and was carried out in secret by just two men. Other hangings in central Texas likewise lacked the support of local citizenry. In 1877 Allen Bowen's body was found hanging from the limb of a tree in Coryell County. Bowen had testified against Bill Green during Green's trial for horse theft in Waco, and Green's friends, not an enraged citizenry, no doubt hanged him.[24]

These cases complicate an understanding of extralegal justice in central Texas. Defenses of lynching and vigilantism there traditionally portrayed the region's vigilantes as moral agents whose actions represented the will of the people. Outsiders, they argued, could not understand circumstances that compelled mob violence. "It is all very easy for the editor of the *News* to write so denunciatorily [sic] of these unlawful combinations, sitting securely in his office in Galveston," the Hill County Expositor noted in 1875. Living on the frontier, the newspaper assured readers, altered one's perspective.[25]

Vigilantes pursued justice against criminals who could not be brought to trial by constituted authorities and thus performed a necessary and important role in society. The hangings of both Dickson and Bowen (as well as those of Covington, Tucker, and Garner) challenge that image and suggest that lynch mobs acted from a varied and diverse set of motives. The imperfection of lynching was recognized by observers such as Leroy Dean, who remarked that in "those days of hasty judgment, there were perhaps many men who suffered from the crimes of others."[26]

* * *

The complicated causes of mob violence in central Texas are perhaps best illustrated by the many acts of vigilantism whose origins can be found in the sectional crisis. Before and during the war, mobs in the region targeted whites suspected of endorsing abolitionism, supporting the Union, or evincing disloyalty toward the Confederacy.

The causes of this sectarian violence are complex and at least partially rooted in tensions between slaveholders and nonslaveholders dating from the antebellum period. As in the rest of the South, central Texas slaveholders—approximately one-quarter of the adult white male population—had legitimate reasons to fret over their minority status. Simply put, most white men could vote during the antebellum period. The Texas Constitution of 1845 established voting privileges for every free male person, twenty-one or older, who met certain minimum residency requirements.[27] Imbued with political power, poor white Texans guarded their interests closely.

For planters, the critical issue was yeoman support for slavery. Land speculator Jacob de Cordova encouraged migration to Texas from all parts of the United States, assuring his audience that "no man need own slaves, or even employ them." Cordova made clear, however, that any migrant must be willing to tolerate the peculiar institution. "All that is asked of the non-slaveholder," he stated, "is that he shall pursue the even tenor of his way, mind his own business, and leave his neighbors to attend to theirs."[28] The loss of yeomen's support for bondage could have been devastating to slaveholders. In theory, an antislavery majority in the voting population might have had the gravest of consequences—emancipation. Although there seemed to be little interest in ending slavery in Texas, slaveholding interests took time to draft constitutional protections against such a measure in the constitution of the Republic of Texas.[29]

The second, certainly more pressing, reason that slaveholders needed state political power was the problem of controlling unfree laborers. Slaveholders needed to pass and enforce legislation and establish slave patrols, jails, and other civil institutions to help in the capture of fugitives. Central Texans realized, quite correctly, that political power was an absolute prerequisite for the continued stability and prosperity of their plantation society. In the South, where the numerically superior nonslaveholders could vote, planters had to work hard to ensure that local and state governments continued to protect their property in human beings.

The task of reconciling small farmers to life in a slave society was a problem that confronted nearly all planters in the South. In Texas, however, the developing nature of the young society forced planters to forge close alliances with a large number of pioneers who had no direct connection to slavery but had often earned respected positions in local society through their roles in settling the region. Complicating matters, the local institutions that planters often dominated by tradition in earlier-settled states—such as county governments—had to be created anew on the edge of the South. Yet in 1861 most of central Texas's nonslaveholders joined with their planter neighbors in voting for secession and fighting a war to protect, among other things, the Southern right to hold slaves. How did planters overcome these difficulties and consolidate their power on the frontier?[30]

Nonslaveholders in central Texas gave support to the development of the region's burgeoning slave society for five reasons. First, and most important, poor white men and women in the South shared the racist assumptions of their slaveholding neighbors. Thus, nonslaveholder support of slavery often had less to do with warm feelings for wealthy planter allies and more to do with white views on the proper role for blacks in Southern society. Planters encouraged belief in black inferiority, and the consequent legitimacy of slave society, by participating in and shaping the most important cultural institutions of early central Texas, particularly the region's churches. Second, white men of all classes shared a belief in a form of republicanism that legitimated the power and wealth possessed by planters and slaveholders. Whereas class divisions in other regions of the South had punctured such a republican vision, the social order of central Texas was fluid enough to sustain such theories. Third, the presence of planters offered distinct economic advantages to many nonslaveholders, who often relied on the planters and slaveholders for transportation of their goods to markets, access to skilled labor, and opportunities to purchase needed goods that otherwise would not have been available locally. Fourth, small farmers and stockraisers needed white unity as desperately as did planters because they lived on a dangerous Indian frontier.

Even more than planters who lived in the better-protected river bottoms, yeomen needed state support for a military "defense" force. Fifth, when all else failed, planters refused to allow the development of dissent against slavery in central Texas. Whenever they detected the presence of whites unsympathetic to slavery, they invoked central Texas's culture of violence to silence such opposition.[31]

Resorting to mob violence was a measure of last resort because many whites realized that violence could have a destabilizing impact upon the already tense political climate of the late antebellum period. It was one thing to lynch suspected horse thieves and outsiders without real connection to the local community; it was another to hang a neighbor for dissent from majority opinion. Such caution limited mob attacks on whites in central Texas until 1860. After John Brown's raid on Harpers Ferry in 1859, however, the white majority—fearful of abolitionists inspiring slave rebellions—embraced vigilantism as never before. The most obvious result was the Panic of 1860, and the various vigilante groups formed in the summer of that year did not disappear when the crisis passed. They remained in place and played an important role in the presidential election that fall, during the subsequent secession crisis, and throughout four years of civil war.

Mass meetings formed in late 1860 to protest the election of Abraham Lincoln and call for secession from the Union. In late 1860 "the people of Coryell County" issued a resolution warning that the Republican administration would support "the abolition of slavery and the equalizing of the white and black population" and cause the "destruction of society" and "corruption of the pure Anglo-Saxon blood of the white race." The meeting then formed a committee to oversee the organization of armed companies to defend the region from attack and prepare "for any emergency that might arise."[32]

Throughout the winter Texas secessionists used every means at their disposal to convince their neighbors to approve the ordinance of secession passed by the Texas legislature. A Presbyterian minister named Thaddeus McRae recalled the intimidation surrounding the issue. McRae had left Mississippi for Texas because he thought Texans "as a whole were opposed to the Southern Revolution" and would remain neutral in the coming conflict with the North. To his dismay, the election "on the issue of secession" was "supported widely by Vigilance Committees in different portions of the state" and was regarded by Union men "as a farce without any legal sanction." McRae wrote that he and thousands of other Unionists refused to vote, but "Vigilance Committees and other desperate measures" forced the "dazed" majority to accept the election's results.[33]

Vigilance committees continued their work after Texas joined the Confederacy and the war began. The "people here are as much united as they will ever be," wrote Wallace Oakes of central Texas, but "a dozen discontented tories" would "if they were not afraid" support Lincoln and the Union. "You may expect to hear of the death of some tories at Waco before many weeks," Oakes concluded, "if they do not speedily hold their peace."[34]

Not everyone followed Oakes in suggesting the lynching of suspected Unionists. Many hoped that law and order could be maintained through the courts, but that was not easy because the courts had to adjust to a new government that lacked a number of experienced officials and leaders who had entered the Confederate Army.[35]

The problems courts faced during the Civil War are made clear by the case of Charles Warren. On 27 August 1861 Warren stabbed an Englishman named John Burton several times with a knife and killed him. Authorities quickly indicted Warren for the murder, although he claimed that he killed Burton because he was "an abolitionist and an alien enemy of the Southern Confederacy." In his request for a continuance of the trial Warren promised that the testimony of C. J. Tinsley would verify Burton's "being an alien enemy." Neither Warren's allegation that Burton was an abolitionist nor his defense that Burton had threatened his life moved the jury. They found him guilty of murder and sentenced him to be executed by hanging.[36]

Although the courts had found Warren guilty, the court of public opinion was more divided. Aided by a company of Confederate soldiers, Warren escaped from jail and joined the Confederate Army. McLennan County officials sought him throughout the war and finally found him in 1864. By that time, however, neither state nor Confederate officials were eager to give up a veteran soldier. The Texas secretary of state wrote about the case to the clerk of McLennan County's district court on 25 March 1864. Warren's commanding officer, he noted, "speaks in high terms of Warren"; moreover, the murder of Burton may have been committed "under excitement induced by drunkeness." Before considering whether to surrender Warren to McLennan County, the secretary of state requested "the facts in the case and the opinion of your county in regards to the subject." Warren was not turned over to local authorities, and he returned to Texas after the end of the Civil War, relocating to Lampasas County. In 1885 McLennan County officials discovered Warren—now sixty-five—and arrested him once again. He was returned to Waco twenty-four years after killing John Burton. Warren's friends petitioned the governor, who pardoned the Confederate veteran. According to the local newspaper the general population of Waco welcomed the governor's action and the case being ended once and for all.[37]

Warren's crime was not the only such case facing central Texas courts. In late 1861 Demetrius Hays and Eli Ensor were killed while awaiting trial in McLennan County. Hays had been recently indicted for harboring an escaped slave, and Ensor had been indicted for "fornication with a person of mixed color." Authorities reacted strongly to these extralegal executions and, attempting to maintain control of the situation, arrested and indicted seven men for the murder of Hays and eight men for the killing of Ensor. The alleged mob leader in both cases was William R. Johnson, who was eventually found guilty of killing Hays and sentenced to five years in prison. Like Warren, however, it is not clear that Johnson actually served any time. He died in 1866 and before his appeals were exhausted.[38]

These cases illustrate that the central Texas legal system was in crisis. Citizens openly challenged the courts by freeing a prisoner sentenced to death and executing others not yet convicted by a jury. Supporters of law and order grew frustrated. The courts seemed unable to either punish criminals or fairly investigate suspected Unionists. Central Texans had long believed in the importance of direct citizen action. Not surprisingly given the circumstances, the region's vigilante movement grew.

On 17 March 1862 Bosque County authorities largely suspended operation of the courts and organized a committee of safety. According to the minutes of its first meeting, the committee worried that the county harbored "persons hostile to our institutions, consequently enemies of our country, and its cause, besides characters who have no love of our county." The committee pledged that "should any man now living in our midst, and who has been or who may hereafter be guilty of using language derogatory of the Southern Confederacy or its cause, or by any act giving evidence that he is unfriendly to the Confederate government," he would be compelled to either join the Confederate Army or immediately leave for the "Lincoln government." If he failed to do either, the committee would regard him "as an alien enemy and a spy for which he shall be executed."[39]

The Bosque County vigilance committee, like most others in central Texas during the war, was composed of some of the region's most respected citizens. Vigilance committees hoped to follow basic rules of investigation and appear fair to the general populace while at the same time silencing dissent. They were often effective. One Texas Unionist wrote that "surrounded as I was, in order to save my life, I was compelled to chime in with my surroundings." Even though "mildly speaking," he was "threatened with the Vigilance Committees" and only saved because of the mob's "regard for my personal friends."[40]

Vigilante leaders, however, sometimes lost control over members of their groups. Such was the case in McLennan County in 1862. A number of men accused a Northern-born printer living in Waco of being an abolitionist. One of these men was C. J. Tinsley, whom Charles Warren claimed would support his claim that John Burton was an abolitionist. The McLennan County committee of safety investigated the charge and declared the printer, whose name was Wood—and who had lived in Texas for many years—to be innocent. Several men, including Tinsley, disagreed with this finding and decided to lynch Wood anyway. They dragged him out of his house on 20 May, "tearing him away from his screaming wife and little son." Then they took him "to the nearest tree and hanged him." Vigilance committee leaders were furious that their verdict had been ignored and tracked down the men. On 23 May, three—Tinsley, J. T. Russell, and Henry Russell—were captured and riddled with bullets. A fourth who was able to convince the committee that others had forced him into the act was allowed to join the Confederate Army. The other two men—unidentified in the sources—escaped. Within a few days a vigilance committee decision not to lynch someone had sparked events that led to the deaths of four men by mob violence.[41]

The situation only deteriorated as the war dragged on and resistance to the war increased. Many who opposed secession decided to support the Confederacy after Texas left the Union, but some local Unionists never backed the new government. John D. Johnson of McLennan County was one such man. Johnson followed the example of Sam Houston—he supported neither the Confederacy nor the Union.[42] Other central Texans also refused to fight or serve the new government. A local historian wrote that almost from the beginning of the war "droves of eligible men" had disappeared. At first they fled to avoid public pressure to enlist; later they dodged the actual Confederate draft.[43]

Whatever the size of this initial group of dissenters, there is no doubt their numbers grew during the war. In 1863 one central Texan informed the governor that many individuals from other parts of the South had recently arrived, "endeavoring to shirk Confederate service."[44] As the home lives of their families grew more desperate and the Confederacy's battlefield results grew more disappointing, many soldiers in the Confederate Army added to those numbers by deserting. An 1864 petition to the governor urged that those "who were drafted or who volunteered" be allowed to return to help "defend the Women and children from Indian depredations."[45] That same year a traveler reported that four to five thousand deserters, armed and defiant, were waiting in the "brush" for the end of the war.[46] By early April in 1865 a Union officer noted that "the demoralization of the rebel army in Texas is very extensive."[47]

Confederate and state officials met the crisis with a range of approaches, including lynching. In the spring of 1864 James Buckner Barry began to "hunt out deserters" in north central Texas. "This was merely the beginning of a drive which was to make, at least, renegades, deserters, and over-stayers-of-leave decidedly uneasy during the year," he wrote.[48] A Confederate officer observed in 1862 that Texas Unionists constituted a serious threat that might have "to be crushed out, even if it has to be done without due course of law."[49]

Eyewitnesses and U.S. officials confirmed the dangers facing Texas Unionists. Thaddeus McRae wrote that the murder of Unionist "suspects" was frequent in Texas.[50] In 1862, after interviewing refugees from Texas, the U.S. consul in Mexico reported the hanging of six men and concluded, "I am confident no portion of the United States has been so badly oppressed as the Union men of Texas."[51] That bleak assessment was seemingly confirmed in October of 1862, when vigilantes in the north Texas town of Gainesville lynched at least forty-four alleged Unionists. No place before or since has seen the mass lynching of so many men.[52]

No such lynching took place in central Texas, but deserters and Unionists did face the danger of mob violence if caught in the region. The Texas Home Guard—the "Heel Flies"—captured three deserters late in the war who were alleged to have been heading for "Camp Safety," a hideout for deserters and Unionists in the central Texas brush. In the process of returning the fugitives to the proper authorities, the Home Guard camped near two companies of Confederate soldiers on a small lake in Bell County. The next morning's dawn revealed the bodies of the three men hanging from a pecan tree. Members of the Home Guard blamed the lynching on the nearby Confederate soldiers although others suggested that local residents hanged them.[53]

By the end of the Civil War, vigilantism, murder, and lynching were widespread in central Texas. The underlying motive for most of these acts of mob violence was that the victim was not properly supportive of the Confederate government. The impetus for lynching was further strengthened by the fact that courts and local governments were in disarray. Most observers astutely reasoned that order would not be easily restored during Reconstruction. "I see," wrote one Texan, "famine, robbery, assassination and misrule, anarchy for long, long years."[54] Even such pessimistic predictions, however, failed to prepare the region for the violence of the postwar era.

* * *

The violence of the Reconstruction era was considerably more complicated than the mob violence of the Civil War years. During the war, the political nature of vigilantism was often transparent and even encouraged by Confederate authorities. After the war the level of politically motivated violence actually increased, but the presence of the Federal Army led mob leaders to be more secretive. They hesitated to tout their actions and reveal their underlying motives. Moreover, it is quite clear that many acts of violence during Reconstruction were not strictly about politics. Economic and social disruption throughout the former Confederacy led many outlaws and criminals to migrate to central Texas. Once there, they often committed horrible acts of violence out of a desire for revenge or money.

Outlaws targeted white Unionists and Republicans for several reasons. They blamed them for a variety of offenses, ranging from Confederate defeat to the death of former comrades to their own economic ruin. More important, however, they knew they could freely target such men without fear of upsetting local authorities. Leaders of the white community in central Texas tolerated violence during Reconstruction so long as it helped destabilize the Republican government, whose policies they abhorred and whose regime they wanted to topple.

"Contemporary observers and later historians alike," wrote one scholar, "held that Texas was the most lawless of all the states in the Reconstruction South."[55] As violent as the state was in the late 1860s, the Upper Brazos River valley was even more violent. Between the close of the Civil War in 1865 and the end of Texas's Reconstruction in 1873, residents of Bosque, Falls, Hill, and McLennan counties murdered more than a hundred people.[56] Given their combined population of 35,785 in 1870, this means that central Texas experienced a level of murder and violence during Reconstruction that set the region apart.[57] An area that contained only 4.4 percent of Texas's population in 1870 committed 10 percent of all murders in the state between 1865 and 1868.[58] Moreover central Texas violence was not limited solely to murder. McLennan County inhabitants, according to reports, committed more crimes between January 1866 and April 1870 than did the residents of any other Texas county.[59]

The political violence sparked by the Civil War flowed into the era of Reconstruction with a vengeance. Many victims of that wave of violence were recently emancipated freedpeople. Antiblack violence during Reconstruction, however, was accompanied by attacks on white Unionists that were so frequent that they defy easy calculation.

When Matthew Young, an agent for the Freedmen's Bureau, arrived in Bell County in 1867 he wrote that Union men in the region "were afraid" to reveal their beliefs "in word or deed" because of the threat of "mob law and personal violence."[60] Numerous episodes confirm that assessment. On 4 January 1867 John McCormick was shot at a ball in McLennan County. After he later died from the bullet's wounds, a Freedmen's Bureau official wrote that "McCormick was murdered because of his Union connections."[61] In

1867 two Hill County men approached Jesse Rose, called him a "Radical," then shot and killed him "deliberately" because of a "political quarrel."[62] In 1868 vigilantes ordered William H. Adams to leave central Texas because he was born in the North. When Adams disappeared, a Freedmen's Bureau agent investigated and concluded that he was "probably murdered."[63] The most infamous lynching of suspected white Republicans was probably the 1868 execution of seven Unionists by vigilantes described at the beginning of this chapter.

Vigilantes sometimes went to great lengths to get their man. Five or six men hunted down and shot James Bishop, a Bell County resident and rebel deserter who had fled to Mexico and joined the Second Texas Regiment of the Union Army during the war, after he returned to Bell County.[64] The protracted search for Bishop paled in comparison to the efforts extended to murder James Christian, whose father was a justice appointed by military authorities in Bell County. The younger Christian fled the region under threat of violence because of "his union proclivities," but assassins tracked him to Springfield, Missouri, and "waylaid and murdered him."[65]

To the number of white Unionists killed in central Texas should be added those who survived assassination attempts. In McLennan County, J. C. Caldwell declared that "he could whip any damn radical in Texas" before attempting to shoot and kill former U.S. lieutenant John Blinn. Caldwell was unable to live up to his boast, however, because his pistol misfired.[66] Clark Jones also failed to kill his target when he walked into the house of Theodore Rice, a registrar for Falls County, and shot him.[67] Intimidation and violence against Unionists was hardly limited to assault and murder. George W. Patten, a farmer and Unionist, had his mill burned to the ground four times before he gave up on rebuilding it.[68]

The threat and impact of such violence was significant. Throughout central Texas, Unionists depended heavily on the army for protection. "It would not be safe to go a mile from town without an escort," wrote agent F. B. Sturgis from Marlin in 1867.[69] A Hill County mob later threatened Sturgis himself for criticizing lynching.[70] Charles Stiles wrote that he had underestimated the number of troops needed in Bell County, declaring "were it not for the presence of troops a union man or a freedman would not be safe in life or property."[71]

White Unionists and army officers were not always innocent victims in the violence of the late 1860s. Bitter tensions on both sides often led to feudlike turbulence, as illustrated by the story behind the lynching of Unionists Jonathan and Newton Lindley. In the summer of 1866 the bodies of Jasper Lindley and Sam Miller were found in Little River in Bell County. According to one rumor, vigilantes shot the men for horse theft; what role their support for the Union played in their deaths is unknown. Clearly, however, U.S. soldiers and Jasper Lindley's family were outraged. On 13 July, Jonathan and Newton Lindley, Jasper's father and brother, set off with fifteen U.S. soldiers to arrest the men they believed had orchestrated the murders. They found two of them, pulled them from their homes, and shot them in the middle of the prairie. After much protest the Lindleys were placed in the Belton jail, and soon thereafter a mob broke in and shot them in their cells.[72]

The Lindley lynching is typical of the Reconstruction-era violence in central Texas that often mixed political difference, personal animosity, and economic desperation. The region hosted many outlaws whose actions cannot be understood in strictly political terms. "There was a great deal of lawlessness in the country," remembered Edward Rotan, a businessman. "Waco had the reputation of being the most lawless city in the state."[73] Another longtime Waco resident, William Sleeper, concurred, recalling that the area "was infested with many desperate and dangerous characters."[74] One of the more gruesome episodes was the 1867 murder of a white widow in Bosque County by a mob of nineteen outlaws known to "murder white and black indiscriminately."[75] Local officials battled outlaw activity for years after the Civil War but with little success. As late as 1873 the adjutant general of Texas noted that "Hill County is infested with a band of lawless characters, who in disguise and under cover of night, go about outraging whoever incurs their displeasure."[76]

The most obvious explanation for the rise of outlaw activity rests on the poverty and frustration created by the postwar economic depression. As Edward Rotan reported, "We forded the Brazos River and I went to the only hotel in Waco. There were so many deserted houses or shacks used before the war," and things "had gone to the bad and grass grew up on the square of Waco after the war. Half the public houses were idle."[77]

Although central Texas had in some ways expanded during the Civil War, the local economy crashed along with the Confederacy. In 1860 the total value of property in the four central Texas counties of Bosque, Falls, Hill, and McLennan amounted to $7,428,846. In 1866 the total valuation of property in those same four counties was estimated at $2,542,178, a third of what it had been six years earlier. The greatest single cause of the downturn, of course, was the sudden emancipation of thousands of slaves. The region's nearly four and a half thousand slaves had been valued in 1860 at $2,747,180—the single most significant form of property in the region. In 1860 slaves counted for more than 40 percent of the region's total wealth and even out-valued the land holdings of the Upper Brazos River valley. Freedom may not have eliminated all obstacles facing blacks in central Texas, but it surely dissolved the finances of many of the region's planters. In addition to losing the unpaid labor of slaves, they saw the value of land plummet. Property value in the four counties had grown steadily every year before the war, reaching a peak at $2,548,218 in 1860; six years later, however, the value of land in the region sank to $1,210,994.[78]

Given the economic situation, it is not surprising that many of the region's outlaws were just as interested in their victims' money and livestock as their racial identities and political affiliations. Republican J. W. P. Doyle, for example, may have "in politics differed with a majority of his fellow citizens," but the mob that murdered the former judge and his son was certainly interested in the reputed fortune the family stored in their home. After killing the two men, the mob found and promptly stole some $13,000 from the Doyle home in Hill County.[79]

The immense social and economic disruption caused by the Civil War was often linked by whites to accompanying political upheavals. The change in political leadership gave native Anglos a convenient scapegoat for their economic woes. John Martin Parks provides one example. Since his move to Texas, Parks had been unable to rise above renting a farm. In 1869 he was living in McLennan County. His cattle had been stolen, two years' worth of his crops had been lost to flooding, and the poor-quality cotton that survived fetched low prices. Although Republicans were hardly the ones responsible for these difficulties, Parks directed his anger at the political situation: "I am disfranchised whilst Sambo and a few demagogue office seekers and other little landowners are enfranchised."[80] The historical record does not reveal what finally became of John Martin Parks, but it is safe to say that many men like him lost respect for the authorities. Their personal difficulties made it easier for them to consider becoming outlaws.

To the number of law-abiding men turned into bandits must be added a great number of desperate characters who immigrated to central Texas at the end of the Civil War. In 1867 a government agent wrote from Falls County that the area "seems to be filled with a set of cut throats from the other side of the Mississippi river" who added to "the Bad men already in the State" and swelled the number of outlaws.[81] Such testimony was confirmed several hundred miles away by Samuel Pointer, who testified during the investigation into the Ku Klux Klan of South Carolina that several wanted men could not be found because they had moved to Texas.[82]

Although some central Texans welcomed these men, others fled the increasingly violent region. The turnover in the number of whites during the 1860s was astounding. According to a sample comparison of the 1860 and 1870 censuses, fewer than 20 percent of whites who resided in McLennan County in 1860—the most economically successful and resilient county in central Texas—still resided there ten years later.[83] Of the 402 males eight years of age and older who lived in McLennan County in 1860, only 80 lived there in 1870, a persistence rate of 19.9 percent. A small number of the 322 no longer living in the county had moved only as far as a neighboring county. An additional one-quarter of former McLennan County residents in 1860 remained in the state but no longer lived at its heart. In the end, however, more than half of the antebellum residents of McLennan County were missing, had left Texas, or had departed the earth entirely by 1870.[84]

That mobility combined with the influx of "bad men" and a postwar depression surely had an impact on violence in central Texas. Ultimately, however, those factors cannot fully explain the rise of postwar outlaw activity there. One critical component in central Texas's Reconstruction-era violence was that citizens who normally organize to contain such violence—especially the economic and social elite who usually favor stability and order—accepted it because it served their political needs, specifically the destabilization of the Republican Party. "I am obliged to fight the whole county," Freedmen's Bureau agent Charles Haughn wrote in 1868, "Lawyers, Doctors, Philosophers, & all."[85]

The impact of such middle-class resistance was felt most acutely in the central Texas court system, and what particularly encouraged violence was the courts' failure to convict known criminals. Edward King noted during his travels through the state that "respectable" men could commit acts of murder without loss of public esteem. "The courts do not mete out punishment in such cases with proper severity," he observed, "sometimes readily acquitting men who have wantonly and willfully shot their fellow-creatures on the slightest provocation."[86] James Jay Emerson, an agent for the Freedmen's Bureau, echoed that sentiment when he wrote in 1867 that union men would not get "justice in the civil courts, owing to the class of men now sitting as Judges, Justices of the Peace, etc."[87] Another outraged agent, D. F. Stiles, noted in 1868 that civil officers could "neither protect or give justice to loyal men" and were "of no earthly account for the simple reason that they cannot get a jury to convict any one."[88]

The story of John W. Oliver illustrates the failures of the court system during Reconstruction. Oliver was the kind of man that conservative white Southerners labeled a "scalawag." He was born in Mississippi but had become a Republican and was living in Houston in 1870 when Republican governor E. J. Davis appointed him judge of the Thirty-third Judicial District. By 1871 the district was composed of McLennan, Falls, and Limestone counties. Local Republicans no doubt hoped that the courts would finally crack down on the region's outlaws, and Oliver struggled to do just that. He often found, however, that local authorities hostile to the Republican government blocked the path of justice. No conflict loomed larger than his struggle to increase the size of the sheriff's force. Oliver correctly believed that central Texas needed more officers to contain the region's violence. His request for additional peace officers was blocked, however, by the county court. Oliver retaliated by jailing the entire court on contempt charges, promising to release them when they authorized his force. Not surprisingly, white conservatives in Waco loathed Oliver, and when he jailed the court "a movement was started, headed by the younger men, to lynch Oliver."[89]

Before Oliver could be lynched, however, another plan emerged. A group of local leaders convinced the Waco medical board to testify that Oliver was insane and recommend that he be removed from the bench. Fearing both the lunacy charge and the lynch mob, Oliver released the men from jail in exchange for the dismissal of the lunacy complaint. Conservative central Texas whites also petitioned the state legislature to ask that Oliver be removed. The house voted 43–31 to impeach him, but the legislature adjourned before any action could be taken. The struggle to remove Oliver had failed, but local conservatives continued to block many of his initiatives. The courts remained divided, weak, and unable to curb the region's violence.[90]

The story of John Oliver gives support to local Unionist-turned-Republican A. J. Evans, who held that the reason for central Texas's lawlessness was that many law-abiding citizens gave Republican authorities no help in capturing fugitives. Instead, recalcitrant Anglos praised, nurtured, and shielded white outlaws. Evans wrote to the governor, asking help in arresting a "young, athletic man, desperate in every sense of the word, and a splendid shot," who was being "fed and succorred by friends."[91] Evans was correct. The upsurge of outlaw activity in central Texas after the Civil War was allowed to grow because of widespread community support for—or at least acceptance of—mob violence.

Why did the local elite tolerate such violence? Many central Texans would have argued that it was necessary, a matter of survival, during Reconstruction. Yet the white majority did not find itself in a truly kill-or-be-killed situation. The danger of violence against white conservatives by recently emancipated freedpeople or white Republicans was consistently exaggerated. Local white citizens opposed the Republican government because they believed it to be illegitimate and because they also believed that Republicans were pursuing specific policies that they abhorred.

In the eyes of many white citizens, the Republican Party threatened to create a central Texas in which native whites had too little political power and too few economic opportunities. Republican economic policies in particular did not sit well with many whites in central Texas. One such policy concerned confiscating Confederate property. A textile mill had been built in Waco during the Civil War to provide uniforms and other goods to the Confederate Army. The mill itself, central Texans argued, was not owned by the Confederacy but rather by a local family. After the war an agent nevertheless "seized the cotton factory mill and foundry formerly owned by the so-called Confederate States."[92] Thomas Harrison, a former slaveowner already reeling from the financial blow of emancipation, wrote a vigorous letter of protest to the governor.[93]

Other than confiscation of Confederate property, the critical financial issue for most whites in the 1860s was taxes. They did not care much for the financial needs of a state government attempting to rebuild a war-torn society and integrate thousands of former slaves into free society. What they cared about was their own pocketbooks. For many native whites, adjusting to the new postwar era was an economic challenge all by itself. For them, paying higher taxes to "sleek-looking, well-clad" Republican officials would only make their lives more difficult.[94]

During the summer of 1871 a group of prominent white Texans called for meetings at the county level to discuss the issue of state taxation. Ninety-four counties sent delegates to the Tax-payers' Convention. McLennan County resident George B. Erath served as temporary chair before giving up his seat to the former governor of Texas, E. M. Pease. Although the convention discussed various problems with the Republican government, the key issue was rising taxes. In 1866, the convention claimed, taxes were but 15 cents per $100; five years later under the Republicans, state taxes had reached more than $2 per $100. The sitting governor, E. J. Davis, refused either to recognize the convention or meet with its special committee to discuss reducing state expenditures.[95] Although no detailed study of the issue exists, it seems that taxes under Reconstruction governments played an important role in galvanizing white opposition to Republicans. Of course, it is equally clear that some whites saw participation in the taxpayer's conventions as a convenient way of attacking a Republican Party whose primary sin was allowing black participation.[96]

Immigration was another critical Republican policy that angered many central Texans. Because the black population of Texas was less than a third of the state's total population after the Civil War, Republican electoral success hinged on forging a coalition between Unionist whites, Mexicans, and blacks. Although a number of whites were willing to join the Republicans in Texas, party officials believed that chances of success would greatly increase by attracting sympathetic and liberal whites from outside the state. The *Waco Register,* a Republican newspaper, proudly espoused that plan: "Thousands and thousands of immigrants are now pouring into our State from Illinois, Missouri, Iowa and Kansas. . . . Let it be understood that Texas is to be a Republican State, and it will receive such an influx of immigration as has never been known before in the history of any State of the Union. We have a climate and soil unequalled by any State, in variety and products. Convince the people that we are to be governed by true representative, American ideas and they will come."[97]

The *Register* was not alone in actively recruiting immigrants to Texas; the Republican Party itself created an aggressive bureau of immigration designed to do the same. Loyal Unionist agents were dispatched to New York City, St. Louis, and New Orleans in hope of luring potential immigrants.[98]

The most prominent Northern-born immigrant to central Texas during Reconstruction was David F. Davis, a Dartmouth-educated teacher from New Hampshire who arrrived in 1866 to aid the Freedmen's Bureau. Davis quickly became a Radical Republican and served as president of the Radical Republican state convention in 1868. His Republican friends later appointed him to a judgeship in McLennan County when a sitting judge resigned to take a seat in the legislature. Davis was a nightmare for conservative central Texans. He attempted to remove local officials stained by "rebel proclivities" and replace them with Republicans. He also wrote to the governor to request appointments for civil positions in central Texas, arguing that "I want a German, a Yankee, a true Southerner & a colored man."[99]

Davis's coalition politics seemed the worst of all possible worlds to the former rebel, white majority of central Texas, and they often blamed Reconstruction troubles upon northern immigrants like Davis. One conservative explanation was typical: "There would have never been any trouble between the Negroes and the white people if it had not been for the carpetbaggers from the North to stir them up and aggravate any feeling of hostility that might have existed."[100]

Although white conservative central Texans treated men like Davis as if they were the advance scouts of an invading army, the region was not inundated with northern immigrants after the Civil War. Despite the efforts of the Republican Party, white arrivals from former Confederate states outnumbered immigrants from Europe and the North by three to one.[101] Even these arrivals were far from sympathetic to Republicans, and many adopted their new white neighbors' views on critical issues. George Ogden, for example, grew up in Iowa but later moved to Texas. He remembered that the racial violence in the South first "struck him as odd, but in time I assumed the same attitude as the southern man toward the Negro."[102]

It seems certain that the vast majority of immigrants to central Texas—both northern- and southern-born—helped bolster the position of conservative white southerners in the region rather than weaken it. Still, the formulation of an aggressive immigration policy by Republicans at the state level and open advocacy of such a plan by Republicans in Waco did much to provoke local white fears of carpetbaggers. They continued to decry the influence of carpetbaggers, but conservative central Texas leaders realized that southern-born supporters of the Republican Party were more numerous than northern immigrants. "The governing men were not all carpet-baggers but they [the Republicans] got some [local] citizens and the result was constant clashes."[103]

Who were these southern men and women who—in the eyes of the white majority—betrayed their region and race by joining the Republicans? Conservative whites charged that they were mere opportunists, and some no doubt were. Many others who joined the Republican Party were loyal Union men who had always opposed secession. There were also a few former rebels who joined out of conviction for the party's ideas. It was the men—and women—of this third group who frightened local conservatives the most.

One such man was Albert R. Parsons, the brother of the fire-eating secessionist William H. Parsons. According to U.S. Census records, Albert Parsons was born in Montgomery, Alabama, in 1845. Both of his parents, however, died while he was very young, and he moved to Texas to stay with his brother, William. Although William eventually settled in Hill County, Albert was kept on the move, attending school in Waco and serving as an apprentice to a printer in Galveston. Influenced by his older brother and his guardian in Galveston—both secessionist leaders in Texas—Albert Parsons joined the Confederate Army in 1861 and fought to preserve slavery. He, by his own admission, believed strongly in the South and its values, opinions that would change when he returned to Waco after the war.[104]

Shortly after his return, twenty-year-old Albert Parsons reached the turning point of his life. Because of a former slave who had belonged to the William Parsons family and had been, Albert Parsons recalled, "my constant associate and [he] practically raised me, with great kindness and a mother's love," Parsons became convinced of the depth of African American desire for freedom. He became, in a stunning change, one of the region's strongest advocates for black rights. That radical turn led Parsons to support black suffrage and help organize freedpeople against oppressive landlords. During a trip to Bell County, he "told the negroes many things that would, under some circumstance, have provoked them to violence. He told them they were the equals if not the superiors of the white people, and advised them to assert their rights, without reserve or hesitation, and to trust to the republicans in power for protection. The white citizens here became somewhat alarmed, and were in favor of hanging Mr. Parsons."[105]

Parsons's radical credentials included joining the Republican Party, editing a party newspaper in Waco, and marrying a former slave named Lucy Gathings. His activities did not go unnoticed by local whites, and he was shot in the leg on one occasion and nearly lynched on another.[106]

Albert Parsons—whom historian David Roediger calls "America's foremost native-born revolutionary labor leader"—was no doubt a unique individual in the history of central Texas.[107] Yet the story of Albert and Lucy Parsons touches directly on what many local whites considered to be the most obnoxious of all Republican policies: the attempt to form an alliance between whites and freedpeople. Mob attacks upon white Republicans were only part of the strategy to prevent that alliance. Assaults on the freedpeople were equally vital to the white majority.

* * *

Given the importance of political and sectional conflict in white-on-white mob violence, what explains the continued lynching of whites after the collapse of Texas's Republican government in 1873? Lynch mobs executed more than two dozen white men between 1873 and 1894. Although the white community was never completely unified, the old causes of so much white-on-white violence—political tension exacerbated by the sectional conflict, the Civil War, and Reconstruction—seem unlikely explanations.

One case concerns a sensational lynching in 1875 for the crime of murder in Bosque County. During the summer, two white men named Wood and Ledwell began to worry that news of their romances with Samantha Smith would get back to her husband, Amos Smith, and they hired an African American to murder him. The plot came undone, however, when the would-be assassin confessed. A mob of thirty men formed to lynch all three men, and guards were stationed to prevent interference with the proceedings. After an investigation, the mob hanged each man on a tree in the town of Iredell. Before leaving the scene they carved a message—"HUNG SURE AS HELL"—into a wooden sign and hung it on the tree alongside the bodies.[108] There are many possible explanations for this mob violence—vengeance by family, neighbors, and friends of the husband; desire to deter future crime in the area; and pessimism in the local court system. Political conflict, however, does not seem to be among them.

One reason that central Texans remained predisposed toward mob violence even after the collapse of the Reconstruction governments is the strong local historical memory that nurtured and preserved a culture of violence. Central Texas's early settlers were praised for their battles with Mexicans and Indians (chapters 1 and 2), and Texans lavished applause those who fought in the Civil War. One such figure was Lawrence Sullivan Ross, "one of the heroes of the war from Texas." Ross, in Corinth, Mississippi, and "with a small force" only, had "held back ten thousand Union soldiers." A town was named after his family in central Texas, and in 1886 he was elected governor.[109]

During the early twentieth century, central Texans formed associations where settlers and pioneers could meet, recall, and pass on their stories. In 1901, for example, Hill County residents formed the Confederate Veterans and Old Settlers Association. Ten years later, several men in Falls County followed suit and formed the Old Settlers and Veterans Association to honor the region's pioneers and the area's Confederate soldiers.[110] Pride in the Confederate past persisted throughout the twentieth century. In 1963, for example, central Texans established the Confederate Research Center in Hillsboro.[111] Whether they praised Confederate soldiers who fought in Virginia and Mississippi or those who defended Texas in the Home Guard, the message was much the same: Brave men embrace violence when necessary to defend their community.

The connection between historical memory and the justification of violence is probably most evident in the local memory of the followers of William C. Quantrill. During the Civil War, Quantrill and his men had committed a number of infamous attacks on Unionist civilians. Most of their attacks were confined to Missouri and Kansas, but they entered Texas in 1863 and terrorized suspected Unionists there as well. Some of the group decided to move to central Texas after the Civil War, and during Reconstruction they helped guide the local population in vigilante attacks on Unionists. One central Texan fondly remembered them, saying that "men who belonged to Qunatrell's Organization were among the first to help to make Texas a place unsafe for criminals."[112] Such praise encouraged the young men of central Texas to believe that violence was both necessary and honorable.

The historical memory of Reconstruction was more complicated than the memory of the Civil War. On the one hand, whites were proud of the vigilantism that was so important in restoring Democratic rule. That pride might be demonstrated in vocal and overt support for vigilantes or in more subtle ways. The historical marker in the town of Moffat, for example, hints at the vigilantism that took the life of the town's founder. Dr. Chauncey Moffet was an immigrant from New York who founded the small Bell County town in

1857. Moffet, however, remained loyal to the Union and even served in the Union Army during the Civil War. He was almost certainly killed by central Texas vigilantes after he returned to the region. As the marker puts it, "He disappeared mysteriously after returning to the Moffat community in 1868."[113]

On the other hand, whites in central Texas did not want to overemphasize the deep political divisions that existed during Reconstruction but rather to strengthen the region's racial solidarity in the late nineteenth century. Thus the historical memory of Reconstruction often minimized the political dimensions of much white-on-white violence. One central Texan remembered that when Reconstruction ended, "peace descended upon us" after the "negro soldiers and guards were done away with" and "once more" the "white men" were "given back their citizenship."[114] When Mrs. George Fowler discussed central Texas's Reconstruction-era violence with her Works Progress Administration (WPA) interviewer, she focused on the killing of three individuals. The first was Merritt Trammell, a freedman "of robust personality" who was alleged to have killed so many people "it was impossible to know the exact number." The second was a northern-born man named Heaton who "had come down to buy cheap land" and cattle, and the third figure was Milt Brothers, who was hanged for cattle theft.[115]

In the memories of these and other central Texas, the violence of Reconstruction was the result of northern-born carpetbaggers, meddling Union troops, white outlaws, and out-of-control freedmen. Southern-born white supporters of the Republican Party were either ignored or portrayed as insane. One of the few white Unionists to appear in local histories of central Texas is John W. Oliver, the judge who jailed the county court and was then accused of being insane by local physicians.[116] Edwin Punchard recalled the conflict as an "amusing and interesting" incident between the "radical" Judge Oliver and the "prominent" men of the county court.[117] Waco's best local historian, Patricia Ward Wallace, described the clash between the Republican Oliver and his Democratic opponents as "Waco's most controversial, and most entertaining, Reconstruction incident."[118] Historical memory also portrayed the southern-born, former-Confederate Albert Parsons as a deviant. Near the end of Parsons's life, a local Waco newspaper recalled that he was a "crank" who was "argumentative," "discontented," and "little disposed to hard work."[119] Such portrayals might make for compelling reading but do little to reveal the real divisions that existed among whites in central Texas during Reconstruction.

Historical memory edited out the political dimension of so much Reconstruction-era violence, but central Texans did not erase memories of white-on-white vigilantism. Quite to the contrary, the historical memory of lynching in central Texas—as demonstrated in local histories and the interviews conducted by the WPA—is filled with recollections of white-on-white mob violence.[120] Instead of emphasizing political conflict, Anglos chose to frame that white-on-white vigilantism within the old and reliable framework of a frontier society beset by the twin problems of frequent outlaw activity and a weak court system. Historical memory in central Texas thus praised vigilantes not so much for their role in stifling political opposition to the Democratic Party but for their work in combating horse and cattle thieves. During the late nineteenth century, central Texans explained vigilante episodes both in the past and the present along these lines. The most startling example may be the historical marker erected near the old Belton jail in 1967. The notice proudly recalls the lynching of nine men in 1874 and concludes that this "citizens' attack was regarded as a major factor in ending lawlessness in Bell County during the 1870's."[121]

Central Texas mobs lynched whites in the late nineteenth century because they believed they were fulfilling their duties to maintain order and enforce the will of the people. They embraced mob violence not for its political utility but because it was an accepted and even honored tradition in local culture. The historical memory of the region from its settlement through Reconstruction privileged those men who took justice into their own hands, and members of pioneer lynch mobs were local heroes. It is not surprising that lynching persisted into the next generation. Given a culture that often reified violence as a positive good, it would have been remarkable had central Texans abandoned vigilantism during the late nineteenth century.

* * *

Although historical memory nurtured a culture of violence and vigilantism in central Texas throughout the late nineteenth and early twentieth centuries, political and social changes had an impact on the frequency and trajectory of lynching in the region. Texas had become a very different place when Reconstruction came to an end in 1873. On the state level, central Texan Richard Coke—a secessionist, Confederate, and Democrat as well as an opponent of Reconstruction—became governor. Locally, the reviled Republican judge John W. Oliver stepped down from the Thirty-third Judicial District Court and died a little more than a year later of tuberculosis. Albert and Lucy Parsons wisely left Texas for Chicago, where they continued their pursuit of radical politics. Parsons spent the next fourteen years of his life as a labor organizer before he was executed in 1887 for his role in the infamous Haymarket bombing.

With the removal of their most bitter foes, and with near-complete political power, local conservative leaders became less tolerant of mob violence. Yet the power of central Texas's culture of violence was such that lynching and mob rule continued for decades. White-on-black violence in particular remained ingrained during the next half century. Never again, however, would so many central Texans support the indiscriminate murder of whites on the scale seen during Reconstruction. In the twenty years that followed it became less and less acceptable to lynch white men.

The reasons for the decline of white-on-white violence can be traced to justifications so long used to defend mob violence and their declining appeal. Perhaps most important, the sectional conflict that had for two decades given rise to fear, paranoia, and vigilantism receded when Texas's Republican government fell in 1873. When the last Republican government in a former Confederate state ended in 1877, the white majority in central Texas breathed even easier. The potential for violence of course still existed because animosities from the Civil War remained, but local leaders had a different attitude toward rampant violence and murder now that such activities would undermine a Democratic, not a Republican, government. Consequently, law enforcement and the courts received greater support from the region's former Confederates. Central Texas outlaws found it harder and harder to escape capture and punishment.

Political differences were not the sole reasons for lynching in central Texas, however. Vigilantes executed many whites before and after the Civil War for crimes such as theft of livestock and murder, and those incidents continued longer than politically motivated white-on-white assassinations. After 1873 central Texas mobs lynched at least twenty-eight Anglos. These acts of mob violence, however, became less frequent as the nineteenth century drew to a close. Fourteen whites were lynched between 1873 and 1879, but only seven Anglos in the 1880s, just six in the 1890s, and only one after 1900.[122]

One reason for the decline is that an increasingly effective court system undermined the traditional justification of lynching. Central Texans routinely justified mob violence as necessary because of the unsettled state of the region. In the words of central Texan William Monroe Graves, nineteenth-century Texas was then "still wild and unsettled," and it was the "day of the cattle thieves." Texas was also infested, he noted, with "criminals from other states." Because Texas was "still in its infancy," those who captured the outlaws "did not stand back on ceremony." "One morning," Graves recalled, "I looked out from my window to a post oak tree in my view and saw seven men hanging to this tree."[123]

Graves's defense of lynching echoed the justifications for mob violence that had been used at different times throughout the United States. The "frontier defense" of lynching begins by locating the scene of a lynching as being along an "unsettled" frontier and in a region not yet fully civilized by the relentless push westward of European American settlers. Next, criminals are alleged to have congregated in the area because of its rough frontier conditions. Finally, resourceful and practical settlers, faced with a bevy of uncontrolled outlaws, dispensed with the formal operation of the law. The act of lynching was seen as a necessary evil because it promoted order and justice at a time when the civil authorities were too weak to do so.[124]

Such defenses, of course, do not always mesh with the historical record. Vigilantism in central Texas peaked not in the earliest years of settlement but during the 1860s, a generation later. Moreover, mobs executed a number of men after local authorities had placed them under arrest. Although the "frontier defense" may not be entirely accurate, its justification was important for local residents. As the conflict over the courts during Reconstruction faded and the judicial system expanded during the final three decades of the nineteenth century, the "frontier defense" became less viable as a justification of lynching. Although other factors remained for spurring mob violence, the inability to make a compelling justification for lynching whites led to the phenomenon's slow decline in central Texas.

The expansion of the court system in central Texas was, then, critical for the decline of lynching in the region. A detailed examination of thousands of court records—principally from McLennan County—between 1851 and 1916 helps trace the court's transformation. Before the 1890s, civil authorities in central Texas failed to bring to trial more than two-thirds (68 percent) of those indicted by grand juries for murder. The reasons for that failure varied. Courts and law officers often found themselves at odds during Reconstruction. Republicans and Union officers charged that former Confederates blocked the apprehension of suspects, and those opposed to Reconstruction policies charged the courts with corruption and bias. Even more significant was the inability of officers to locate suspected criminals. Demographic instability caused by both flight out of the region and movement within it disrupted the administration of justice. That applied not only to those indicted for crimes but also to potential witnesses. It was frequently difficult to locate individuals to testify once a trial was set. Even when alleged murderers were brought to trial, they were more likely to be found not guilty (55 percent) than guilty (45 percent). Finally, juries sometimes assigned relatively weak punishments for serious crimes. Only about half of the men indicted for rape before 1890 stood trial.[125] One of them was Ed Busby. In 1881 a jury found Busby guilty of the rape of Emma Bentley, and he received two years in prison. Three years later Busby again found himself on trial for sexual assault. Again, a jury found him guilty, this time for assault to commit rape. Despite his previous record Busby received only a seven-year sentence.[126]

These patterns changed dramatically after 1890. Over the next thirty years, persons in McLennan County whom grand juries indicted avoided trial far less, only about one-third of the time (32 percent). In addition, juries now found defendants guilty (57 percent) more often than not guilty (43 percent). Punishments also increased in severity. Juries awarded the death penalty and life sentences more frequently. Three men were sentenced to life in prison for sexual assault after 1890. At least according to the surviving records, no sentence for sexual assault before 1890 exceeded Ed Busby's seven years.[127]

Changes in the judicial system were evident not only in the courtroom but also in the penitentiary. According to the records of the Texas State Penitentiary, the seven central Texas counties of Bell, Bosque, Coryell, Falls, Hill, Limestone, and McLennan sent nearly 2,500 persons to the penitentiary between 1891 and 1920. The records, admittedly incomplete, list only 613 individuals from those counties received at the penitentiary before the 1890s.[128]

Thus, the legal system in central Texas underwent four significant changes after 1890: a greater likelihood for criminals to face trial, more frequent guilty verdicts, increasingly severe punishments, and an ever-greater flow of convicts to the Texas State Penitentiary. Together those changes undermined the intellectual defense of mob violence that William Monroe Graves and many other central Texans had used. The charge of an ineffective legal system no longer had the same resonance.

The impact of the changes on central Texan attitudes toward the courts is demonstrated by the reaction to the lynching of Edward Cash, an alleged fence cutter, in 1894. In early April, Cash was taken out of his bed by some ten men. Despite the pleas of his sick wife, the mob shot him twenty-five times and then hanged him. The *Waco Evening News* published a strong condemnation of the lynching on 11 April. "Coryell County was, in the past," noted the editorial, "all too used to assassinations," but "law-abiding people" had hoped that this spirit "had been stamped out." The return to "old-time lawlessness [had] aroused" citizens, and "they will never rest until the assassins are brought to justice." The next day the newspaper reported that five men had been arrested for Cash's murder.[129] Although it is not clear that the courts ever convicted them, the strong reaction the lynching generated illustrates that central Texans perceived the region to have entered a new era and no longer required "old-time lawlessness." Mobs in central Texas did not lynch another Anglo for more than twenty-seven years, and reaction to that event—the hanging of Curley Hackney in 1921—confirmed the transformation of local attitudes.

Late on the evening of 13 December 1921, a mob of two or three hundred armed men approached the McLennan County jail in Waco, which housed

Curley Hackney, a white man accused by an eight-year-old girl of having committed sexual assault a few hours earlier. The nervous chief of the jail's night staff tried to delay the mob by urging them to respect the law. Meanwhile, other officers quickly took Hackney out of his cell and hid him inside a room normally reserved for African American inmates. At first the mob was confused. The vigilantes were, however, determined to lynch Hackney, and on their third search of the jail he was found and seized.[130]

The mob placed Hackney in a car and drove him three miles out of town to a grove of trees. Smoking a cigarette, he joked with the mob as they prepared to hang him. He instructed them on how to fasten the rope around his neck and told them that he was looking forward to shaking their hands in hell. After the hanging, several members of the mob fired their pistols into Hackney's body. The mob dispersed, and the corpse was taken to a local undertaker. A justice of the peace ruled that Hackney "came to his death as a result of hanging by parties unknown."[131]

At the time of his death Hackney was an unemployed former circus performer who had lived in Waco for less than a year. He had been unable to leave with the circus because of a gunshot wound in his leg. Hobbling around on a crutch, Hackney was an outsider who made few friends in Waco. When the daughter of one the few local families to befriend him accused him of sexual assault, he became the first white man lynched in central Texas in more than a quarter of a century.[132]

It is not surprising that Hackney was lynched. His alleged crime—sexual assault of a young girl—often spurred the creation of a mob in the South. Furthermore, Hackney was an outsider and had few friends in central Texas to come to his defense. Judging by newspaper reaction, most residents had little doubt about his guilt. Such conditions frequently led to lynching in the early twentieth century. Yet one thing about Hackney's lynching is surprising. He was white. Central Texas mobs lynched several African Americans under similar circumstances but never a white man.

Hackney was not the only white man accused of sexual assault in central Texas. Many in the region—both white and black—had been charged with that crime during the previous half-century.[133] One of the most infamous cases involved a young woman named Antonia Teixeria. A visitor from Brazil, Teixeria was staying with the family of the president of Baylor University in 1895. To the shock of Wacoans, she became pregnant during her stay and accused H. S. Morris, who was white, of raping her on multiple occasions. Morris was charged with rape in 1895, and his case went to trial several months later. "I fell to the ground when he pulled me out [of the house]," Teixeria testified, "and he then got on top of me and had illicit intercourse with me." Such testimony was not enough to convict a son of one of central Texas's leading families. Morris was found not guilty on 20 May 1896.[134]

A victim's social status could also play a role in the outcome of a central Texas sexual assault case. One grand jury indicted A. F. Gazley for sexual assault upon a "female under the age of ten," but he was never convicted. A possible reason is that a witness claimed that the victim, Minnie Daura, was "of loose, bad character, [and] associated with boys in Waco away from her home both day and night, under such suspicious circumstances."[135]

Differences were significant between Hackney's case and earlier cases involving whites charged with rape. The young girl who accused Hackney was neither seen as an outsider like Antonia Teixeria nor as a person of dubious morals like Minnie Daura. Hackney, unlike H. S. Morris, could not call upon well-placed friends and family to protect him because he was an unemployed stranger in Waco. Members of the mob must have thought the lynching of a white man under those circumstances would be tolerated, so reaction to the death would have been quite a surprise.

On 14 December, the day following Hackney's lynching, the county attorney's office conducted a hearing into the event. Law officers and other witnesses testified, and the county attorney decided to prosecute those who had murdered Hackney. A few days later two central Texas judges lectured on Hackney's hanging. James Alexander denounced the lynching "in scathing terms" and condemned those actions that "lose respect for the law and the courts." Meanwhile, the city commissioner of Waco attempted to remove the chief of police, two detectives, and a policeman for allowing Hackney to be taken from the jail and failing to report the incident to the board of commissioners. In January, Judge Monroe urged the grand jury to indict members of the mob that lynched Hackney.[136]

Despite these vigorous protests the grand jury did not indict those men who led the mob on 13 December. Neither did the board of commissioners remove any officers involved in the affair. Although mob members had once again escaped legal punishment in central Texas, public denunciation of the act by so many public officials was unprecedented in the region. There are several reasons for the outcry. First, the development of the court system had undermined traditional justifications for lynching white men in central Texas. Second, a coordinated and systematic attack on lynching had emerged throughout the United States during the early twentieth century. Led by African American civil rights activists, the antilynching movement had widespread support within the South, throughout the United States, and even internationally. Communities that allowed lynching were seen as "uncivilized" and "backward" places, images not welcomed by central Texas leaders. Third, and perhaps most important, Hackney was white. In central Texas, lynching blacks did not elicit the same reaction as lynching whites did. Mobs that lynched African Americans operated under different assumptions, defended their actions with different justifications, and engendered different reactions from the larger community.

5. "No Justice in It": Racial Violence and Reconstruction

On the night of 26 September 1868 a mob of white men went on a brutal rampage of racial violence in McLennan County. Several sexually assaulted three young black women, Ann White, Susan Bowie, and Eliza Amos. Then the mob turned their attention to seven-year-old Dolla Jackson, also black. Although they broke off their attempt to rape her, they contented themselves by depriving her of the 25 cents she possessed. Disappointed with her meager earnings, they turned on seventy-five-year-old Lotta Brown. After pistol-whipping her, they found that she held little more money than Jackson. They took her 75 cents. Before daybreak the white mob had severely beaten at least twenty black women.

Black women seemed to be the special target of this mob, but they did not hesitate to attack the eight black men who got in their way. The mob assaulted them, knocked them over their heads with pistols, and robbed them of any money they carried. Their thieving netted $99. When they found that freed-man Warren Hunter possessed no money for them to take, the mob stripped him of his clothes and then burned them in front of him. The message was unmistakable. Although no longer slaves, the freedpeople of central Texas were to understand that freedom did not mean emancipation from violent attacks by white men. It did not mean safety for black women from white sexual desire. It did not mean that freedpeople would be allowed to accumulate wealth. Witnesses identified four members of the mob, but civil authorities never made any arrests.[1]

Although this episode of mob violence was not the last or even the most brutal racial outrage to have occurred in central Texas, it epitomized the reign of terror that began after the Civil War. Before 1865 vigilantes and mobs in the region rarely executed blacks, but between 1865 and 1921 they lynched at least sixty-four (table 6). The methods, style, and justifications of postwar violence drew heavily on earlier patterns of mob law, but emancipation and the Civil War fundamentally transformed extralegal violence in central Texas.

Surveying and analyzing the extralegal executions of African Americans in central Texas is so important that the topic cannot be fully explored in a single chapter. This chapter and the two that follow are devoted to examining why white mobs attacked African Americans in central Texas. Here, I will focus on the years following the North's victory in the Civil War, when an orgy of racial violence swept across the South. That was especially true of central Texas, where lynch mobs and outlaw bands executed an unknown number of former slaves. Although records from this era are less complete than those for the one after 1873, the period nonetheless accounts for nearly one-third of the known victims of mob violence in central Texas. Historical memory of vigilantism and extralegal violence informed the actions of Reconstruction mobs, but the primary cause of so much bloodshed was the revolutionary struggle between the area's Democrats and Republicans.

The twenty-five years following the collapse of Reconstruction form the second period of racial violence in central Texas. During those years racial violence began to take on a different character, and mobs began justifying themselves on different grounds. Whites constructed memories of the Reconstruction era that glorified mob violence and began to infuse lynching rhetoric with the charge of rape. The combination helped make the 1890s an especially deadly decade for African Americans.

A decline in the number of lynchings at the turn of the century signaled the birth of a third era in central Texas's history of lynching.[2] Although there were fewer lynchings, those that did occur attracted larger mobs and con-

Table 6. African American Lynching
Victims by Decade

Decade	Number of Victims
1860–69	16
1870–79	9
1880–89	5
1890–99	20
1900–1909	5
1910–19	7
1920–29	2
Total	64

Source: Appendix A.

tained extensive acts of ritualized sadism and torture. As lynching became increasingly a public spectacle, community leaders began to criticize mob violence. After the lynching of Jesse Washington in 1916, the historical memory of lynching in central Texas shifted, and the legitimacy of the practice began to erode. By the middle of the twentieth century, whites were attempting to erase lynching from their historical memories. African Americans, however, were placing the memory at the center of the black freedom struggle.

These chapters should be read against the discussion in chapter 4 about white-on-white violence. Mob violence against African Americans at times paralleled and at other times diverged sharply from mob violence against whites. One area of interest concerns the reasons that lynch mobs gave for their acts (table 7). On the one hand, no matter what the person's race, mobs often justified violence with the charge that the victim had committed murder. On the other hand, mobs that lynched whites regularly alleged horse or cattle theft, whereas those that lynched blacks made that accusation hardly at all. At the same time, African Americans were often executed for sexual assault, but whites were rarely lynched for that crime.

A second area of comparison and contrast involves the size and actions of mobs during lynchings. Mobs frequently executed both whites and blacks by either hanging or shooting, executions that were sometimes ritualized. In the case of African Americans, however, ritualized acts of torture such as burning and mutilation were more common. Likewise, lynch mobs varied greatly in size from case to case for both blacks and whites, but central Texas's largest appeared only when a victim was African American.[3]

Table 7. African American Lynching Victims by Alleged Crime, 1860–1929

Crime	Number of Victims
Murder	15
Rape or attempted rape	14
Murder and rape	2
Horse or cattle theft	2
Nonsexual assault	2
Resisting arrest/trying to escape	2
Attempted murder	1
Threatening to murder	1
Entering room of white woman	1
Competing against whites for jobs	1
Unknown	22
Total	64

Source: Appendix A.

The most striking comparison between the lynching of whites and blacks, however, is one of chronology. The late 1860s were a time of deadly violence for both groups. By contrast, lynching patterns after 1890 could not have been more different. White-on-white mob violence was in rapid decline by the 1890s; only one Anglo was lynched in central Texas after 1894. Mob attacks on blacks, however, escalated greatly in the 1890s and continued regularly in the early twentieth century. Blacks numbered only about a quarter of central Texas's population, but they accounted for more than half of the region's victims of mob violence after the Civil War.

Murder, lynching, and vigilantism, then, became increasingly racialized in the late nineteenth and early twentieth centuries. That is because, as I will argue here and in the next two chapters, the white majority continued to perceive African Americans as a threat to the social and political order, whereas fears of white dissenters receded. The era encompassing the sectional crisis, the Civil War, and Reconstruction was a time of revolutionary upheaval that pitted Confederates and Democrats against Unionists and Republicans. By the turn of the century the division among the white population was not so deep, and the triumphant white majority rested more securely in its power. In that environment, it was willing to trust the legal system to punish and control white criminals. Persistent resistance from blacks in the region, however, meant that whites were not yet ready to relinquish punishment to the courts. Only after the lynching of Jesse Washington brought national and international attention to central Texas did white leaders seriously reconsider the role of lynching in regulating the region's African Americans.[4]

* * *

Mob violence against blacks in central Texas was overwhelmingly a crime of the postbellum period. It would be inaccurate, however, to suggest that white mobs in central Texas never executed an African American before the Civil War. In Colorado County, location of a suspected slave rebellion, five rebellious slaves died in 1856 at the hands of a vigilance committee. Moreover, in 1860 an unknown number of African Americans in Texas, possibly some in central Texas, were executed in a panic over their alleged activities in a series of purported slave uprisings.[5] To those executions should surely be added a number of black victims felled far from the public eye by cruel masters, vicious overseers, and zealous patrollers.[6]

Even the highest estimates of the number of blacks that white mobs killed under slavery cannot compare, however, with the amount of African American blood spilt after emancipation. During the late 1860s the murder of African Americans became commonplace, and in 1866 federal agents began to investigate and report on violence in Texas. Those reports—both those filed for the Bureau of Refugees, Freedmen, and Abandoned Lands and those completed for the United States Army's Department of Texas and the Fifth Military District—have been preserved in the National Archives. From the beginning, the reports record episode after episode of violence perpetrated upon central Texas's freedpeople. Sometimes agents found trees hanging with black corpses. At other times agents never found the bodies of black victims. Freedmen were sometimes ambushed and shot on the road; at other times mobs assassinated them on their own doorsteps. Some were killed by bands of masked men whose identities were never determined. Still others were killed by men who openly boasted of their actions.[7]

Reports from Falls, McLennan, Bosque, and Hill counties confirm that at least forty-six African Americans were killed between 1865 and 1869.[8] Because the black population in those counties was just 10,642 in 1870, that number represents a very high level of violence.[9] Between 1865 and 1869, forty-four of the forty-six (96 percent) blacks murdered in the four counties were killed by whites.[10] Blacks in the four counties composed 4.1 percent of the state's black population in 1870, but the forty-four central Texas blacks killed by whites between 1865 and 1868 represent 11.8 percent of the 373 blacks killed by whites throughout the state during that same period.[11] Randolph Campbell has summarized the state of affairs in central Texas accurately in concluding that freedpeople in McLennan County "faced a level of violence virtually unparalleled in any other Texas locality."[12]

Freedpeople became the objects of racial violence in Reconstruction central Texas for two primary reasons. First, many whites believed mob violence to be necessary to the overthrow of the Republican government in the South. Second, a significant number of the local elite, especially officials who oversaw the courts and law enforcement, agreed on the need to undermine or eliminate the Republican Party from central Texas. Other factors, including deep anger generated by Confederate defeat and frustration born out of economic collapse, also played roles in the era's mob violence. The historical memory of violence, especially attacks on Native Americans and Unionists, influenced events as well. Nevertheless, Reconstruction's violence was fundamentally a political struggle over who would control the region—a coalition of freedmen and white Republicans or conservative white Democrats.

To understand the sudden rise in white-on-black violence after the Civil War, one must realize that freedom meant that former masters had much less interest in the welfare of their "black families" than had been the case earlier. During the antebellum period, masters regulated their slaves' lives with violence and the threat of violence, but the financial investment in the slaves themselves almost always convinced slaveowners that killing them outright was unwise. Calvin Kennard, a former slave, remembered that "dey tended to us good w'en us sick cause a good nigger was worth money."[13] With emancipation, the financial connection disappeared between those who were once slaves and those who were once their masters. Although bonds of shared experience and even affection persisted between some, emancipation revealed just how shallow many "paternal" connections were. Many freedpeople were quite willing to abandon their masters, and many former masters were quite willing to murder their former slaves.

The story of how the bondsmen and bondswomen of the Upper Brazos River valley learned of their freedom foreshadowed the difficulties that would attend Reconstruction. It was not until 19 June 1865, more than two months after Robert E. Lee had surrendered to Ulysses S. Grant at Appomattox, that Union general Gordon Granger notified Texans that slavery no longer existed in their state. Although former slaves would come to celebrate the date, "Juneteenth," as the day of their emancipation, the reality was that even Granger's late pronouncement had no impact on many of their lives.[14]

"De folks down in Texas didn't seem ter hear 'bout de war bein' over w'en de odder states up nearer de North did," recalled former slave Annie Whitley Ware. "Us un gits freed 'bout er year later dan de slaves in de ole states."[15] Nearly three months after Juneteenth, Freedmen's Bureau officials confirmed that many whites in central Texas still forcibly held blacks as slaves. One "says to his negroes and others that his negroes are not free, and that he will kill them before they shall be." Another former slaveowner compelled "his former slaves to work for him without compensation." The freedmen of a third central Texan were "nearly naked," and "he refused to pay them wages, clothe them, or allow them to work for others and so clothe themselves." Three other central Texans were so confident of being able to defy federal law that they purchased a total of six slaves late in the summer of 1865. These men were certainly not alone. After reporting that two other individuals refused to acknowledge the freedom of their former slaves, agents despaired that their quest to catalog such men had "by no means been exhausted."[16] More than a year later, Philip Howard wrote, the problem still remained. On 25 September 1866 he reported from his post in Meridian in Bosque County, "I heard of two men above here some forty miles that yet holds their Blacks in Bondage. Their names are John Anderson and Alfred Lloyd. I sent them orders to release the Blacks. They sent me word back that they had paid for the Negroes and the Government should not [help] them in any such way."[17]

Most whites in central Texas were more creative in their quest to undermine the practical impact of emancipation, and in 1865 and 1866 conservatives turned to the court system for help. Before the Civil War, whites had routinely permitted masters to administer punishments to slaves for non-capital crimes such as theft. That system, of course, began to collapse with the end of slavery. In the first two years following emancipation, courts indicted freedmen for petty crimes that had never before merited indictments (table 8).[18]

Many freedmen indicted for theft could not be found and brought to trial. Those who were arrested, however, often received harsh sentences. Freedmen Jack Harris and Eli Bradly were both sentenced to two years in prison. Harris had stolen a pair of shoes, and Bradly had absconded with a cake.[19] Despite such sentences, the conservative white majority was never satisfied with the courts as a mechanism for controlling the freed population. What little faith there was in the court system evaporated in 1867, when the Union Army replaced moderate and conservative judges with ones more favorable to white and black Republicans.[20]

Dissatisfaction with the Reconstruction-era courts was not particular to central Texas. The Upper Brazos River valley, however, seemed filled with especially recalcitrant slaveholders who were especially willing to abandon the legal system for extralegal justice. Perhaps that was the case because refugee

Table 8. Selected Indictments in McLennan County, 1866–67

Crime	Indicted
Theft of lard	Bob Drury
Theft of one quart of whiskey	Thomas Brown
Theft of one pair of shoes	Jack Harris
Theft of two chickens	Arthur Woodman
Theft of one cake	Eli Bradly
Theft of one hat	Elisha Smith
Theft of plank	James Dragoo
Theft of corn	Jerry Blackwell
Theft of one bushel of corn	Sheppard Renfro
Theft of coat	James Reagan
Theft of a cloak	Vina Downs

Sources: *State of Texas v. Bob Drury* (case no. 518), *State of Texas v. Thomas Brown* (case no. 520), *State of Texas v. Jack Harris* (case no. 521), *State of Texas v. Arthur Woodman* (case no. 522), *State of Texas v. Eli Bradly* (case no. 525), *State of Texas v. Elisha Smith* (case no. 527), *State of Texas v. James Dragoo* (case no. 538), *State of Texas v. Jerry Blackwell* (case no. 547), *State of Texas v. Sheppard Renfro* (case no. 574), *State of Texas v. James Reagan* (case no. 632), and *State of Texas v. Vina Downs* (case no. 636), all in Civil and Criminal Minute Books, vols. D and E, McLennan County Archives, Waco, Tex.

slaveowners who arrived from other parts of the South during the Civil War were so intent on forestalling emancipation that they were willing to remove their slaves to the very edge of the South. How many refugee masters moved to Texas during the war will never be accurately known.[21] Their influx into the Upper Brazos River valley, however, gave the region a high number of southerners unwilling to face the realities of emancipation. Given such reluctance, it is not surprising that many local blacks only learned of their freedom after the Union troops arrived. "We didn't know we wuz free till we saw some soldiers in blue come into de country," recalled former slave President Wilson. "Our master tol' us then that we wuz free."[22]

A significant number of former slaves bolted immediately. They did so for a variety of reasons, but memories of cruelty under slavery were among the most important. "Marse Tom been dead long time now," William Moore recalled in the 1930s. "I guess he is in hell. . . . Seems like that is where he b'longs. He was a turrible mean man."[23] Not all, however, left as soon as they became free. Many left gradually over a period of months or even years. S. L. Love, a former slaveowner of Milam County, reported in 1869 that it was "doubtful this morning whether a single one of the old hands will remain on this place."[24]

In the immediate wake of emancipation many, probably most, former slaves decided to remain and work as freedpeople for their former masters. After the exultation of first freedom, most of the "oldes' ones, dey calmed down 'bout de nex' mawnin' an' den dey begin ter ask 'Whar us gwine stay, an' how us gwine eat?'" noted one.[25] Many freedpeople in central Texas began to realize that their problems did not disappear with emancipation. The former slaves faced the harsh realities of making their way in an economically shaken world inhabited by an alarming number of bitter, vicious, and armed racists. Given the circumstances, many were willing to stay with their former masters if they showed willingness to treat them as something more than slaves.

Even when the former slaves remained with former masters, most embraced a far different form of farm life than they had known before emancipation. Before the Civil War most slaves worked as part of gangs under the direct daily supervision of their master, an overseer, or a slave foreman. After 1865, they became, by and large, sharecroppers who had varying degrees of autonomy in the organization of their daily labor practices. In October 1865 a group of former slaves in Falls County signed a sharecropping contract that required them to "remain on, prepare, plant, and cultivate, gather and prepare for market the crop on one hundred & twenty acres of land" belonging to the estate of Willis Lang and overseen by J. H. Anders and J. B. Billingsley.

According to the contract, they agreed that the crop "shall be planted and cultivated by the advice of the said J. H. Anders" and that they would not "ride the mules or horses without the consent of the said J. H. Anders." Although such restrictions were no doubt plotted to keep some semblance of the old order on the Billingsley plantation, the method of punishment was undoubtedly new. If "any of us fail[ed] to do our duty, the Foreman [was] to report him or her to J. H. Anders [who would] then appoint six of us to try the accused and if found guilty [was] to leave the place and forfeit his part of the crop." The former slaves would "get one-half of everything that [was] raised on the 120 acres of land for the year 1866."[26]

Despite such agreements, the development of sharecropping in central Texas proceeded poorly. Former slaves and former masters had difficulty adjusting to the postwar world. "Mos 'ob dem didn't know noddin' 'bout ow to make a livin' an' dey jes' had a lot ob fool notions 'bout how the yankees gwine do so much for dem," recalled Janey Landrum.[27] Another freedwoman concurred, suggesting that too many slaves "think de Government is goin' to take keer of dem."[28] One remembered that many freedpeople "think dey don't have to work any more."[29]

Unfortunately, they were not the only ones reluctant to embrace the new era's harsh realities. In 1865 central Texan George F. Sparks told his former slaves that "he would kill any one who attempts to leave."[30] Sparks attempted to make good on his word by shooting a freedwoman named Mariah.[31] Although Mariah did not die from her wounds, another freedman who had left his master to find work in the Bosqueville area of McLennan County died mysteriously at the hands of parties unknown. His body was found "lying in the road."[32] A white man, Charles Barlow, shot and wounded a freedman named Sandy Lockridge who had "persuaded another freedman not to work for him."[33] B. C. Dorsey murdered a freedman in 1868 over "the weight of a cotton basket."[34] Dick Maine, Hiram Reed, and another white man named Smith attempted to murder Moses Gibbons because the freedman had reported to the authorities that Reed owed him wages.[35]

Most labor disputes in central Texas did not end in the death of a former slave, but a great many did involve the use of violence to intimidate black workers. One central Texan sent a letter to a freedman "ordering him to leave the county by 12 o' clock on the 14th of April, or he would bring on a party with him."[36] During Reconstruction, whites attempted to chart the limits of black freedom by forming vigilance committees and whipping any freedperson who got out of line. "A gang of men about thirty in number mostly painted black, whipped the freedman Matthew Solomon very severely," reported Freedmen's Bureau agent Charles Haughn. He "did not recognize any of them."[37] Between 1865 and 1873, white mobs in central Texas punished at least seventeen black men and fourteen black women in this way.[38]

Although labor disputes between whites and blacks were often an essential backdrop to postwar violence, whites continually justified violence on the grounds that freedpeople were violating what whites considered to be acceptable social norms— acting "out of their place." White central Texans, by and large, reluctantly accepted the freedom of the region's blacks, but virtually all steadfastly refused to acknowledge that African Americans had been elevated to anything close to civil or social equality.

Former slaves recognized the dangers of challenging white society, but many braved those dangers because they refused to accept their former master's limited definition of freedom. Time and time again freedpeople who remained on the plantations of their former owners and those who left for towns chose to test the limits of their freedom. One former slave remembered these efforts as attempts to "sit up like de w'ite man."[39] Anderson Jones observed that the actions of many freedpeople made little sense unless one understood that they felt "dey must try dey freedom."[40]

The white majority in central Texas was determined not to tolerate black assertiveness. One-time slave Sam Forge recalled that white mobs would take blacks "out an' whips dem or hangs dem to a tree where dey kin be in sight of de other niggers. . . . dey has lots of trouble for three or four years after freedom."[41] In 1866 a black man in Bosque County was "whipped nearly to death for saying he was as free as any man."[42] In McLennan County, Hal Evans beat his black domestic servant for "slandering him."[43] A freedwoman named Fanny was shot for giving "some sassy words to her mistress."[44]

Whites often gave no reason for attacking freedpeople. In 1868 D. F. Stiles reported that the freedman Sam Robinson had been gunned down "on the public square of Waco [with] no provocation given."[45] Robinson was not alone. A "Freedman and his wife were riding along the roads, when there appeared a white man following them, who from the roadside commanded them to halt & before they knew his purpose shot this Freedman, inflicting a severe wound in the shoulder & arm," a planter in Falls County reported to the governor.[46] What offense had the couple committed? They had dared to exercise their rights to travel on public roads. Black resistance to such assaults prompted deadly counterattacks. When a freedman named Gibson in Bosque County "resisted and refused to be tied up and whipped" by a white mob, he was shot.[47] Fear of violence from whites became a way of life for many blacks in Reconstruction Texas.[48]

Blacks were determined to alter the antebellum pattern involving the role of black women. On most plantations before the Civil War, black women worked in the fields alongside black men. When they returned to the quarters at night, however, they had the greater share of housework, cooking, and child-rearing. As difficult as that "double burden" was for enslaved women, an unknown number of them faced something far worse: sexual assault and exploitation by white men. Not surprisingly, both black men and black women were eager to distance themselves from these aspects of slavery. Black families favored sharecropping because it allowed individual families to divide their own labor. Husbands and fathers were particularly eager to duplicate the model long common in free families throughout the South and segregate the work duties of the sexes. Black families also favored sharecropping because it minimized interaction with white men and thereby limited their access to black women.[49]

Whites made a special effort to disabuse freedmen of the idea they could protect black women, who, although only limited records exist, were victims of at least twenty-three attacks by whites in central Texas during the years after emancipation.[50] According to one Freedmen's Bureau agent, central Texan C. S. Denton attacked a black woman and beat "her nearly to death."[51] In 1868 three white men "got drunk and attempted to rape" the wife of freedman Thomas Wilson. While the three men were breaking the couple's dishes, turning over their tables, and generally destroying their household, Mrs. Wilson escaped to warn her husband, who was away at church. As Thomas Wilson returned the white men shot him dead.[52] The clearest example of white attacks on black households, of course, was the 26 September 1868 mass rape and assault in McLennan County.[53]

Even as white men jealously guarded their own access to black women they fervently protected white women from black men. In 1866, for example, a white mob castrated Tony McCray, a freedman from Bosque County, for alleged attempted rape.[54] A freedman named Daniel was whipped an unbelievable total of one thousand lashes by A. C. Pearce for allegedly attempting a sexual assault.[55]

Assaults on black children could also be interpreted as attacks on the authority of black heads of household. In June of 1865, Luke Adams, fourteen, was whipped by William Richard until he died. Another white man, Mason Jones, "flogged and kicked [a] little freedman, six years old," reported Philip Howard of the Freedmen's Bureau. "The little fellow was found four days afterward in the woods nearly dead—his hip was dislocated."[56] It is hard to believe that anything in the bloody history of racial violence in central Texas angered or frightened the region's freedpeople more than such attacks on their children.

Attacks on black women and children, it can be argued, were designed to show freedpeople that no one was safe from white violence. This message of vulnerability was also extended to the most successful and loyal former slaves. In 1868 a white mob attacked a family of former slaves that lived near the Unionist planter B. G. Shields of Falls County. "Both the freedman and his old master are examples of sobriety, industry and high moral character," Shields assured the governor in a letter protesting the violence. One "of the men shot it is supposed will recover, the other is in a very critical condition," and no "one can conjecture what reason or motive could have instigated the assailants to make such an assault, nor can it be ascertained who they were."[57] As this evidence suggests, white mobs targeted blacks not at random but in ways that helped serve the larger purpose of frightening freedpeople into submission to white authority.

As powerful as the desire to reassert authority over former slaves was, it was not the only influence on postwar violence. Other factors—particularly the social, political, and economic disruption caused by the Civil War—combined with white racism to promote mob violence. Frustration with the collapse of central Texas's economy sent many whites searching for a scapegoat for their anger, and African Americans proved a relatively powerless and convenient target. White rage had roots that stretched far beyond the quickly emerging color line.

As former slave Allen Manning explained the origins of central Texas violence to an interviewer in 1937, "Them whitefolks done had everything they had tore up, or had to run away from the places they lived, and they brung their Negroes out to Texas and then right away they lost them too. . . . They didn't see no justice in it, and most of them never did until they died. The folks that stayed at home didn't straggle all over the country [and] had their old places to live on and their old friends around them, but the Texans was different."[58]

The bitterness and frustration that many whites experienced in the postwar world often translated into violence. Simpson Dixon, known as "Dixie," sought to avenge the wrongs done to the South by terrorizing blacks in central Texas. "He proceeded unrestrained to murder Negroes whenever and wherever he caught them conveniently," reported Walter Cotton.[59] The ranks of those Dixie killed include two old black men, Seymour Abrams and Norville Rhodes, and a black woman shot in the back after being made to dance for him. Although Union soldiers and local blacks eventually killed Dixie, others took his place.[60] The most feared was a McLennan County gang, called the "Fishbackers" after the group's leaders, Bud and Bill Fisher. "If a Negro insulted a white woman or 'sassed' a white man or in any way acted objectionably," Ida Leggett Hall recalled, "one or more of these men would call on the injured white to learn the exact nature of the trouble, and a few days later the black would be reported as found shot to death."[61]

The question of how well-organized the terrorist bands were is open to debate. The Ku Klux Klan, for example, was surely active in the region, and many freedmen in central Texas reported its activities. Hattie Gates said, "I kin 'member w'en de niggers make a little money an quits picking cotton an' de Ku-Klux parades down de street in Waco wid de signs dat dey must go ter work or leave town."[62] Joe Oliver remembered that "de Ku Klux Klan, dat got to whippin' de niggers so bad after freedom dat my daddy moved nearer to Hillsboro."[63]

One wonders, however, how often Joe Oliver and other former slaves identified all white terrorists as being part of the Klan. Moreover, the more recent activities of the Second Klan during the 1920s no doubt clouded the memories of former slaves who attempted to recall in the late 1930s the activities of the Klan during Reconstruction. Yet even if their testimony is not a reliable indictment of the Klan itself, they still tell a frightening tale of locally sanctioned, white-on-black violence. "Let a colored man steal a horse in this country and, if he escapes lynching, he is sure of coming to Huntsville [the state penitentiary] for five to fifteen years," a letter writer from Texas noted. But if "a white man kills a freedman, it is a small affair."[64] As one historian summarized the situation, white outlaws, whether they belonged to the Klan or not, "thought no more of shooting a Negro who didn't jump to one side of the road quickly enough than they thought of shooting a sheep-killing dog."[65]

* * *

It is difficult to imagine a scenario in which white central Texans would not have translated their bitterness at defeat, their anger over emancipation, and their frustration with economic conditions into violence against the region's former slaves. It is also difficult to imagine that the political conflicts of Reconstruction did not magnify this violence significantly. The struggle for political control in central Texas exacerbated white-on-white violence, and the attempt to encourage black political participation amplified white-on-black brutality.

An early assessment of Reconstruction in Texas by the *Houston Union* concluded that the Republican administration in Texas had "been met with a storm of opposition" that was "unequaled" in any other state.[66] A Freedmen's Bureau agent from Belton maintained that the freedmen in his district possessed the "well-grounded fear" that they would be unable to vote "unless sustained by the military."[67] Another agent noted in April 1868 that planters were driving freedmen from their farms without compensation as punishment for political activity. "Already some planters are saying to them, you went & voted God damn you! Now lets see what the Yankees can do for you."[68] The *Freedmen's Press* of Austin advised in 1868 that "men are murdered daily for no other reason than because they are loyal to the government."[69] In Navarro County an unknown band of whites murdered a freedman because he was the county's registrar.[70] In 1871 the Texas correspondent for *The New Era*, a national newspaper devoted to black rights, observed that the "chief interest for the country in Texas politics just now is the growing spirit of Ku Kluxism."[71]

David F. Davis, a Dartmouth-educated Republican, understood both the dangers and the importance of the political struggle. He knew that the white majority would never support Reconstruction or the Republican Party but believed that his party could win control of central Texas by uniting black voters with disaffected whites and sympathetic immigrants. Writing to the governor, Davis outlined his plan for the Republican Party in central Texas. A "general conversion of the native whites you need not expect," he advised, but if "we hold the colored vote & the living elements among the whites & the accessions from abroad [we] will permanently bury the old ideas."[72]

When congressional Republicans took over the administration of Reconstruction in 1867 they opened the door for Davis's plan by providing for black suffrage throughout the South. Local Republicans in central Texas quickly began courting black allies and voters. A. J. Evans, a white Republican, helped organize local blacks in Waco when he spoke at a political rally on 11 May 1867 and called upon "all our citizens" to join the Republicans.[73] Beginning on 10 July 1867, Nathan Patten and George B. Dutton, white Republicans also, headed up the board of registrars in McLennan County. When registration closed on 30 August, more blacks (1,003, or 53 percent) than whites (877, or 47 percent) could vote.[74]

The impact of black suffrage in central Texas can hardly be underestimated. First, black votes helped power radical white Republicans into office at both the local and state levels. Davis may have exaggerated his own influence when he wrote that not "one colored man in the county would knowingly vote against me," but enough blacks voted for this white teacher from the North that he became the new district clerk.[75] In February of 1868, central Texas blacks helped elect A. J. Evans, Nathan Patten, and William E. Oakes, another white Republican, to the constitutional convention. Even in late 1869, when white voters outnumbered black voters, a coalition of white and black Republicans gave McLennan County a majority in favor of the radicals. The radical nominee for governor, E. J. Davis, beat out the moderate candidate, A. J. Hamilton, in local returns.[76]

Black voters often supported the white leaders of the Republican Party,

but black central Texans also used their voting power and political influence to place members of their own race in positions of power during Reconstruction. In 1869 they sent Giles Cotton, David Medlock Jr., and Shepard Mullens to the Twelfth Legislature of the state of Texas. These men were
three of only thirteen blacks elected in the state.[77]

Cotton and Medlock represented Limestone County and the Eighteenth
District. Cotton was born in South Carolina but came to Texas as a slave in
1852. He became a successful farmer after emancipation. Medlock, originally
from Alabama, had also been a slave. He came to Texas in 1846 and rose to
prominence because of the position of his family; his father had served as a
minister during the difficult years of bondage. The senior Medlock's greatest moment came in the wake of emancipation when he helped guide many
fearful freedpeople into the postwar world. A number of fellow former slaves
believed that his sermons had "saved them from destruction."[78]

Born around 1830, Mullens came to Texas as a slave in 1854. He would
eventually become the most successful black politician in central Texas. As
a slave, Mullens had been trained as a blacksmith, a skill that served him well
in freedom. He was able to acquire a significant amount of property, including a town lot in Waco and eight acres of land elsewhere in McLennan
County. In addition to serving in the legislature, Mullens served on the Platform and Resolutions Committee of the Republican state convention in 1867,
was a delegate to the constitutional convention of 1868–69 (replacing William Oakes when he died), and was vice president of the Radical Republican state convention in 1869.[79]

Whether in the state legislature or in convention, Mullens consistently
supported the radicals of the Republican Party. In 1867 he pushed for a plank
in the party's platform calling for confiscation of planter property and creation of a homestead bill that would have secured a "portion of the unap-
propriated public domain" for all citizens "without distinction of race or
color."[80] In the legislature, Mullens was a member of the Radical Republican
Association, a secret group pledged to pursue the radicals' agenda.[81]

In addition to elected positions, black central Texans served in a number
of important appointed offices. One local trial jury in May 1867 consisted of
three whites and nine blacks. In November of that same year, Gen. Joseph
Reynolds appointed two freedmen—Mullens and twenty-seven-year-old
Stephen Cobb, a minister from Waco—to the court of county commissioners in McLennan County. They were, according to Randolph Campbell,
"among the very few blacks to hold that office anywhere in Texas."[82] A freedman named Thomas Ford served as supervisor for the public schools—both
black and white—of central Texas's Seventh District.[83] Three more blacks, Wil-

liam Blocker, Shadrack Willis, and Lewis Graves, were Waco aldermen during Reconstruction.[84]

Although the mere achievement of political power was a radical departure, most of the region's black leaders did not attempt to transform the basic economic and social structure of the Upper Brazos River valley. Instead, they focused on protecting the civil rights of freedpeople and creating social institutions for the black community. As one black Texan wrote in 1871, "We must labor by ourselves, through ourselves, and for ourselves, while the progress of civilization is gradually developing the idea of the equality of citizens, irrespective of color or previous condition, from an article of political faith into a rule of social practice."[85]

Mullens, for example, hoped and struggled for radical change but of necessity supported moderate legislation. When he was unable to get his homestead bill incorporated into the Republican platform, he pushed for modest legislation such as an act supporting the Greenwood Institute, an early school for blacks in central Texas. One bill he wrote was to prohibit "the sale of ardent spirits within two and one half miles from the Greenwood Institute of McLennan County."[86]

Like many other central Texas blacks, Mullens was concerned with establishing black schools. After the Freedmen's Bureau acquired land for one in Waco, the state of Texas named Mullens, Stephen Cobb, William Blocker, and other local black leaders as commissioners of Howard Institute, "an institution of learning for the community of McLennan County."[87]

Black churches were another early focus of central Texas's African American leadership. Cobb, Mullens's fellow county commissioner, was the founder and first minister of New Hope Baptist Church in Waco, but he was hardly alone among black leaders in focusing on the region's religious institutions. Between 1866 and 1875 blacks organized at least fifteen churches in McLennan County alone.[88]

Although most people would hardly consider an emphasis on social institutions such as schools and churches to be radical, conservative whites in central Texas bemoaned the rise of black institutions. One Waco newspaper observed in 1869, "We are decidedly in favor of the black people educating their children when able to do so and not neglect their duties. But we do not approve their sending their children to school from a mere hifalutin idea of making them smart and like white folks."[89] According to the former slaves, white central Texans physically attacked black schools and black churches. "Services were sometimes disturbed by lawless people of the other race," recalled a church member of New Hope Baptist. On "one Sunday night while Rev. Cobb was conducting a heated revival some desperados fired two shots through a window of the church."[90] Between 1867 and 1873 juries regularly indicted individuals in McLennan and Hill counties for disturbing religious worship. Most were never punished.[91]

Harassment of black churches was only surpassed by attacks on black schools. There "was some trouble 'bout the schools when 'mancipation came," William Moore recalled. His "brother Ed was in school then when the Ku Klux came" and drove "the yankee lady and gentleman out and closed the school."[92] A black school in Waco was burned to the ground during Reconstruction.[93] Three men in McLennan County attempted to shoot and kill a black man named Warren Hunter because he taught school.[94] After surveying the Freedmen's Bureau schools, Alton Hornsby concluded that hostility "displayed by many white Texans, especially as expressed through acts of violence, constituted the most serious and persistent problem confronting the Bureau's schools in the state."[95]

Hostility might have destroyed the schools completely had they not been protected by armed black civilians, the U.S. Army, and, eventually, a Republican-organized state militia. Local whites saw the soldiers and officers as unjustly establishing military rule in place of a white majority government. "When the military administration came in," recalled one central Texan, "there was a change in most of the county offices throughout the state and the government in Austin put in its own force and henchmen."[96] Union troops occupied central Texas for the first time in January 1866, when forty cavalrymen arrived under Lt. Eugene Smith. Although the soldiers and their leadership changed frequently, they were an important part of the landscape throughout Reconstruction in central Texas.

Protests of native whites to the contrary, the army's ability to protect freedpeople and white Republicans in central Texas was inadequate. Local Republicans, the U.S. Army, and the Freedmen's Bureau were continually overmatched by white resistance. In 1871 a congressional investigation of an election in Limestone County found that—despite the presence of federal troops—"a state of excitement and fear existed in this county at the time of the election," causing freedmen to abstain from voting "for reasons which most men would consider good and sufficient."[97]

Black leaders who chose not to follow these "good and sufficient" reasons were killed. Merritt Trammell, one of central Texas's most radical black leaders, was a man who "was looked on by the white folks as a person who spread dissension among his group."[98] Trammell had written to tell state authorities of the dangers blacks faced in the region and ask for reinforcements. Although Democrats were murdering women and children in central Texas, Trammell wrote that blacks in the region were not going to be forced to leave.[99] One pioneer remembered that whites so despised Trammell that "every crime that was committed was thought to be thro' him."[100] He was well aware that his life was in danger. While urging blacks to resist white violence, Trammell "preached with his shotgun leaning against the pulpit." In the end, neither the U.S. Army, the Freedmen's Bureau, nor Trammell's shotgun saved him. A white man named Hargrave killed him in 1875.[101]

Trammell was not alone. In 1868 a special committee on lawlessness and violence reported to the Constitutional Convention of Texas. After extensive research into government records, it concluded that "the mass of testimony is so overwhelming that no man of candor can for a moment question" that freedpeople were "wantonly mistreated and slain, simply because they are free, and claim to exercise the rights of freemen." These conclusions were accompanied by claims that the courts were ineffective if not obstructionist. The committee on lawlessness reported that courts had only convicted five of the 249 men indicted for murder in 1865, 1866, and 1867. Furthermore, some counties were staffed by officers who were "themselves involved in these acts of violence, or connive at them, or willfully neglect to make arrests."[102]

Such reports finally convinced the Republican leadership that something needed to be done. In order to combat the "practice, which has become common, of mobs of lawless men assembling and operating in disguise," Gov. Edmund J. Davis called for the establishment of "a police system that will enable the officers of the law to follow up and arrest offenders" in 1870.[103]

Although Davis's state police provided local officials with needed manpower, the state militia infuriated conservative whites for a number of reasons. To begin with, freedmen commonly served in the state police, composing as much as 40 percent of the total membership.[104] A rural newspaper in central Texas reported after the mustering of the state police that white citizens were now in danger of the "aggressions of an armed ignorant negro mob."[105] A resident of Groesbeck wrote that they were "having quite a bad time" because the "negro policemen have been arresting citizens of this place ever since Wednesday."[106]

Some of the most famous battles between whites and the state police took place in central Texas during the early 1870s. On the night of 6 August 1870 a band of young white men brazenly robbed a black-owned grocery store in the presence of its proprietor and even returned to the store to pilfer it a second time. Blacks attempted to stop the second theft but were unable to prevent the young whites from committing the crime. Angered, the blacks gathered an armed force at the store that included a member of the state police named William Mason, also black. When the whites returned for a third time, allegedly to pay for some melons at the behest of a white policeman, the blacks opened fire and killed the owner of a local saloon. The whites shot back, injuring and capturing Mason. Thirty armed blacks surrounded the hotel where Mason was taken, agitating for his release. When federal troops stationed in Waco arrived, they demanded that the black mob surrender. There was an exchange of gunfire, and the blacks were turned away.[107]

After the incident, the *Democratic Tri-Weekly State Gazette* wrote that African Americans in Waco "have ever been with some few exceptions, peaceable and well disposed. One bad man, however, in the State Police changes the condition of affairs by his influence and example and a reign of terror is at once instituted."[108] The argument was a warning to local whites that they were not safe with blacks in positions of power because blacks could not handle such positions properly.[109] Conservative frustration increased when Mason, having recovered, was later acquitted of murder.

The "Waco Riot" was but one of the many clashes to occur between armed blacks and local whites. One white pioneer remembered that her father and his neighbors helped shelter a white man named Steward after he had murdered a black soldier in Limestone County. In January 1871 whites in Hill County captured a group of the state police while they were attempting to locate two persons for the murder of a black couple. Another incident occurred in September 1871 when a black member of the state police shot and killed a white citizen in a barroom brawl. In both cases the governor prevented massive mob violence only with military force.[110]

In the end, the long campaign of violence, manipulation, and intimidation directed at freedpeople paid political dividends for the white majority of central Texas. Historian Carl Moneyhon notes that in 1873 "for the first time violence had made inroads against black votes." Throughout those areas of central Texas with potential black voters, the strong support for Republicans that had existed in the late 1860s and early 1870s suddenly disappeared, and votes for Democratic candidates surged.[111]

Not all central Texas's postwar violence, of course, could be attributed to politics. Much of it had roots in an antebellum culture of violence shaped by both slavery and conflicts with the Indians. Moreover, the racial upheaval of emancipation and the economic disruption of the Civil War, regardless of corresponding political changes, no doubt sparked many regional episodes of violence. Yet, ultimately, it is impossible to separate these factors from the political realities of Reconstruction Texas. Race, economics, and older traditions of mob law fed and nurtured a culture of violence intimately connected with the struggle between Democrats and Republicans.

*   *   *

In December 1873 crowds of white men and women took to the streets of Waco to celebrate the news from Austin. One of their own had become governor of the state of Texas. Less than nine years after the defeat of the Confederacy, Richard Coke—a former captain in the rebel army—prepared to move into the governor's mansion. Coke was born in Williamsburg, Virginia, in 1829. After attending the College of William and Mary, he moved to Waco, where he began a law practice. In the years leading up to the Civil War Coke proved to be an ardent supporter of slavery and a leading secessionist. After serving in the Confederate Army, he returned to central Texas, where he opposed the Reconstruction policies of the Republican Party. Coke finally triumphed over his foes when he out-polled E. J. Davis in the 1873 election for governor. As leader of the white Democratic conservatives (who referred to themselves as the "Redeemers") Coke served notice that the old order had returned to power in the Lone Star State.[112]

Republicans appealed to the federal government to investigate the fairness of the election, but when the government refused to intervene Republicans understood that the experiment of Reconstruction was over in Texas. Some radical leaders like Albert and Lucy Parsons fled the region and the state. Others, like David F. Davis and Stephen Cobb, fought on. They found it difficult, however, without support from the state or national governments.[113]

Coke's election foreshadowed developments in central Texas for the rest of the century. While the Republican Party's dream of a coalition of blacks and Unionist whites crumbled under the weight of violent intimidation and racial politics, the Democratic Party's coalition of conservative and moderate whites tightened its hold on power. In the last quarter of the nineteenth century that white majority—although rarely challenged politically—reinforced its dominance by continuing to sanction racial violence and insisting on the system of discrimination and segregation that would eventually be known as Jim Crow. Politics, not historical memory, had been the key cause of Reconstruction's mob violence. During the late nineteenth century, however, historical memory of Reconstruction would become an important part of justifying continued white-on-black violence.

6. "A New Crime": The Changing Character of Mob Violence in the Late Nineteenth Century

On 15 June 1874 a band of vigilantes lynched two unidentified black men for alleged horse theft in Coryell County. A month later the *San Antonio Express* reported that five white men—without "provocation"—shot and killed two more blacks, a married couple, outside Mexia in Limestone County. The murder of these four African Americans brought that year's toll of mob violence in central Texas to thirteen, nine whites and four blacks.[1]

Although each of the year's episodes had its own unique characteristics, the pattern of mob violence in 1874 was little changed from patterns in previous years. Two decades later, however, the character of mob violence was strikingly different. In August 1897 more than a hundred men hanged a black man named Wesley Johnson, whom they charged with the attempted rape of a white woman. Johnson was the fourth victim of vigilantism that year. All the victims were African Americans. All were charged with rape or sexual assault of a white woman. All were murdered by mobs numbering at least a hundred persons.[2]

Mob violence in central Texas changed dramatically during the late nineteenth century. Between 1870 and 1900 vigilantes lynched thirty-four blacks and twenty-eight whites. Such numbers, however, do not convey the extent of the transformation. Central Texas mobs lynched twenty African Americans in the 1890s, a number greater than the total of the previous two decades. At the same time, the number of white victims steadily declined from fifteen victims in the 1870s to seven in the 1880s to six in the 1890s.[3]

The narratives justifying the lynchings also followed different trajectories. The primary reason given for lynching whites—a weak and ineffective court system—had less and less resonance as the nineteenth century drew to a close (chapter 4). The growing effectiveness of the court system, however, did not convince whites that they should dispense with extralegal punishment for blacks. Instead, as the nineteenth century drew to a close they believed African Americans to be more violent, more likely to commit crimes, and less likely to be controlled by the courts. The result of those changes was the racialization of lynching. A punishment that was at one time meted out to both whites and blacks became by 1900 a punishment for blacks administered by whites.

* * *

Whites in central Texas believed in the importance of law and order. Mob violence, for most residents, was justifiable only when courts were ineffective.[4] If the white majority came to believe that courts could adequately contain those who threatened the post-Reconstruction social order, central Texas might have witnessed a slow decline in racial violence during the late nineteenth century. To some extent such violence did decline. Never again, for example, would the numbers of murders and lynchings in central Texas reach those associated with the late 1860s. The region's new leaders, however, did not consistently renounce mob law but openly encouraged the use of extralegal violence. White central Texans, it is clear from the historical record, believed that mobs still had an important role to play in regulating black behavior during the late nineteenth century.

The level of racial violence that blacks experienced during the late nineteenth century will never be known for a number of reasons. First, people who wrote the vast majority of documents used to study racial violence—notably, newspapers—were not always aware of all a region's violence. Acts of racial violence often played themselves out secretly in many small villages, out-of-the-way towns, and rural hamlets. For example, Bob Hall disappeared from a McLennan County convict gang in 1885 after an escape attempt. Although Hall was shot while trying to escape, no one knew if he had recovered from his wound and made his escape or had died from the wound and been quietly buried somewhere down along the river.[5] Similarly, authorities discovered the corpse of a black man named Gebe Austin on 2 June 1883. Although Austin had been strangled and shot, no further details of his death emerged.[6]

Second, even when white newspapers knew all the details about an act of racial violence, they did not always report them. The *Waco Examiner* vowed to report McLennan County's violence but noted that "the papers of some counties have preferred to with-hold from their columns, all mention of the crimes occurring around them, and consequently very many lawless acts and deeds have occurred, of which the general public has no knowledge."[7] Although some newspapers like the *Examiner* kept fairly detailed reports on racial violence, the daunting task of looking through day after day of the hundreds that have survived in Texas (not to mention the thousands that have survived in other lynch-prone states) has prevented historians from fully investigating the topic of racial violence.[8] Despite the incomplete nature of the evidence, surviving documentation nevertheless reveals that mob violence was endemic in central Texas during the late nineteenth century.[9]

In describing mob violence against blacks, historians often focus on lynching, but this most violent form of racial harassment was not the most common. Random assaults by whites on blacks became a daily feature of life.[10] Another frequent form of racial violence tolerated by the white majority was robbery. Many whites took umbrage at black success, although some pointed to prosperous African Americans as a sign that blacks could "progress" in a segregated society.[11]

Just as stealing black property was acceptable to many whites, so was destroying it. In 1898 a group of white policemen came across a group of white boys in the act of throwing rocks at the home of a black domestic servant. Despite being caught "in the act of violating the laws," the boys were not arrested.[12] In the eyes of the law, destruction of black property was the work of "pranksters," not criminals. Such "pranks" could easily escalate from throwing rocks to shooting guns. One local historian recalled that "adventurous white men and boys who were on the lookout for excitement made it a point to hunt out . . . Negro dances and shoot them up."[13]

Some acts were spur-of-the-moment reactions to unfolding events. Others involved considerable premeditation and planning. One of the most organized forms of racial intimidation and violence was the phenomenon known as whitecapping, in which a group of disguised men would threaten and terrorize local inhabitants who refused to accede to the mob's wishes. Although illegal, whitecapping was always the result of rational planning. Unlike most lynchings—where the mob's clear purpose was nothing less than the death of the victim—murder was a threat and a last resort in most whitecappings. Whitecappers usually issued a warning, urging victims either to desist from some specific activity or leave the region. Whitecappers in McLennan County, for example, posted a warning in 1883: "You are ordered not to fence in the Jones tank, as it is a public tank and is the only water there is for stock on this range. . . . No good man will undertake to watch this fence, for the Owls will catch him."[14] A notice issued by Falls County whitecappers read: "Change your trade or move and be damn quick. . . . By complying with this notice you will save your backs and necks. Take warning, Your friends."[15]

Most often, these terrorist groups were content when their victims left the region. In Hill County a group of whitecappers gave four alleged thieves thirty days to leave but warned that if they did not, "ropes and six-shooter balls are prepared for you."[16] In 1891 a mob "allowed" an African American named Matt Watkins to leave town with his life after he got into a dispute with a white man.

Whitecappers, however, were more than willing to murder if their wishes were not met. James Wilson, a black porter at the Pacific Saloon in Waco, was told "to be careful about how he talked to a white man [because] some men might take a shot at him." Wilson chose not to flee after the warning and paid the price when he was later assassinated by a white man.[17]

White horse thieves and fence cutters sometimes suffered at the hands of such vigilantes, especially in other parts of the South and West, but victims of whitecapping in central Texas were most often black or Mexican. In 1898 whitecappers posted a "Notice to Mexicans" that read: "You all have got ten days to leave in."[18] Blacks were often targeted on the basis of race. William Cowper Brann, who published a nationally read news magazine in Waco, wrote in 1895 that southern whites "must take a day off and kill every member of the accursed race that declines to leave the country."[19]

Although Brann's race war was never fully implemented, something like it was reported to have occurred in Limestone County in 1875. A white pioneer, John Cox, remembered the trouble "with the freed negroes" there and called the struggle a "race war."[20] A white newspaper reported that a black man was taken out of jail in Groesbeck on 22 May 1875 and shot. A black leader reported that whites were killing blacks—men, women, and children—throughout the county.[21] "The raid on the colored people of Limestone County, which commenced in May of last year and continued for several weeks," reported former Gov. E. J. Davis in 1876, killed "some forty or fifty men, women, and children."[22]

Events in Limestone County and the position of William Brann were extremes. Most central Texans were not in favor of murdering or chasing out all blacks. Instead, they hoped to shape the blacks' behavior to the liking of the white majority. If blacks would "stay in their proper place, be respectful and courteous . . . [and] have nothing to do with those who will not work," wrote the *Waco Times-Herald*, "law-abiding people would so frown upon any threats of violence toward them that whitecapping would immediately cease." The article concluded that it "is only the insolent, impudent, worthless negroes who are in danger of whitecaps anyway."[23]

Local whites thus insisted that only they could save blacks—and only then if they acted according to vague and arbitrary standards. Three central Texas farmers kindly offered a more specific suggestion. They would "solve" the whitecap problem by shielding all endangered blacks from attackers if the blacks would pick cotton for them.[24]

Racial violence in central Texas was not limited to whitecapping. White mobs chose to attack blacks for a variety of offenses, and they did not always warn their victims to leave. In October 1876, for example, a band of masked men approached the cabin door of Jesse Estelle, a black man living on Aquilla Creek in McLennan County, and asked him to come outside. When he refused they attempted to force their way into his home. Failing to gain entry, they then riddled the house with bullets. The mob left, thinking that their victims were dead. Much to the mob's dismay, Estelle and his family, although wounded, survived and later fled to Waco for safety.[25]

Unpremeditated attacks are also replete in the historical record. In 1877 a half-drunk white man named Harris Burney shot "an unoffending negro" named John Jackson in the back of the head as he was walking out of a saloon. Jackson had made the mistake of refusing to share a drink with Burney.[26] One of the worst cases of such racial violence occurred on 17 September 1877, four miles outside Waco. An elderly black man named Asa Brinkley had retired on a portion of a plantation after a life of "hard work and close economy." He had been fortunate enough to accumulate "considerable property," including a "fine gray mare." When two white men rode up to a pasture near Brinkley's home and attempted to capture the horse, they urged him to help them steal the animal. According to Brinkley's wife, one man said, "You damned old gray headed son of a bitch you go and catch me this gray mare or I will shoot your damned fool head off." When Brinkley refused to help, Andrew McCarty unloaded his revolver and "scattered the old man's brains out" in front of his wife and two grandsons.[27]

Although killings such as Brinkley's were all too common, historians have devoted attention to the less frequent but more disturbing spectacle of lynching. The public support and ritual associated with lynchings, especially the largest and most organized ones, have often been used to distinguish that form of murder from the many others that existed in the late nineteenth century.

Using the definition of lynching later adopted by the NAACP, I have found that at least thirty-two African Americans died at the hands of mobs in central Texas between the end of Reconstruction and the turn of the century. Most victims were male, but three were female. They were lynched for a variety of reasons. Sexual assault, either real or imagined, was the justification for the deaths of eleven black men. In the lynchings of seven black men and two black women, the mob's victim was allegedly involved in a murder. Two black men were lynched for horse theft. Although details are scarce, one black died for not following the orders of whitecappers, one was lynched for attempted murder, another for resisting arrest, and yet another for threatening a white man. A black couple, a husband and wife, were assassinated without provocation according to the newspaper account that reported the attack. The crimes justifying the lynching of four blacks were unknown to the sources reporting the mob violence.[28]

* * *

Understanding and explaining the racial violence that plagued central Texas during the late nineteenth century requires attention to several factors. The place to begin, at least in central Texas, is with the election of Richard Coke as governor in 1873. Social and historical memories of Reconstruction shaped late-nineteenth-century attitudes toward mob violence, particularly mob violence against blacks. White southerners constructed a narrative that blamed the Republican Party and the military for the lawlessness of Reconstruction. The end of slavery, from their perspective, encouraged chaos by removing blacks from the "civilizing" influence of slavery. This narrative viewed the men of the Democratic Party as "Redeemers" who were forced to take drastic action to restore order and peace. Although that basic historical narrative was much the same for whites throughout the South, men and women shaped it to specific needs and local circumstances. Most frequently, they inserted memories of specific events and particular individuals from the history of their states or communities. In central Texas, this regional narrative was interwoven with the election of a local hero, Richard Coke.

The enshrining of Coke in local historical memory began immediately upon his victory in 1873. Most whites in central Texas applauded the election. The region's most successful newspaper wrote that Coke "entered the executive chair free from the vices of the trained politician, and with no purpose to accomplish, save that of redeeming his State from Radical ruin, and restoring the prosperity of the people."[29] Longtime central Texas resident George Erath cheered Coke's ascendancy and took joy in the fact that the enemy was "evacuating" the capital.[30] Coke's coattails helped white Democrats sweep into local county offices throughout most of the state, including central Texas. Finally, the *Waco Daily Advance* roared, the region had "in all its offices men who are undoubtedly the choice of the people."[31]

Coke's place in central Texas's historical memory grew over time. White pioneers in the 1930s remembered Reconstruction as a time of oppression and suffering and the election of Richard Coke as one of the greatest moments of their lives. During Reconstruction, "lawlessness" reigned, and thieves were

"numerous and bold" until the "Hon. Richard Coke of Waco was made Governor," recalled a resident of Falls County. "I think the happiest times was
when Richard Coke of Waco was elected over what we called the carpet-
bagger governor Davis" remembered a central Texas woman. A man who had
memorized Coke's inaugural address repeated the words with pride: "For the
first time since the disaster of the Civil War, Texas has a government chosen
by free vote of the people." He then wondered whether "the present generation know what a grand man Richard Coke was."[32] John Henry Brown included Coke in his list of "Eminent Texans" and described him as "a man of
massive brain and great intelligence with finesse and honor as a base."[33]

Why is Coke's memory important to the history of mob violence in central Texas? Those who revered him and what they called his "redemption"
of Texas understood that violence and vigilantism had been vital to his election. As central Texans prepared for the election, the *Waco Daily Examiner*
wrote that long "years of oppression have not quelled the fires of manhood
in their bosoms, nor has a decade of Radical prostitution brought any other
feeling than one of disgust." Urging readers to action, the *Examiner* proph-
esied that they would "destroy as with a keen sword the Radical cabal, which
has ruined us and now insults us. The black flag is up—we take no prisoners."[34] One Coke supporter thought it "high time for an enraged and outraged people to take the law into their own hands as a means of seeking re-
dress for the manner in which they have been outraged, robbed, threatened,
murdered, abused and vilified for the past ten years."[35]

Many central Texans agreed and understood that restoring Democrats to
power required not only voting for Coke but also preventing blacks from cast-
ing ballots. It was quite obvious that black voters had been "persuaded" to either stay home or vote Democratic—pro-Coke forces admitted as much. Radical sympathizers could "install his Excellency, E. J. Davis, 'the man without
a country,' as president of the negro republic, and go, all in a solid wad, to San
Domingo, where they [could] enjoy, under a tropical sun, the unadulterated
odor of the children of Ham, with no Ku-Klux to molest or make them
afraid."[36] A campaign of intimidation had been waged against Republican
voters.

Not only did most whites approve of such tactics at the time but they also
continued to glorify such violence in their long-term memories. Looking back
on events six decades past, Sarah Ann Pringle remembered that in "the campaign of 1873 when Richard Coke of Waco ran against Davis we had some real
exciting times." White men, she explained, "were instructed to come armed,"
and one person "decided to try shooting to scare the negroes off and so he
started shooting, I think, on the Court House lawn." When blacks who had

come to vote heard the shooting, "they piled into their wagons and buggies and left town." Then the "white men went ahead and had their vote." Looking back on events a half-century old, she concluded that the "way was made much better for us after the Klan began to operate."[37] Whether events occurred exactly as Pringle remembered is not as significant as the memory itself. Whatever the actual role of racial violence, central Texas's whites believed that violence and the threat of it saved them from the tragedy of Reconstruction.

In the years following Coke's election, whites came to trust that racial violence was not only useful for intimidating black voters but also a critical resource in shaping the social order in central Texas. In 1874, for example, congressional lawmakers considered legislation that would bar discrimination based on race in public places. The *Waco Daily Advance* warned against this extension of civil rights to blacks. When a black man "attempts to force himself on a social equality with the whites, to enter their schools, churches and homes," wrote the editor, "he will step upon ground that will open a grave at his feet." If the civil rights bill were passed, the *Advance*'s editor predicted that "blood of the best men of the South may run in torrents but every acre of land from the Ohio to the Rio Grande will be covered with dead carcasses of negroes ere this damnable outrage can be consummated."[38]

White leaders in the region continued to support mob violence against blacks, at least in part because such violence was glorified in the region's historical memory. It was believed to have been a central part of the "redemption" of the Democratic Party and the return of "civilization" to the prairies of central Texas. In choosing to remember racial violence in that way, the white majority came to believe, rightly or wrongly, that it was one of the best resources for maintaining power. During the remaining years of the century there was no hesitation in tapping into that resource whenever the slightest threat was perceived to white political, economic, and social authority. The result was a powerful culture of mob violence.

* * *

A large and diverse number of central Texans recalled Richard Coke and helped contribute to his special place in the area's historical memory. Not everyone, however, had equal influence on the region's collective memory. Law officers, judges, juries, and newspaper editors in central Texas had a disproportionate impact on the historical memory of mob violence there. What these figures did and did not do, what they said, and what they did not say greatly shaped the way in which acts of mob violence were remembered. One of the striking differences between central Texas's late-nineteenth-century mob violence and the region's Reconstruction-era violence centers on the decline in the number of Anglo American and Native American victims. Before the 1870s, white posses and mobs had dispatched at first Indians and later whites as often, if not more often, than blacks. The reason for the decline in the number of Native American victims is clear. Their numbers decimated by disease, warfare, and immigration, very few Indians were left in central Texas after 1870.

The decline of both forms of violence was critical to the rise of white-on-black lynching during the late nineteenth century. The enormous mobs that lynched African Americans could not have gathered without widespread support in the white community. Before 1880 the Anglo settlers of central Texas were often divided. In the beginning, they struggled over the proper strategy for dealing with the region's native inhabitants, and later they became embroiled in debates over disunion and Reconstruction. Early patterns of racial violence reflected the tension. Before 1860 few central Texans were lynched because full attention was focused on conflict with the Indians; after 1860 mobs began to target whites and blacks but were usually small and secretive. They differed markedly from the mass mobs that emerged in the twentieth century and culminated with the midday killing of Jesse Washington before a crowd of thousands. Such spectacle lynchings, one historian has observed, are only possible when a community possesses considerable unity. That unity was lacking in central Texas until the 1880s.[39]

The solidarity that emerged among whites in the crucible of Reconstruction was a necessary step for the mass lynchings of the late nineteenth century, but it was not a sufficient step. Other communities possessed even greater unity than central Texas but not its history of racial violence. Part of the answer for the mob violence against African Americans after Reconstruction can be found in examining the actions and attitudes of central Texas officials and leaders toward such violence.

Many who study lynching have long focused on what happened before a lynching.[40] Precipitating events are undoubtedly important, but examining the aftermath of lynching may be even more valuable in getting at causality. In short, the behavior of white leaders after a lynching may indicate the value they found in promoting racial violence. The days and weeks that followed a lynching are critical. Did community leaders defend or condemn the event? How were lynching episodes to be remembered? Were members of the mob portrayed as heroes who completed a grim but necessary task, or were mob leaders criminals worthy of punishment and rebuke? In areas where mob leaders were convicted or at least prosecuted, mob violence may well have declined rapidly. Even where leaders at least spoke out consistently against lynching it seems likely that mob law suffered a decline. But in areas where local leaders defended lynching on a consistent basis it is not surprising to find that historical memory endorses it and a vibrant culture of mob violence persists.

Court officials and law officers played a central role in determining reaction to a lynching episode. Did the sheriff and his fellow law officers attempt to prevent the mob violence or look the other way? Did the justice of the peace and others in the legal system seek out, indict, and prosecute members of the mob?

The historical record suggests that law officers and court officials in late-nineteenth-century central Texas exerted little effort to prevent mob violence and other attacks on African Americans. In 1886 the *Waco Day* reported that four officers "closely guarded" a black prisoner named Bill Harris until they realized "the hopelessness of their efforts" and turned him over to the mob without firing a shot. The newspaper praised this "strong effort to protect the prisoner" and simultaneously endorsed the subsequent hanging. The newspaper praised the mob as having "done something" to deter black criminal behavior, and the grand jury refused to indict anyone for the murder of Bill Harris.[41] Newspaper editors, law officers, and local officers took a similar approach to the lynching of Henry Davis in 1889. A local newspaper praised the court of "Judge Lynch" for "the shortness of its shifts and the celerity of its executions." The law officers from whom Davis was taken testified that they were powerless to protect their prisoner. The mob leaders who hanged Davis were not indicted by the grand jury.[42]

Not only did law officers do little to prevent racial violence but they were also active themselves in attacks on African Americans. In 1876 a police officer shot and killed a black man named Miles Butts who was fleeing arrest. The *Waco Examiner* reported that no "blame whatever attaches to Constable Holcomb" because the death of Butts "would not be regretted by any one."[43] Shooting at blacks in flight was standard operating procedure for local law officers. Anthony Bidwell, a nineteen-year-old African American, had allegedly stolen $8 from a white man in 1876. A year later the police spotted him and gave chase. "Despairing of catching him by this means," recounted the local newspaper, "they concluded to try another method, and drawing their pistols fired five shots after the fugitive."[44]

Although Bidwell was only injured, Sim Woods was not so lucky eight years later. Woods, like Bidwell, had been sought for stealing from a white man. After a search of at least a year, four policemen finally found him in 1885. According to the testimony of Woods's stepmother, he "did not make any demonstrations toward the officers; he only ran to get out of their way." Despite the unarmed Woods's lack of aggressiveness and the cries of his son not to "shoot my pappa," the police shot and killed Woods as he climbed the banks of Waco Creek.[45] That killing provoked outrage in a local newspaper. "The negro, it is true, was under the ban of the law," argued the *Examiner,* "but if arrested, tried and convicted, he could not have been hanged or otherwise put to death for the crime of which he had been charged."[46] The *Examiner* continued, noting that there "have been many instances of this sort of official murder [and it] is time to call a halt."[47] Despite such strong words, Sim Woods's killers were not indicted. In fact, after a grand jury had finished considering the case, its members and the judge dined with one of Woods's killers, a police officer named William Ish. Even the *Examiner* quickly forgot about its hard-line stance against police violence; later the same year its editors endorsed Ish for sheriff of McLennan County.[48]

In overlooking cases of police misconduct against African Americans and failing to prosecute mob leaders, central Texas judges and juries followed the desires of the region's white public opinion. As early as 1857 a newspaper correspondent writing from Falls County recognized the critical role that public opinion played in supporting a culture of mob violence. He believed that residents of Texas would not be allowed to "assert the rights of freemen without fear of assassination . . . until the public journals of the day shall condemn, in unmeasured terms, the unjustifiable murders and assassinations so prevalent in the land."[49] Decades later in 1893, the editor of the *Waco Weekly News* confirmed the importance of local reaction to lynching. "Lynching," wrote J. N. Bennett, "becomes chronic and contagious." Young men "follow the example set them by their fathers" and reach adulthood "with the idea, ingrained in them that lynch law is right and proper, and worthy of applause."[50]

* * *

The support, or at least tolerance, of racial violence by local white leaders helped the culture of violence endure in central Texas during the late nineteenth century. The fact that mob members could lynch victims and escape punishment encouraged future acts of extralegal violence. Still, additional justifications and forces were at work, and they were critical in motivating central Texans to join vigilante groups and lynch mobs. The end of Reconstruction undercut one primary justification used in the 1860s. During that time, black political participation and concern over the loss of white mastery motivated racial violence. Members of the Ku Klux Klan did not have to give long speeches outlining the group's positive contributions to white majority rule and felt no need to leave notes pinned to their victims, spelling out their reasoning. After 1873 that implicit justification of racial violence no longer functioned because local whites had regained political power and significant social control.

Postbellum central Texas was a place of both continuity and change. Although Richard Coke's election was a sign that political power had shifted back to the men who had led Texas into the Civil War, the antebellum elite was never completely destroyed. Throughout the era of Reconstruction ample numbers of the old elite found ways to persevere and prosper in the New South.[51] As Richard Coke's career demonstrates, many in central Texas's ruling families emerged from this era of rapid change with their status and relative economic strength intact. Upon his return from the Civil War, Coke was treated quite well by his former battlefield foes, who appointed him district judge in 1865; he was elected to the state supreme court in 1866. Although removed from that position after a year by Radical Republicans, Coke was able to return to a profitable law practice in Waco. In 1873 he became governor and then, four years later, a U.S. senator.[52]

Just as startling as the amount of political power regained by one-time rebels was the extent to which the antebellum elite controlled central Texas's post-Reconstruction economy. More than half of McLennan County's wealthiest families in 1865 retained their status fifteen years later. Specifically, fifteen of the twenty-nine white families that constituted the wealthiest 5 percent in 1865 remained in the top 5 percent in 1880.[53]

"Redemption" meant a return to power for many of the old elite, but it meant something quite different for black central Texans. The post-Reconstruction world reduced the vast majority of them once again to a state of subservience. After 1873 the door of opportunity for local blacks—never wide open—was shut once again.

One of their most significant setbacks was the undermining of black suffrage during the 1870s. Conservative whites had attempted to discourage blacks from voting during the 1860s, but the power of the Republican government and federal soldiers provided some protection. In the early 1870s, however, the removal of these allies left black central Texans with little defense.[54] After the election of Richard Coke in 1873, a local historian noted that "the Negroes have not been in charge of the ballot boxes nor much voted in Waco."[55]

Local whites did little to hide their contempt for the concept of voting rights for African Americans. A conservative, pro-Democrat newspaper in Waco, for example, confirmed the intimidation of black voters. On 11 January 1876 the *Waco Daily Examiner* reported on a conversation held the previous morning between a freedman who had presented himself at the polls in East Waco and the election overseer.

"Are you a Democrat?" asked the white man.

"Dat's my affair," replied the freedman.

"Without you are a Democrat, and promise to support the Democratic party in the coming election, you can't vote here."

"Well, I would like to know what hab come ob de rights ob de culled cit'zen, dat dey can't vote for whatsomever dey want to. I'm a Republic[an], and I'm votin' dat ticket, every time, and I'm gwine to see if I haven't got de right to vote jes' as I sees fit."

The freedman, like other former slaves, was learning that blacks in post-Reconstruction central Texas did not necessarily have the right to vote. Many protested their disfranchisement. C. M. Thompson, an African American from Waco, wrote to President U. S. Grant in 1876, objecting to the intimidation of black voters in the region during the recent presidential contest pitting the Republican Rutherford B. Hayes against the Democrat Samuel Tilden. "Sir, I thought that I would write you a few lines about this election. Gov. Hayse [sic] was knock out of about four or five hundred votes Here in Waco, Texas." The Democrats, Thompson continued, told local blacks that on the day of the election "to go on in the field and Go to work," because "if they went to town that day to vote" they would "drive them off."[56] The few blacks who attempted to vote in Waco, Thompson added, were turned away after being forced to admit that they planned to vote for the Republican candidate.

Thompson understood that he had a constitutional right to vote, but knowledge of his rights mattered little in a world where the federal government was retreating from Reconstruction and where his neighbors were more committed to the subordination of African Americans than to the fundamental principles of democratic government. Some central Texas blacks overcame such obstacles and managed to keep voting during the late nineteenth century, but white intimidation meant that it would be a hundred years before blacks would again vote as freely as they did during the late 1860s.[57]

Economic prospects were also exceedingly poor under post-Reconstruction politics. Although revolutionary gains had never materialized, a significant number of blacks in Texas had managed to acquire property between the end of slavery and the end of Reconstruction. In 1860 only eighteen blacks in the entire state owned real estate; by 1870, however, there were 1,508 African American landowners in Texas.[58] Yet with the withdrawal of federal troops and the end of the Republican-created state militia, already-bleak conditions for blacks turned bleaker. White planters and merchants increasingly wielded the upper hand in negotiating tenant and sharecropping arrangements.

Sharecropping had become the dominant mode of agricultural organization in central Texas before the end of Reconstruction. After 1873, however, it increasingly became a form of near-bondage as white landowners successfully tied black tenants to the land with the credit system. Sharecropping was a process in which a landlord allowed a family to till and cultivate a section of the landlord's property in exchange for a portion, often half, of the year's crop. Historians have argued that white southern planters employed sharecropping as a primary method in their successful attempt to retain the coercive and exploitative system of plantation agriculture.[59]

Some blacks in central Texas, however, did manage to acquire land and property. In 1880, shortly after the end of Reconstruction, 16 percent of those McLennan County blacks designating themselves as farmers claimed land-ownership.[60] But they struggled against enormous problems that mounted as the turn of the century approached. Whites throughout the South did not look favorably on black property ownership.[61] Problems began when they refused to sell land to blacks.[62] Even those few blacks fortunate enough to acquire land found that it was "often of poor quality or located in remote sections."[63] The properties owned by central Texas blacks did not compare to the land typically owned by their white neighbors. As late as 1900 the average size of black land-holdings in Texas was only 58.6 acres compared to 425.5 for whites.[64]

The failure to secure financial loans also impeded black landholding, making it difficult for black real estate owners to stay afloat in years of poor production or low prices. With no institution to loan them money, blacks were often forced to sell their land. Such a cycle unfortunately seems to have plagued black property owners in central Texas more than their peers in other regions of Texas and the South. In 1880 McLennan County had 639 black property owners. Ten years later, however, the number had declined to only 435. Black-owned property was also worth less in 1890, falling to $124,180 after a total of $134,802 in 1880. During that same time the number of white land-holders increased by 36 percent, and their property values increased by 44 percent. By 1890 only 4.1 percent of McLennan County blacks owned property.[65]

Blacks in the city of Waco fared little better than those in the countryside. Faced with mounting discrimination and nearly insurmountable obstacles to progress, most city blacks worked jobs that white society deemed acceptable for African Americans. Texas had the lowest proportion of wage-earners to black population of any state. White craftspeople were opposed to competition from blacks and refused to give apprenticeships to them. Opportunities to enter the professions or to own a business were even narrower because blacks generally did not have access to the necessary capital or the patronage of whites, often the bulk of a city's population. Black professionals were restricted to being teachers and ministers, and black business owners were restricted to special operations, such as barber shops, deemed acceptable by the white population.[66] According to a sample from the 1880 manuscript records of the U.S. Census, skilled craftspeople and professionals accounted for only 10 percent of the working black population in Waco. Of blacks in the professions, 82 percent were teachers, ministers, or barbers. The vast majority of local blacks worked either as domestic servants or unskilled laborers. Those two groups, in fact, contained 84 percent of the working black population of Waco.[67]

A third area of change for African Americans in the post-Reconstruction period involved the courts and legal system. Although they found themselves battling against a racist and discriminatory justice system soon after emancipation, blacks did serve on juries in McLennan County during Reconstruction. Furthermore, the courts were often headed by sympathetic white Republicans such as Judge J. W. Oliver.[68] After 1873, however, blacks no longer had allies on the courts and were not considered as part of the venire from which jurors were selected until the twentieth century.[69]

The most abusive legal discrimination heaped on black central Texans was the convict lease system. During the fifty years following emancipation southern courts did not usually send convicts to prison but rather packed them off to farmers and businesses who were in search of cheap labor.[70] The convict lease system blended perfectly with the plans of Richard Coke and his fellow Democrats. By providing the state with both additional revenues and a cheap, dependable labor force, the system allowed Redeemers to ease taxes while funding costly projects such as railroad construction. Nearly all convicts in this innovative scheme were black.[71] Although they made up roughly half the prison population in Texas during the late nineteenth century, "farm labor was assigned almost exclusively to black prisoners."[72]

The local court system aided in the policy of racial control by providing inmates for the lease system and sentencing blacks to long prison terms for petty crimes. Redick Brown, for example, was sentenced to two years in prison for stealing a cut of bacon.[73] Although the treatment meted out to convict gangs no doubt varied, the experience of the gang leased by a man named Darwin in McLennan County was typical. "It is alleged that Lessee Darwin does not conduct the convict farm with due regard to humanity," reported the conservative *Waco Day*, "and reliable persons state that the food furnished is insufficient while the labor imposed is very heavy."[74]

Before local criminals could be sent off to receive a diet of meager rations and hard labor, they had to survive what may have been the even more dire conditions of the McLennan County jail. The grand jury of McLennan County reported in 1876 that "all the prisoners, forty-six in number, [were] huddled together in the upper room, most of them in a cell less than twenty-six feet square." Criminals "of every grade, the least as well as the greatest, the weak and the strong, the sick and the well and—with shame be it told, regardless of sex—are crowded together in this narrow apartment."[75]

The legal system intimidated blacks in numerous other ways as well. In general, white society used the law to ensure continued performance of prescribed tasks. The *Waco Times-Herald,* for example, announced in 1906 that the "city calaboose is about chuck full of some of the finest cotton pickers known ... about twenty or twenty-five healthy, robust negro men in that place just at present as a direct result of the proceedings of the city court this morning." The *Times-Herald* explained that "there is a demand for cotton pickers, and the scarcity almost reached a serious stage." Fortunately for local planters, authorities had spotted many blacks on the streets of Waco, "the majority of them well-dressed and sleek looking, but with no visible means of support." Thanks to the efforts of the local police, no vagrant "escaped this morning and if farmers do not come forward and pay fines for some of the darkies in order to secure them for cotton pickers, there's going to be some splendid material at work on Waco's streets the next twenty days."[76]

Unfortunately, there were even worse abuses of the legal system. The courts could be deadly. In what historian George Wright has called "legal lynchings," the central Texas legal system often executed blacks suspected of violent crimes on the thinnest of evidence and with what amounted to no legal defense.[77] In 1877, for example, Perry Davis was hanged in Waco for the murder of a policeman.[78] With the meager legal defense given him, the Republican *Waco Register* sarcastically wrote that there was little difference between a lynching and Davis's hanging because he "could have been hung without law about as well as with it." According to the *Register,* "The pathway of the colored man to the gallows in this State, once he gets started, is easy. No obstructions are thrown in his way."[79]

In 1887 a black man named Conrad Jackson was sentenced to be hanged for the murder of his white employer. Jackson, however, claimed that another person had committed the crime. The state's evidence was admittedly circumstantial, and there were no witnesses. These problems, however, did not delay "justice." The jury "returned a verdict which is highly acceptable to the public."[80] Seven months later the executioner's rope snapped Jackson's neck in front of a select crowd that had managed to obtain tickets of admission from the sheriff.[81]

Although Lee Robinson did not die at the hands of central Texas courts like Davis and Jackson, his trial was a display of even less interest in black legal rights. Robinson was accused of the assault and attempted rape of a white woman named Ella Robertson. Robinson was indicted on Tuesday. His trial was set for Friday. George Barcus, his lawyer, was not appointed to the case until the day of the trial and, not surprisingly, failed to put together much of a defense for his client. Instead, Barcus told the jury that the trial had been fair, and he was sure a just verdict would be delivered. Barcus must have thought that Robinson's sentence of 1,001 years in prison was just, because he made no appeal.[82] The legacy and impact of such legal maltreatment were a level of mistrust between blacks and the court system that persists to this day.[83]

Discrimination against blacks in local political life, in their working lives, and in the courts meant that African Americans in central Texas after Reconstruction appeared in many ways to be hardly better off than they were under slavery. Whites continued to deny free blacks, like slaves, certain fundamental rights accorded to most citizens of the United States, most notably the right to vote. Economically, blacks continued to have little power and little hope for improvement. In the cotton fields, where blacks had worked on plantation gangs, they now served as tenant farmers and sharecroppers or as hired hands. Few owned their own land, and those who did were slowly folding to outside pressures. White landowners found debt bondage to be an effective alternative to enslavement. Moreover, with a prejudicial rather than a judicial legal system, blacks in central Texas found themselves reduced to second-class citizenship and confined, as before, to the lowest caste of society.

It is against this backdrop of increasing white control that central Texas's late-nineteenth-century racial violence must be explained. Blacks continued to press for political rights long after 1873, but the threat of political power was insignificant for the next one hundred years and did not directly provoke whites to mob action during the late nineteenth century. Yet racial violence did not decline. Indeed, whites persisted in believing that mob violence was necessary to control black behavior. Black resistance to white rule continued to fuel lynching in central Texas, but that resistance did not take the direct political form it had during Reconstruction. The resilience of racial violence in the late nineteenth century had more to do with new and reinvented justifications of racial violence (albeit ones linked through social memory to earlier central Texas history) than with justifications specific to the period after the Civil War.

* * *

Whites in central Texas often justified mid-nineteenth-century campaigns of violence against Indians and Mexicans as necessary steps in protecting the women and children of Anglo households. Before the Civil War, however, vigilante action against blacks was rarely based on such justifications. That is not surprising. After all, African Americans—as slaves—were part of the households of the antebellum South. Justifying mob reprisals against blacks on the basis that they posed a danger to white women and children would have called into question the entire system of slavery. With the destruction of the peculiar institution, however, central Texas whites were free to justify attacks on blacks in the same way they had long justified attacks on Indians and other ethnic minorities—through a gendered appeal to white racism.

Yet whites in central Texas did not immediately begin to portray freedmen as rapists; a decade lapsed before that would be the case. Few blacks in the four counties of the Upper Brazos River valley, for example, were assaulted for sexual transgressions during Reconstruction. Although central Texas blacks fell victim to at least 165 acts of violence between 1865 and 1873, whites justified only two of those acts with the charge that a black man had sexually assaulted a white woman. Although one can hardly describe the mob's extralegal punishments as lenient, those involved chose not to murder either alleged rapist. Instead, they castrated one of the freedmen and whipped the other one severely.[84] Such a story contrasts strikingly with events of the late nineteenth century, when the charge of black sexual assault was not only heard much more often but was also almost always fatal to alleged rapists.

White central Texans did not discover the "black rape fiend" overnight. Questions revolving around gender, sexuality, and race had been among the most contested of Reconstruction. How would black households be refashioned after emancipation? Would white men still have sexual access to black freedwomen? Would freedmen's quest for equality lead to intermarriage with white women? These questions were first raised and fought over during Reconstruction. Yet white central Texans did not choose at that time—most of the time, at least—to defend violence against freedpeople with explicit references to those gendered questions. It was not until the end of Reconstruction, when the overt and obvious political justification for white-on-black violence disappeared, that whites reached for gender to justify attacks on African Americans.[85]

One of the first post-Reconstruction references to a black man sexually assaulting a white woman in central Texas can be found in the 10 September 1875 edition of the *Waco Examiner and Patron:* "a negro man attempted to commit rape upon the person of Mrs. Horn." The "black fiend threw her down several times but failed to accomplish his base purpose," noted the report. A search for Horn's attacker failed to locate him.[86] Several things about this first reference are of interest to historians of racial violence. First, the story did not appear on the front page but was buried in small print under the headline "Attempted Rape." Second, there is no evidence that neighbors and friends of the victim made much of a search for the alleged criminal. No additional stories followed up on the crime, and authorities were apparently never alerted. Ten or twenty years later the attempted assault on Mrs. Horn would have drawn front-page coverage and surely have sparked a massive manhunt leading to the capture of a black man (one way or another) to sate the anger of the mob. But that was not the case in 1875. Whites, in central Texas at least, had yet to develop the hair-trigger response to the charge of rape that would dominate the New South during the 1890s.

This relative inattention is confirmed by an examination of central Texas legal records. Sexual assault appeared only infrequently in the central Texas courts of the 1850s and 1860s. Before the 1870s, hardly any indictments for sexual crimes appear in the fragmentary records of Bosque, Hill, and Falls counties, and even the more complete record books of McLennan County hold only one indictment for rape before 1870.[87] Courts began to pay greater attention to sexual assault in the 1870s, but most who were indicted were not convicted. Those found guilty typically received two years in prison. During the 1880s and the 1890s, however, courts began to indict a greater number of individuals for sexual assault. Sentences began to increase in severity as well, climaxing with the case of Lee Robinson, who in 1905 was sentenced to 1,001 years in prison for rape.[88]

Increasing legal attention to sexual assault paralleled growing attention in the press and popular culture to illicit black-white relationships. One step on the road to the hysteria of the 1890s was escalating intolerance for black men and white women engaged in consensual relationships.[89] In 1877 the *Waco Daily Examiner* announced that "Big Lou, an abandoned white woman, . . . was married last Sunday morning to a negro named Bill Warner, and the pair are now domiciled on Waco Creek." The newspaper urged authorities to arrest and punish the two.[90] Intermarriage between blacks and whites, especially between black men and white women, was infrequent, but a new determination to eliminate such unions emerged in the late nineteenth century. In 1878 a Texas newspaper justified the lynching of a "Negro Seducer" for living with a sixteen-year-old white girl in Walker County. The lynchers were merely following "the first law of nature—self-defense—in protecting their daughters from the unhallowed approaches of brutes, and visiting vengeance on those who outlaw the sanctity of their household."[91] White Texans convinced themselves that no white woman would ever willingly live with a black man. No such union could be a consensual one. Any black man involved with a white woman was a "seducer." Within a few years they would be called rapists.

Throughout the 1880s white central Texans became increasingly alarmed by reports of attempted sexual assaults by black men. In 1884 a local mob for the first time lynched a black man for rape. On 23 June three hundred men in Hill County surrounded the county jail in Hillsboro. They extracted Zeke Hadley from his cell. Hadley was scheduled for a preliminary examination the next morning on a charge of sexual assault. The mob hanged Hadley and asked that a written justification appear in the next issue of the *Whitney Messenger.* "We regret the necessity of having to step beyond the limits of the law in the execution of this negro," began the note, "but we have positive proof of his guilt and think the crime justifies the act." Furthermore, we "dedicate this precedent [*sic*] to the *defense and protection of woman,* feeling that we owe the mothers, wives, and daughters of this community, the extreme measure to which we have resorted."[92] The most fascinating aspect of Hadley's lynching is that the "three hundred citizens" who wrote the notice were aware that lynching a man for rape was a "president" in central Texas, and they felt need to justify their actions in the press. Lynch mobs during the years ahead did not often go to such lengths to defend themselves.

Despite the actions of the Hillsboro mob, the charge of rape—even when the victim was a white woman and the alleged assailant was a black man—did not always lead to mob violence in the 1880s. In 1884 an unidentified man broke into the "residence of a widow lady" in Marlin and "attempted to commit an outrage on her." After the widow gave an alarm the "brute" fled. Although the story received front-page coverage in the *Waco Daily Examiner,* authorities soon gave up the search for the assailant because the victim was unable to identify her attacker.[93]

Two years later, on 27 March 1886, the *Waco Daily Examiner* reported that Maggie Schuster, a young German "ignorant of the ways of the wicked world," was the victim of "some brute's vile desires." In a detailed and well-placed article the *Examiner* told readers that the likely suspect was a "bright mulatto" barber named Tom Burney. Schuster had spoken to Burney several times on the street and had visited with him in her room before the incident. Schuster, however, "thought all the time that Burney was a white boy." When warned of his race and his "vile intentions," though, she began to shun Burney. Unlike the attack on Mrs. Horn more than a decade earlier, police authorities worked swiftly to locate and jail Burney.[94] Burney, however, was not lynched. In fact, he did not even go to prison. The case eventually ended in a hung jury.[95]

When seen in light of the attention devoted to sexual assault in the 1870s, Burney's story revealed heightened sensitivity to the charge of sexual assault. The assault was detailed in the local newspaper, and Burney was quickly arrested. Yet his ultimate fate proved that white central Texans still treated the charge of rape with some degree of discretion. No mob lynched Tom Burney, and authorities eventually set him free.

Such was not the case with Bill Harris, the second alleged rapist to be lynched in central Texas. Just after dusk on 3 August 1886 hundreds gathered near Whitehall church in rural McLennan County to wreck "swift and terrible vengeance" upon Harris, a black porter from Waco. He had been identified by Mrs. Fred A. Heitmeiller as the man who assaulted and robbed her. Although some members of the gathering mob attempted to bring Harris to Waco for imprisonment and trial, a "throng of men" with "blazing eyes and set lips" wrested the alleged criminal from these guards. He was taken to a grove behind the church, where the mob placed a rope around his neck. "Hundreds of willing hands" helped pull the "negro ravisher" off his feet and waited until his "death rattle had ceased to gurgle in his throat." Harris's body remained suspended from the tree all night, a public reminder of the punishment awaiting those who would violate central Texas's social order.[96]

Harris and Hadley were not alone. Although there had been no recorded lynchings for sexual assault for many years following emancipation, the hangings of Bill Harris and Zeke Hadley inaugurated a new trend. Between 1884 and 1897 white mobs in central Texas lynched ten black men for rape. One of the alleged criminals was Henry Davis, whom a white mob, more than one hundred persons strong, lynched on 18 July 1889. Davis's crime was "laying his hands" on the young wife of a Robinson farmer. Although the young black man fled when she screamed, a mob of whites pursued him. Dressed in long robes, their faces concealed, the mob took the prisoner from law officers, hanged him near a black church, and then shot the body full of bullets. As a final touch a note was pinned to the body: "Take Warning! Executed by 150 men for seven attempts to rape white women!" How the mob defined "attempts to rape white women" is unknown.[97] Although a white newspaper reported that opinion "in the Robinson neighborhood is said not to be unanimous in regard to the guilt of Davis," such information did not spur much investigation into the identity of the mob's leaders. The inquest resulted in the verdict that the crime was committed by "persons unknown."[98]

By the end of the century, central Texas had developed a culture of violence that condoned and supported the lynching of black men accused of raping white women. In 1886 the *Waco Day* urged readers to spare the county "the tedium and delay of a formal trial" when Bill Harris was captured.[99] In 1888 the *Waco Evening News* commented that the "law's slow delay seems unable to cope with the monstrous practice of intermarriage between whites and blacks, and hence the operation of a higher sovereignty."[100] In 1892 the *Waco Weekly News* reported that "justly enraged neighbors and friends" of a murdered man would spare McLennan County "the expense of a criminal prosecution" should the black men who committed the "hellish deed" be caught.[101] In 1893 newspaper editor J. N. Bennett wrote that "negroes themselves provoke lynching by their brutal crimes, the *News* does not approve of lynch law, but, at the same time, it makes allowances for the acts of men maddened by passion and outraged feelings."[102] In 1898 the *Waco Times-Herald* noted that a black man had attacked a white woman on 16 February. "Should the negro be caught," the newspaper predicted, "it is quite likely that a hanging bee will be held in Waco."[103] In addition to support from the region's white newspapers, lynch mobs consistently found sympathy among central Texas's civil officials. Juries called out to investigate lynchings almost invariably failed to indict anyone involved.

As central Texans became increasingly obsessed with the crime of sexual assualt, almost all attention focused on alleged black rapists. White men charged with sexual assault did not often arouse public anger. In 1892, for example, a white postmaster, A. L. Scott, was charged with attempted rape. Had Scott been black, his crime would have been blazed across the headlines of local newspapers, and he likely would have been hanged without much delay. But Scott was not black. So the newspaper reported the case under the headline "A Grave Charge" and wrote that "the public should withhold judgment till he has had a fair and impartial trial and not jump at the conclusion of his guilt simply because he is charged."[104] In 1895 William Holmes was indicted for attempted rape of a girl under the age of twelve. He was found guilty of aggravated assault and fined $30.[105] The sharply contrasting attitudes of central Texans toward white and black rapists underline how racialized lynching was in the late nineteenth century.

* * *

Growing concern over alleged African American rapists during the 1880s and 1890s was not limited to central Texans. Especially in the South, the late nineteenth century was beset with white paranoia on the topic. Many explanations have been offered to explain this development. At the time, white southerners claimed they were reacting to a black crime wave, a viewpoint several central Texans endorsed. Among them was John W. Stevens. "Insanity was almost unknown among the negroes in slavery," wrote Stevens, but there "must be insane asylums in every Southern state now for the colored insane." Stevens claimed that "the younger generation of negroes" were "already the most criminal class in our population" and had developed a "mania" for "assaulting white women," a "new crime" that Stevens assured readers "was unheard of in slavery."[106]

Historians have successfully questioned the "sudden black crime wave" explanation for the rise of lynching in the 1890s. Instead, scholars at various times have linked lynching to the release of white frustrations and aggression, to the success or failure of the cotton economy, to deep psychological problems about race and gender among white southerners, and to the legacy of honor and patriarchy in the South.[107] There is little doubt that all those factors played some role, but what has been overlooked or downplayed is equally important: grassroots resistance by African Americans.

Although white authorities rarely sought to prevent the lynching of blacks or even to punish whites who orchestrated mob violence, African Americans in central Texas took steps to protect themselves. Their successes and failures are among the most important but least studied stories in the late-nineteenth-century South.[108]

Most scholars do not believe that blacks could sustain serious organized resistance to white power in the late nineteenth century. For resistance to lynching, most historians have turned to one of two places. First, they have focused on black efforts to resist white degradation by creating "an increasingly separate institutional and cultural life." This independent black culture provided subtle opportunities to resist white authority through religion, work, music, and humor.[109] Second, numerous scholars have focused on the antilynching campaigns led by twentieth-century national organizations such as the National Association for the Advancement of Colored People, the Commission for Interracial Cooperation, and the Southern Women's Society for the Prevention of Lynching.[110] Both forms of resistance deserve significant historical attention, but by concentrating on them so exclusively scholars have reinforced the idea that overt, local black resistance did not exist in the postwar South.[111]

One form of local resistance to lynching that has been acknowledged is flight.[112] Blacks began organizing to leave central Texas soon after the end of Reconstruction, and in 1877 the Colored Emigration Society called a meeting at Howard Institute in Waco to discuss establishing a black colony in another portion of Texas.[113] A few blacks in the region considered leaving the United States entirely by settling in Mexico or in parts of Africa.[114] No evidence survives of these groups' efforts to leave central Texas together, but many individual blacks left the Lone Star State, settling instead in places like Kansas, Oklahoma, and the Indian Territories.[115] Immigration from lynch-prone central Texas was the result of several different factors, but mob violence and insistence on black subordination played their roles.[116]

Unlike flight, scholars have rarely associated participation in local politics with black resistance after Reconstruction. The assumption has been that such participation disappeared in the wake of the violent harassment leveled against blacks during the collapse of Republican rule in the 1870s.[117] Central Texas's white leadership understood that to be far from true. "White people," warned the *Waco Daily Advance*, "do not delude yourselves with the fanciful, lulling belief that the masses of negroes will never endorse such measures."[118] Although continuing intimidation made political life especially challenging, African Americans did not retreat from political participation in the mid-1870s. Some worked to revive the party of Lincoln. Others embraced newly created third parties. Still others threw their support behind the Democratic candidates they deemed most sympathetic to black interests.

The Republican Party survived in central Texas during the late nineteenth century largely on the loyalty of the region's African Americans. Year after disappointing year, in the 1870s, 1880s, and 1890s, blacks returned to the polls to reaffirm their right to suffrage and show electoral support for Republican candidates. Even when it became clear that that the unification of the white majority behind the Democrats made victory for their candidates highly unlikely, blacks continued to cast their ballots.[119]

Although most felt some degree of loyalty to Republicans, some were more than willing to join other political organizations. In 1878 black central Texans joined a small number of local whites in supporting the Greenback Party in local elections. Seventy-five black and thirty-six white delegates met in August at the McLennan County courthouse to nominate candidates for county elections. An October barbecue organized by Thomas Nelson, chair of the party's black supporters, attracted some 1,200 African Americans and a small number of whites such as former Republican David F. Davis. Despite numerous attempts to harass the Greenback campaign, many local blacks managed to vote in November's county election. They did so by approaching the polls as a group.

Greenbackers, however, only attracted a small percentage of local whites. The vast majority continued to support the Democratic Party, resulting in a victory for the Democrats by a margin of two to one.[120] Another third-party effort that saw blacks and whites join hands in central Texas was the Prohibition Party during the 1880s. According to an optimistic black orator at a prohibition rally in 1885, African Americans were "ready and willing to join hands with the whites in the cause of prohibition" and prepared "to break down the republican and democratic parties in order to clear the field for the fight against the whiskey demon."[121]

The most famous third party in the late-nineteenth-century South, the Populist Party, also drew black supporters. The Farmer's Alliance rose to prominence in central Texas during the mid-1870s, but until at least 1888 the local alliance in McLennan County did not allow blacks to join.[122] During this early period the Alliance used its influence to support political candidates who favored agricultural interests. By the early 1890s, however, the Alliance had developed into the Populist Party, and in their struggle to defeat the entrenched Democratic Party, Populists began active recruitment of black voters. Although the number and influence of black Populists was limited in the state, McLennan County was one of the few centers of their organizing.[123] Populists won few victories in central Texas, however, and gained little political power in the region.

When the third-party coalitions failed to be serious threats to the dominance of the white majority, blacks in central Texas willingly worked within the Democratic Party. In fact, black Wacoans agitated in favor of the primary system because they believed it would allow them a voice in the nomination of Democratic candidates. On 16 May 1890 the *Waco Weekly News* announced that it opposed the switch to the primary system because "negroes could participate in the nominations in primaries while in a convention they could not."

When blacks did have opportunity to choose among several white candidates, they made their voice known. Gov. James Hogg won the support of many for his hard-line stance against lynching. L. M. Sublett, a central Texas black leader, argued in 1892 for the support of the incumbent Hogg. "In my judgment," he noted, "he has been governor of the whole people and not of any class; he has not discriminated in favor of railways, rich corporations and monied syndicates; he has enforced the laws, causing them to bear equally upon all alike,—rich and poor, black and white." Sublett concluded that although Hogg was "a straight democrat, he is honest and able, and I prefer to support him with his consistent and manly record."[124] Many blacks joined Sublett in this election and, according to some election observers, gave Hogg his margin of victory over Wacoan George Clark, a former Confederate and long-time friend of Richard Coke. The editor of the *Waco Day* bitterly remarked that "the patriotism, decency, and refinement of the state stood by Clark like a stone wall. Without the 'coon' and purchasable vote the governor would not have been in it at all."[125]

Despite the continued participation of African Americans in central Texas politics during the late nineteenth century, their political influence alone was never enough to counteract the region's continuing mob violence, end local legal discrimination, or clear many hurdles to black economic progress. Blacks in central Texas thus joined their political activities with a number of extrapolitical strategies, including work strikes and slowdowns, especially during cotton picking season. In 1900 one central Texas farmer remarked that the "negroes, that is many of them, who have been picking our cotton for us have demanded higher wages; they want 75 cents a hundred and in many instances 85, and we will not pay that much."[126] A few years later the local press reported that "cotton planters find that the negro field hands, in advance of the cotton picking season, are organizing unions."[127] Unfortunately, additional details of such labor agitation have not survived in the historical record.

Public protest was another significant form of black resistance during the late nineteenth century. In 1874, when the Houston and Texas Central Railway threw a black man named J. O. Ford off the train he was riding to Waco, Ford brought suit against the company.[128] In 1885 two black women unsuccessfully protested their removal from a section reserved for white women in the Garland House, a theater in Waco.[129] In 1905 several African Americans quit their jobs at a Waco hotel in protest over a recent lynching.[130]

Black central Texans also took the time to oppose racism in the local white press. H. T. Kealing, president of Waco's Paul Quinn College, an institution of higher learning founded by the African Methodist Episcopal Church, wrote to the *Waco Day* to protest that newspaper's reprinting of an article that labeled blacks an inferior race. Kealing noted the achievements of Egyptians; cited the names of black artists, writers, and inventors; and offered evidence that blacks in the United States were making considerable progress despite being only a generation removed from slavery.[131]

Unfortunately, such protests had little impact. Legal segregation on railroad cars continued, black women were denied the right to sit with white women in central Texas theaters, and a white man responded to Kealing with the prediction that black progress would doom the South to a "future where the elevation of the Ethiopian meets the degradation of the Anglo-Saxon, at last, in a seething, festering, rotting mass of mulattos fit only for organ grinders, banana sellers, and barbers."[132]

Black protest also risked encouraging reprisals and even higher levels of white-on-black violence, because white central Texans jealously guarded a double standard that treated blacks not just as a separate people but as second-class citizens. In 1878 two men, one white and one black, watched the legal execution of a white man from a Waco rooftop. The black man stood up after the execution and proclaimed his satisfaction that "de law bars eben all around." That simple declaration that the law should treat people equally so angered the white onlooker that he struck the black man with his fists and knocked him off the roof, injuring him.[133]

Because the double standards of white society rested on a foundation of violence, the most dangerous form of black resistance was self-defense. Scholars have yet to realize just how frequent such resistance was. In 1885 black onlookers—wary of another Sim Woods–like killing of an unarmed black by white police officers—helped a young black boy, John Matthews, escape arrest. When a policeman named Falwell attempted to arrest Matthews on an old charge, a nearby African American rushed to Matthews's aid and wrested the gun from the officer. When another white man attempted to help the policeman, "he was thrown to one side by a crowd of negroes." Before fleeing with Matthews, the black man gave the gun to a white onlooker, who later returned it to the officer. One member of the black crowd was arrested.[134]

Despite the dangers that such acts of resistance posed, spontaneous resistance occurred often. In 1898 in the city of Marlin in Falls County, for example, a pair of black men took action when a group of whites threw a stone into a black restaurant. Angry at such recurring attacks on black-owned businesses and homes, two men seated inside got up and confronted their white antagonists. The fight that erupted led to the paralysis of one of the white men. The two African Americans escaped lynching when the local sheriff hurried them out of the county.[135]

African Americans in rural areas also defended themselves from white attacks. At about the same time of the restaurant incident in Marlin, another black man injured a white attacker in rural Falls County. Roden Long, a farmer who "had just received notice from whitecaps to leave," shot a man who appeared on his doorstep at 2 on a Sunday morning. When a strange voice requested that Long open his door so he might stay the night or get a drink of water, Long declared "it was no place for a white man" and refused to allow entry. Soon after the exchange the force gathered outside attempted to break down the door to Long's house. He responded by taking his Winchester rifle and firing through the door, striking and injuring a white man. Police arrested Long the next day despite his belief that "there were other white men with this man and the object was to do him violence."[136]

Spontaneous acts of self-defense were probably more common, but black central Texans sometimes organized complicated plans of retaliation against belligerent whites. In 1889 reports reached Waco that sixty blacks living in the Brazos bottoms of McLennan County had organized themselves "with the avowed purpose of doing up three" of the men who orchestrated the lynching of Henry Davis.[137] No evidence remains that the group took action.

That, however, was not the case with the black men who protested the lynching of Charles Beall in Falls County two years later. On 2 January 1891 a mob of some two hundred white men hanged Beall, one of four black men accused of assaulting and robbing Mrs. Joseph Fisher in Lang, Falls County. Not satisfied with the lynching of one of the four alleged criminals, the mob continued to search for the others. In the wake of Beall's lynching, the black community of Falls County organized to defend itself. "The negroes around Lang have organized and are breathing threats against the whites" reported the *Waco Daily News* on January 5. In fact, a daring trio of black men had already struck back. During the night of 4 January, three shot George Taylor, "whom the negroes accused of leading the lynchers," and left him bleeding to death on the doorstep of his home. They then fled the region for parts unknown, possibly Mexico.[138]

Whites in central Texas were outraged by Taylor's murder. "George Taylor, because he had the manhood to lead his fellows to the defense of the life and virtue of his white sisters . . . [was] shot down under cover of darkness by a party of negroes to avenge the death of one of their black brothers," cried a local paper.[139] Whites quickly organized to avenge Taylor. Conjuring up an image of a racial massacre, the *Waco Daily News* reported that the "farmers and ranchmen are under arms for miles around and it is expected that there will be more dead negroes in the Pond Creek valley than were dead Indians at Wounded Knee."[140] White mobs estimated to number between five hundred to a thousand prepared to enter the black community and lynch the three men who allegedly aided Beall in the robbery and the men who murdered Taylor.[141]

Blacks, however, were determined to defend themselves. One white newspaper reported that blacks around Lang, even after Taylor's murder, were "noisy and violent."[142] They were said to have "the upper hand" in the confrontation with the white mob, especially after blacks from other towns came to the defense of Lang's black community. The local white press reported that the blacks congregated in Falls County intended "to abet the outragers, or to shield them from lynching." The black mob made its intentions clear. "If it were necessary this correspondent could furnish affidavits of fifty good citizens who saw them [and] heard them explain their mission."[143]

At least in this case, a show of black militance forced whites to stand down, and no additional mob violence occurred in the region after Taylor's murder. White policemen captured the other three black men accused of the assault on Mrs. Fisher and escorted them safely out of the region. Apparently, the black men who killed Taylor were never found or punished. Those who had come to the region to protect the black community left the area, having apparently succeeded in deterring additional white mob violence. That a group of blacks could murder a white man in his own home and escape both legal and extralegal punishment undermines any picture of a victimized, powerless, cowering black community in late-nineteenth-century central Texas. Yet such acts of black retaliation were rare—and the safe escape of defiant blacks was even rarer.[144]

The story of Abe Phillips reveals that for most local African Americans the cost of black resistance to white authority could be very high. Phillips and his brother, Wesley, fell into a dispute with a white neighbor named Philip Arnold in the middle of April 1895. In a gun battle between the three men, Arnold and Abe Phillips both suffered fatal bullet wounds. Angry at Arnold's death, local whites decided that the Phillips family had to be sent a message about resisting white authority—despite the fact that Abe Phillips had also been killed and the sheriff of Falls County had arrested and jailed Wesley Phillips. A three-month wave of terrorism against the Phillips family ended on 20 July 1895 when an unknown party of whites placed a dynamite bomb in Phillips's house. Heard for miles around, the explosion killed Abe Phillips's widow, Mary; three children; and two black men who were staying at the house. Another unidentified man was critically injured and later died.[145] The explosion was so powerful that, a local German-language newspaper reported, it killed birds in the area.[146]

The murder of an entire family, however, failed to intimidate local blacks intent on resisting white authority. "In a specially-called meeting, Negroes [in Falls and McLennan] counties stated that the whole incident was a 'deliberate conspiracy on the part of several white men to exterminate the family.' Many blacks expressed their determination not to pick cotton in the precincts near the explosion."[147] Whites became so worried about the black strike that they offered a reward for the capture of the men who planted the bomb, and authorities released Wesley Phillips from jail. Nevertheless, the parties who orchestrated one of the most deadly acts of mob violence in the history of central Texas never faced justice.

* * *

The nineteenth century ended on a gloomy note for most African Americans in central Texas. The great changes wrought by emancipation had not entirely disappeared, but the meaning of that freedom had been greatly limited. Despite considerable effort and resistance on the part of local blacks, the greatest continuity in their lives between 1865 and 1900 was not slow progress toward full and equal citizenship but rather thirty-five years of resilient racial violence.

If anything, racial violence was worse during the last decade of the nineteenth century. Although central Texas leaders criticized mobs that lynched Anglos, they praised vigilantes who executed African Americans. Black resistance to white supremacy and violence was a primary spur to the era's violence, but white mobs chose to portray their actions as necessary in combating a "new crime": the rape of white women by black men. Escalating fear of black rapists spurred greater and greater numbers of central Texans to participate in the region's culture of extralegal violence. Like the "Indian fighters" who settled the region a generation earlier, central Texans justified their actions as necessary to defending their households and families. That call to defend the honor of white womanhood resonated with thousands, and during the twentieth century lynch mobs in central Texas swelled to unprecedented numbers. The execution of African Americans became an increasingly ritualized spectacle of community violence.

7. "A Damnable Outrage": Mob Violence in Twentieth-Century Central Texas

On 7 August 1905 a mob of five to six hundred white central Texans lynched a black man for the alleged rape of a white woman named Clintie ("Benny") Robert. For ten days after the alleged sexual assault, the chief suspect, a twenty-year-old named Sank Majors, eluded law officers until finally being captured at his brother's home. Although sentiments for mob violence no doubt existed even then, Majors received a trial in Waco on 2 August. At the trial, the victim could not identify Majors by his face but swore that the scar on his hand was the same one possessed by her attacker. The police obtained a confession that became the key evidence offered at the trial. In less than three minutes the jury returned a verdict of guilty and a recommendation for death. The court-appointed defense lawyer for Majors appealed. He noted that Judge Surratt had "failed to charge the jury that unless they believed the confessions of the defendant were made without compulsion or promises from the officers and without fear or hope on the part of the defendant, they should wholly disregard" the confessions.[1] Judge Marshall Surratt reluctantly agreed to set a new trial date for 9 August 1905. Angered by this judicial delay, whites planned to lynch Majors on the night of 7 August.[2]

When the mob came to Waco's city jail late that evening, they were armed and silent. They carried crowbars and sledgehammers and were not dissuaded by local officials' pleas to await the trial. As one told a reporter, "We are for protection of the women of our country, even to the extent of our lives and our liberty."[3] Using their sledgehammers, members of the mob broke through five steel doors. When they broke through the last barrier, officers fought them "hand-to-hand" and with "blows of fists."[4] This remarkable resistance failed, and the mob dragged Majors from his cell. They proceeded to the city square, where preparations were under way to burn him. As the mob headed to the square one man quipped, "New trial granted, and change of venue from Waco to Hell."[5]

The mob tied Majors to a stake in the center of the town square and prepared to burn him, but Majors's alleged victim, Robert, asked that he be hanged, not burned. The mob cut him loose and took him to the Washington Street Bridge, where they secured a noose around his neck. After being set upon a horse, mob members led the horse away and Majors dropped. Angry men and—according to one account—a woman stabbed the body with knives. Several men cut off fingers as souvenirs. The rope used to hang Majors was sliced into short pieces and distributed among those who led the lynching. An hour after the crowd dispersed Waco law officers (who had witnessed the lynching) removed the remains.[6]

At first glance it is difficult to perceive the importance of the lynching of Sank Majors. In the previous half-century, central Texas had hosted numerous acts of mob violence and vigilantism. The size of the mob, the charge of rape, and the complicity of law officers all conformed to patterns of racial violence that had emerged during the late nineteenth century. On closer inspection, however, the murder of Majors was far more complicated. Sank Majors was the first victim of extralegal violence in central Texas in eight years, and his lynching initiated a new era of racial violence in the region.

Between 1897 and 1905 there is no evidence of an act of mob violence in central Texas. A region rich with a history of vigilantism suddenly abandoned the practice. Such a development is even more remarkable when one considers that racial violence flourished during this same period in many other parts of the nation. Lynching continued even in other parts of Texas. According to the records of Tuskegee University, mobs in the Lone Star State lynched more than fifty persons between the extralegal executions of black central Texans Wesley Johnson in 1897 and Sank Majors in 1905.[7]

The murder of Sank Majors was not an isolated case. His lynching was not the exception that proved mob violence was on the decline. Rather, the event marked the return of racial violence. After 1905 mob attacks on African Americans reemerged in central Texas with unprecedented ferocity, and fourteen African Americans were lynched in little more than a decade. No longer content to merely hang a suspected criminal, mobs in the early twentieth century began to burn and torture them. At the same time, the size of mobs grew, routinely numbering in the thousands. That vicious turn of events climaxed with the lynching of Jesse Washington in 1916.

For nearly a decade central Texas was a powerful example of how local leaders and officials could thwart mob violence, even in a region where lynching was ingrained in historical memory and seen as a vital resource for maintaining order. Subsequently, however, central Texas became internationally renowned for lawlessness, racism, torture, and brutality. The momentary fall and the vicious return of racial violence is a complicated story involving national and regional developments peculiar to the early-twentieth-century United States. Key factors included changing immigration patterns, demographic shifts, technological changes, formalization of disfranchisment, implementation of rigid residential segregation, and the rise of a new consumer culture. At the same time, the history of lynching in early-twentieth-century Texas underscores the importance of the immediate local context. Indeed, the region's racial violence combines many central themes of this book: the role of grass-roots black resistance, the place of historical memory, and the impact of the courts and local officials.

* * *

To understand the absence of mob violence in central Texas between 1897 and 1905 it is necessary to explore what happened between 1895 and 1897, when racial violence exploded in the area and at least twelve African Americans died at the hands of "parties unknown." One lynching in particular, the murder of a young black man by whitecappers in 1896, provoked protest from local authorities. During the dead of night of 19 August a band of masked men approached a hut on a farmstead in the McLennan County community of Hillside. Sleeping inside were five African American cotton pickers employed by James Kendrick. The masked mob roused the men with gunfire, shooting and killing Anderson Vaughn. Armed with whips and leather straps, the mob beat "to a brutal degree" the remaining four men and told them to flee. They ran for their lives. Satisfied, the mob retreated, leaving Vaughn's corpse for the authorities.[8]

The fact that this whitecapping episode included the shooting of a black man was not unusual. What was unusual was the reaction the murder generated. Local authorities clearly resented the act of racial violence. The sheriff and the justice of the peace conducted an investigation, and the local newspaper reported the attack under the headline "A Damnable Outrage." The strongest action taken, however, came from the Fifty-fourth District Court representing McLennan and Falls counties. Instructing the grand jury, Judge Samuel R. Scott ordered an investigation into the region's racial violence. "The worst stain on the fair name of the county," said Judge Scott, "was the whitecapping case." Jurors were not to let the "prominence of the parties who might be concerned" shield them from investigation, warned Scott, because the "treatment given the Hillside negroes was outrageous and should be investigated to the very bottom." Moreover, "the men who did the whitecapping were ten times worse than the victims of their wrath" and the "country should be rid of them at all costs."[9]

The grand jury complied with Scott's plea and indicted ten men for the murder of Anderson Vaughn. In the previous half-century, central Texas courts had rarely indicted anyone for an act of mob violence. Although they had never indicted a white man for lynching a black man, in 1896 they indicted ten. The case was dismissed because, after a year's search, the four African Americans who suffered from the mob could not be located to testify. The failure of the courts to convict the mob should not obscure the significance of the grand jury's action. They stripped the masks from the ten men and issued a powerful warning to those who might consider mob violence in the future. It is not a coincidence that nearly nine years elapsed before another lynching was reported in McLennan County.[10]

There are two important reasons for the strong reaction to the whitecapping of Anderson Vaughn. First, the episode followed a particularly gruesome episode of racial violence a year earlier. The bombing of the Phillips home in 1895 resulted in the deaths of seven persons, including a mother and her daughter. The carnage warned of the dangers of uncontrolled mob violence and no doubt worried local white leaders. Second, evidence suggests that whitecappers murdered Vaughn not because he had committed a particular criminal act but because he and his friends threatened to pick cotton more cheaply than others in central Texas. Although white mobs had murdered African Americans over labor disputes in the past, they had usually acted to intimidate those who were recalcitrant. This case was different. Many central Texans viewed the attack as an assault on the business rights of James Kendrick, the white farmer who employed Vaughn. Genuine outrage at the brutal murder of innocent blacks thus combined with anger over the attempt to use violence to limit the supply of workers in the region. The result was the indictment of Vaughn's murderers.

At the turn of the century, the central Texas court system showed signs of improving on a decades-old history of racial bias. Beginning with the surprising indictment of the ten white men for lynching Anderson Vaughn in 1896, the courts' treatment of African Americans startled many. Judge Scott in particular continued to shock white Wacoans. In 1904 he dismissed a burglary case against a black man named Henry Green after learning that the police had beaten a confession out of him. The local white newspaper endorsed Scott's decision, arguing that it "makes no difference that the victim was a negro [because] the next victim of police brutality may be another negro or it may be a white man."[11] Although such logic hardly eschewed racism, the motion was a clear improvement over earlier practices.

The most famous turn-of-the-century case involving black legal rights was the trial of Will King, a black Wacoan accused of killing a white police officer. In many communities King would not have lived long after 28 October 1900, the day he shot and killed William Mitchell, who was off-duty at the time. Thanks to the prevailing feelings against mob law in central Texas, however, King's case was allowed to come to trial. Once before the courts, he benefited from the expert legal counsel of a team of lawyers and activists, both white and black. Attorneys Charles Sparks and Wilford H. Smith headed the defense effort. Sparks, a white northerner, was a respected lawyer described by the local press as "an old citizen, well and favorably known."[12] Smith, an African American from Texas, was described by the black press as "an instrument of honor in the uplift of the race."[13] Two key witnesses for the defense included a black woman named Celeste Mitchell and a black man, N. E. Anderson.[14]

When King's case began in November, his lawyers immediately motioned that both the grand jury indictment and the trial were unfair and unconstitutional. On 8 November his attorneys charged that the jury commissioners had "excluded" all "persons of color, or of African descent, known as negroes, because of their race and color."[15] The prosecution responded by taking the curious position that "no special discrimination" existed against King because blacks had not been on any juries in the county for twenty-five years or more. The defense's motion was overruled, and King was sentenced to death. But his lawyers had made an unprecedented attack on one of the bastions of white supremacy, the all-white jury.[16]

Sparks and the rest of the legal team did not give up. They appealed for a new trial. Once again they charged discrimination in the selection of both the grand and petit juries, and this time testimony was solicited from jury commissioners. One testified that when "I came to a one I knew to be a darkey, I skipped them because I knew he was a darkey and it was not customary to put them on the jury." Another commissioner and a former sheriff testified that "when I came to a name marked colored, I passed it by."[17]

After much consideration Judge Scott granted a new trial on the basis that no blacks had been considered for the juries that indicted and convicted King. Scott claimed that based on the testimony before him, precedents set down by the Supreme Court and the Texas state court of appeals, he had little choice.[18] In January, for the first time since Reconstruction, ten blacks were part of the venire from which the new jury was selected.[19] One African American—A. J. Moore, an educator—sat on the second grand jury. Although the second petit jury contained no African Americans, the trial nevertheless resulted in a hung jury. One juror, George Lambin, refused to support the death penalty and favored only a ten-year sentence because he believed the defense argument that King was temporarily insane.[20]

At this point, for the first time in King's legal case, the white public began to cry for him to be lynched. "Most people were dissatisfied with the verdict in the King case" understated the *Waco Weekly Tribune*. The sheriff temporarily avoided trouble by removing King from the city.[21] As preparations for a third trial began, local newspaper editor A. R. McCollum wrote that if "the negro Will King is brought back here for trial and is lynched nobody need experience surprise [because this case] has aroused public feeling to an unusual degree."[22]

With King absent, frustrated whites turned on the legal team defending him. An angry justification of mob law appeared in the newpaper on 9 February 1901. "By the efforts of a tricky lawyer and a chicken-hearted juror, this case is put off from time to time, negro jurors are foisted upon the people of this county for the first time in twenty-five years, and threats of mob violence are heard on every side," observed a correspondent from McLennan County. If "mob law is necessary to purify the moral atmosphere of the courts in this county," he continued, "let them give a liberal dose of Manila hemp to a certain class of shysters and jurors."[23] Defense witness Celeste Mitchell maintained "that she had been threatened on more than one occasion if she did not desist in her efforts in this case."[24]

Mitchell and the others did not give in to pressure. In fact, they went further, protesting that the token African American representation provided in the second trial did not go far enough. "One-fourth of the population of this county is composed of negroes" charged the defense, and King was "entitled to be tried by a grand jury composed proportionately" of his race.[25] The motion failed, and King's third trial ended in the death sentence. The defense launched yet another appeal, arguing that "the defendant could not get a fair and impartial trial in the county" because of the atmosphere created by McCollum's threatening editorial and other warnings of possible mob violence. Lambin testified for the defense that his life had been threatened on the previous jury for refusing to change his verdict.[26] Sparks also noted that the court erred in failing to authorize a change of venue and in allowing the prosecution to draw conclusions and lead witnesses. The defense's best efforts, however, had no impact this time. Judge Scott overruled all appeals. On 25 October 1901 Will King was legally hanged.[27]

Many blacks in central Texas would have agreed that King was guilty of murder, but they no doubt knew that his execution was intimately tied to his race. Even the local white newspaper admitted that others would have gotten off on the same evidence and that "a calm and impartial analysis of the tragedy leaves no other lesson than that it was mainly due to drink craze and the too-common practice of carrying deadly weapons."[28] Despite such sober

reasoning, local whites continued to favor a legal system that meted out justice to black wrong-doers while simultaneously doling out leniency for white
criminals.

Although the accomplishments of the King trial were bittersweet at best
for the defense team and King's family, they indicated that white lawyers and
white judges were willing to extend more legal rights to blacks than had been
the case in more than a quarter of a century. Even more important, they
helped set a number of precedents in favor of black legal rights in McLennan County. Before Will King's execution, his case had already led to blacks
being considered for grand juries. In at least two cases in 1901 a black juror
was actually one of the final selections for a McLennan County grand jury,
something that had not happened since Reconstruction in central Texas. Although Sparks and his fellow lawyers were unable to save King's life, they
forced local whites to face some of the inequalities of their legal system.[29]

Blacks throughout Texas and the United States cheered the King trial. The
African Methodist Episcopal Church Review heaped praise on Waco and remarked that the killing of a white police officer by a black man normally
inflamed "the most violent prejudice," but in this case "the prisoner was not
lynched" and had even been given a new trial "because no Negroes were in
the [jury] box."[30] Fifteen years later African Americans throughout the United
States would come to have a very different view of race relations in Waco.

* * *

Central Texans had avoided mob law for eight years. Why did racial violence
and lynching return in 1905? The leaders of the mob that lynched Sank Majors would surely have emphasized the alleged crime committed. White men
in the early-twentieth-century South believed that the rape of a white woman
required defense of their honor and reaffirmation of masculine authority.
The crime in this case, however, was not the sole cause of the lynching. No
mob lynched Lee Robinson, the African American sentenced to 1,001 years
in prison for the rape of a white woman a few months before Majors was
lynched. And Sank Majors, it should be noted, did not face the danger of
lynching until he was granted a second trial.

The chain of events that led to the lynching of Sank Majors probably
began not in the farmhouse where he was alleged to have assaulted Mrs.
Robert but in the courtroom, where four years earlier Will King's lawyers
had assaulted white supremacy. There can be little doubt that the legal struggles of Will King's defense team greatly angered local white residents. Some
were probably also angry that a mob did not lynch King when he was granted
a new trial. Four years later it seems almost certain that central Texans had

not forgotten King's trial and the successful appeals of his lawyers. Whatever their reasoning, they worked quickly to make sure that Sank Majors, unlike Will King, never reached a second trial. The reporter who covered the story for the *Dallas Morning News* noted that the lynching must be "ascribed" to the "new trial" because the mob began to organize as soon as "it became known that a legal hitch" had developed.[31]

In the wake of the lynching central Texans seemed pleased with the work of the mob, certain that the region's black population needed a vivid lesson that assaults on white women would not go unpunished because of a judicial technicality. The Sank Majors lynching was deemed reasonable and justified. Even Majors's defense attorney concurred when he claimed, "I am a white man and a Southern man, and that is all that need be said. Had I been one of the crowd that hunted him before his capture I have no doubt I would have helped kill him."[32] It was the *Waco Weekly Tribune*'s opinion that it "was just, it was right, it was imperative that he die."[33] The *Waco Times-Herald* argued that "the act was justifiable—fully so, in all respects."[34]

The key issues concerning lynching in central Texas converge in the lynching of Sank Majors. First, the connection between lynching and historical memory is clear in Majors's murder. The men who participated in the lynch mob of 1905 grew up in a world that praised their fathers and grandfathers by reciting tales of battles with Indians and honoring strong men who had taken the law into their own hands for the safety of the community. To these well-established memories the young men of central Texas now added recent memories of a judicial system too lenient and tolerant of black civil rights. Memories of past vigilantism in general, and memories of the trial of Will King in particular, helped create the mob that lynched Sank Majors.

Second, black resistance was also critical. The trial of Will King mattered so much to white central Texans because it represented a serious attack on white supremacy. The lawyers and activists in the King trial had come remarkably close to toppling such bastions of segregation as the all-white jury. When one white juror agreed with the defense's argument and refused to sentence King to death, the defense had opened a small crack in the white unity that had largely prevailed since Reconstruction.

The third issue that was so critical in Majors's lynching and the subsequent wave of mob violence in the area was the role of local officials and leaders. Not only did the law stand idly by while viewing the lynching but authorities, by failing to indict or punish members of the mob, also helped ensure that the event was not an isolated incident. Emboldened by that lack of censure, white central Texans inaugurated a new era of racial violence.

In the years following the death of Sank Majors, mobs of whites in central

Texas hanged, burned, and shot many more blacks. In April 1906 a white mob searching for an African American who had entered the room of a young white woman came across Lincoln Porter near Groesbeck in Limestone County and shot and killed him without even bringing him before his alleged victim for identification.[35] A few months later, a group of white men in Falls County hanged a black man named Mitchell Frazier for cutting a white man named Frank Hess in a fight.[36] The mob was not satisfied, however, with lynching Frazier. One white man attacked a black man who had argued that Frazier had a right to defend himself. The black man narrowly survived the encounter despite having his face cut nearly from ear to ear.[37] The mob continued its rampage by corralling three black girls, who, the local white press reported, were "seized and beaten and used in such a manner that they were glad to be released and allowed to go." The mob's actions soon drove out "all other Negroes in town."[38] A third lynching followed in 1909, when some fifty men in Falls County removed a black man named Coke Mills from his jail cell on the night of 20 December. While being arrested Mills had shot and seriously wounded a city marshal. The mob completed the lynching quickly and left his body hanging from the tower at the fire department.[39]

* * *

These acts of racial violence, also unchecked by local authorities, helped build and intensify central Texas's increasingly brutal culture of mob violence. The lynching of Jesse Washington, however, must also be understood in light of the region's shifting demographic character during the early twentieth century. The movements of thousands of people—black, white, and Mexican—were transforming Waco and its surrounding countryside.

The most obvious demographic change was the growth of the city itself. The regional economy of central Texas, like many parts of urbanizing America, was becoming increasingly centered on its largest city, and the migration of area farmers to Waco had begun to produce a density of population never before seen in the region. In 1890 it was the largest city in the seven counties of central Texas, with a population of not quite fifteen thousand. By 1920 the city had swelled to 38,500.[40] The racial and ethnic dimension of central Texas's demographic transformation, however, may have been even more important than urbanization in providing the unsettling backdrop to racial violence after 1910.

Migration into and out of central Texas was not new. What may have been new was the connection between the migrations of blacks and Mexicans and racial violence. The early-twentieth-century movement of African Americans was, at least in part, a reaction to central Texas's history of racial violence. The return of lynching appears to have been the last straw for a number of area blacks. After the lynching of Sank Majors, a group of black hotel workers quit in a mass protest.[41] A black man named Jim Lawyer spoke out against the mob violence and was visited by approximately twenty men on the night of 9 August and given 150 lashes with a whip. A resident stated that there was "not much danger of any of the Negroes who attend to their own business and keep their mouths shut being disturbed," but there were those who "must be checked by some means or other."[42]

Anger with the region's mob violence clearly accelerated the exodus of African Americans from central Texas, and more than ever left the region during the first decade of the twentieth century. Although black migrants continued to pour into Waco during the early twentieth century, it was more than balanced by those who left during the same period (table 9).

The surging black community and expanding economy of the city of Waco beckoned to many, but more than a few African Americans preferred to leave the region entirely, and by the early twentieth century they were doing so in record numbers. Between 1900 and 1910, for the first time in the history of central Texas, more blacks left Waco than arrived.

Table 9. Population of Waco by Race, 1870–1930, and Estimated Compounded Annual Rate of Growth, 1870–1930

Year	Black Pop.	Black Pop. Increase	Est. Black Pop.	Est. No. of Migrants	White Pop.	White Pop. Increase Attributable to Natural Increase	% Black of Total Pop.
1870	1,091	——	——	——	1,914	——	36.3
1880	2,562	1,471	150	1,321	4,729	2,815	35.1
1890	4,069	1,507	353	1,154	10,365	5,636	28.2
1900	5,818	1,749	561	1,188	14,839	4,474	28.1
1910	6,067	249	802	-553	20,333	5,494	23.0
1920	7,726	1,659	836	823	29,762	9,429	20.1
1930	9,370	1,644	1,065	579	41,171	11,409	17.7

Sources: Raw data of population increase compiled from *Ninth through Fourteenth Censuses of the United States, General Population Statistics* (Washington: Government Printing Office, 1872–1921); Ansley J. Coales and Norfleet W. Rives Jr., "A Statistical Reconstruction of the Black Population of the United States 1880–1970: Estimates of True Numbers by Age and Sex, Birth Rates, and Total Fertility," *Population Index* 39 (Jan. 1973): 26; the Coales-Demeny West Female Level 6 Model Life Table; Samuel Preston and Michael R. Haines, *Fatal Years: Child Mortality in Late-Nineteenth-Century America* (Princeton: Princeton University Press, 1991), 81–87.

Note: A 1.3 percent growth rate is used above and based on the difference between a 43.4 per thousand birth rate and a 30.5 per thousand death rate. The birth rate was estimated at 43.4 per thousand, the life expectation at 32.5 years, and the death rate at 30.5 per thousand.

Black out-migration was nothing new. At least as early as 1877 black central Texans had organized to fund and organize the creation of a colony outside the region.[43] In the early twentieth century, however, out-migration became much more commonplace. After noting that a thousand blacks had already left by 1902, one local newspaperman wrote that "it seems as if there is a wholesale emigration of the colored race from this part of the state."

The efforts of white and black leaders to slow the pace of out-migration amounted to little. "The exodus of the colored people from this city still continues," worried an observer, the "territories are the mecca and there is hardly a day but a large party does not leave."[44] Stories of better wages and dreams of better treatment continued to push many blacks to leave central Texas during the early twentieth century, an exodus that peaked during World War I in the Great Migration. "Many of our readers may not know it," reported the *Waco Semi-Weekly Tribune* on 30 June 1917, "but negro men are leaving Texas daily in groups of hundreds, going north."[45]

The labor shortage created by black out-migration was of great concern to local farmers and civic leaders. In the middle of 1903 central Texans feared that cotton picking prices would rise because during "the past ten months, a large number of able-bodied farm laborers, white and colored, have left McLennan County for homes or work elsewhere."[46] In 1917 a white newspaper noted that "Texas cannot afford to lose" so many African Americans because they "are part and parcel of the economic wealth of the state."[47]

The danger of racial violence was, of course, not the only reason black central Texans fled the region. They also sought better jobs in the booming economies of the North and West and left to join family members who had departed Texas years earlier. In the final analysis, however, intensifying discrimination and hardening segregation galvanized the black exodus. The return of racial violence in 1905 paralleled the erosion of gains in the legal system. Turning their back on the precedents established in the Will King case, central Texas courts returned to a policy of ignoring the rights of black defendants. The 1906 trial of a young black man named Jesse Jones serves as an example.

Local police in the city of Waco possessed few clues in the murder of white Jewish storekeeper, Mat Block. Nevertheless, an employee named Jesse Jones quickly became a suspect.[48] Without any material evidence, law officers needed a confession from Jones. They obtained one. Incredibly, the sheriff testified to his office's strategy at the trial: "When I was talking with the defendant we gave him some whisky; also told him that if he would confess we would protect him from the mob. We kept him up all night" and told him that "there was a crowd gathering downtown" and that it contained "too many men for that time of night." Another officer suggested that Jones should confess because "he might be in hell tomorrow night." That dubious confession became the centerpiece of the case against Jones.[49]

At the behest of an angered citizenry Waco officials quickly arranged for the trial and sentencing. During the trial, which was brief, the defense brought forth two witnesses who testified that Jones kept company with them during the time of the murder, testimony the judge and jury ignored. Jones, based on his coerced confession, was found guilty of Block's murder and sentenced to death by hanging on 25 September 1906. Two months later lawmen hanged him from a scaffold in downtown Waco as a throng of spectators looked on approvingly.[50] The way in which law officers carried out the investigation of Block's murder, their quick deduction of Jones's guilt, his sentencing on insufficient evidence, and the festival-like public hanging all suggest that Jones's trial was actually a "legal" lynching. His rights were discarded not by a howling mob on the streets of Waco but by local officials and an all-white jury inside a courtroom.[51]

Blacks in the region were certainly more likely to suffer Jesse Jones's fate than were whites. Even when black central Texas criminals survived their trials, however, they still suffered unequal treatment by the legal system. According to the findings of sociologist John Gordon, between 1880 and 1920 African Americans convicted of murder in McLennan County received an average sentence of fifty-one years in prison. Whites convicted of the same crime during the same period received an average prison sentence of twenty-nine years.[52]

Perhaps the most frustrating encounter with the law for black central Texans during the era was when a white bandit robbed the Farmers' Improvement Bank on 13 January 1927. Robert L. Smith's treasured creation was one of the region's most important African American institutions. Police arrested W. E. Ratliff for the crime. Despite the positive identification of Ratliff by the bank's black bookkeeper and corroborative testimony placing Ratliff at the scene of the crime from a city official, the all-white jury acquitted him on 11 April 1928. Although Smith had wisely taken out insurance, the failure of the judicial system to convict Ratliff greatly angered the local black community. A black who robbed a white bank, they had no doubt, would not have been acquitted on the same evidence. Ratliff's acquittal especially sapped the energy and optimism of those committed to improving themselves by developing and investing in their own institutions. The case of the Farmer's Improvement Bank was yet another sign that whites in central Texas did not favor a world where they and blacks were "separate but equal." More than ever, local blacks recognized that they lived under a system of racial apartheid where whites manipulated the legal and political system to maintain dominance.[53]

Given the situation it is not surprising that thousands of African American workers fled central Texas during the early twentieth century, and their loss created a crisis for the region's labor-heavy agricultural economy. Fortunately for local landlords, more cheap labor was readily available across the border. As a local observer noted, "In the place of the departing negroes are coming tens of thousands of Mexicans."[54]

Although Mexico had never ceased to influence the Texas prairie, very few central Texans in the late nineteenth century were born in Mexico. As late as 1900 the U.S. Bureau of the Census documented only 238 Mexican-born residents in seven central Texas counties (table 10). All that changed at the turn of the century. Between 1900 and 1930 central Texas's Mexican population increased rapidly. More than a thousand Mexicans moved to the region between 1900 and 1910, and more than three thousand arrived during the following decade.

By 1930, the first census year for which there are statistics for Mexican Americans born in the United States as well as those born in Mexico, the migration had begun to have an impact on race relations in central Texas, and nearly twelve thousand Mexicans lived there. In Falls County, Mexicans and Mexican Americans made up nearly 10 percent of the total population; Bosque County had one Mexican for every three African Americans. The impact of their arrival cannot be comprehended, however, from statistics alone. Mexican immigrants' impact on race relations surpassed their overall demographic impact because the vast majority were concentrated in jobs traditionally held by blacks. Lorenzo Greene, an African American bookseller who visited Waco in 1930, observed that "Mexicans have greatly cut Negro

Table 10. Population Born in Mexico for Seven Texas Counties, 1870–1920, and Mexican Population in Seven Texas Counties, 1930

Year	Bell	Bosque	Coryell	Falls	Hill	Limestone	McLennan	Total
1870	5	2	0	50	2	3	12	74
1880	30	2	0	23	0	4	6	65
1890	25	10	7	13	4	42	34	135
1900	82	6	48	27	11	47	17	238
1910	257	71	59	379	84	72	496	1,418
1920	717	159	107	1,283	387	556	1,502	4,711
1930	1,722	168	353	3,567	946	988	4,156	11,900

Source: Elizabeth Broadbent, "The Distribution of the Mexican Population in the United States," Ph.D. diss., University of Chicago, 1941.

working opportunities." They work for lower wages than blacks, he continued, and thus "nearly all the picking about Waco is done by Mexicans."[55]

How and why did these men and women decide to immigrate to central Texas? As with any important demographic change, there were a number of factors. Political and economic developments in Mexico played a key role. During the late nineteenth century, railroad construction and general industrial development attracted many farmers to northern Mexico. The growth of the Mexican population closest to the Texas border combined with the phenomenal growth of the American economy naturally helped increase migration to the United States. Unrest in Mexico was another factor. A report compiled by the U.S. government concluded that many Mexican immigrants came north because of "the intolerable living conditions in Mexico."[56]

During the nineteenth and early twentieth centuries most Mexican immigrants remained in south Texas. After 1910, however, more and more moved into the state's interior. One reason for doing so was the Mexican revolution, an event that triggered a decade of political and economic upheaval in both Mexico and south Texas.[57] Waco in particular became a meeting ground for Mexicans fleeing the racial violence of south Texas and the revolutionary violence of Mexico. One of the most famous was Jesús M. Rangel, a revolutionary supporter of the Mexican Liberal Party (PLM) and a member of the radical International Workers of the World (IWW). Rangel worked in the hotel and restaurant business in Waco while plotting his return to Mexico. From central Texas he supplied revolutionaries in Mexico with arms, ammunition, volunteers, and provisions until the U.S. Army captured one of Rangel's Mexico-bound expeditions in south Texas in 1913. When the court sentenced Rangel to life in prison and gave many of his men particularly long terms, Mexicans in Texas were outraged and protested.[58]

Some along the border suffered even more than Rangel and his men. After 1910 south Texas became an especially dangerous place for Mexican nationals and Mexican Americans.[59] Lynching and anti-Mexican mob violence had been a consistent characteristic of south Texas since the mid-nineteenth century, but such attacks exploded in the second decade of the twentieth century. In 1911, for example, a mob of a hundred Anglos beat, tortured, burned, and hanged a fourteen-year-old Mexican boy named Antonio Gomez in Thorndale, Texas. After murdering Gomez, the mob dragged his corpse through the streets of the town.[60]

Conditions deteriorated further after a series of raids by would-be Mexican revolutionaries in 1915. The raids sparked panic among the white population along the border. Texas Rangers and citizen posses went on a brutal binge of retaliation, summarily killing hundreds of Mexicans without due process of law. One of the most brutal acts of violence was the massacre of fifteen Mexican men at Porvenir on Christmas in 1917. Texas Rangers and U.S. soldiers took the men from their homes, beat them severely in an attempt to extract confessions from them, and then shot each in the head, point-blank.[61]

The Porvenir massacre has been especially well documented, but it was not an isolated incident. The lynching of Spanish speakers was a routine occurrence in south Texas. The *San Antonio Express* observed that the "finding of dead bodies of Mexicans, suspected for various reasons of being connected with the troubles, has reached a point where it creates little or no interest."[62] There are numerous stories of mobs, often with the aid of Anglo lawmen, taking Mexicans out of jail and executing them.[63] "The death toll among Mexican Americans cannot be determined with any precision" wrote a former deputy sheriff of Hidalgo County. "Twenty years later," he continued, "rows of skeletons with bullet holes in the skulls were still being found in the countryside."[64] As a result of such violence many Mexicans fled south Texas; most retreated back across the border, but some were drawn toward central Texas.

One of the ironies of central Texas history was that blacks and Mexican migrants passed there, one group leaving the region while the other entered. Both were in flight from the threat of mob violence, and central Texas, renowned for its brutal violence against blacks, offered many Mexicans a refuge.

White farmers in the region had actively sought Mexican laborers as early as the turn of the century. In the fall of 1900 the farmers, frustrated with a strike organized by black cotton pickers, began to look elsewhere for labor. "We have decided to let the negroes go and get other help," related one. After compiling a list of farmers who needed hired hands, a party left for San Antonio, hoping to return with three hundred Mexican laborers. Unfortunately for them, they arrived too late, having been outpaced by other prospective laborlords. The Texans served notice, however, to the local Mexican population that they would be welcomed in central Texas with work should they decide to go north in the future.[65] One migrant recalled that "the promising news was heard that there was a great demand for cotton picking hands in central Texas."[66]

During the coming years many followed such news to the fields of the Upper Brazos River valley. By 1925 Mexican workers were so important to the local economy that the *Waco News Tribune* railed at any attempt to block the northward flow of immigrants: "If the national lawmakers agree to [restrict Mexican immigration] where will the people of the southwest get their yearly supply of rough workers?" Central Texas landlords, the newspaper warned, "depended upon the willing hands of the Mexican wage earner."[67]

Many white landlords welcomed the cheap labor, but a number of central Texans worried openly about the social repercussions of Mexican immigration. W. P. Meroney, a Baylor University professor, warned that the "Mexican inrush" was transforming central Texas. "Are we to witness a change from the present fine intelligent admixture of city and country around Waco, to a condition of landlordism in the cities and peasants in the country?" he asked.[68] Meroney's comments reveal what Mexican immigrants quickly learned upon arrival: Local demand for Mexican labor did not mean that local whites would treat Mexican workers as social or political equals. The immigrants did not question that they would continue to suffer discrimination at the hands of the region's Anglos. What they did not know was the extent of that discrimination.

The treatment of Mexicans in Texas varied greatly by region. Mobs in south Texas frequently lynched Spanish speakers. An accurate count of the numbers of Mexicans executed without resort to the law by civilian posses and the Texas Rangers will never be calculated. Mexicans in early-twentieth-century south Texas may have been in greater danger of mob violence than blacks anywhere in the South. By contrast, mob violence against Mexicans in central Texas was infrequent. There is only one documented case of mob violence against a Mexican in the seven central Texas counties at the heart of this study. In 1872 a party of eight or nine men in Limestone County approached the home of a Mexican couple; after searching unsuccessfully for a gun, they took the man and hanged him near their house.[69]

To say that there were few lynchings of Mexicans in central Texas is not to say that violence against them was rare. The relatively small number of Mexicans in central Texas suffered frequent attacks by Anglos in the late nineteenth and early twentieth centuries. In 1894 a mob extracted a Mexican from the Belton jail. Instead of lynching their victim, however, the mob whipped him. In 1897 Drew England killed Ramon Alcantra in a dispute over Alcantra's daughter, and in 1904 an unknown Mexican man was found dead on the railroad tracks in Waco.[70] Despite the frequency of such incidents, Mexicans in central Texas did not live with the same fear of mob violence as did their fellow Spanish speakers in south Texas or their black neighbors in central Texas.[71]

Explaining why blacks but not Mexicans suffered mob violence in central Texas requires an understanding of several factors. First, throughout the nineteenth and early twentieth centuries, far fewer Mexicans lived in central Texas than in south Texas. Second, those who did live in central Texas often had been recruited by Anglo landlords and were thus highly valued workers. Much like the murder of Anderson Vaughn in 1896, the lynching of a compliant Mexican worker would have provoked outrage from local leaders. Third, the historical memory of anti-Mexican mob violence in central Texas was weak by the early twentieth century. Unlike Anglos in south Texas, Anglos in central Texas had not lived with a substantial population of Spanish speakers since the days of the War for Texas Independence. Stories of Mexican "banditry" surely reached central Texas, but they had less resonance than they did elsewhere. The historical memory of mob violence in the region revolved around whites, blacks, and Indians but not Mexicans. Without a powerful narrative justifying it, the anger and energy necessary to bring about mob violence against Spanish speakers did not materialize in early-twentieth-century central Texas. Mexicans who came there were thus able to escape some of the worst aspects of life in south Texas.

The absence of mob violence did not mean, however, an absence of discrimination. One central Texan remembered that often "we were told, 'We don't serve Mexicans here.'"[72] Many Mexican Americans in central Texas fell victim to such racism and discrimination. "We had places here in Texas that wouldn't even allow us in their cafes," recalled Tomas Arroyo. "You had to go out in the kitchen just like a nigger."[73]

Texas law defined everyone except for African Americans as "white," but Mexicans suffered formal as well as informal discrimination. In 1915 Mexican workers in Waco protested that white workers in the city were not only attempting to block their pursuit of public works jobs but also to drive them out of town altogether.[74] The courts indeed discriminated against Mexicans. Rangel's life sentence was the most infamous, but they often received particularly severe sentences compared to Anglos.[75] At the same time, courts were tolerant of Anglos who committed crimes against Mexicans. In 1911, for example, John Anderson stabbed a Mexican man to death. The courts, however, sentenced Anderson to only three years in prison. Anderson was so pleased with the verdict that he thanked the jury for their lenience. Grover Ross, who killed two Mexican men with a shovel, did even better. His case never came to trial because authorities were unable to locate several key witnesses.[76] The school system also discriminated, sometimes allowing Mexican children to attend white schools but at other times forbidding them from doing so. Julia Duron recalled discrimination in the central Texas school system against Mexicans but noted, "The blacks got worse than the Mexican people."[77]

Such comparisons were common. Mexicans in central Texas were keenly aware that most Anglos regarded Mexicans as racially inferior. At the same time, they understood that whites, at least in central Texas, treated Mexicans somewhat better than the area's African Americans. As historian Neil Foley has concluded, Mexicans eventually came to live in an "ethnoracial middle ground between Anglo Americans and African Americans, not white enough to claim equality with Anglos and yet, in many cases, white enough to escape the worst features of the Jim Crow South."[78]

The introduction of thousands of Mexican workers may have solved the labor crisis provoked by the migration of blacks, but it did not change the perception of central Texas whites that their world was in a state of dangerous flux. The carefully constructed world of segregation, labeled with neat "white" and "colored" signs, had never reflected reality. The simplistic illusion of segregation was being replaced by the uncomfortable realization that the world was a more diverse, a more complex, place than whites desired. In short, W. P. Meroney was far from the only person upset with these changes no matter how necessary they were for the economic health of the region.

Central Texas whites reacted to the changing world in a number of ways, one of which was to support and participate in increasingly brutal mob violence. Extralegal action was, however, not the only means of coping with the problems of the early twentieth century. A brief exploration of alternative forms of tightening social control helps deepen understanding of the world in which Jesse Washington was lynched. As the region became more urbanized and more racially diverse, local leaders might have abandoned their rigid binary vision of race relations. They did not. Instead, they struggled to enforce white unity, standardize discrimination, and reinforce the system of segregation. During the early twentieth century the growth of white solidarity, so important to the creation of large lynch mobs, reached its climax. Nothing symbolized the growing white unity better than residential segregation and disfranchisement.[79]

Whites and blacks were becoming physically distant from each other in the early twentieth century. During slavery they had lived in close proximity, but after emancipation they began to live in separate neighborhoods. Segregation, however, was never complete and was not accomplished by political and legal means. That changed during the twentieth century. Until then, most attempts to create white-only neighborhoods involved white landlords evicting or refusing to lease to black tenants.

Whites had always had difficulty, both philosophically and legally, in clearing black property-owners out of white neighborhoods. During the early twentieth century they overcame reservations about violating the sanctity of property. "The efforts of the white citizens toward more concentrated segregation of the colored people," wrote local sociologist Ida Hall in 1928, "is shown in the efforts of civic organizations to remove Negroes from certain localities." Between 1906 and 1907 a private group led by a Baylor professor and the president of the local chapter of the Daughters of the Confederacy organized the South Waco Park Association, which received funds from the city of Waco and the help of local officials. At the urging of the association, Judge J. N. Gallagher condemned a black neighborhood on South Fifth Street. The association then moved or tore down the houses, forcing the black residents to seek shelter elsewhere and creating the space for their park.[80]

Although the efforts of the South Waco Park Association reflected the deteriorating state of relations in central Texas, the struggle over residential segregation paled in significance next to turn-of-the-century attempts to disfranchise local blacks. During the nineteenth century, central Texas whites had employed largely informal methods to deter black voters. Indeed, most considered the formal disfranchisement of African Americans to be a constitutional impossibility. In 1889 a local white newspaper despaired of solving the race problem at all. "Deportation is impossible; disenfranchisement is equally impossible and miscegenation is still more impossible," wrote the *Waco Evening News*.[81] As late as 1898 the *Waco Times-Herald* argued that all talk of black "disfranchisement because of his race is folly" due to the Fifteenth Amendment.[82]

The hesitancy of central Texans to embrace disfranchisement was not based on belief in African American rights. Indeed, local whites considered black voting to be the heart of the "race problem." One observer spoke for many whites when he wrote that giving "the ballot to the newly freed slave was a deplorable mistake."[83] According to a local white newspaper, the "whole trouble between the two races in the South lies simply and purely in unrestricted negro suffrage, which is a constant menace and source of irritation."[84]

For whites, the difficulty with disfranchisement was not intellectual but practical. How could they find a constitutionally acceptable way to disfranchise all blacks without disfranchising some whites? The literacy test, endorsed by two local newspapers in 1889, was troublesome because it disfranchised some, but not all, blacks while simultaneously pulling the ballot away from many whites.[85] Mississippi's "understanding" clause allowed illiterate whites to vote if they could prove they "understood" a section of the state constitution when it was read to them. That plan received the endorsement of the *Waco Times-Herald* in 1898 because illiterate whites were not to be grouped with illiterate blacks. All white men should be able to vote, justified the newspaper, because each "was a descendant of generations of free-born and self-governing people."[86] Despite that endorsement the "understanding" clause and the literacy test were never fully embraced in central Texas. In 1898 a group of city leaders formed a "Committee of Six" and a "Good Government Club" in an effort to win local elections and push through disfranchisement measures. This movement was narrowly defeated at the polls. The nineteenth century closed with some blacks voting in local elections.[87]

African American suffrage did not survive long into the twentieth century, however. On 21 July 1900 Democrats in the city of Waco met to discuss a resolution: "Provided, that all white citizens who are or may be qualified voters and none others, shall be entitled to vote at such primary election or elections." Fearful of constitutional problems, some launched a debate over the direct nature of racial exclusion, specifically the use of the term *white*. Worried that the direct use of "white" would risk a constitutional confrontation, these men convinced their fellow Anglos to replace "white" with "Democratic." The semantic difference mattered little because Anglo leaders of the Democratic Party had decided then and there that only certain citizens would be allowed to participate in local primary elections.[88]

This de facto form of restricting black suffrage was soon bolstered with legal sanction through the development of the white primary in county and state elections. In 1905 the legislature of the state of Texas passed the Terrell Election Law, which required introduction of the primary system to nominate candidates. This law gave the Democratic Party the green light to block black suffrage, and in 1904 it recommended that only white Democrats be allowed to vote in these primaries (white being defined as "all men except Negroes").[89] Blacks could still vote in general elections but were now blocked from the Democratic Party in a region where Democratic nomination was, in practice, election to office.

The lack of regard for African American rights that allowed whites to remove blacks from their homes and deny them the right to vote was not new in central Texas. What was new, however, was the cultural distance and alienation that resulted from these and other changes. In 1933 the editor of a black-owned newspaper looked back on the changes of the early twentieth century and recalled that events had increased "the ignorance of white people concerning the general psychology of colored people."[90]

Such ignorance easily translated into frustration and anger. By the early twentieth century a new generation of whites, reared in the aftermath of southern defeat and economic collapse, confronted a new generation of blacks, born, educated, and reared in freedom. Whites saw a growing black community that was slowly improving and opening black-owned and operated institutions and businesses in central Texas.[91] They recognized a growing militancy among the region's blacks, represented most clearly by the rapid growth of NAACP branches in central Texas after World War I.[92]

Such changes added to the discomfort that many whites were experiencing with the changes of the early twentieth century and, not surprisingly, coincided with a turn for the worse in white attitudes toward blacks. During the half-century following the abolition of slavery the majority of central Texas Anglos slowly embraced the view that African Americans—and to a lesser extent Mexican Americans—possessed an unalterable set of racial characteristics that inclined them to violence and crime.

One way to illustrate the subtle change in anti-black sentiment is to examine white attitudes toward Juneteenth, the annual black Texas holiday celebrating emancipation. In the 1870s and 1880s white newspapers of central Texas consistently reported, year-in and year-out, on the activities held on Juneteenth. They also often gave warm praise to the black holiday. Emancipation "was celebrated in Waco in a very becoming manner, by about two thousand men, women and children of color" wrote the *Waco Daily Examiner* in 1876.[93] In the late nineteenth century, well-respected white citizens often attended and spoke to the black celebrants. Dr. W. H. Wilkes, "a gentleman of high standing in the community, and a former slave owner," spoke in 1877. During this period, local newspapers often reprinted the speeches of Juneteenth speakers like Wilkes, who urged his black audience to "educate and elevate your children."[94] White attitudes toward Juneteenth continued to be basically positive as late as 1886, when the *Examiner* reported that the anniversary of emancipation was marked by "peace and good order."[95]

Those attitudes, however, began to change. In the 1890s white newspapers began to ignore the holiday, a sign of the growing wall of segregation between white and black central Texans. The *Waco Tribune* printed one of the last detailed and favorable reviews of Juneteenth by a white newspaper on 24 June 1899. From that point until the onset of the Great Depression, white newspapers in central Texas ignored the celebration entirely, gave it the shortest possible mention, or ridiculed the celebrants. In 1901, for example, a one-sentence line replaced the long excerpts from speeches that were once printed in the newspaper following 19 June: "Warm and clear—This being Emancipation day, the colored people celebrated the occasion at Golden Gate Park in South Waco and at Busch park in North Waco."[96] In 1904 the *Waco Weekly Tribune* failed to cover Juneteenth at all.[97] When white newspapers did cover the event in the early twentieth century, black-on-black violence was their theme. In 1926 the only mention of Juneteenth was that a black man was shot to death during the celebration. A year later the *Waco Times-Herald* attempted to humor readers with a report on the lack of violence that year: "Juneteenth was celebrated Sunday by Waco negroes without any tragedies or near tragedies occurring."[98]

The growth and evolution of white supremacy was not limited to the subtle changes underlying coverage of Juneteenth celebrations. A series of overt public figures defended white supremacy in central Texas during the late nineteenth and early twentieth centuries as well. In 1888 the *Waco Evening News* quoted a story about Africa: "Almost every village of pagan Africa, particularly toward the west coast, has a fetish house, a grim and ghastly building, often ranged with human skulls in every stage of decomposition, and a fetish man, who is its highest priest."[99] Whites also blamed the poor living conditions that most central Texas blacks endured on racial characteristics. Claiming that blacks "have a maternal instinct below the average, and a low estimate of the value of human life" as well as "loose, careless habits," a local newspaper concluded that "the race question will solve itself in time, the black race eventually disappearing."[100]

In addition to espousing racism on a daily basis, central Texans occasionally composed extended studies of the "race problem." One central Texan who thought extensively on the subject was Wacoan W. F. Cole. In 1900 he spoke at a convention in Chattanooga, Tennessee. Cole wrote that it "seems the destiny of the white man to rule the colored races, because they have not the power to resist."[101] The African, said Cole, has "been heavily handicapped by nature, because his ancestors were not compelled to struggle for existence like those of the white man."[102] In 1905 John C. Stephenson, a resident of Waco for more than thirty years, published *The Negro Problem,* which defended white supremacy. His goal was to promote "a good understanding between the races and to advise a state of affairs that will conduce to the welfare of the negro and yet safeguard the interests and assure the supremacy of the white race."[103] Stephenson suggested that African Americans remain in the countryside, avoid big cities, and work as farmers. He also reexamined and reasserted the long-held assertion of whites that black men and women formed a distinct race from the rest of humanity because they suffered from the curse of Ham.

The demographic changes of the early twentieth century led whites to embrace an increasingly vicious racism and to strengthen segregation. The changes also help account for the brutal racial violence of central Texas's second decade. This violence should be seen as equally a product of the region's past and the changing world of the early twentieth century. For eight decades central Texans supported extralegal violence as necessary to secure the social order. By participating in lynching whites could connect to the venerable tradition of frontier justice. At the same time, this connection to the past was probably more important than ever given the uncertainties caused by the demographic and social changes of the early twentieth century.

Encouragement to mob violence came not only from memories and oral traditions of frontier Texas but also from national and regional stories printed in local daily newspapers. Newspapers expanded in size and circulation in the early twentieth century and began to carry more stories from outside the local area. Stories of lynching no matter their place of origin filled the columns of local dailies. These stories about mob violence helped create a public eager for the "amusement" of lynching and also provided rituals and tropes that helped to unify lynching and lynching tales across the South. Lynching photography was another hallmark of twentieth-century mob violence. Postcards emblazoned with the images of black lynching victims passed back and forth throughout the South, sometimes finding a final resting place in a family photo album. Other twentieth-century technological changes, particularly the telephone and the automobile, made communication about and participation in mob violence far easier than in the nineteenth century, when news of plans was spread on horseback and person to person.[104]

Twentieth-century technological change created the potential for a lynching to become a spectacle, an "amusement" attended by thousands and orchestrated according to widely approved regional and national rituals. Although such changes were necessary, they were not sufficient to create spectacle lynchings. Only certain communities at certain times passed from the stages of reading about to performing acts of racial violence. Those communities varied greatly in demographic structure, economic orientation, and participation in the new consumer culture of the twentieth century. The story of any particular spectacle lynching must be found in the intersection between national and regional patterns and local history. Understanding the brutal racial violence of central Texas between 1910 and 1916 requires understanding both America and central Texas. It also requires understanding the changing character of the twentieth century and the lingering legacies of the nineteenth.

Lynching in central Texas reached new levels of brutality and participation during the second decade of the twentieth century. Thousands joined in the burning and torture of alleged black criminals, then sliced off fingers as souvenirs and posed for photographs. "What was strikingly new and different," wrote historian Leon Litwack, "was the sadism and exhibitionism that characterized white violence." Killing the victim was "not enough, the execution needed to be turned into a public ritual, a collective experience, and the victim needed to be subjected to extraordinary torture and mutilation."[105] These spectacle lynchings flourished throughout the South in the early twentieth century, but few regions matched the horrors orchestrated in central Texas.

On 22 July 1910 a mob of several thousand burned the body of a black man named Henry Gentry on the public square of Belton in central Texas. Gentry's crime was an alleged attempt to enter the home of a white woman. Given the lynching of Lincoln Porter a few years earlier for a similar transgression, Gentry had decided to go out firing. While being sought by the authorities, he killed a local constable. Despite the shooting, Gentry was unable to escape, and the posse-turned-mob tracked him down. The mob dragged Gentry's body around the square, then carefully placed the body on the pyre. As he was being burned, several hundred people fired shots into his corpse.[106] Photographers captured the scene and underscored the deliberate nature of the burning by making sure to include an unused, hand-operated fire truck in the foreground. Due to the fear provoked by Gentry's lynching, white employers had to escort black workers to and from their homes. As one central Texan remembered after the burning, "The Negroes who worked for us were afraid to come to work."[107]

Even more brutal than Gentry's death was the lynching of a black man named Will Stanley in Temple in the early morning hours of 30 July 1915. Stanley stood accused of murdering three young white children from the Grimes family. The evidence for Stanley's guilt was far from conclusive, but the mob was determined to lynch him. They broke into the jail, removed Stanley, and were in the process of burning him alive when a member of the mob shot him. The mob then dragged the corpse through the fire until very little remained. Men photographed the charred corpse. Larger than Gentry's mob, the active participants and spectators at Stanley's lynching totaled between five and ten thousand. "The streets were filled with pedestrians and automobiles loaded with onlookers," reported a newspaper. "Trees fringing the street on the side of the square nearest the burning were filled with boys, and scattered through the crowds were many young girls."[108] After the mob burned Stanley to death on the town's public square, they hung what remained of his charred body from a nearby telephone pole.[109]

Stanley's death shocked many in the United States, but the horror of his death was soon replaced by the even more infamous lynching of Jesse Washington. Perhaps no lynching in American history received so much attention. Washington's murder was a turning point in the history of mob violence in central Texas. To be sure, Washington was not the last central Texan to be lynched. In 1919 a mob of three to four hundred used a telephone pole to batter down the doors to the Hill County jail. They soon found their victim, a black man named Bragg Williams who had been convicted of murder, pulled him from the courthouse, and burned him alive. Photographers once again captured the grisly scene.[110]

The mass lynchings of Bragg Williams, Jesse Washington, Will Stanley, and Henry Gentry attracted widespread participation and support in central Texas. Tens of thousands participated and viewed these gruesome scenes. Individuals were so proud of their participation that they sought souvenirs of the experience. Fingers and teeth were especially prized, but photographs were the most common. One central Texan who purchased a postcard of Will Stanley's burnt corpse scrawled, "This is the Barbecue we had last night. My picture is to the left with a cross over it. Your son, Joe."[111]

This is the
Barbecue we
had last night
my picture is to
the left with a
cross over it your
son Joe.

A postcard commemorating the lynching
of Will Stanley, Temple, Texas, 30 July 1915.

(Collection of James Allen and John Littlefield,
Without Sanctuary: Lynching Photography in America)

Central Texans also displayed approval for the lynching by failing to prosecute mob leaders. Mobs did their work unmasked, in the light of day and in full view of thousands of witnesses. Nevertheless, authorities failed to indict any of them. The *Waco Morning News* wrote that it "opposed lynching under any circumstances" but "readily recognize the provocation that prompted" the Temple mob to lynch Will Stanley.[112] In his report on the lynching of Bragg Williams for the National Association for the Advancement of Colored People, G. N. T. Gray wrote that sentiment in Hillsboro among local officials and "members of the white race is all but unanimous in favor of lynching and burning Negroes."[113]

* * *

The brutality and violence exhibited in Waco and central Texas were, unfortunately, duplicated in other parts of the South. Similar combinations were conspiring to ignite mass lynchings throughout the former Confederacy. Far from unique, central Texas was one of many parts of the South that embraced the burning and mutilation of African Americans in the early twentieth century. Yet it was probably not pure accident that central Texas hosted some of the South's largest and most sadistic mobs.

The culture of mob violence that supported the lynching of Jesse Washington was eight decades old in 1916. Central Texans had long justified extralegal killing as a necessary fact of life. In the earliest days of white settlement such violence was administered not by lynch mobs but by citizen posses in pursuit of "encroaching" Native Americans or "invading" Mexicans. As the region became more settled, a tradition emerged of administering justice without recourse to the still-developing court system. During the sectional conflict, vigilance committees sought out suspected slave insurrectionists, abolitionists, and Republicans. After emancipation, whites continued to rely on mob violence as a means of maintaining order over freedmen who had become, in the minds of whites, dangerous murderers and rapists.

Lynching and mob violence, in short, had been praised for generations. Historical memory in central Texas accorded great prestige to the region's Indian fighters, to those who helped collapse the Reconstruction government through violence, and to the men who defended the honor of white womanhood. Participation in a well-ordered lynch mob was, for the region's Anglo Americans, a rite of passage, a public duty, and a source of prestige. During the twentieth century shifting demographic patterns inside the region and national and regional influences from outside the area helped shape ideas about the proper form and ritual of mob violence. The result was the participation of some fifteen thousand central Texans in the lynching of Jesse Washington.

Epilogue

Ironically, the moment of central Texas's most brutal act of racial violence became a turning point in the region's history of race relations. The local, national, and global reaction to the murder of Jesse Washington prompted civic leaders to reconsider their tolerance of central Texas's culture of violence. Although mob law did not end there overnight—indeed, racial violence persists to this day in the region—the burning of Jesse Washington ended an era eight decades old. No longer would central Texas's leaders publicly support, praise, and encourage the use of extralegal violence. Eventually, that cultural and intellectual change led to a decline in the size and frequency of the region's lynch mobs. The memory of central Texas's history of racial violence, however, remained. The struggle over the local memory of the region's racial violence continues, a reminder that we are never completely free of the past.

* * *

In the immediate wake of Jesse Washington's lynching, neither black nor white central Texans could forget their region's act of mob violence. At least some whites in the city wanted the incident to be seen as an object lesson for local blacks. The day after the lynching, Augustus R. McCollum, editor of the *Waco Semi-Weekly Tribune*, argued that although lynching was brutal and revolting, in this case it was justified. Black criminals were "freaks of nature," and Washington deserved to be put to death. Furthermore, "the protection of our women is the first thought of this people," and the black community as a whole should take note of "Judge Lynch's" justice.[1]

McCollum's comments suggest that some white central Texans viewed the lynching as a means of controlling the black community, a way to keep them in their "place." Many wanted a message of racial domination to linger in the black community, but a large contingent of civic-minded whites preferred that the rest of the country forget Waco's outbreak of lawlessness. Neither of central Texas's two largest daily newspapers, the *Morning News* and the *Times-Herald,* printed an editorial on the issue of mob violence.

Washington's lynching, however, received widespread exposure in the state, national, and even international media, preventing white central Texans from forgetting the incident. Almost all major national newspapers, both black and white, reported on the event. Although many members of the mob were from Robinson and other central Texas communities surrounding Waco, most newspapers targeted the city in their editorials. The fact that the lynching had taken place in the public square of a "New South" city that had an expanding economy and a reputation as a religious and educational center was particularly galling to many observers.[2]

Not surprisingly, some of the harshest denunciations came from black-owned newspapers. The *New York Age* charged that "there was not the least shadow of excuse" for Washington's lynching and declared that those who perpetrated and witnessed it were "lower in the human scale" than "any other people who at present inhabit the earth."[3] In an editorial, the *Chicago Defender* said that "Waco has disgraced itself, the state, the nation." In an illustration accompanying the editorial, the *Defender* highlighted the contrast between the burning of Jesse Washington and Waco's religious image as the home of Baylor University, the world's largest Baptist college. In the drawing, white men surround a young black man as he is being burned at the stake; above the flames and smoke, looking down on the scene, is a weeping angel.[4]

But black newspapers were not alone in denouncing the mob action at Waco. In Harrisburg, Pennsylvania, a newspaper reported that the burning of Jesse Washington was "a disgrace to the state of Texas" and a "blot upon the civilization of the entire United States." The *New Bedford Standard* of Massachusetts declared that the "shame of Texas is felt throughout our country," and the *Battle Creek News* of Michigan declared that Wacoans would one day realize "the stain that they have placed on the good name of the city."[5]

Criticism came from newspapers published inside as well as outside the South. The *Montgomery Advertiser* wrote that no "savage was ever more cruel; no stoneman was ever more heartless" than "the men who participated in this horrible, almost unbelievable episode." The *Birmingham Christian Advocate* worried that some members of the mob "were church members" who "have disgraced their state" and "humiliated the whole South" and concluded, "May God help us."[6] Central Texas was not even immune from the criticism of other Texans. The *Houston Chronicle* published a scathing review of the racial violence of 16 May. "Not a word of defense is there to offer," wrote the editor, "there was not the slightest excuse for mob violence on the threadbare plea that justice was about to be outraged." He noted that the lynching "was not a secretly planned affair; not an assault upon an unprepared jail," and the burning had occurred during "daytime, in the courthouse, in open and deliberate defiance of law and order."[7]

Harsh criticism from fellow white Texans surprised central Texans, but local residents still hoped to put the incident behind them. The investigation of the National Association for the Advancement of Colored People, however, made that impossible. Outraged by the incident in Waco, the NAACP sent Elisabeth Freeman, a field agent and suffragist, to Waco to conduct a full-scale investigation. In July the NAACP published Freeman's findings in "The Waco Horror," a special July supplement to its newspaper, *The Crisis*. W. E. B. Du Bois, the editor, argued that "any talk of the triumph of Christianity, or the spread of human culture, is idle twaddle so long as the Waco lynching is possible in the United States of America."[8] The story drew such a response that the NAACP decided to make the lynching its centerpiece in the 1916 drive to procure a federal antilynching law. As Joel E. Spingarn, chair of the NAACP's board of directors, wrote, "The publicity we gave Waco has roused a fighting spirit we must not let die."[9]

In addition to the NAACP's continuing efforts, prominent national journals persisted in discussing the lynching of Jesse Washington for months and years after his death, fostering in the minds of readers a picture of Waco as a center of racial brutality. A 1917 issue of *Survey* magazine noted that whereas the South from 1915 to 1916 experienced a decline in the overall number of lynchings, Texas had witnessed an increase in mob violence.[10] Citing the lynching of Jesse Washington, *The Nation* argued that the state of Texas indulged in far more brutal lynchings than other southern states.[11] In August *The Nation* relayed the findings of the NAACP's investigation into Washington's death. There "is not enough manhood in Waco," challenged the editor, "to cause one [person] to rise up in defense of the law."[12]

Letters commenting on Jesse Washington's lynching continued to appear in the pages of *The Nation* throughout 1916. At the end of the year, the magazine admitted that some Wacoans had denounced the lynching but reiterated that "Waco cannot hold up its head until the criminals are punished."[13] Four years after Washington's death, W. E. B. Du Bois published a short story about an escaped black convict who, after being falsely accused of assaulting a farmer's wife, died at the hands of a lynch mob. Du Bois chose to entitle the story "Jesus Christ in Texas," and he began it with a chilling first line for those central Texans hoping to distance themselves from the past: "It happened in Waco, Texas."[14]

Many central Texans believed that the national publicity of Jesse Washington's lynching had shaped a national image of Waco as a brutal, lawless, and racist backwater. Indeed, until the tragedy involving the Branch Davidians in 1993, the only mention of Waco in American history textbooks was in reference to the region's brutal racism.[15] Over the next several decades the Jesse Washington lynching was a tragic highlight in books on the history of the South and the history of lynching in the United States. As recently as 1998, the student-run newspaper of the University of Texas at Austin, the *Daily Texan,* ran a story about Jesse Washington entitled "Waco Still Haunted by Lynching."[16]

The continuing reputation of Waco and central Texas as a center of racial violence was not due solely to the attention of outsiders; actions of white central Texans themselves bolstered a negative image of the region. Acts of racial violence, exemplified by the lynching and burning of Bragg Williams, persisted well after 1916 and continued to attract media attention.[17] In Freestone County on the edge of central Texas, a brutal act of racial violence occurred in May 1922. A mob in Kirven burned three black men alive, then went on a monthlong binge of racial intimidation and terrorism. Meanwhile, local authorities concealed the identity of the probable white murderers.[18] Another devastating blow to the reputation of the region was the 1922 murder of a young black man named Jesse Thomas in the city of Waco.[19]

Despite their own role in fostering Texas's violent image, whites were distinctly unhappy with lingering memories of Jesse Washington and the region's racial violence. One white Wacoan recalled that "Waco . . . had a lot of people that thought highly and acted mannerly and everything . . . that [the lynching] was a kind of nasty slap at the reputation."[20] Even without massive national publicity, the lynching of Jesse Washington by an estimated fifteen thousand men and women would have been impossible to forget in central Texas. But national exposure changed the way the event was remembered, especially by the civic-minded white leaders and businesspeople of Waco. Ironically, a town once known as the "Athens of Texas" and the "City with a Soul" had become associated with barbarism and savagery.

White Wacoans' long-term memories of the incident centered on the damage done to the city's reputation as a result of the racial violence. After Waco had received six months of negative criticism over the Jesse Washington affair, one civic leader, Dean John Kessler of Baylor, attempted to put a new face on the racial violence of 1916: "Waco has a conscience, but it happens here as elsewhere that the criminal minority takes us unawares; and here as elsewhere there is an irresponsible element that misrepresents the community."[21] Kessler's story of an "irresponsible element" seemed hard to swallow because the number of participants and witnesses to Washington's lynching had numbered in the thousands, making it difficult for white Wacoans to pin the blame convincingly on the backs of the city's poor and uneducated.[22]

Perhaps in response to the difficulties of dealing with Waco's image and the estimated fifteen thousand participants, a steady wave of local historical revision has attempted to lower the number over the years. The first attempts occurred shortly after the lynching, when it became clear that the national press wanted to cover the incident. Elisabeth Freeman reported to the NAACP that "when I first went to Waco they admitted that fifteen thousand saw the lynching, but before I left this number had reduced to five hundred."[23] In 1968 William Curry produced the first history of Waco to mention the incident. The volume celebrated Waco's violent past and nickname, "Six-Shooter Junction." Curry devoted two pages to the story of Jesse Washington and claimed that "a crowd of a thousand people gathered where the execution took place."[24] In 1983 Patricia Ward Wallace published a history of Waco that declared "an estimated crowd of four hundred" witnessed the event.[25]

One of the most remarkable "misrememberings" of the Washington lynching was offered by Lewis Delony, a former peace officer called to guard Washington at his trial. In his memoirs, Delony correctly recounts the basic outline of the lynching. He recalls, for example, that the young black man he guarded had been accused of the murder of a white woman. He also remembers that the mob took their victim from the court after someone shouted "get the nigger." The mob, Delony wrote, then mutilated Washington on the way to the pile of dry-goods boxes that had been prepared for his execution. After the mob "roasted him," a man on horseback dragged the corpse through the streets of Waco. Delony claimed that 150 men on horses followed the body through the streets and that it "was the most terrible and brutal murder ever committed in Texas."[26]

Delony's narrative, however, departs frequently from the standard accounts. He places, for example, the date as January 1919 instead of May 1916, but such factual errors are not as interesting as the other changes Delony introduces. As one of the men assigned to guard Washington, he clearly sought to exonerate himself and other law officers involved in the affair. Numerous witnesses and court records confirm that the trial and sentencing concluded before the crowd seized Washington. Delony, by contrast, remembers that the mob refused to wait for the trial to even begin. The mob took Washington, according to Delony, shortly after the judge appointed two defense lawyers in the case. The judge, in Delony's memory, jumped in front of the mob and told them to release Washington. The mob then struck the judge down with a cane. Delony, for his part, remembers that "I hit several with my pistol before they got me down." He later claimed that he sought out a doctor to treat the wounds he suffered in defending Jesse Washington. Like Kessler's letter, Delony's memoirs suggest that white central Texans were increasingly uncomfortable with the lynching. Instead of glorifying it as had been done for generations, some central Texans now remembered the lynching as a shameful moment. The heroes of these reconstructed narratives attempted to stop, not start, lynchings.[27]

Most central Texans did not follow Delony in recording their memories of Jesse Washington's lynching. Most whites apparently hoped to forget the incident altogether. Elisabeth Freeman wrote to Roy Nash, executive secretary of the NAACP in 1916, that Waco's leaders "think they are right in trying to forget" the lynching of Jesse Washington "and fancy the world will do so too."[28] Roger Norman Conger, the city's premier historian, did not mention racial violence in his many histories of McLennan County and Waco. In a telephone interview he maintained that there was no need to bring up aspects of Waco's history that reflected poorly on the city.[29] When an interviewer for Baylor University's Institute for Oral History talked to Harold Lester Goodman, the interviewer complained that white Wacoans, seemingly old enough to remember the incident firsthand, were "very evasive on this issue."[30] "I don't think people really like to remember these things," Goodman explained. "We don't like to remember the horrible things that go on."[31] Clearly, some white Wacoans desired to forget unpleasant memories of racial violence in their city.

In a unique history of the city, however, one Wacoan decided not to ignore or minimize the lynching. Madison Cooper, a wealthy businessman, wrote two novels about Texas in the later years of his life. The first, *Sironia, Texas,* was published in 1951. Readers at the time noted the similarity between the fictional Sironia and Cooper's hometown, Waco. Not until he died, however, was it possible to learn of the close connections between Sironia and the real Waco. An examination of Cooper's unpublished papers makes it clear that he based almost every character in the lengthy novel on real-life people from Waco. Similarities between plot events in the book and actual historical events locally were not coincidental.[32] In fact, Cooper conceded to a friend that "many of the happenings are adapted from those which actually occurred."[33]

One of the central events—in many ways the climax—of *Sironia, Texas* is the lynching and burning of a black man in the city square. In Cooper's fictionalized account, the Southern Patriots—a Klan-like organization—orchestrate the lynching of Bennie Henderson, an innocent young black man. Cooper portrays the leader of the Patriots, Pete "Splice" Rogan, as a crooked and evil man who has been the victim of society. In making Rogan and his group responsible for the lynching, Cooper has presented a fictional argument for Dean Kessler's thesis that a small and unrepresentative element overpowered the "best" people of Waco in the lynching. Cooper portrays the lynching as a regrettable incident that served notice to Waco's leaders that they needed to be more careful lest undesirable elements bring disgrace upon the entire city.[34]

Cooper does not put blame solely on the white community for the problems of race relations in Sironia; peace would be ensured as long as blacks "know dey place."[35] In his notes for the book, Cooper wrote that the key to maintaining a harmonious society in Waco was "the interweaving of the black and white threads in the texture of southern life, mutually interdependent, although one is stronger than the other."[36] By articulating such views, Cooper suggested that the lynching was unfortunate, but such incidents might not occur if blacks could just accept their "place" in society.

In many ways Cooper's work represents a common southern response to lynching. Like many southerners, Cooper realized the randomness of white violence against blacks. Yet he still placed a large amount of blame for such incidents on an unruly black community. That viewpoint suggests how lynchings thrived in the South. Many, if not most, whites were unwilling to incite or directly participate in racial violence. But they were also unwilling to risk their lives in defense of rebellious blacks who were disrupting the social order. Mob violence, they realized, undermined the supremacy of the law, but black criminals also needed to be punished.

Sironia reveals that by 1951, despite a determined attempt by many central Texans to forget about the lynchings of the early twentieth century, the events still held a firm grasp on the white mind. Madison Cooper, and undoubtedly many more central Texans, continued to struggle more than three decades after the lynching of Jesse Washington with what went wrong and what could have been done to avoid the incident. Cooper, however, chose to frame his discussion of Waco's racial violence under the veil of fiction. Although he felt he must include the story of the lynching in his account, he did not want to draw further attention to his city. Even Madison Cooper, one of the few white voices to attempt to make sense out of Waco's violent past, felt the need to protect the city from further attacks by disguising it and its action under a fictional cover.

Like Madison Cooper, most white central Texans could not forget their region's history of racial violence and the national backlash it generated. Beginning almost immediately after Washington's lynching, the area's business elite committed themselves to preventing future outbreaks of racial violence and any further erosion of the region's image that such incidents might provoke. An opportunity to display that new commitment soon arose.

In June 1917 a crowd of men beat Elijah Hays to death with a piece of wood on the streets of Riesel in McLennan County. According to the press report, Hays had refused to pay a white man named Oliver Courtrade 75 cents, and in the midst of the dispute struck Courtrade in the head with a piece of iron. The aftermath of that act of mob violence proved quite different than the one the previous year. The local press assailed the lynching, hyperbolically calling it "one of the most brutal and cruel, unwarranted outbursts of violent lawlessness that has occurred here." The editor called for "an absolute, impartial, fearless investigation." Authorities complied by arresting, jailing, and placing on trial several men accused of leading the mob, including Oliver Courtrade. Although it appears that none were found guilty, the modest step of putting members of a lynch mob on trial must be seen as progress in early-twentieth-century central Texas.[37]

The change in attitude toward men who committed acts of mob violence eventually helped prevent lynchings. On two separate occasions in 1919 white women charged that they were assaulted by black men. Neither case, thanks to the authorities, ended in a lynching.[38] An even more impressive case occurred in 1929, when local officials shielded an African American migrant worker named Jordan Scott from mob violence. Scott had confessed to murdering a white husband and his wife when they refused to give him a drink of water. Authorities rushed Scott out of McLennan County when a mob threatened to lynch him, and local officials continued their vigilance throughout Scott's first trial. Tensions mounted again when Judge Richard Munroe dismissed the first jury's guilty verdict because the district attorney had used "inflammatory language" and described Scott as a "colored negro, brute and black assassin." City officials persevered and protected Scott through his second trial, which also ended in a guilty verdict and a death sentence.[39]

Success at preventing lynching in Texas can be traced to the state's leaders' changes in attitude. The *Wichita Falls Times* remarked on the shift throughout the state, noting that there "has been a change of sentiment in many of the larger communities in reference to lynching." Officials in the past, the editor continued, regarded mob violence with "complaceny," but there "has now grown up a sentiment" that "doubtless prevented lynchings in recent months in several Texas cities."[40] In sharp contrast to Governor (and Wacoan) Richard Coke, Governor (and Wacoan) Pat Neff denounced lynching in 1922. Neff remarked that every "lynching party strikes a deadly blow at civilization" and hoped both for the passing of antilynching legislation and the execution of "about a dozen high-grade lynchers."[41] In 1930 the *Waco Times-Herald* wrote that mob law "cannot be condoned by civilized men and women" and "should be crushed in Texas and mobites handled without gloves."[42]

The most powerful testimony concerning the changing attitudes of white leaders came from the *Waco Messenger*, an African American newspaper. In 1937 the editor wrote that some "years ago this community became mob infested," and several "Negroes and at least one white were lynched." He remembered that many "blamed the Ku Klux movement, but the real trouble was in the unhealthy attitude of Waco and McLennan county business, civic and political leaders toward law enforcement." But when "the situation got extremely bad and something had to be done," the editor concluded, "this element acted and the country has since witnessed an era of total freedom from mobs."[43]

The memory of Waco's lynchings, however, extended even beyond the end of mob violence in the region. Evidence in the white community suggests that recollections of national exposure, and the negative reviews mob violence evoked in 1916, helped unify the white community as it attempted to avoid a similar fate during the end of the Jim Crow era. Like many communities across the South, Waco's civic leaders watched the image of cities such as Little Rock attacked nationally for their attempts at preserving Jim Crow. Although they may not have known what path to take toward desegregation in their city, all Waco's leaders knew they did not want to imitate Little Rock's example. They knew firsthand from 1916 that negative press coverage of any local incidents would mean a tarnished image and heavy economic losses. In 1961, when blacks threatened violence and protest, Waco's white citizens moved to contain the situation. These reluctant progressives realized the potential danger that Waco would acquire a negative national image for its approach to race relations. Although they did not really want desegregation, they feared violent conflict even more. Garry Hamilton Radford, a black dentist who in 1966 was elected to the first of three consecutive terms on the Waco city council, recalled that the "power structure" was interested in racial harmony and avoiding racial violence "because there was so many of the white people who were disgusted after that lynchin'."[44] These civic-minded business leaders, who came to call themselves the Committee of Fifty, decided to intervene to ensure a quiet transition to post–Jim Crow Waco.[45]

Desegregation and the civil rights movement in Waco is a story that cannot be fully told here, but a few incidents reveal the white leadership's desire to avoid local violence. From the very beginning, the leadership imposed a ban on media coverage of any protests such as sit-ins or picketing that occurred in Waco, and the ban was observed. Even at the height of Waco's civil disobedience, a three-month sit-in and picket at a convenience store in East Waco, white Waco newspapers remained silent.

From a white perspective, the most volatile desegregation event occurred when a Dallas newspaper reported on segregation in Waco. That exposure threatened to undermine the image of peaceful race relations that Waco's leaders had worked so hard to maintain. Fanning the fears of economic damage, the Veteran's Administration and more than two hundred workers threatened to leave after the Dallas story. Urged on by this and other rumors that employers might relocate over the issue, white leaders put renewed pressure on recalcitrant businesses. When describing why they decided to desegregate the city, civic leaders cited fear that black students would picket downtown restaurants, causing a counterdemonstration by segregationists and resulting in violence. Spurred further by black protest, the rest of Waco's businesses eventually complied.[46]

* * *

White Wacoans were not alone in shaping their memories of Jesse Washington and their city's violent past. Blacks in Texas and throughout the United States saw central Texas and Waco through the prism of lynching. Seven years after Washington's murder, the *Houston Informer,* a black newspaper, wrote that Waco was "better known" as "Barbecueville." When central Texas authorities could not locate a suspect in a murder, the newspaper asked, "What is the matter with the peace officers of Waco and McLennan County that they cannot apprehend the customary 'scape-goat'?" The editor wondered why authorities had not yet found that "huge Negro" lounging on a "lonely county road." Perhaps, the *Informer* concluded, it was because all young black men in the area had already been "lynched, burned at the stake, or deported."[47]

Black central Texans remembered Jesse Washington, but they also remembered the many other lynchings endured over the years. They knew that "lynchings" and racial violence had not ended with Jesse Washington. In fact, black central Texans often focused on another powerful incident of racial violence that occurred in Waco in 1922, six years after Washington's death. On 25 May the press reported that a black man had killed a white man, Harrell Bolton, and sexually assaulted his companion, the widowed Maggie Hays, while they were out driving near Waco on the Corsicana Road. Posses swarmed the countryside, going as far as Fort Worth to seek the assailant. Hays was able to provide a limited description of the attacker, said to be of medium build, a "yellow" as opposed to black "negro," and possessing a gold tooth. The authorities immediately went through Waco, rounding up all blacks who fit that description, and by the following morning four were in jail as suspects. Constable Leslie Stegall, however, suspected a black named Sank Johnson because he lived close to the scene of the crime. Johnson was arrested and became the chief suspect when his shoes fit some footprints the police had identified as those of the assailant.[48]

By the afternoon of 26 May a crowd of about four hundred had formed outside the city jail after learning Johnson had been arrested. Many suspected a lynching would be attempted that night. Officers hoped Maggie Hays— who waited in the home of her father, Sam Harris—would identify one of the five blacks in the jail before nightfall. Officials had already brought two of the four imprisoned African Americans to Harris's house in the morning, but she could not identify either of them.[49]

About 4:30 P.M., a deputized citizen named McClure and his wife spotted a local black man named Jesse Thomas around the City Hall Plaza. Thomas answered the description of the assailant. On the pretext of hiring someone to cut his lawn, McClure approached Thomas. Unaware of his predicament, Thomas agreed to do the work, climbed in McClure's car, and drove away toward the house of Sam Harris. Upon entering the house, Mc-Clure warned Harris that he had brought a suspect to be identified. Harris retrieved his gun. Hays was brought down for the identification, and when she saw Thomas, she cried out. Hays's father pulled out his gun, and Thomas scrambled for the back door. Eight shots from Harris found their mark and left Jesse Thomas dead in a pool of blood.[50]

Multiple narratives exist of the moment of Hays and Thomas's meeting. According to the local white newspaper, the *Waco Times-Herald*, when Thomas was brought before Hays she responded, "That's him, Papa."[51] But Willie Long Smith—a lifelong resident of Waco born in 1890—claimed that the newspapers tried to cover up the story because Thomas was innocent. "When they took him [Thomas] in to identify him," Smith said, "they [Thomas and Hays] were good friends and it frightened her for the police to bring him in and she screamed and they killed him." Thomas was a yardman in that area, remembered Smith, and was well known by many of the whites, including Hays and Harris. Smith said that Hays screamed because she was confused. She apparently suspected that there might be impending mob violence and was unprepared for seeing her acquaintance, Jesse Thomas, as a suspect.[52]

The newspaper's and Smith's accounts coincide regarding events after the shooting. Waco officials removed the body to a local undertaking firm, and when the crowd milling around the city jail, now enlarged to two thousand, heard about the shooting, they hurried to Harris's house, where they learned the location of Jesse Thomas's corpse. They dragged it behind a truck from the undertaking firm to City Hall Plaza. As five thousand spectators now cheered, the body was burned. Then the remains were dragged through the streets of Waco. As the body was paraded around the city, Waco's blacks retreated to their houses.[53]

The next day, 27 May, Sam Harris turned himself in to Constable Leslie Stegall, but no charges were filed. The black prisoners remained jailed because law enforcement officials believed that Thomas was not the guilty party. Thomas's relatives provided evidence that he could not have been at the scene of the crime. Stegall reportedly still believed that Sank Johnson was the guilty party. Strangely, there is no mention in the newspapers that authorities ever took Sank Johnson before Maggie Hays. His jailers eventually released him on 3 June 1922. More than a year later law officers captured Roy Mitchell, a black man from the Waco area. Mitchell confessed to the murder of Bolton and the assault on Hays. He was publicly and legally hanged under festive conditions before a crowd estimated between seven and ten thousand on 30 July 1923.[54]

The white community in Waco failed to respond to the murder of Thomas. Sam Harris was never indicted. The *Austin Statesman* reported on 28 May 1922 that "no person in Waco of course, would deny that Harris was justified in shooting the Negro, no matter how much doubt there may be as to which Negro did the killing and assault on the Corsicana Road." Local businessman Harold Goodman recalled that no "attempt was ever made by any group of the city to do anything for his widow and children."[55] The Waco Baptist Pastors' Association, the Waco Methodist Pastors' Association, and the American Legion did issue resolutions censuring the mob action that occurred on 26 May. But Joseph Dawson, one of the leaders of the Waco Baptist Pastors' Association, recalled in 1971 that "when they [white people in Waco] discovered they had burned an innocent man, [and that] they [had now] found the guilty [party], the only comment I heard around town . . . was, 'Well, it's fine. At last they got the right Nigger.'"[56]

The Thomas murder received a fraction of the national and state coverage that the Washington lynching generated. In many ways that allowed white Wacoans to forget about the incident more easily. When Waco's leaders looked back on the racial violence of the early twentieth century, the incident that stood out in their minds was the lynching of Jesse Washington and the national exposure it generated, not the murder of the innocent Jesse Thomas.[57]

For the black community in Waco, however, the tragedy of the murder of Jesse Thomas went beyond the personal effects on his family and friends. Although undoubtedly race relations were poor in Waco before Thomas's murder, Waco's blacks looked upon the Thomas affair as insufferable, a wound that could not be healed. According to Willie Long Smith, race relations were never the same in Waco after the murder of Thomas. She said, "Everything was downhill after that." Blacks were able to accept many injustices, said Smith, but the murder of the innocent Jesse Thomas combined with the lack of prosecution of Harris was more than they could tolerate. "They were terribly upset," she remembered, but "couldn't do anything about it."[58] As a black minister in Waco recalled, "I have heard some of the laymen now who were youngsters then, they say what a horror it [the mob violence] was and maybe what distress it brought to them during those early periods."[59] Knee-land Clemons, born a few months after Thomas's murder, said that "the fire never died" in the hearts of blacks in Waco, but that they kept their resentment until they died.[60]

The murder of Jesse Thomas held a tighter grip on the mind of black Wacoans than did the lynching of 1916. Jesse Washington did not live in or come from Waco. Instead, he was a young black man whose family had only recently moved to Robinson, a rural area outside the city. By contrast, Thomas lived in the city itself, and both blacks and whites in Waco knew him and his family. Furthermore, black Wacoans knew the Harris family. The mob leaders who supposedly led Washington's lynching went home to Robinson, but Harris stayed in Waco and continued to lead his life, an enduring example of Waco's refusal to bring wrong-doers to justice. Black Wacoans recognized both Washington and Thomas as members of the same race, but the black community perceived Jesse Thomas as more than a fellow victim of racial oppression. His murder left black Wacoans feeling that their community itself had been personally attacked.[61]

White Wacoans would not allow black Wacoans to openly denounce the mob violence involved in the killings.[62] In 1916 a young black reporter "took the city to task" over the Washington lynching. A. T. Smith, a columnist for the local newspaper associated with the black Paul Quinn College, suggested that Jesse Washington was innocent of murdering Lucy Fryer and that the true murderer was her husband, George Fryer. "It is evident," wrote Smith, "that the boy did not commit the crime." Smith blamed the "thirsty blood crackers of the city" and declared that black lynching victims were innocent in "nine cases out of ten." White reaction was swift. George Fryer sued Paul Quinn College for libel. The college escaped with a fine of only $1, but the court sentenced Smith to a year of hard labor on a county convict labor gang.[63]

Such repression did not mean that black Wacoans forgot about the lynching of Jesse Washington and Jesse Thomas. Sam Price, a jazz pianist, recalled how blacks in Waco improvised new words to a familiar tune, creating an outlet for the anger that had been generated in the black community after Washington's lynching. "I'll never forget the first song I ever heard to remember," Price recalled. "A man had been lynched near his home in a town called Robinson, Texas. And at that time we were living in Waco, Texas,—my mother, brother and myself. And they made a parody of this song and the words were something like this: 'I never have, and I never will / Pick no more cotton in Robinsonville / Tell me how long will I have to wait / Can I get you now or must I hesitate?'"[64]

In the intervening decades, black memories of the lynchings of Washington, Thomas, and other victims of mob violence blurred together, eventually becoming one horrible racial catastrophe in the minds of most black Wacoans.[65] The memories became tales as they passed down the story of the lynching to their children and newcomers to the area. The repression of local criticism of lynching meant that blacks were not likely to write down their memories and feelings about lynching. Instead, they passed stories privately, through oral tradition, inside the black community. It is difficult to determine how these stories evolved during the first decades after racial violence because no written records of the tales exist. We do know that black memories of the lynching transformed dramatically with the arrival of a tornado.

No Wacoan living at the time will forget 11 May 1953. Mary Denkins certainly never forgot. She remembered vividly how her father hastily crossed the Brazos River bridge in Waco in an old Model A Ford. A tornado, the radio warned, could touch down in the city at any moment. Anxious to pick up his daughters, Mary's father pulled into the parking lot of the all-black Moore High School. Racing home with him, eleven-year-old Mary watched the sky grow darker and darker. Arriving home, she and her sister joined her younger brother and sister. Mary's mother made them all climb into their parents' bed together. Do not waste time taking your clothes off, not even your shoes, she instructed. No radio played in the background, and no sound could be heard. Mary's mother turned toward the children and said, "God is fixin' to work, so you all be quiet." Scarcely fifteen minutes later Mary heard the roaring of the tornado as it ripped through Waco's downtown. Within moments she heard the sirens of rescue vehicles rushing to help victims of what would be labeled the worst disaster in the United States during 1953. She did not know then, but the tornado killed 114 people and caused $51 million in damage, destroying Waco's downtown.[66]

History works in strange ways. Few could predict that one of the greatest repercussions of the tornado would be neither blows to the economic health of the city nor the human suffering of its victims and their families but the transformation of the memory of Waco's African American community. Like Mary's mother, blacks in Waco interpreted the disaster as the work of God, a punishment to white Waco for the mob violence it had perpetuated and allowed to occur in the early twentieth century. The proof, according to black Wacoans, rested in the path of the tornado as it destroyed Waco's downtown. It followed, they said, the exact same route that the mob took when it dragged its corpse through the streets, terrorizing the black community. One local black woman recalled that the mob "dragged him through the streets from downtown, stopped on Bridge Street to be sure the blacks would see, and then went on out Elm Street, and turned left on Garrison, and came back. And that's the route the tornado took."[67] Another black Wacoan said, "I remember my grandparents and my parents telling me . . . the way they drug his body around the square was exactly the way the tornado came."[68]

Although the path of the tornado served as the central element in the telling of the story, other elaborations developed. For example, the tornado completely destroyed the R. T. Dennis furniture building, killing more people in that one structure than in any other. One variation of the folktale claimed that God turned his special wrath on the four-story Dennis building because it displayed a carving of the lynching in its window. Others recalled that the deaths of Washington and Thomas and the appearance of the tornado had all fallen in the middle of May.[69]

Not all of the 114 people who died in Waco on 11 May 1953 were white. Many black businesses located downtown on Bridge Street had been destroyed by the tornado. How did local blacks reconcile the tornado's wrath with the fact that a number of blacks had died in the disaster and several black businesses had also been destroyed? One version of the folktale claimed that God had sent a messenger to warn blacks about the impending danger. Mary Denkins recalled, "Before the tornado came, there was a man, a black minister, I don't remember his name and nobody knows where he came from [who] . . . came to our church." The mysterious messenger said, "God told me to tell you" that "there is something awful going to happen to Waco" and that blacks should "get as far away from Waco as possible" because "something is going to happen and happen soon." Denkins noted that after the warning "it was less than a month that this tornado came and destroyed Waco." The underlying assumption in this version of the folktale is clear: Those blacks killed in the tornado had failed to heed God's warnings.[70]

Other black accounts of the tornado ignored the deaths of local African Americans and the destruction of black businesses. The tornado "just flattened Bridge Street," recalled Maggie Washington, "and Bridge Street was where they stopped to show blacks that they had dragged him."[71] Finding meaning in natural disasters has long strained the human imagination, and recollection is always a selective process. Many black Wacoans chose to forget certain troubling aspects of 11 May's destruction and fashioned a vision of the tornado that reached three decades into the past.

The enduring memory of the lynching was made possible in great part through the creativity and strength of African American religion. Black Christianity assumed a central place within African American culture well before the end of slavery. During the late nineteenth and twentieth centuries, African Americans continued to turn to the spiritual world in the struggle to resist white domination. As W. E. B. Du Bois once noted, for blacks "God was real. They knew Him. They had met Him personally in many a wild orgy of religious frenzy, or in the black stillness of the night."[72] For black Wacoans, as for many blacks throughout the South, God could be invoked to protect them and attack others. As Johnetta Ray, a well-traveled black woman born in Virginia, explained the meaning of black religion, "[W]hen it shall please Him to cut down the wicked that flourish, no man, especially *the* man, can hinder Him! . . . [W]e rely on Jesus lynched, who is nowise just Christ crucified! It is the Lord wronged, the good 'buked and scorned we sing of mostly. It is not so much that we are healed by His stripes as it is that by keeping alive by singing and shouting and raging the memory of His scourging, we incline the ear of Jesus, the conquering king, to our own fresh scars."[73]

The attribution of a natural disaster to the hand of God has been a staple of human cultures for thousands of years, and African Americans in central Texas were not alone in adapting it to their own particular persecution at the hands of whites. African Americans throughout the nation viewed the sinking of the *Titanic* in 1912 through the lens of race. The famous African American bluesman Hudie Ledbetter recorded a song about the *Titanic* in which he concluded, "Black man oughta shout for joy / Never lost a girl or either a boy."[74] Jeff Place, a musicologist, has observed that "African-Americans, in particular, found it noteworthy and ironic that company policies had kept Blacks from the doomed ship; the sinking was also attributed by some to divine retribution."[75]

In seeing the wrath of God in the tornado of 1953, central Texas's African Americans may have been traveling familiar ground. They saw God retaliating for the injustice whites had inflicted upon the black community and reaffirming their moral superiority even as they continued to suffer from white oppression.[76] As one black minister in Waco put it, "Religion brought our people through."[77]

Although direct connections between the spiritual resistance embodied in the tale of the tornado and more overt forms of resistance are often difficult to find, it is clear that the tale of the tornado coincided with a period of black protest against Jim Crow. From the boycotting of department stores to acts of sabotage to flight from the region, black Wacoans provided almost daily evidence that they were not content with segregation. And they combined such everyday resistance with more coordinated forms of protest. Soon after Jesse Washington's 1916 lynching, black Wacoans—in conjunction with a postwar statewide campaign—formed a local branch of the National Association for the Advancement of Colored People. Beginning in 1919, local black leaders led a determined effort to undermine the white primary and reacquire equal voting privileges. Black activism continued into the 1930s, with new members joining a reinvigorated local branch of the NAACP. After World War II, local blacks began an extended campaign to end segregation and acquire electoral power. In 1973 Waco became the first metropolitan city in Texas to have a black mayor.[78]

How did the tale of the tornado bolster black resistance? It did so by helping blacks remember racial violence on their own terms. One definition of memory is the use of the past for present needs, a definition that could apply to the tale of the tornado. Scholars of racial violence have argued persuasively that lynchings are political acts designed to intimidate African Americans.[79] Whites were eager to use the memory of racial violence to intimidate blacks and encouraged them to remember lynchings as warnings to "stay in your place." Whites, however, worked against dissenting interpretations of lynchings, especially local black narratives that portrayed mob violence as a brutal and criminal act. So, in connecting the tornado's wrath to the murders of Jesse Washington and Jesse Thomas, black Wacoans challenged the intimidation at the foundation of racial violence. And in their inability to control how lynching was or was not remembered, white Wacoans came face to face with the limits of their power in central Texas.[80]

By the early 1950s, when the tornado myth was first created, the end of World War II had initiated a new wave of black resistance throughout the South. Members of the civil rights generation needed, however, the tools of resistance and survival present in African American religion. In the creation of the tornado tale, black Wacoans fashioned more than a tale of survival. They created a vision of black men and women empowered, liberated, and preserved by God. The message behind the tale of the tornado could not have been more clear for activists: God has arrived in Waco, and the time for protest is now.

The point here is not that the folktale itself changed the consciousness of a generation of black Wacoans but that the tornado represented an important example of a transformation in black thought. There may well have been an active role for the myth of the tornado in subtly shifting the ideology of black protest in Waco, but what is more certain is that changes in the meaning of the tornado tale revealed a significant shift in black attitudes in Waco. In other words, the changing ideas about the tornado tale illustrate a shift in black thought, generational as well as ideological, that was occurring more or less simultaneously.

The clearest indication of the significance of the tornado folktale is its remarkable persistence. It still lives in the black community of Waco a half-century after the 1953 tornado and more than eighty years after the murder of Jesse Thomas. Furthermore, it is not only the elderly members of the community who know the tale. Mary Denkins, born in 1941, provided one of its most elaborate tellings, suggesting that the tale is expanding as time passes. Significantly, even newcomers to Waco's black community know of the connections between the tornado and the path of the lynch mobs. As recently as 1993 James Leeper, a native of Tennessee who had lived in Waco for only five years, recounted the story of the tornado's vengeance.[81]

The phenomenal endurance of the legend of the tornado in the minds and memories of younger black Wacoans like Mary Denkins and James Leeper indicates that more than one generation has adopted the story and passed it along. Why has the folktale survived? At its deepest level, the narrative of the tornado was a survival mechanism designed to help black Wacoans cope with the lynching of Jesse Washington and the murder of Jesse Thomas. But the tale of the tornado was more than a psychological tool of protection. By forging an alternative vision of Waco's early-twentieth-century lynchings, blacks attacked one of white society's justifications for oppressive race relations. The tale of the tornado countered the depiction of blacks as deserving of mob violence, and black Wacoans also portrayed whites as brutal, criminal, and deserving divine retribution. In short, through the tale of the tornado, they weaved a powerful moral and religious critique of white Waco that affirmed their moral superiority and challenged the intellectual underpinnings of Jim Crow.

* * *

The heritage of violence in Waco was racialized, taking different forms in the white and the black communities of the city. For whites, the memory of the national exposure and criticism Waco received after the lynching of Jesse Washington seared in their minds a desire to avoid any further tarnishing of the Waco image. When the civil rights era approached, white civic leaders sought a peaceful solution to the issue of desegregation, not because they wanted to end Jim Crow but because their memories sparked fear of the consequences of a violent black-white encounter in their city.

For blacks, the heritage of violence could have been a tragic one of submission and fear. Indeed, many scholars have assumed that the intimidation at the heart of white mob violence was largely successful. Flight has, virtually alone, received scholarly attention as a form of resistance to lynching.[82] Many black Wacoans did, in fact, use that form of resistance and left the city after the racial violence of the early twentieth century.[83] Few scholars, however, have explored resistance to lynching by those who remained in their communities. Yet many black Wacoans—bound by ties to relatives, friends, and institutions—chose to continue their lives in central Texas. One quietly highlighted his determination to stay and fight for his home when he said, "It did no good to run from trouble."[84]

Although more vocal and successful, African Americans are not alone in challenging the dominant narrative of central Texas history. Mexican Americans, for their part, contest the black-white model of the region's history because it portrays them only as recent interlopers. The early settlement of the region by Mexicans is little remembered now. Few whites remember that in the early nineteenth century Anglos from the United States were the first "illegal immigrants" in central Texas. Men and women of Mexican descent have returned to central Texas and they remember how they have been treated as "strangers in their native land." The return and growth of the Spanish-speaking population contrasts sharply with the region's Native Americans. Too few survive today in central Texas to challenge the historical memory of their conquest. The Texas Ranger Hall of Fame and Museum in Waco glories in the heroism of the Rangers in settling the West, but the region's Native Americans are largely ignored.

The battle over the memory of central Texas's violent past continues to this day. Black men and women in the region persist in passing on the story of the tornado's wrath, even as the tale enters academic discourse. Moreover, the struggle over the memory of Jesse Washington has reappeared in central Texas's public debate as well. In 1998 Waco City councilman Lawrence Johnson called for the city of Waco to issue a statement denouncing Washington's lynching and proclaiming a commitment to racial harmony. According to an Associated Press report, local officials were uneasy with memorializing what they called a "shameful" event.[85]

In 2002 the battle over remembering Jesse Washington reached the McLennan County Commissioner's Court. The struggle erupted when the court voted to spend $22,000 to refurbish a sixteen-panel mural in the county courthouse. A hanging tree is pictured on one of the mural's panels. County Commissioner Lester Gibson argued that the noose and the tree was a "symbolic" representation of "what would happen to people of color if they got out of line." Citing the treatment of African Americans "not just in Waco but all over the country," Gibson introduced a resolution that would acknowledge Washington's lynching and offer a "conciliatory atonement." The plaque, according to Gibson, would be placed on the wall near the mural with the hanging tree. No one seconded Gibson's resolution, however, and it died. He complained that the white population of central Texas preferred to ignore and forget the racial violence that marked the area for so many years. County Commissioner Wendall Crunk disagreed with Gibson's interpretation and maintained that the mural did not symbolize racial violence but rather a long-gone era of vigilantism that claimed victims of all backgrounds.[86]

There is no doubt that the image of a hanging tree symbolizes different pasts to different people, hardly surprising because black and white central Texans have been constructing separate pasts since at least 1916. The collapse of legal segregation during the 1960s did lead to significant changes, changes represented by Lawrence Johnson and Lester Gibson themselves. But those changes did not bridge, to use Scott Ellsworth's phrase, the "segregation of memory."[87]

This debate—whether acts of racial violence should be remembered or forgotten—is not limited to Waco. Communities across the nation are struggling to deal with memories of their violent pasts. Part of the impetus for the prominence of the discourse over memory and violence can probably be traced to an increasing realization that racial violence still plagues the United States. At one time many hoped that racial violence had largely ended, but more recent media attention to racial hate crimes, especially the racially inspired murder of such men as James Byrd Jr. in east Texas in June 1998 and the burning of black churches throughout the 1990s, have dispelled that myth.

Although we have little control over the actions of extremists and assassins, we have much more control over how we remember racial violence. Because those whose ancestors suffered that violence cannot and will not forget the impact of racial violence on their lives, the refusal of Anglo Americans to come to terms with their violent past will continue to be a stumbling block in building better race relations. Disclosure of the nation's violent past need not be because of the necessity of finding someone to blame but of building a new foundation for race relations, one based on acknowledgment of past mistakes and centered on mutual trust. There are signs that some communities are ready to begin this process. The investigation of the Rosewood race riot by the Florida state legislature is one example. White leaders have been reluctant to take such steps in the past, arguing that the era of racism is over and looking backward can only provoke greater feelings of racial antipathy. That optimistic viewpoint fails to acknowledge the continued presence of racial violence in society and, more important, misunderstands the role and importance of historical memory in chartering civic society. W. E. B. Du Bois wrote that the problem of the twentieth century was the color line. The problem of the twenty-first century might well be called the memory line.

Notes

Introduction

1. *Waco Morning News*, 16 May 1916; *Waco Times-Herald*, 15 May 1916; *State of Texas v. Jesse Washington*, District Court of McLennan County, Tex., Fifty-fourth Judicial District, March term, 1916, case no. 4141. A comprehensive study of the immediate events surrounding Washington's lynching is James M. SoRelle, "'The Waco Horror': The Lynching of Jesse Washington," *Southwestern Historical Quarterly* 86 (1983): 517–36. Also see Rogers M. Smith, "The Waco Lynching of 1916: Perspective and Analysis," master's thesis, Baylor University, 1971.

2. *Waco Times-Herald*, 15 May 1916.

3. *Waco Morning News*, 16 May 1916; "The Waco Horror," special supplement to *The Crisis* 12 (July 1916): 1–8.

4. The time of Washington's death was placed at 11:50 A.M. Death certificate of Jesse Washington, 16 May 1916, Bureau of Vital Statistics, Waco–McLennan County Public Health District, Waco, Tex.

5. D. W. Meinig, *Imperial Texas: An Interpretive Essay in Cultural Geography* (Austin: University of Texas Press, 1969), 93, 108–9. It is important to point out that the long-settled plantation counties of the Lower Brazos River valley are not included in my definition of central Texas. McLennan County, home to Waco, was not only the most populous of these seven counties, it also possesses the best surviving records. For these reasons this study often concentrates on McLennan County. For additional discussion of how particular sources were chosen, see Appendix C, "Terms, Sources, and Methods."

6. Although western and southern historians have examined the conflicts between Anglo-Americans, Mexican Americans, Native Americans, and African Americans, few studies have plumbed the comparative benefits of exploring these encounters simultaneously. Western historians have focused on conflicts between Anglos and either Mexicans or Indians, whereas southern historians have devoted attention to the black-white struggle that has plagued their region. Although both southern and western historians have been reluctant to borrow from one another, many scholars of the borderlands have begun to combine the two fields, particularly in the study of the state of Texas. They have drawn

together the complex issues of racial and class conflict—long the focus of southern history—with the legacies of conquest and colonization, the heart of new western history.
In bridging these fields and rejecting the old picture of the Southwest, these scholars have
presented a "counternarrative" to the one of triumphal Anglo domination and divinely
sanctioned Manifest Destiny. Despite their success, however, many southwestern historians have yet to draw as much as they could from comparing the southern and western
pasts. David Montejano's prize-winning *Anglos and Mexicans in the Making of Texas,
1836–1986* (Austin: University of Texas at Austin Press, 1987), for example, ignores almost
entirely the presence and influence of African Americans in Texas history.

Many Texas historians have been content to remain within the geographical subdivi-
sions of the state. Southern historians have concentrated on the eastern half of the state,
where cotton agriculture and an African American population tended to predominate.
Borderlands scholars have focused on south Texas, which witnessed more cultural contact
between Mexico and the United States than other regions. And the best ethnohistory of
Texas Indians has focused on the west Texas plains and the Oklahoma hills. Yet one region holds particular promise for the exploration of southern and western influences in
the Lone Star State: central Texas. For specific details and an expanded account of more
modern Texas historiography, see the introduction to William D. Carrigan, "Between South
and West: Race, Violence, and Power in Central Texas, 1836–1916," Ph.D. diss., Emory University, 1999.

7. *Bellville Countryman,* 31 May 1862.

8. Interview with Dave May in *American Life Histories: Manuscripts from the Federal
Writer's Project, 1936–1940,* U.S. Works Progress Administration Federal Writers' Project
and Historical Records Survey, Manuscript Division, Library of Congress. Digital fac-
similes accessed through the American Memory Collection Web site at <http://www
.memory.loc.gov>.

9. It is important to note that this study does not rely on the inventories compiled by
the *Chicago Tribune,* Tuskegee University, the National Association for the Advancement
of Colored People, or the Association of Southern Women for the Prevention of Lynching. Scholars who rely on those inventories fall victim to the fact that each group pursued its own definition of lynching and that even within groups the definition of lynching changed over time. This study is based on research into the original sources themselves
and does not rest on how intermediaries defined lynching. Of course, all historians work
through intermediaries of some sort. My sources—local newspapers, court records, and
government reports—constitute an incomplete record of actions that took place in central Texas. No study of mob violence can escape that limitation. Thus, none can claim to
have definitively listed all victims of "lynching." Nevertheless, information acquired
through careful attention to sources (and the words they use and do not use) is well worth
the effort. Additional discussion of how I applied my definition of lynching in this study
can be found in Appendix C, "Terms, Sources, and Methods." For discussion of the definition of lynching by activists and scholars, see Christopher Waldrep, *The Many Faces of
Judge Lynch: Extralegal Violence and Punishment in America* (New York: Palgrave, 2002);
Christopher Waldrep, "Word and Deed: The Language of Lynching, 1820–1953," in *Lethal
Imagination: Violence and Brutality in American History,* ed. Michael Bellesiles (New York:
New York University Press, 1999), 229–58; and Christopher Waldrep, "War of Words: The

Controversy over the Definition of Lynching, 1899–1940," *Journal of Southern History* 66 (2000): 75–100; see also W. Fitzhugh Brundage, "Lynching," in *Violence in America: An Encyclopedia,* ed. Ronald Gottsman (New York: Charles Scribner's Sons, 1999), 297–303.

10. David Thelen, "Memory and American History," *Journal of American History* 75 (March 1989): 1118.

11. Recognition of memory as an active process emerged first among psychologists. In 1932 Frederick C. Bartlett's *Remembering* attacked old conceptions of memory as a passive recall mechanism. His fellow psychologists, however, did not catch up with Bartlett for forty years. During the 1970s, the work of Jean Piaget and Ulric Neisser finally destroyed the old conception of memory. Jean Piaget, *Memory and Intelligence,* trans. Arnold J. Pomerans (New York: Basic Books, 1973); Ulric Neisser, *Memory Observed, Remembering in Natural Contexts* (San Francisco: W. H. Freeman, 1982).

Over the next two decades, historians came to embrace psychologists' new understanding of memory. European scholars, particularly those studying the impact of the world wars of the twentieth century, were among the first to examine social memory in this new light. Examples of a rich literature include Paul Fussell, *The Great War and Modern Memory* (New York: Oxford University Press, 1975), 310–35; Saul Friedlander, *When Memory Comes,* trans. Helen R. Lane (New York: Farrar, Straus, Giroux, 1979); Christa Wolf, *A Model Childhood,* trans. Ursule Molinaro and Hedwig Rappolt (New York: Farrar, Straus, Giroux, 1980); Lawrence Langer, *Holocaust Testimonies: The Ruins of Memory* (New Haven: Yale University Press, 1991); and Henry Russo, *The Vichy Syndrome: History and Memory in France since 1944,* trans. Arthur Goldhammer (Cambridge: Harvard University Press, 1991).

12. Among the most significant calls for the study of historical memory in the history of the United States are those from Michael Frisch, "The Memory of History," *Radical History Review* 48 (1981): 9–23; David Thelen, "Memory and American History," *Journal of American History* 75 (March 1989): 1117–29; Edward Ayers, "Memory and the South," and Scot A. French, "What Is Social Memory?" both in *Southern Cultures* 2 (1996): 5–18; and Elizabeth Lapovsky Kennedy, "Telling Tales: Oral History and the Construction of Pre-Stonewall Lesbian History," *Radical History Review* 62 (1995): 58–79. An important collection of work on historical memory and African American history is *History and Memory: African American Culture,* ed. Geneviève Fabre and Robert O'Meally (New York: Oxford University Press, 1994).

13. Other scholarly explorations of memory and racial violence at the local level fail to trace developments over the long view, which this study embraces. Scott Ellsworth, *Death in a Promised Land: The Tulsa Race Riot of 1921* (Baton Rouge: Louisiana State University Press, 1982), 98–107; David Godshalk, "In the Wake of Riot: Atlanta's Struggle for Order, 1899–1919," Ph.D. diss., Yale University, 1992.

14. George Santayana, *The Life of Reason, Reason in Science* (New York: Scribner's, 1932), 45.

15. Significant works explaining the cultural origins of violence in the American South include Kenneth S. Greenberg, *Honor and Slavery: Lies, Duels, Noses, Masks, Dressing as a Woman, Gifts, Strangers, Humanitarianism, Death, Slave Rebellions, the Proslavery Argument, Baseball, Hunting, and Gambling in the Old South* (Princeton: Princeton University Press, 1996); David Hackett Fischer, *Albion's Seed: Four British Folkways in America* (New York: Oxford University Press, 1989); Grady McWhiney, *Cracker Culture: Celtic Ways in the*

Old South (Tuscaloosa: University of Alabama Press, 1988); Bertram Wyatt-Brown, *Southern Honor: Ethics and Behavior in the Old South* (New York: Oxford University Press, 1982); and Dickson D. Bruce Jr., *Violence and Culture in the Antebellum South* (Austin: University of Texas Press, 1979).

16. W. Fitzhugh Brundage dismantled many traditional sociological interpretations of lynching in his 1993 monograph (*Lynching in the New South: Georgia and Virginia, 1880–1930* [Urbana: University of Illinois Press, 1993]). Now, work on lynching by sociologists correctly asserts that much work by historians remains overly narrative and undertheorized. The broad patterns and generalizations suggested by sociologists, however, fail at capturing the complexity of lynching. On sociologists and lynching, see Brundage (1–16); James W. Clarke, "Without Fear or Shame: Lynching, Capital Punishment and the Subculture of Violence in the American South," *British Journal of Political Science* 28 (1998): 269–89; Stewart Tolnay and E. M. Beck, *A Festival of Violence: Lynching in the South, 1882–1930* (Urbana: University of Illinois Press, 1995); and Roberta Senechal de la Roche, "The Sociogenesis of Lynching," and Larry J. Griffin, Paula Clark, and Joanne C. Sandberg, "Narrative and Event: Lynching and Historical Sociology," both in *Under Sentence of Death: Lynching in the South,* ed. W. Fitzhugh Brundage (Chapel Hill: University of North Carolina Press, 1997), 24–47, 48–76.

Chapter 1. "*Texas Shall Be . . . Americanized*": Mob Violence in the Conquest of Mexican Texas

1. José María Tornel y Mendívil, "Relations between Texas, the United States of America, and the the Mexican Republic," in *The Mexican Side of the Texan Revolution,* trans. Carlos E. Castañeda (Washington: Documentary Publications, 1971), 334.

2. Editorial, "Annexation," *United States Magazine and Democratic Review* 17 (July–Aug. 1845): 7. Traditionally, this editorial has been attributed to the *Democratic Review*'s editor, John O'Sullivan. In 2001 historian Linda S. Hudson suggested that the editorial may have actually been written by another proponent of western expansion, Jane McManus Storm Cazneau. Linda S. Hudson, *Mistress of Manifest Destiny: A Biography of Jane McManus Storm Cazneau, 1807–1878* (Austin: Texas State Historical Association, 2001).

3. On the seventeenth-century decline and transformation of Spain, see John Lynch, *The Hispanic World in Crisis and Change: 1598–1700* (Cambridge: Blackwell Publishers, 1992). For a critical account of the Bourbon reforms that contrasts them with the earlier Habsburg state, see Colin M. MacLachlan, *Spain's Empire in the New World: The Role of Ideas in Institutional and Social Change* (Berkeley: University of California Press, 1988). For a work which suggests that the impact of the Bourbon reforms varied widely across Spanish America, see John R. Fisher, Allan J. Kuethe, and Anthony McFarlane, eds., *Reform and Insurrection in Bourbon New Granada and Peru* (Baton Rouge: Louisiana State University Press, 1990).

4. Richard White, "*It's Your Misfortune and None of My Own*": A New History of the American West* (Norman: University of Oklahoma Press, 1991), 37–39.

5. David J. Weber, *The Mexican Frontier, 1821–1846: The American Southwest under Mexico* (Albuquerque: University of New Mexico Press, 1982), 122–57.

6. Weber, *The Mexican Frontier,* 158–78; Eugene C. Barker, *The Life of Stephen F. Austin: Founder of Texas, 1793–1836* (Austin: University of Texas Press, 1969), 119–20.

7. Statistics for the importation of slaves into Spanish America come from Philip D. Curtin, *The Atlantic Slave Trade: A Census* (Madison: University of Wisconsin Press, 1969), 268; Randolph B. Campbell, *An Empire for Slavery: The Peculiar Institution in Texas* (Baton Rouge: Louisiana State University Press, 1989), 14, 19.

8. Thomas Cooper (?) to Dr. Cohen, 9 April 1830, Thomas Cooper Papers, South Caroliniana Library, University of South Carolina, Columbia.

9. Campbell, *An Empire for Slavery*, 20.

10. In January 1823, the Imperial Colonization Law emerged with provisions greatly undermining bondage in Texas. Article 30 read: "After the publication of this law, there may be no sale or purchase of slaves which may be introduced into the empire. The children of slaves born in the empire shall be free at fourteen years of age." The enforcement of this article would have greatly limited the profitability of slavery in Texas, but the overthrow of Emperor Iturbide in February led to the entire Imperial Colonization Law being annulled. When, in August of 1824, the new government passed a revised immigration law that contained only a vague restriction on the slave trade, the institution of slavery seemed safe at the federal level. H. P. N. Gammel, comp., *The Laws of Texas, 1822–1897* (Austin: Gammel Book Co., 1898), 1:30.

11. Stephen F. Austin to Jose Antonio Saucedo, 11 Sept. 1826 in *The Austin Papers*, ed. Eugene Barker (Washington: Government Printing Office, 1924–28), 1:1452. On 11 March 1827 the final draft of the Constitution emerged, and it was neither as hostile to slavery as the Anglos feared nor as supportive as they desired. The children born to all slaves after publication of the Constitution were free, and the government would only permit the introduction of new slaves for six more months. Although the law did not eradicate slavery in Texas, it did greatly slow immigration from the southern states in 1827 and 1828. Southerners feared for the future of slavery under a government that was openly hostile to the institution. The political downturn of 1827 did not prompt the Anglo colonists to revolt or to abandon Mexico and return to the United States. After all, a Texas plantation owner whose capital rested primarily in a mobile force of slaves could always retreat to the comforts of a slaveholding United States. It made more sense to the Anglos to search for a way around the legal roadblock constructed by the Mexican government than to raise arms against it. In 1828, they found such a loophole. Because the Mexican government had not outlawed indentured servitude, slaveholders began to rig labor contracts for their servants that technically gave them freedom but which in reality could never be paid off in their lifetimes. On 5 May 1828, the Congress of Coahuila and Texas approved this legal fiction and made slavery practically as safe in Texas as in the southern United States. The decree stated: "All contracts, not in opposition to the laws of the State, that have been entered into in foreign countries, between emigrants who come to settle in this State, or between inhabitants thereof, and the servants and day laborers or working men whom they introduce, are hereby guaranteed to be valid in said State." Gammel, *The Laws of Texas*, 1:213, 1:424.

12. Lockhart, "The Slave Code of Texas," 16–17; Campbell, *An Empire for Slavery*, 25–32.

13. Good accounts of the slow and mixed reaction to the centralization of the Mexican government can be found in Weber, *The Mexican Frontier*, 242–72; and Paul D. Lack, *The Texas Revolutionary Experience: A Political and Social History, 1835–1836* (College Station: Texas A&M University Press, 1992), 3–37.

14. In March, Santa Anna ordered a drastic reduction in the state militia, a move that

little affected Texas but indicated Santa Anna's intent to break the back of state resistance. In May, the Mexican congress announced the rewriting of the Constitution of 1824, the document that many Anglo Texans believed was the legal foundation for their autonomy. Regarding local administrators, an official at Liberty issued a public defense of the right of Mexico to collect revenues. The clearest sign of Mexico's desire to bring greater control over Texas came when Anglos intercepted secret communications detailing plans to bolster the Mexican forces in Texas with reinforcements. Weber, *The Mexican Frontier,* 244, 248; Lack, *The Texas Revolutionary Experience,* 24.

15. Weber, *The Mexican Frontier,* 248; Stephen F. Austin to Mary Austin Holley, 21 Aug. 1835, in *The Austin Papers,* ed. Barker, 3:102.

16. Barker, ed., *The Austin Papers,* 3:102. For an insightful discussion of Austin's views on slavery, see Gregg Cantrell, *Stephen F. Austin: Empresario of Texas* (New Haven: Yale University Press, 2000), 8–9, 189–91, 340–45.

17. Resolution of December 22, 1835, originally published in the *Telegraph and Texas Register* (San Felipe de Austin), 23 Jan. 1836, 102–3, reprinted in David Weber, *Foreigners in Their Native Land: Historical Roots of Mexican Americans* (Albuquerque: University of New Mexico Press, 1973), 105–8.

18. Resolution of December 22, 1835, in *Foreigners in Their Native Land,* 105–8.

19. Weber, *The Mexican Frontier,* 250–51.

20. Gammel, *The Laws of Texas,* 1:1079.

21. Ibid.

22. Ibid.

23. Robert A. Calvert and Arnoldo De León, *The History of Texas* (Arlington Heights: Harlan Davidson, 1990), 75, 90–91.

24. Calvert and De León, *The History of Texas,* 92–93. On the role of sectionalism in the annexation debate, see William W. Freehling, *The Road to Disunion: Secessionists at Bay, 1776–1854* (Oxford and New York: Oxford University Press, 1990), 353–452. Some southerners embraced annexation precisely because it would exacerbate sectional tensions. One fire-eater wrote that in the wake of nullification's failure, the "Texas question may prove to be a God-send, and in this view of it, I shall vote for annexation." (?) to (?), 7 April 1844, George McDuffie Papers, South Caroliniana Library, University of South Carolina, Columbia.

25. Unpublished memoirs, George Barnard Erath Papers, Center for American History, University of Texas at Austin.

26. Noah Smithwick, *The Evolution of a State; or, Recollections of Old Texas Days* (Austin: Gammel Book Co., 1900), 282.

27. Calvert and De León, *The History of Texas,* 93–94.

28. Ibid., 93–96. On the participation of central Texans in the U.S.–Mexican War, see Lillian Schiller St. Romain, *Western Falls County, Texas* (Austin: Texas State Historical Association, 1951), 31.

29. *Texas Democrat,* 9 Sept. 1846.

30. Walter Prescott Webb, *The Texas Rangers: A Century of Frontier Defense* (New York and Boston: Houghton Mifflin, 1935).

31. For the importance of lynching and extralegal violence across regions in the United States, see Christopher Waldrep, *The Many Faces of Judge Lynch: Extralegal Violence and Punishment in America* (New York: Palgrave, 2002), esp. 6.

32. The tradition of violence and vigilantism in the American South is discussed in: John Hope Franklin, *The Militant South, 1800–1861* (Cambridge: Harvard University Press, 1956); Richard Maxwell Brown, *The South Carolina Regulators* (Cambridge: Harvard University Press, 1963); and Edward L. Ayers, *Vengeance and Justice: Crime and Punishment in the 19th-Century American South* (New York: Oxford University Press, 1984). Also, see Kenneth S. Greenberg, *Honor and Slavery: Lies, Duels, Noses, Masks, Dressing as a Woman, Gifts, Strangers, Humanitarianism, Death, Slave Rebellions, the Proslavery Argument, Baseball, Hunting, and Gambling in the Old South* (Princeton: Princeton University Press, 1996); David Hackett Fischer, *Albion's Seed: Four British Folkways in America* (New York: Oxford University Press, 1989); Grady McWhiney, *Cracker Culture: Celtic Ways in the Old South* (Tuscaloosa: University of Alabama Press, 1988); Bertram Wyatt-Brown, *Southern Honor: Ethics and Behavior in the Old South* (New York: Oxford University Press, 1982); Dickson D. Bruce Jr., *Violence and Culture in the Antebellum South* (Austin: University of Texas Press, 1979).

33. Phillip Shaw Paludan, *"A People's Contest": The Union and the Civil War, 1861–1865* (New York: Harper and Row, 1988), 11.

34. Dozens and dozens of life histories of nineteenth-century Texas settlers can be found in the holdings of the Bancroft Library. Sherwood A. Owens, who arrived in Sacramento in 1849, later moved to San Francisco, and finally settled in Waco in 1857, is one example. Sherwood A. Owens, Texas Dictation, P-024, Bancroft Library, University of California, Berkeley. John Henry Brown clipped a newspaper story on the return of "thousands" from California and their settlement in Texas. "Frontier Sketches No. 1," John Henry Brown Family Papers, Center for American History, University of Texas at Austin. The 1850 manuscript census also illuminates the connection between the California goldfields and the Texas prairies. In Navarro County, the census enumerator listed Elvira Williams as the head of her household but noted that her husband was in California. Seventh Census of the United States, 1850, schedule 1, "Free Inhabitants," Navarro County.

35. David B. Edward, *The History of Texas; or the Emigrant's, Farmer's, and Politician's Guide to the Character, Climate, Soil, and Production of that Country; Geographically Arranged from Personal Observation and Experience* (Cincinnati: J. A. James, 1836), 277.

36. Frank Owsley, "The Pattern of Migration and Settlement of the Southern Frontier," in *The South: Old and New Frontiers: Selected Essays of Frank Lawrence Owsley*, ed. Harriet Chappell Owsley (Athens: University of Georgia Press, 1969), 3.

37. Frederick Law Olmsted, *A Journey through Texas; or, A Saddle-Trip on the Southwestern Frontier, with a Statistical Appendix* (New York: Dix, Edwards, 1857), 124.

38. According to the *Handbook of Texas*, the "initials GTT ('Gone to Texas') came into use in the first half of the nineteenth century, when Texas had the reputation for producing and harboring outlaws. The letters were often chalked on the doors of houses in the Southern states to tell where the occupants had gone, but the exact date at which they came to be a synonym for 'at outs with the law' is not known." "GTT," in The Handbook of Texas Online at <http://www.tsha.utexas.edu/handbook/online/articles/view/GG/pfg1.html> (accessed 22 Feb. 2002).

39. Charles W. Webber, *Old Hicks, the Guide; or Adventures in Camanche Country in Search of a Gold Mine*, 2 vols. (1848, repr. New York, 1855), 311. My analysis of Webber borrows heavily from Henry Nash Smith. For his analysis and for additional examples of the

image of Texas in nineteenth-century literature, see *Virgin Land: The American West as Symbol and Myth* (New York: Vintage, 1950), 77–81, esp. 80.

40. Emma Elliot to Carrie H. Jenkins, 19 June 1858, Micah Jenkins Papers, South Caroliniana Library, University of South Carolina, Columbia.

41. A. W. Moore, "A Reconnaissance in Texas in 1846," *Southwestern Historical Quarterly* 30 (April 1927): 271.

42. Walter Allison to T. L. Treadwell, 5 March 1845, Aldrich Collection, Archives and Special Collections, J. D. Williams Library, University of Mississippi.

43. Moore, "A Reconnaissance in Texas in 1846," 271.

44. Olmsted, *A Journey through Texas,* 124, 126.

45. For a discussion of the Black Legend and the roots of Anglo-American prejudice against Mexicans, see David J. Weber, "'Scarce More Than Apes': Historical Roots of Anglo-American Stereotypes of Mexicans in the Border Region," in *Myth and the History of the Hispanic Southwest* (Albuquerque: University of New Mexico Press, 1988), 153–67; Philip Wayne Powell, *Tree of Hate: Propaganda and Prejudice Affecting United States Relations with the Hispanic World* (New York: Basic Books, 1971).

46. McLean, ed., *Papers Concerning Robertson's Colony in Texas,* 12:36.

47. Resolution of 22 December 1835, originally published in the *Telegraph and Texas Register* (San Felipe de Austin), 23 Jan. 1836, 102–3.

48. The poster is reprinted in Geoffrey C. Ward, *The West: An Illustrated History* (Boston: Little, Brown, 1996), 75.

49. Editorial, "Annexation," *United States Magazine and Democratic Review* 17 (July–Aug. 1845): 7. The editorial is not signed, but it seems certain that at the very least its content was endorsed by editor John O'Sullivan. Some of the ideas and the words, however, may have come from others working for O'Sullivan, notably Jane McManus Storm Cazneau. Hudson, *Mistress of Manifest Destiny.*

50. U.S. Congress, Senate, *Congressional Globe,* 30th Cong., 1st sess., 1848, 98.

51. Dozens and dozens of travel accounts from Texas—too many to list individually here—were published before 1860. For an extensive discussion of the travel literature on Texas published before 1860 see Marilyn McAdams Sibley, *Travelers in Texas, 1761–1860* (Austin: University of Texas Press, 1967). Many accounts of Texas, of course, were published after 1860. They continued to contain negative portrayals of Mexicans and to shape the impressions of would-be settlers. See, for example, Nathaniel Alston Taylor, *The Coming Empire; or, Two Thousand Miles in Texas on Horseback* (New York: A. A. Barnes, [1878]), esp. ch. 3. For a comprehensive account of the attitudes of white Americans toward Mexicans in the nineteenth century see Reginald Horsman, *Race and Manifest Destiny: The Origins of American Racial Anglo-Saxonism* (Cambridge: Harvard University Press, 1981).

52. David G. Gutiérrez, "Significant to Whom? Mexican Americans and the History of the West," in *A New Significance: Re-Envisioning the History of the American West,* ed. Clyde Milner II (New York: Oxford University Press, 1996), 68–69; Don L. Meyer, "Early Mexican-American Responses to Negative Stereotyping," *New Mexico Historical Review* 53 (Jan. 1978): 75–91.

53. There are literally hundreds of published diaries, memoirs, and accounts from Anglos in the gold rush. Representative examples of accounts that have negative stereotyping of Mexicans include Theodore T. Johnson, *Sights in the Gold Region and Scenes by the Way*

(New York: Baker and Scribner, 1849), 197, 240; Bayard Taylor, *Eldorado; or, Adventures in the Path of Empire* (1850, repr. New York: Knopf, 1949), 109; Walter Cotton, *Three Years in California* (New York: A. S. Barnes, 1850); Daniel B. Woods, *Sixteen Months at the Gold Diggings* (New York: Harper and Brothers, 1851), esp. 192; James H. Carson, *Early Recollections of the Mines* (Stockton: Published to accompany the steamer edition of the *San Joaquin Republican,* 1852), esp. 25–26; Eliza W. Farnham, *California: In-Doors and Out* (New York: Dix, Edwards, 1856); Alonzo Delano, *Life on the Plains and among the Diggings* (New York: Miller, Orton, 1857), esp. 364–65; and L. M. Schaeffer, *Sketches of Travels in South America, Mexico, and California* (New York: James Egbert, 1860), esp. 90–91, 102, 225.

54. W. Eugene Hollon, *The Southwest: Old and New* (Lincoln: University of Nebraska Press, 1961), 107–8.

55. Mary J. Jaques, *Texan Ranch Life* (London: Horace Cox, 1894), 361.

56. McLean, ed., *Papers Concerning Robertson's Colony in Texas,* 12:668–675.

57. Brawn, "The History of Falls County," 31–32.

58. *Debates of the Texas Convention* (Houston: J. W. Cruger, 1846), 235.

59. *Texas State Gazette* (Austin), 21 April 1855.

60. *American Flag* (Brownsville), 20 Aug. 1856, quoted in *Reports of the Committee of Investigation Sent in 1873 by the Mexican Government to the Frontier of Texas,* translated from the official edition made in Mexico (New York: Baker and Godwin, 1875), 131–32.

61. *Texas State Gazette* (Austin), 14 Oct. 1854.

62. Paul D. Lack, "Slavery and Vigilantism in Austin, Texas, 1840–1860," *Southwestern Historical Quarterly* 85 (1981): 1–20.

63. *Texas State Times* (Austin), 27 Sept. 1856; *Dallas Herald,* 27 Sept. 1856.

64. *Reports of the Committee of Investigation Sent in 1873,* 179.

65. *San Antonio Herald,* 18 Aug. 1857, quoting story from the *Goliad Express.*

66. Olmsted, *A Journey through Texas,* 164.

67. Manuel Robles to Lewis Cass, 14 Oct. 1857, Office of the Governor, box 26, folder 47, Records of Elisha Marshall Pease, RG 301, Archives and Information Services Division, Texas State Library and Archives Commission, Austin; *San Antonio Herald,* 15 Sept., 25 Nov., and 1, 12 Dec. 1857; Frank W. Johnson, *A History of Texas and Texans* (Chicago: American Historical Society, 1914), 1:515.

68. Seventh Census of the United States, 1850, schedule 1, "Free Inhabitants," Milam County, Navarro County.

69. Dorman H. Winfrey and James M. Day, eds., *The Texas Indian Papers, 1875–1916,* 4 vols. (Austin: Texas State Library, 1959–61), 2:31.

70. During the twentieth century, the seven central Texas counties in this study erected at least twenty-seven historical markers to those who helped secure Texas independence from Mexico. Texas Historic Sites Atlas, Texas State Historical Commission Web site at <http://atlas.thc.state.tx.us/> (accessed 20 Jan. 2003).

Chapter 2. "Necessity Knows No Law":
Mob Violence in the Conquest of Central Texas's Native Americans

1. Amos Lee, "Amos Lee Tells Story of Wilkerson Valley Raid," and Isaac Williams, "Who Killed the Indian?" both printed in E. A. Limmer Jr. et al., Bell County Historical Com-

mission, *Story of Bell County, Texas* (Austin: Eakin Press, 1988), 1:17–19. For additional instances of "volunteer" Indian fighters during the 1850s see *Austin Southwestern American,* 28 July 1852; John Henry Brown to Hardin Richard Runnels, 16 March 1857, Office of the Governor, Records of Hardin Richard Runnels, RG 301, Archives and Information Services Division, Texas State Library and Archives Commission, Austin (hereafter Texas State Archives); and "Frontier Sketches No. 3," John Henry Brown Family Papers, Center for American History, University of Texas at Austin.

2. "Lynching—1916 Discussions," box 2, Lynching Files, Tuskegee University Archives, Tuskegee, Ala.

3. One notable exception is John Ross, "At the Bar of Judge Lynch: Lynching and Lynch Mobs in America," Ph.D. diss., Texas Tech University, 1983.

4. W. W. Newcomb Jr., *The Indians of Texas: From Prehistoric to Modern Times* (Austin: University of Texas Press, 1961), 333–63; F. Todd Smith, *The Caddo Indians: Tribes at the Convergence of Empires, 1542–1854* (College Station: Texas A&M University Press, 1995), 103; E. A. H. John, *Storms Brewed in Other Men's Worlds: The Confrontation of Indians, Spanish, and French in the Southwest, 1540–1795,* 2d ed. (Norman: University of Oklahoma Press, 1996), 459.

5. Newcomb, *The Indians of Texas,* esp. chs. 6, 7, 10, and 13.

6. Stephen F. Austin to Josiah H. Bell, 6 Aug. 1823, in *The Austin Papers,* ed. Eugene Barker (Washington: Government Printing Office, 1924–28), 1:682.

7. Stephen F. Austin to Militiamen, ca. 1 May 1826, in *The Austin Papers,* ed. Barker, 1:1317.

8. Stephen F. Austin to the Cherokees, 24 April 1826, and Stephen F. Austin to Mateo Ahumada, 8 May 1826, in *The Austin Papers,* ed. Barker, 1:1307–9, 1:1323–25.

9. "List of Lands Deeded in the Nashville Colony 1834 and 1835," 14 Jan. 1836, in Malcolm D. McLean, ed., *Papers Concerning Robertson's Colony in Texas* (Arlington: University of Texas at Arlington Press, 1985), 12:668–675; Walter W. Brawn, "The History of Falls County," master's thesis, Baylor University, 1938, 27–28.

10. Disposition of J. G. W. Pierson in *Papers Concerning Robertson's Colony in Texas,* ed. McLean, 9:47.

11. Robert I. Chester to his wife, 3 Jan. 1836, in *Papers Concerning Robertson's Colony in Texas,* ed. McLean, 12:540.

12. Juan N. Almonte, "Statistical Report on Texas," *Southwestern Historical Quarterly* 28 (Jan. 1925): 205.

13. J. W. Wilbarger, *Indian Depredations in Texas* (Austin: Hutchings Printing House, 1889), 216, 219 (quotation).

14. Brawn, "The History of Falls County," 30; George W. Bonnell, *Topographical Description of Texas* (1840, repr. Waco: Texian Press, 1964), 47–48.

15. John Love in *The American Slave: A Composite Autobiography: Supplement, Series 1,* ed. George P. Rawick (Westport: Greenwood Press, 1979), 7:2438.

16. Bonnell, *Topographical Description of Texas,* 47–48; Brawn, "The History of Falls County," 30.

17. Despite its rather unappealing appellation, Bucksnort benefited from the wave of Anglo immigration sparked by Texas independence. By 1840, a topographer reported that

a nearby fort had been established, its security encouraging the settlement to grow to ten to fifteen families. In addition to a boarding house, the little community offered the services of a post office and a blacksmith shop. Throughout the period of the Republic, Bucksnort and the lands immediately below the Falls of the Brazos River continued to attract a small but determined number of immigrants. Roy Eddins narrative, Center for American History, University of Texas at Austin; Bonnell, *Topographical Description of Texas*, 47–48; Brawn, "The History of Falls County," 30.

18. Cheves Family Papers, 10 mss, 8 June 1808–25 Sept. 1836, South Caroliniana Library, University of South Carolina, Columbia.

19. McLennan County Civil and Criminal Minute Books, vols. A-C, McLennan County Archives, Waco, Tex.

20. David B. Edward, *The History of Texas; or the Emigrant's, Farmer's, and Politician's Guide to the Character, Climate, Soil, and Production of that Country; Geographically Arranged from Personal Observation and Experience* (Cincinnati: J. A. James, 1836), 41.

21. *Southern Literary Messenger* 2 (1836): 597.

22. The quotation comes from an account of Ross's life compiled by his granddaughter. "YA-A-H-H-OO: The Life and Adventures of Captain Shapley P. Ross and a Biographical Sketch of Lawrence Sullivan Ross," Elizabeth Ross Clarke narrative, unpublished typescript, Center for American History, University of Texas at Austin.

23. During the nineteenth and well into the twentieth century, most Texas historians largely portrayed the settlement of Texas as white pioneers saw it—in sympathetic and heroic terms. According to this school of interpretation, a hardy band of resourceful Texans forged a rich, sprawling, democratic republic by overcoming a barbaric and ruthless Indian enemy and a corrupt and dictatorial Mexican government. These historians placed Texas within the larger framework of America's relentless westward expansion toward "manifest destiny." Two of the most important proponents of this view are bestselling author T. R. Fehrenbach, who portrayed the Indians as "savages" who needed to be removed so "Super Americans" could begin to properly exploit the fertile land of Texas, and Walter Prescott Webb, who paid particular homage to the Texas Rangers. T. R. Fehrenbach, *Lone Star: A History of Texas and Texans* (New York: Macmillan, 1968); Walter Prescott Webb, *The Texas Rangers: A Century of Frontier Defense* (Boston: Houghton Mifflin, 1935). Since the 1980s, a number of revisionist scholars have challenged this portrayal and emphasized the aggressive nature of the Anglo-American conquest of the Southwest. Patricia Limerick in particular has drawn attention to the revisionist attack in *The Legacy of Conquest: The Unbroken Past of the American West* (New York: Norton, 1987) and *Something in the Soil: Legacies and Reckonings in the New West* (New York: Norton, 2000). Limerick and her fellow "New Western Historians" emphasized the aggressive role of the U.S. government in westward expansion; the brutality of federal Indian policy; and the nation's mistreatment of Mexicans, Chinese, Japanese, and other minorities in the American West. In addition to Limerick, notable works in a rich revisionist literature include Reginald Horsman, *Race and Manifest Destiny: The Origins of American Racial Anglo-Saxonism* (Cambridge: Harvard University Press, 1981); David Montejano, *Anglos and Mexicans in the Making of Texas, 1836–1986* (Austin: University of Texas Press, 1987); Thomas D. Hall, *Social Change in the Southwest, 1350–1880* (Lawrence: University of Kansas Press, 1989); Richard Griswold del

Castillo, *The Treaty of Guadalupe Hidalgo: A Legacy of Conflict* (Norman: University of Oklahoma Press, 1990); and David J. Weber, *The Spanish Frontier in North America* (New Haven: Yale University Press, 1992).

24. *Belton Independent,* 2 April 1859; E. A. Limmer Jr. et al., Bell County Historical Commission, *Story of Bell County, Texas* (Austin: Eakin Press, 1988), 1:40–42.

25. McLean, ed., *Papers Concerning Robertson's Colony in Texas,* 12:36 (quotation), 12:31–36, 12:102–5, 12:138, 12:196.

26. Webb, *The Texas Rangers,* 22–24.

27. M. B. Menard to Sam Houston, 9 Aug. 1836, in *Papers Concerning Robertson's Colony in Texas,* ed. McLean, 15:128.

28. Bonnell, *Topographical Description of Texas,* 47–48.

29. Dictation of Jackson Puckett, P-O 78, Bancroft Library, University of California, Berkeley.

30. John Love in *The American Slave: Supplement, Series 1,* ed. Rawick, 7:2439.

31. One of the boys died in captivity of "cruel treatment." The other, John, was eventually restored to his uncle, Neil McLennan. Petition from John McLennan, Petition Files, Texas State Archives; Roy Eddins narrative, Center for American History, University of Texas at Austin.

32. John Love in *The American Slave: Supplement, Series 1,* ed. Rawick, 7:2441.

33. Michael L. Tate, "Indian White Relations in Texas, 1821–1875," in *The Indian Papers of Texas and the Southwest, 1825–1916,* ed. Dorman H. Winfrey and James M. Day, 5 vols. (Austin: Texas State Historical Association, 1995), 1:ix.

34. Tate, "Indian White Relations in Texas, 1821–1875," 1:x; Conger, *Highlights of Waco History,* 23.

35. John Love in *The American Slave: Supplement, Series 1,* ed. Rawick, 6:2441.

36. Francisco Ruiz to Antonio Elosúa, 6 Aug. 1831, in *Papers Concerning Robertson's Colony in Texas,* ed. McLean, 6:335.

37. Francisco Ruiz to Antonio Elosúa, 21 Aug. 1831, in *Papers Concerning Robertson's Colony in Texas,* ed. McLean, 6:377.

38. John Holland Jenkins, *Recollections of Early Texas: The Memoirs of John Holland Jenkins,* ed. John Holmes Jenkins (Austin: University of Texas Press, 1958), 19–20; Noah Smithwick, *The Evolution of a State; or, Recollections of Old Texas Days* (Austin: Gammel Book Co., 1900), 241–42.

39. Jenkins, *Recollections of Early Texas,* 24–26, 26 (quotation).

40. Watt, "The Waco Indian Village and Its People."

41. Tate, "Indian White Relations in Texas, 1821–1875," 1:xi.

42. Dictation of Jackson Puckett.

43. Ferdinand Roemer, *Texas with Particular Reference to German Immigration and the Physical Appearance of the Country,* trans. by Oswald Mueller (San Antonio: Standard Printing, 1935), 14.

44. Winfrey, ed., *Texas Indian Papers, 1825–1916,* 1:25–26.

45. Ibid., 22–28.

46. Edward, *The History of Texas,* 92–93.

47. Winfrey, ed., *Texas Indian Papers, 1825–1916,* 1:24.

48. *Waco Daily Examiner,* 29 June 1878.

49. Quoted in Thomas W. Kavanagh, *Comanche Political History: An Ethnohistorical Perspective, 1706–1875* (Lincoln: University of Nebraska Press, 1993), 306; Tate, "Indian White Relations in Texas, 1821–1875," 1:xi–xiii.

50. Quoted in Kavanagh, *Comanche Political History,* 309.

51. Tate, "Indian White Relations in Texas, 1821–1875," 1:xi–xiii.

52. A. J. Strickland et al. to Elisha Marshall Pease, 8 May 1854, Office of the Governor, Records of Elisha Marshall Pease, RG 301, Texas State Archives.

53. Unpublished memoirs, George Barnard Erath Papers, Center for American History, University of Texas at Austin.

54. W. L. Jones et al. to Elisha Marshall Pease, 16 Nov. 1857, Office of the Governor, Records of Elisha Marshall Pease, RG 301, Texas State Archives.

55. John S. Ford to Hardin Richard Runnels, 2 June 1858, Office of the Governor, Records of Hardin Richard Runnels, RG 301, Texas State Archives.

56. *Belton Independent,* 16 April 1859.

57. *Belton Independent,* 14 Nov. 1857, quoted in Zelma Scott, *A History of Coryell County, Texas* (Austin: Texas State Historical Association, 1965), 53.

58. George B. Erath to Hardin Richard Runnels, 10 Jan. 1859, and Edward J. Gurley to Hardin Richard Runnels, 3 Feb. 1859, Office of the Governor, Records of Hardin Richard Runnels, RG 301, Texas State Archives; Helen McLure, "'I Suppose You Think Strange the Murder of Women and Children': Gender and Lynching in Texas, 1858–1926," unpublished paper presented at the annual meeting of the Texas State Historical Assn., 4 Mar. 2004.

59. George B. Erath to Hardin Richard Runnels, 10 Jan. 1859, Office of the Governor, Records of Hardin Richard Runnels, RG 301, Texas State Archives.

60. Edward J. Gurley to Hardin Richard Runnels, 3 Feb. 1859, Office of the Governor, Records of Hardin Richard Runnels, RG 301, Texas State Archives.

61. George Barnard to Hardin Richard Runnels, 4 May 1859 (quotation), John Henry Brown to Major B. G. Neighbors, 14 July 1859, Robert Neighbors to Captain John Henry Brown, 17 July 1859, John Henry Brown to Major Neighbors, 19 July 1859, John Henry Brown to Hardin Richard Runnels, 22 July 1859, John Henry Brown to Hardin Richard Runnels, 19 Aug. 1859, John Henry Brown to Hardin Richard Runnels, 12 Sept. 1859, J. R. Plummer to Hardin Richard Runnels, 26 July 1859, and John Henry Brown to J. R. Plummer, 28 July 1859, all in Office of the Governor, Records of Hardin Richard Runnels, RG 301, Texas State Archives; *Dallas Weekly Herald,* 1 June 1859; *Belton Independent,* 2 April 1859; *Waco Southerner,* 8 June 1859.

62. On the removal of the reservation's Indians and the assassination of Robert Neighbors, see George Klos, "'Our People Could Not Distinguish One Tribe from Another': The 1859 Expulsion of the Reserve Indians from Texas," *Southwestern Historical Quarterly* 97 (April 1994): 598–619; Kenneth S. Neighbors, "The Assassination of Robert S. Neighbors," *West Texas Historical Association Yearbook* 34 (1958): 38–49; Kenneth S. Neighbors, "Robert S. Neighbors and the Founding of the Texas Indian Reservations," *West Texas Historical Association Yearbook* 31 (1955): 65–74; Kenneth S. Neighbors, *Indian Exodus: Texas Indian Affairs, 1835–1859* (Austin: Nortex, 1973), 118–39; and Rupert Norval Richardson, *The Frontier of Northwest Texas, 1846 to 1876* (Glendale: Arthur H. Clark, 1963), 195–212.

63. John Henry Brown, *Indian Wars and Pioneers of Texas* (1880, repr. Austin: L. E. Daniell, 1978).

64. Wilbarger, *Indian Depredations in Texas.*

65. Lillian Schiller St. Romain, *Western Falls County, Texas* (Austin: Texas State Historical Association, 1951), 29.

66. James K. Green, ed., *Buck Barry: Texas Ranger and Frontiersman* (Waco: Moody Texas Ranger Library, 1978). The newspaper quotations appear in the preface of this edition on page xiii. Additional clippings praising Barry can be found in James Buckner Barry Papers, 1847–1917, Center for American History, University of Texas at Austin.

67. Jenkins, *Recollections of Early Texas;* George Barnard Erath, *The Memoirs of Major George B. Erath* (Austin: Texas State Historical Association Press, 1923); "YA-A-H-H-OO: The Life and Adventures of Captain Shapley P. Ross and a Biographical Sketch of Lawrence Sullivan Ross," Elizabeth Ross Clarke narrative, Center for American History, University of Texas at Austin.

68. Clippings of the Collier stories can be found in John Henry Brown Family Papers, Center for American History, University of Texas at Austin. Brown used these clippings and other sources to compile an early three-volume history of Texas.

69. Ibid.

70. *Waco Examiner and Patron,* 29 Oct. 1875.

71. Interview with Mrs. William Price, Folklore Project, WPA Federal Writers' Project, Manuscript Division, Library of Congress, Washington (hereafter MFWP).

72. Interview with Belle Little, MFWP.

73. For examples of interviews that discuss Indian fighting in central Texas, see interview with Emma Falconer, MFWP; and Nelson Taylor Densen, John Love, and Felix Grundy Sadler, all in *The American Slave: Supplement, Series 1,* ed. Rawick, 4:1168–92, 6:2431–43, and 9:3415.

74. Numerous additional markers exist praising Texas Indian fighters. In Bosque County, J. J. Cureton is noted as an "Indian fighter," William Berry Smith is honored as a "veteran of the Indian Wars," and John R. Baylor's marker identifies the man as a "colorful Indian fighter" who was stripped of his rank when he ordered that his men kill, instead of capture, "troublesome Apaches." All information on historical markers, including numerous towns named after men involved with "Indian defense" in central Texas, can be found at the Texas Historic Sites Atlas, a Web site maintained by the Texas State Historical Commission at <http://atlas.thc.state.tx.us/> (accessed 20 Jan. 2003).

75. Fort Parker, Fort Griffin, Fort Smith, Fort Gates, Texas Historic Sites Atlas.

76. Waco Cotton Palace, Texas Historic Sites Atlas.

77. John Love in *The American Slave: Supplement, Series 1,* ed. Rawick, 6:2419–20.

Chapter 3. "Slavery with a Will": Slave Resistance and the Origins of the Panic of 1860

1. "Texas Troubles" is in the Handbook of Texas Online Web site at <http:www.tsha.utexas.edu/handbook/online/articles/view/TT/vetbr.html> (accessed 27 June 2001).

2. Not all historians agree that the events of 1860 were more imagined than real, but my reading of the evidence follows that of Donald E. Reynolds and Randolph B. Campbell, who conclude that no actual plot existed. Donald E. Reynolds, *Editors Make War: Southern Newspapers in the Secession Crisis* (Nashville: Vanderbilt University Press, 1970);

Donald E. Reynolds, "Vigilante Law during the Texas Slave Panic of 1860," *Locus: An Historical Journal of Regional Perspectives* 2 (Spring 1990): 173–86; and Randolph B. Campbell, *An Empire for Slavery: The Peculiar Institution in Texas* (Baton Rouge: Louisiana State University Press, 1989), 225. Historians who find evidence of a plot compelling include Bill Ledbetter, "Slave Unrest and White Panic: The Impact of Black Republicanism in Ante-Bellum Texas," *Texana* 10 (1972): 335–50; William H. White, "The Texas Slave Insurrection of 1860," *Southwestern Historical Quarterly* 52 (Jan. 1949): 259–85; Wendell G. Addington, "Slave Insurrections in Texas," *Journal of Negro History* 35 (1950): 408–34; and Herbert Aptheker, *American Negro Slave Revolts* (New York: International Publishers, 1964), 353–54.

3. Reynolds summarizes the evidence against an abolitionist conspiracy in *Editors Make War*, 108–12.

4. Data are compiled from *The 1840 Census of the Republic of Texas*, ed. Gifford White (Austin: Pemberton Press, 1966), 158–63. Randolph Campbell's study found that Robertson County held 292 slaves in 1840, while officials did not even collect statistics in the largely unsettled Milam county that year (*An Empire for Slavery*, 266). I have used White's data because it was sufficiently close to Campbell's reliable data, and his individual listings allowed me to chart owners and size of holdings.

5. Lewis Cecil Gray, *History of Agriculture in the Southern United States to 1860* (Washington: Carnegie Institute of Washington, 1933), 2:907.

6. *Ninth Census of the United States, Statistics of Population* (Washington: Government Printing Office, 1972), 63–67.

7. The following is a statistical breakdown of birthplace of central Texas heads of households based on a personal sample of the original manuscript returns of the Eighth Census. Born in Texas, 9 percent; born in the Upper South, 44 percent; born in the Lower South, 35 percent; born in free states, 9 percent; and other, 3 percent. More than 70 percent of the adults in McLennan County worked in agriculture according to this sample. Birthplace and occupation (as well as other information) was recorded for every fourth household listed in the manuscript census taken in McLennan County. On rare occasions I was forced to alter that pattern when an entry was unreadable. The total number of residents in the sample was 968. That included 464 persons aged eighteen and over and 504 persons under eighteen. There were 173 heads of households. "Manuscript Returns for the Eighth Census of the United States, McLennan County," schedule 1, 1860, NA, Southeast Region Branch, Eastpoint, Ga.

8. U.S. Bureau of the Census, *Population of the United States in 1860: Compiled from the Original Returns of the Eighth Census* (Washington: Government Printing Office, 1864).

9. I take my definition of the frontier from David J. Weber, *The Spanish Frontier in North America* (New Haven: Yale University Press, 1992). Weber defines the frontier as a zone of cultural interaction. One the one hand, this definition differs significantly from a conception of the frontier as a new and "open" wilderness awaiting the next generation of immigrants to tame it, a view held by many settlers, white and black, coming to central Texas. On the other hand, a zone of cultural interaction can also be sparsely settled. Such was the case with the central Texas frontier, a sparsely settled zone of cultural interaction among Anglos, blacks, Mexicans, and Native Americans.

10. The most important work published on fugitive slaves is John Hope Franklin and Loren Schweninger, *Runaway Slaves: Rebels on the Plantation* (New York: Oxford University Press, 1999). Like many who write on antebellum slavery, the authors fail to emphasize

change over time in the decades before the Civil War. In his excellent overview of slavery in the United States, *American Slavery, 1619–1877* (New York: Hill and Wang, 1993), Peter Kolchin mentions the increased likelihood of successful slave flight from the border states, but he does not mention the frontier with regard to slave resistance. Such weaknesses in the literature are long-standing. John Blassingame's pathbreaking *The Slave Community: Plantation Life in the Antebellum South* (New York: Oxford University Press, 1972, 1979) revealed long ago that resistance was commonplace in the Old South, but Blassingame largely failed to consider change over time or within the subregions of the Old South. The same can also be said of the work of Eugene D. Genovese, *Roll, Jordan, Roll: The World the Slaves Made* (New York: Vintage, 1974), and Robert Fogel, *Without Consent or Contract: The Rise and Fall of American Slavery* (New York: W. W. Norton, 1989). Although Genovese notes the appeal of Mexico and friendly Indians for slaves in Texas, Louisiana, and Arkansas, he does not explore the issue at length.

11. This story of slave flight in Texas in the years before the Civil War challenges narratives of southern history that assume a static view of slave resistance in the antebellum South. Although Herbert Aptheker, in *American Negro Slave Revolts* (New York: International Publishers, 1943), argues for the constancy of slave resistance in the antebellum South, there is virtually no historical literature on the chronology of slave resistance during the antebellum period. Most antebellum historians take no stand on whether resistance increased or decreased over time.

12. The editor of the *San Antonio Ledger*, quoted in Frederick Law Olmsted, *A Journey through Texas; or, A Saddle-Trip on the Southwestern Frontier, with a Statistical Appendix* (New York: Dix, Edwards, 1857), 332.

13. Paul Adams, "Amelia Barr in Texas, 1856–1868," *Southwestern Historical Quarterly* 49 (1946): 367.

14. *Corpus Christi Ranchero*, 17 March 1860.

15. Joe Gray Taylor, *Negro Slavery in Louisiana* (Baton Rouge: Louisiana Historical Association, 1963), 175.

16. Earlier settlements by southerners in Texas had not produced dramatic differences in slave resistance. See, for example, Randolph Campbell, *A Southern Community in Crisis: Harrison County, 1850–1880* (Austin: Texas State Historical Association, 1983).

17. Olmsted, *A Journey through Texas*, 105–6.

18. Richard Sutch, "The Breeding of Slaves for Sale and the Westward Expansion of Slavery, 1850–1860," in *Race and Slavery in the Western Hemisphere: Quantitative Studies*, ed. Eugene D. Genovese and Stanley L. Engerman (Princeton: Princeton University Press, 1975), 173–210.

19. For this statistical comparison of family disruption I have used the statistics and the coding system found in Paul Escott, *Slavery Remembered: A Record of Twentieth-Century Slave Narratives* (Chapel Hill: University of North Carolina Press, 1979) and compared them with more than fifty narratives of former slaves from central Texas. Those narratives were carefully selected from the hundreds of Texas interviews found in *The American Slave: A Composite Autobiography: Supplement, Series 1*, gen. ed. George P. Rawick, ed. Jan Hillegas and Ken Lawrence (Westport: Greenwood Press, 1977) and *The American Slave: A Composite Autobiography: Supplement, Series 2*, ed. George P. Rawick (Westport: Greenwood Press, 1979). Of the eleven bound volumes of Texas slave narratives (more than exist for any other

state), two of the volumes were included among the original seven volumes published as *Supplement, Series 1,* and the other nine volumes were published later as part of *Supplement, Series 2.* The nine volumes of *Supplement, Series 2* contain, to the best of my knowledge, all (or nearly all) the narratives published in *Supplement, Series 1.* In many cases the interviews in *Supplement, Series 2* are longer and appear to be less edited than the *Supplement, Series 1* narratives. I have, therefore, concentrated on the more than four thousand pages of narratives found in *Supplement, Series 2.* Of these hundreds of interviews, I selected only narratives that could be specifically tied to the antebellum Upper Brazos River valley. Thus, I was able to derive a base of slave narrative testimony about central Texas to compare with the overall slave experience plotted by Paul Escott. The statistical results of the comparison are hardly definitive. Such statistics are an attempt to place the experience of central Texas slaves in a larger context, but the limitations of the sources, the relatively small sample size, and other problems ensure that the statistics are merely suggestive. Nevertheless, such a technique is valuable because scholars of antebellum slavery pay too little attention to geographic variation within the Cotton South.

20. Henry Caufield to Watt Caufield, 22 April and 25 Sept. 1860, Caufield Family Papers, Texas Collection, Baylor University, Waco, Tex.

21. Green Sims in *The American Slave: Supplement, Series 2,* ed. Rawick, 9:3591.

22. Smith Austin in *The American Slave: Supplement, Series 2,* ed. Rawick, 2:134.

23. This pattern of behavior—initial wariness of a new environment followed by rebellious behavior—fits the traditional definition of culture shock. In fact, the Texas frontier was not the first example of that pattern. Gerald Mullins has explained that recently arrived African slaves often failed to match the level of slave resistance displayed by the more acculturated slaves of eighteenth-century Virginia. The difference, he concludes, sprang from the more seasoned slaves' increased familiarity with their environments. Gerald Mullins, *Flight and Rebellion: Slave Resistance in Eighteenth-Century Virginia* (New York: Oxford University Press, 1972).

24. The term *slave resistance* is indeed broad, encompassing collective rebellion, work slowdowns, sabotage, procurement of extra food rations, and a host of other activities. In central Texas, however, I have focused on slave flight. That decision derives not from a lack of other types of resistance but from the greatly increased incidence of slave flight in central Texas. Slaves in Texas found other ways to resist, but flight presented the most direct attack on the slave system. It is likely that one day a more collective slave rebellion in Texas than has been heretofore recognized will be discovered. In Washington County, for example, a serious plot involving some two hundred slaves was uncovered the day before it was to begin. Addington, "Slave Insurrections in Texas," 408–34.

25. Sworn statement of A. J. Yates, I. N. Moreland, and A. C. Allen, 29 Aug. 1835, in *The Papers of the Texas Revolution,* ed. John H. Jenkins (Austin: Presidial Press, 1973), 1:376–78.

26. James H. C. Miller to the Public, Sept. 1835, in *The Papers of the Texas Revolution,* ed. Jenkins, 6:517.

27. Benjamin R. Milam to Francis W. Johnson, Punto Lampasos, 5 July 1835, in *The Papers of Stephen F. Austin,* ed. Eugene C. Barker (Austin: University of Texas, 1927), 3:82–83; Horatio Allsberry to the Public, Columbia, 28 Aug. 1835, in *The Austin Papers, October 1834–January 1837,* ed. Eugene Barker (Austin: University of Texas Press, 1927), 3:107–8.

28. William Parker to Editor of the Free Trader, Natchez, 29 April 1836, in *The Papers of the Texas Revolution,* ed. Jenkins, 6:123.

29. Antonio López de Santa Anna to José María Tornel, 16 Feb. 1836, in *The Mexican Side of the Texas Revolution,* trans. Carlos Castañeda (Washington: Documentary Publications, 1971), 65.

30. José Enrique de la Peña, *With Santa Anna in Texas: A Personal Narrative of the Revolution* (College Station: Texas A&M University Press, 1975), 104.

31. Additional examples include a fugitive slave who volunteered to serve General Filisola as his coachman, a slaveholder's wife who recalled that four of her husband's slaves ran away to the Mexican army, and slaves who belonged to John F. C. Henderson and Thomas Jamison finding refuge in the Mexican army. After the Mexican army was defeated, at least thirteen fugitive slaves joined the retreat to Matagorda. De la Peña, *With Santa Anna in Texas,* 179; "Reminiscences of Ann Raney Thomas Coleman," Ann Raney Thomas Coleman Papers, Center for American History, University of Texas at Austin; Henderson and Jamison to Editor, *Colorado Gazette and Advertiser,* 18 Jan. 1840.

32. Paul D. Lack, *The Texas Revolutionary Experience: A Political and Social History, 1835–1836* (College Station: Texas A&M University Press, 1992), 245.

33. Frank W. Johnson, *A History of Texas and Texans* (Chicago: American Historical Society, 1914), 1:515.

34. James Gadsen to William L. Marcy, 16 Oct. 1854, in *Diplomatic Correspondence of the United States,* ed. William R. Manning (Washington: Carnegie Endowment for International Peace, 1937), 734.

35. *Clarksville Northern Standard,* 25 Dec. 1852.

36. Olmsted, *A Journey through Texas,* 256–57.

37. *San Antonio Herald,* 29 May 1855.

38. For the above estimates see, Ronnie C. Tyler, "Slave Owners and Runaway Slaves in Texas," master's thesis, Texas Christian University, 1966, 22; Campbell, *An Empire for Slavery,* 180; and Olmsted, *A Journey through Texas,* 324.

39. *Corpus Christi Ranchero,* 17 March 1860; *San Antonio Herald,* 7 Jan., 6 Feb., and 19 May 1858, cited in Arnoldo de León, *Apuntes Tejanos,* vol. 1 (Ann Arbor: University Microfilms, 1978).

40. A. A. Blankenship had captured Jim a month earlier, on 18 December 1860. The sheriff of McLennan County described him as being twenty-nine or thirty, five feet ten inches tall, and 160 pounds. This "very intelligent" slave of "copper complexion" had stolen four horses in his escape attempt. Although Jim belonged to Robert Grant of Mississippi, he had been hired to Jeff Galloway of Shreveport, Louisiana. For his part, Jim had traveled several hundred miles—a long way in search of freedom. He was not hiding out in the woods. He could have been searching for a family member who had been removed to Texas, but he could also have been heading for the Mexican border. *The Southwest* (Waco), 16 Jan. 1861.

41. Wesley Burrell in *The American Slave: Supplement, Series 2,* ed. Rawick, 3:534.

42. Nelson Taylor Densen in *The American Slave: Supplement, Series 2,* ed. Rawick, 4:1172.

43. George Glasker in *The American Slave: Supplement, Series 2,* ed. Rawick, 5:1505. Although this interview indicates that Mexicans attempted to lure away rebellious slaves, evidence does not support that statement, at least for central Texas. Glasker, when questioned

by a white about slave resistance, may have sought to place the responsibility with Mexicans in order that they would not arouse white suspicions about black rebelliousness.

44. Tyler, "Slave Owners and Runaway Slaves in Texas," 7–8.

45. Addington, "Slave Insurrections in Texas," 414.

46. Alwyn Barr, *Black Texans: A History of African Americans in Texas, 1528–1995,* 2d ed. (Norman: University of Oklahoma Press, 1996), 29.

47. Burke Simpson in *The American Slave: Supplement, Series 2,* ed. Rawick, 9:3562. President Wilson, a former McLennan County slave, reported that "lots of slaves run away, but dey'd most always ketch 'em and bring 'em back" (*The American Slave, Supplement, Series 2,* ed. Rawick, 10:4206).

48. George Barnard Papers, Texas Collection, Baylor University, Waco, Tex.; see also John Willingham, "George Barnard: Trader and Merchant on the Texas Frontier," *Texana* 12 (1974): 311; and John K. Strecker, "Chronicles of George Barnard," *Baylor University Bulletin* 31 (1928): 14–15.

49. H. J. Jewett, Austin, to M. B. Lamar, Galveston, Texas, 21 June 1840, in *The Papers of Mirabeau Buonaparte Lamar,* ed. Harriet Smither (Austin: Von Boeckmann-Jones, 1922), 3:412–13.

50. N. B. Hawkins to Rebecca Hagerty, 6 March 1852, Rebecca McIntosh Hawkins Hagerty Papers, Center for American History, University of Texas at Austin.

51. J. D. B. Stillman, *Wanderings in the Southwest in 1855* (Spokane: Arthur H. Clark, 1990), 119–20.

52. H. J. Jewett, Austin, to M. B. Lamar, Galveston, Tex., 21 June 1840, in *The Papers of Mirabeau Buonaparte Lamar,* ed. Smither, 3:412–13.

53. Noah Smithwick, *The Evolution of a State; or, Recollections of Old Texas Days* (Austin: Gammel Book Co., 1900), 325–27.

54. Nelson Taylor Densen, a former slave from Falls County, recalled a host of violent encounters between the whites of central Texas and the Indians. Densen remembered three deadly incidents during which Indians killed a total of eleven white central Texans. In a battle at Brushy Creek between whites and Indians, he recalled, four prominent central Texans died. Former slave Henry Childers said the family that owned him had to leave their home on three different occasions because they feared an Indian raid. Henry Caufield, who lived on the Bosque River, wrote to his brother in 1858 that "the Indians have been committing depredations" and "there have been four white men and two negroes murdered by them." Nelson Taylor Densen and Henry Childers both in *The American Slave: Supplement, Series 2,* ed. Rawick, 4:1172–73 and 3:698; Henry Caufield to Watt Caufield, 30 Jan. 1858, Caufield Family Papers, Texas Collection, Baylor University, Waco, Tex.

55. The Comanches "regarded white and Negro settler alike with ferocious antipathy and even contempt." Kenneth W. Porter, "Negroes and Indians on the Texas Frontier, 1831–1876," *Journal of Negro History* 41 (1956): 208–9.

56. In 1845, soon after the Indian trader George Barnard arrived in the Upper Brazos River valley, a number of free white traders and their Indian employees returned runaway slaves to him in exchange for financial rewards. George Barnard Papers, Texas Collection, Baylor University, Waco, Tex.; see also Willingham, "George Barnard: Trader and Merchant on the Texas Frontier," 311; and Strecker, "Chronicles of George Barnard," 14.

57. In 1839 hostile Indians murdered an enslaved servant of Hamilton White while he

was hauling lumber from Bastrop to Austin. At the same time in central Texas, Indians killed an enslaved member of a surveying crew. In 1843 a group of Indians murdered a slave in Milam County. In Bosque County, Texas Ranger James Buckner Barry recalled that in 1857 the Indians "killed a man named Bean and his negro man." Henry Caufield reported that two blacks were killed by Comanches in 1858. J. W. Wilbarger, *Indian Depredations in Texas* (Austin: Hutchins Printing House, 1889), 266–67; Porter, "Negroes and Indians on the Texas Frontier, 1831–1876," 210; James K. Greer, ed., *Buck Barry: Texas Ranger and Frontiersman* (Waco: Moody Texas Ranger Library, 1978), 96; "Reminiscences," James Buckner Barry Papers, 1847–1917, Center for American History, University of Texas at Austin; Henry Caufield to Watt Caufield, 30 Jan. 1858, Caufield Family Papers, Texas Collection, Baylor University, Waco, Tex.

58. In 1839 an armed Fannin County slave named Smith successfully defended himself when three Indians attacked him in a cornfield, and in 1842 an enslaved woman died fighting Indians at Caney Creek. Porter, "Negroes and Indians on the Texas Frontier, 1831–1876," 197–201.

59. Amos Clark in *The American Slave: Supplement, Series 2*, ed. Rawick, 3:726–727.

60. Anderson Jones in *The American Slave: Supplement, Series 2*, ed. Rawick, 6:2068.

61. George Glasker in *The American Slave: Supplement, Series 2*, ed. Rawick, 5:1505.

62. Fred S. Perrine, ed., "The Journal of Hugh Evans," *Chronicles of Oklahoma* 3 (1925): 194.

63. Porter, "Negroes and Indians on the Texas Frontier, 1831–1876," 194.

64. Ibid., 198.

65. W. M. Williams to M. B. Lamar, 1 April 1840, in *The Papers of Mirabeau Buonaparte Lamar*, ed. Smither, 3:361.

66. "Annual Report of the Commissioner of Indian Affairs, 1848," *House Executive Documents*, 30th Cong., 2d sess. 1 (serial 537), no. 1, 215.

67. Andrew Forest Muir, *Texas in 1837: An Anonymous Contemporary Narrative* (Austin: University of Texas Press, 1958).

68. Sophia Bereall in "Ex-Slaves in Waco," unpublished paper, Baylor University, 1920(?), 14–15.

69. Porter, "Negroes and Indians on the Texas Frontier, 1831–1876," 213–14.

70. According to an estimate by the *Houston Telegraph*, 1,500 former slaves were said to have joined the Comanches on the warpath against Texans. Aptheker, *American Negro Slave Revolts*, 343.

71. John Holland Jenkins, *Recollections of Early Texas*, ed. John Holmes Jenkins III (Austin: University of Texas Press, 1958), 21.

72. Wilbarger, *Indian Depredations in Texas*, 405–11. There are additional examples. In 1838 fugitive slaves, Coshatees, Caddos, and Keechies all fought against Gen. Edward Burleson at Kickapoo Town. A year later, blacks and Biloxi Indians joined forces with Córdova in his attempted insurrection. H. McLeod to M. B. Lamar, 22 Oct. 1838, in *The Papers of Mirabeau Buonaparte Lamar*, ed. Smither, 3:412–13; Wilbarger, *Indian Depredations in Texas*, 151–57.

73. Historian George Woolfolk observes that "the Indian in the western borderlands was to afford the Negro, slave or free, a fruitful alternative to personal discrimination and spiritual emasculation." Kenneth Porter likely provided a more balanced assessment when

he noted "a general pattern of mutual hostility." Even Porter, however, reasoned that the few "examples of cooperation" proved that black-Indian hostility was based more upon cultural conflict than upon racial difference. George Ruble Woolfolk, *The Free Negro in Texas: 1800–1860: A Study in Cultural Compromise*, published for the *Journal of Mexican American History* (Ann Arbor: University Microfilms, 1976), 132; Porter, "Negroes and Indians on the Texas Frontier, 1831–1876," 308.

74. Muriel H. Wright and George H. Shirk, "Artist Möllhausen in Oklahoma, 1853," *Chronicles of Oklahoma* 31 (Winter 1953): 400.

75. Willis Easter in *The American Slave: Supplement, Series 2*, ed. Rawick, 4:1252.

76. An approximate population density of 0.29 for central Texas in 1850 is found by dividing a total population of 8,629 (the number of residents estimated by the U.S. Census for the counties of Robertson, Limestone, Navarro, and Milam in 1850) by a square mileage of 300,000, which is estimated from the map in *Map Guide to the U.S. Federal Census, 1790–1920*, ed. William Thorndale and William Dollarhide (Blane, Wash.: Dollarhide Systems, 1987), 329; J. D. B. DeBow, *The Seventh Census of the United States: 1850, an Appendix* (Washington: Robert Armstong, Public Printer, 1853).

77. Churchill Jones to George H. Daffan, Esq., 25 July 1853, Churchill Jones Letters, Center for American History, University of Texas at Austin.

78. T. Lindsay Baker and Julie Baker, eds., *The WPA Oklahoma Slave Narratives* (Norman: University of Oklahoma Press, 1996), 287.

79. This statistical comparison of family disruption is based on the comparison of my data set of central Texas slave narratives and the published findings of Escott, *Slavery Remembered*. This set of data is an imperfect measure of family disruption and should be regarded as an approximation at best.

80. Calvin Kennard in *The American Slave: Supplement, Series 2*, ed. Rawick, 6:2179.

81. George Glasker in *The American Slave: Supplement, Series 2*, ed. Rawick, 5:1505. The river bottoms were such good hiding places and the region so full of game that one slave recalled fugitives could hide out for as long as a year before returning to their plantation. President Wilson in *The American Slave: Supplement, Series 2*, ed. Rawick, 10:4205. Numerous other former slaves recalled slave flight in central Texas in response to whipping. Wesley Burrell remembered that "we had an overseer so mean de nigger a runned off in de woods." After a violent encounter with their owner, William Moore remembered that a mother and child fled into the woods for "two or three months." Wesley Burrell and William Moore both in *The American Slave: Supplement, Series 2*, ed. Rawick, 3:535 and 7:2768–69.

82. A number of scholars have suggested that slaves resisted the abuse of power by masters, including Genovese, *Roll, Jordan, Roll*; Peter Kolchin, *Unfree Labor: American Slavery and Russian Serfdom* (Cambridge, Mass.: Harvard University Press, 1987); and Charles Joyner, *Down by the Riverside: A South Carolina Slave Community* (Urbana: University of Illinois Press, 1984), 232.

83. Such information does not mean that Texas slaves were somehow less content than those slaves living in the earlier-settled regions of the South. After all, the majority of central Texas slaves had just recently arrived from those states. Most slave communities throughout the South exhibited the same signs of rebelliousness displayed by the central Texas slaves, but those communities did not have the opportunities provided by the Texas frontier.

84. President Wilson in *The American Slave: Supplement, Series 2*, ed. Rawick, 10:4205.

85. For the defense of slavery and its influence, see Drew Gilpin Faust, ed., *The Ideology of Slavery: Proslavery Thought in the Antebellum South, 1830–1860* (Baton Rouge: Louisiana State University Press, 1981); Anne C. Loveland, *Southern Evangelicals and the Social Order, 1800–1860* (Baton Rouge: Louisiana State Press, 1980); William Sumner Jenkins, *Pro-Slavery Thought in the Old South* (Gloucester: Peter Smith, 1960); Larry E. Tise, *Proslavery: A History of the Defense of Slavery in America, 1701–1840* (Athens: University of Georgia Press, 1987); James O. Farmer Jr., *The Metaphysical Confederacy: James Henley Thornwell and the Synthesis of American Values* (Macon: Mercer University Press, 1986); Eugene D. Genovese, *The Slaveholder's Dilemma: Freedom and Progress in Southern Conservative Thought, 1820–1860* (Columbia: University of South Carolina Press, 1992); Willie Lee Rose, "The Domestication of Slavery," in *Slavery and Freedom*, ed. William W. Freehling (New York: Oxford University Press, 1982), 18–36; see also Genovese, *Roll, Jordan, Roll.*

86. Although Texas slaveholders fancied themselves paternalists, recently arrived Texas slaveholders found their organic social philosophy difficult to follow because slavery in the Old South was wedded to an exploitative economic system that demanded production for the world market. Especially for those slaveholders who had borrowed large amounts of capital to move to Texas, planter paternalism had to contend with the material realities of building a plantation and turning a quick profit. This contradiction often led the slaveholders to violate key tenets of the paternal bargain, such as selling off members of slave families, and, thus, undermining any trust that had developed between master and slave. For the financial difficulties involved in moving to the frontier, see Cashin, *A Family Venture.*

87. Charles William Tait Family Papers, Center for American History, University of Texas at Austin. The Tait plantation is discussed in a number of works on Texas, including Abigail Curlee, "A Study of Texas Slave Plantations, 1822–1865," Ph.D. diss., University of Texas at Austin, 1932. Planters did more than merely lay out the rules, they sought to convince their slaves of their legitimacy by fulfilling, both symbolically and physically, the master's role as provider and caretaker. One former slave recalled that Churchill Jones would "wear a long w'ite beard, reach 'bout to he waist. He used to let us climb 'roun him an' I kin recall 'bout a dozen of us, a-settin' on his knee and a-plaitin' an' a-twistin' on his beard." Henry Broadus in *The American Slave: Supplement, Series 2*, ed. Rawick, 2:441.

88. Churchill Jones Letters, Center for American History, University of Texas at Austin.

89. Henry Broadus in *The American Slave: Supplement, Series 2*, ed. Rawick, 2:444.

90. Ned Broadus in *The American Slave: Supplement, Series 2*, ed. Rawick, 2:434–437.

91. Baker and Baker, eds., *The WPA Oklahoma Slave Narratives*, 284.

92. Henry Childers in *The American Slave: Supplement, Series 2*, ed. Rawick, 3:697.

93. Mary Ann Carter to Laura Perry, 5 Oct. 1851, Laura L. Perry Papers, Texas Collection, Baylor University, Waco, Tex.

94. Walter Cotton, *History of the Negroes in Limestone County* (Mexia, Tex.: J. A. Chatman and S. M. Merriwether, 1939), 5.

95. Lou Austin in *The American Slave: Supplement, Series 2*, ed. Rawick, 2:121–32.

96. Jeffrey Kent Lucas, "Hill County History: Early Settlement through Congressional Reconstruction," master's thesis, Baylor University, 1993, 44.

97. Tobe Zollicoffer in *The American Slave: Supplement, Series 2*, ed. Rawick, 10:4323.

98. Wilbarger, *Indian Depredations in Texas*, 580, emphasis added.

99. Rena Maverick Green, ed., *Samuel Maverick, Texan: 1803–1870* (San Antonio: Private printing, 1952), 73.

100. Wilbarger, *Indian Depredations in Texas*, 431.

101. L. W. Kemp, ed., "Early Days in Milam Country: Reminiscences of Susan Turnham McCown," *Southwestern Historical Quarterly* 50 (1947): 366–76.

102. It is true that slave narratives abound with favorable discussion of former slave-owners. If we trust these statements, it seems that a number of slaves accepted the reality of plantation life and acquiesced to its peculiar moral code. Almost one-quarter of the former slaves who lived in central Texas claimed that their masters only punished slaves for justifiable reasons. A third of the former slaves recalled their master in either favorable or very favorable terms. Former bondswomen Becky Evans recalled that "Ole Massa would at the end of the year give us a suit of clothes and feed us good, an would not allow us to be whipped. Why, I lived among the white girls, just like I was one of them. The white boys had to work too. Yes, Honey, the white people were good to us in every way, and they always waited on us whenever we got sick." Any acceptance of the paternal bargain, however, was strictly limited. Even Becky Evans, for example, recalled that she would "go to the woods and stay" if the overseer or her master treated her poorly. Evans's age is unknown, but her interview was probably conducted around 1920. Judging from other details of her life story, she was approaching adulthood, if not already an adult, by the time of emancipation, meaning that she was probably born between 1830 and 1850. Becky Evans in "Ex-Slaves in Waco," unpublished paper, Baylor University 1920(?), 4.

Just as Evans's statement suggests the need to carefully weigh even the most positive statements about slaveholders, one of Churchill Jones's slaves helps explain how slaves reacted to a paternalist. Ned Broadus recalled a slave song that captured acceptance of their condition while simultaneously voicing implicit critique of slavery: "Dey crucified my Lawd / An' He nevah said a word. / Dey crucified my Lawd / An' He nevah said a mumblin' word. / Not a word—not a word—not a word." Jesus' silence did not mean he thought his crucifixion just, and the slaves' quiet did not mean they believed their enslavement to be just. Ned Broadus in *The American Slave: Supplement, Series 2*, ed. Rawick, 2:440.

103. "Ex-Slaves in Waco," 15. The eight to ten slaves not interviewed should be compared with the fifteen interviews completed. Approximately ⅓ to ⅔ of Waco's former slaves refused to talk about slavery, suggesting that the slave narratives should be considered an incomplete, if still useful, sampling of the slave population.

104. Wesley Burrell in *The American Slave: Supplement, Series 2*, ed. Rawick, 3:537.

105. DeBow, *The Seventh Census of the United States: 1850, An Appendix*. Population statistics for the Republic of Texas are sketchy, but an excellent account that pays close attention to the number of slaves is Campbell, *An Empire for Slavery*.

106. George Barnard Papers, Texas Collection, Baylor University, Waco, Tex.

107. For the early political development of Waco, see Walter Baker, "Political History of McLennan County," master's thesis, Baylor University, 1936.

108. The Callahan expedition warned Mexican authorities that Texans would no longer tolerate the harboring of fugitive slaves. Ronnie Tyler ("Slave Owners and Runaway Slaves in Texas") suggests that the warning, in fact, worked. Mexicans, he argues, returned slaves

more often after 1855. The establishment of Fort Belknap on the Texas frontier and the destruction of the Brazos Indian reservation pushed the Native Americans of central Texas to the north and west. On Belknap, see Roger N. Conger et al., *Frontier Forts of Texas* (Waco: Texian Press, 1966), 5–19; on the Brazos reservation, see Kenneth S. Neighbors, "Robert S. Neighbors and the Founding of the Texas Indian Reservations," *West Texas Historical Association Yearbook* 31 (1955): 65–74; and Kenneth S. Neighbors, "The Assassination of Robert S. Neighbors," *West Texas Historical Association Yearbook* 34 (1958): 38–49.

109. Waco's whipping post and auction block are remembered by a number of former slaves, including Aaron Ray and Andy Williams, both in *The American Slave: Supplement, Series 2*, ed. Rawick, 8:3257, 10:4070.

110. Baker, "Political History of McLennan County," 75.

111. "Diary, 24 June–20 July 1855," James Buckner Barry Papers, 1847–1917, Center for American History, University of Texas at Austin.

112. Commissioner's Court Minutes, Falls County, District Court Civil Minute Books, vol. A (1851–56), Texas Collection, Baylor University, Waco, Tex.

113. *Waco Tribune,* 16 June 1895.

114. *Brazos Statesman* (Waco), 3 Jan. 1857.

115. *Southern Democrat* (Waco), 18 Nov. 1858.

116. Ralph A. Wooster, "Membership in Early Texas Legislatures, 1850–1860," *Southwestern Historical Quarterly* 69 (1965): 163–73.

117. *State of Texas v. Simon, a slave of Thomas Alexander,* case no. 214, McLennan County Civil and Criminal Minute Books, vol. C, 100–193, McLennan County Archives, Waco, Tex.

118. *State of Texas v. Fed, a Slave,* case no. 198, Falls County Civil and Criminal Minute Books, vol. B, Texas Collection, Baylor University, Waco, Tex.

119. In most instances Texas law did not require a grand jury investigation for cases involving slaves. Thus it is likely that the surviving court records (incomplete in any event) fail to include a number of legal procedures involving slaves. Nevertheless, the two cases that do appear in the record indicate that the formal legal system was sometimes invoked to punish slaves. Such moments were likely infrequent because these two cases represent fewer than 1 percent of all criminal cases during the 1850s. The surviving minutes books and case files from Bosque, Falls, and McLennan counties contain information on nearly four hundred criminal indictments and cases from 1850 to 1859. McLennan County Civil and Criminal Minute Books, vols. A-C, McLennan County Archives, Waco, Tex.; Falls County Civil and Criminal Minute Books, vols. A-B; Bosque County Civil and Criminal Minute Books, vol. A; Case Files of the Third and Nineteenth District Courts, McLennan County Archives, Waco, Tex.

120. *State of Texas v. Lewis Cooley and Robert Thompson,* case no. 151, fall term 1857, Falls County Civil and Criminal Minute Books, vol. A, 332.

121. *State of Texas v. H. White,* case no. 261, fall term 1859, McLennan County Civil and Criminal Minute Books, vol. C, 270–354, and *State of Texas v. William King,* case no. 265, fall term 1859, McLennan County Civil and Criminal Minute Books, vol. C, 314, both in McLennan County Archives, Waco, Tex.

122. For example, Henry Coleman and Jonathan Pool were fined $5 or less after receiving convictions for attempted murder. *State of Texas v. John J. Long,* case no. 96, fall term 1856, *State of Texas v. L[abor] Dodson,* case no. 105, fall term 1856, *State of Texas v.*

Jonathan Pool, case no. 85, fall term 1855, and *State of Texas v. Henry B. Coleman,* case no. 67, fall term 1854, all in Falls County Civil and Criminal Minute Books, vol. A, 254, 281, 300, 255, 285, 116, and 209.

123. Frederick Douglass, "The Annexation of Texas: An Address Delivered in Cork, Ireland, on 3 November 1845," and "Texas, Slavery, and American Prosperity: An Address Delivered in Belfast, Ireland, on 2 January 1846," in *The Papers of Frederick Douglass,* ed. John W. Blassingame, series 1: *Speeches, Debates, and Interviews,* vol. 1: *1841–1846* (New Haven: Yale University Press, 1979), 73, 120.

124. *State of Texas v. Alexander McGehey,* cases no. 200 and no. 221, spring and fall terms 1858, McLennan County Civil and Criminal Minute Books, vol. C, 30–193, McLennan County Archives, Waco, Tex.

125. *Southern Democrat* (Waco), 18 Nov. 1858. For a discussion of the Penal Code of 1856 as it relates to slavery, see Lockhart, "Slave Code of Texas," 51–54.

126. *State of Texas v. H. White,* case no. 261, and *State of Texas v. William King,* case no. 265, fall term 1859, both in McLennan County District Court Minute Books, vol. C, 270–354, McLennan County Archives, Waco, Tex.; *State of Texas v. Frank, a Mexican,* case no. 200, and *State of Texas v. George White,* case no. 208, spring term 1860, both in Falls County District Court Minute Books, vol. B, 50, 51, 122, ; *State of Texas v. A. H. Cushman,* case no. 284, spring term 1860, McLennan County District Court Minute Books, vol. C, 374, McLennan County Archives, Waco, Tex.; *State of Texas v. James Skein,* cases no. 34 and no. 35, fall term 1860, Bosque County District Court Minute Books, vol. A, 219, 365, 379; *State of Texas v. William Lathrop,* case no. 296, fall term 1860, McLennan County District Court Minute Books, vol. C, 449, McLennan County Archives, Waco, Tex.

127. John M. Clayton to Luis de la Rosa, 21 March, 6 July 1850, and Luis de la Rosa to John M. Clayton, 19 March 1850, both in *Diplomatic Correspondence of the United States,* ed. William R. Manning (Washington: Carnegie Endowment for International Peace, 1937), 9:50, 9:56–57, 9:350; Tyler, "Slaveowners and Runaway Slaves," 19. For an account of the Seminole maroons in Mexico, see Kevin Mulroy, *Freedom on the Border: The Seminole Maroons in Florida, the Indian Territory, Coahuila, and Texas* (Lubbock: Texas Tech University Press, 1993). Historians before Mulroy who focused on the continued resistance of the Seminoles after removal include Kenneth W. Porter, "The Seminole in Mexico, 1850–1861," *Hispanic American Historical Review* 31 (1951): 1–36; Tyler, "Slaveonwers and Runaway Slaves;" Daniel Littlefield, *Africans and Seminoles: From Removal to Emancipation* (Westport: Greenwood Press, 1977); and Richard Allen Sattler, "Seminoli Italwa: Socio-Political Change among the Oklahoma Seminoles between Removal and Allotment, 1836–1905," Ph.D. diss., University of Oklahoma, 1987.

128. Juan Manuel Madlonado to P. H. Bell, 22 Sept. 1851, Office of the Governor, Records of Gov. P. H. Bell, RG 301, Archives and Information Services Division, Texas State Library and Archives Commission, Austin (hereafter Texas State Archives); Jesse Sumpter, *Life of Jesse Sumpter* (Self-published? 1902), ch. 4; Tyler, "Slaveowners and Runaway Slaves," 21.

129. According to a report issued by the Mexican government nearly twenty years after the invasion, "The pretext was the pursuit of the tribe of Lipan Indians of whom the Texans complained . . . [but it] is probable, nevertheless, that one of the incentives was the capture of fugitive slaves." *Report of the Committee of Investigation Sent in 1873 by the Mexican Government to the Frontier of Texas* (New York: Baker and Godwin, 1875), 178. His-

torian Ronnie C. Tyler demonstrated persuasively in 1967 that the capture of escaped slaves was the primary mission of Callahan's foray. Ronnie C. Tyler, "The Callahan Expedition of 1855: Indians or Negroes?" *Southwestern Historical Quarterly* 70 (1967): 574–86.

130. Individuals were more successful than Callahan's party in recapturing fugitive slaves by illegally crossing the border in 1855. For one example, see J. D. B. Stillman, *Wanderings in the Southwest in 1855* (Spokane: Arthur H. Clarke, 1990), 119–20.

131. Tyler, "The Callahan Expedition of 1855: Indians or Negroes?" 574–86.

132. Gammel, *The Laws of Texas,* 1:1385–86, 4:1074–75.

133. *Report of the Committee of Investigation Sent in 1873 by the Mexican Government to the Frontier of Texas* (New York: Baker and Godwin, 1875), 178–92.

134. Porter, *The Negro on the American Frontier,* 463.

135. Some evidence of this can be gleaned from the manuscript returns of the U.S. Census in McLennan County. The census taker did not use the column under the heading "fugitive slaves" to mark down the number of escaped slaves but instead used that column to help him add up the number of mulattos on a given census page. Because we know that at least some slaves were almost surely temporarily "on leave," failure to use that column seems likely to mean that the census taker was unwilling to ask his superiors about this delicate subject. Manuscript Census, McLennan County, schedule 1, "1860."

136. George P. Garrison, *Texas: A Contest of Civilizations* (Boston: Houghton Mifflin, 1903), 273–74.

137. H. S. Thrall, *A History of Texas: From the Earliest Settlements to the Year 1876* (New York: University Publishing, 1876), 146.

138. Olmsted, *A Journey through Texas,* 163. For a discussion of Olmsted's reliability as a witness, see Arthur M. Schlesinger, "Was Olmsted an Unbiased Critic of the South?" *Journal of Negro History* 37 (1952): 173–87.

139. When the plot was discovered, slaveholders punished the slaves immediately and jailed the Mexicans. The jail, however, could not hold the alleged conspirators, and they escaped. *Texas Sentinel,* 3 Oct. 1857, cited in Frank H. Smyrl, "Unionism, Abolitionism, and Vigilantism in Texas," master's thesis, University of Texas at Austin, 1961, 34.

140. Tyler, "Slave Owners and Runaway Slaves in Texas," 68–69; Addington, "Slave Insurrections in Texas," 414–18.

141. *San Antonio Herald,* 6 Feb. 1858, cited in de León, *Apuntes Tejanos.* Anglo warnings of Mexican-slave alliances far exceeded the actual existence of such combinations, but the two groups united just often enough to maintain white apprehensions. In 1838, two years after Thomas Morgan cautioned that black slaves were pursuing an alliance with Indians and Mexicans, "a motley gang" of Mexicans, fugitive slaves, Coushatta Indians, and others attacked an armed force of Anglos under Gen. Thomas Jefferson Rusk near Kickapoo Town. Rusk's force suffered eleven men wounded, but the Anglos killed eleven of the insurgents. A few months later, in March of 1839, fugitive slaves, mulattos, and free blacks fought with the Mexican rebel Vicente Córdova in his attempt to topple the Texas republic. Gen. Burleson and the Texas Rangers defeated Córdova east of Seguin, killing two black rebels and capturing two more. One of the captive black men was a two-hundred-pound "French Negro" named Raphael. The rebel claimed he was a free man who held nothing but hostility for Anglo Texans and refused to acknowledge the legitimacy of their republic. Although his companion was sold into slavery, Raphael's defiant

tone left Texans with little choice but to execute him. H. McLeod to M. B. Lamar, 22 Oct. 1838, in *The Papers of Mirabeau Buonaparte Lamar,* ed. Smither, 2:412–13; Wilbarger, *Indian Depredations in Texas,* 151–57.

142. B. J. White to Stephen F. Austin, 17 Oct. 1835, in *The Austin Papers,* ed. Barker, 3:190.

143. Kenneth Wiggins Porter, *The Negro on the American Frontier* (New York: Arno Press, 1971), 381–82.

144. One newspaper reported that whites in Nacogdoches feared a slave insurrection in 1841. Addington, "Slave Insurrections in Texas," 413.

145. *Texas State Gazette* (Austin), 15 Nov. 1856.

146. *Galveston News,* 11 Sept. 1856, quoted in Olmsted, *A Journey through Texas,* 503.

147. *Texas State Times* (Austin), 27 Sept. 1856; *Dallas Herald,* 27 Sept. 1856; *True Issue* (La Grange), 5 Sept. 1856, reprinted in Olmsted, *A Journey through Texas,* 504.

148. Addington, "Slave Insurrections in Texas," 417–18.

149. Randolph Campbell describes them as "more imaginary than real" in Campbell, *An Empire for Slavery,* 184. Clarence Mohr discusses a similar panic in Georgia in Clarence L. Mohr, *On the Threshold of Freedom: Masters and Slaves in Civil War Georgia* (Athens: University of Georgia Press, 1986).

150. Quoted in Addington, "Slave Insurrections in Texas," 418.

151. Annotated newspaper clipping from the *Courier* in 1860, John Henry Brown Family Papers, Center for American History, University of Texas at Austin.

152. *Galveston News,* 24 Sept. 1857, quoted in Edna Junkins, "Slave Plots, Insurrections, and Acts of Violence in the State of Texas, 1828–1865," master's thesis, Baylor University, 1969, 21.

153. Richard Coke et al. to the Legislature of Texas, undated (1860), Petitions File, Texas State Archives.

154. *The Southwest* (Waco), Wednesday, 17 Oct. 1860.

155. Ibid.

156. *Texas State Gazette* (Austin), 1 Sept. 1860, cited in Smyrl, "Unionism, Abolitionism, and Vigilantism in Texas," 72.

157. *Texas State Gazette* (Austin), 25 Aug. 1860, cited in Edna Junkins, "Slave Plots, Insurrections, and Acts of Violence in the State of Texas, 1828–1865," master's thesis, Baylor University, 1969, 79.

158. "Diary, 13, 23–25 July 1860," James Buckner Barry Papers, 1847–1917, Center for American History, University of Texas at Austin.

159. Philip Howard, Sub-Assistant Commissioner, Meridian, Texas, to L. K. Morton, 15 Sept. 1866, in "Record of Criminal Offenses Committed in the State of Texas," Records of the Assistant Commissioner for the State of Texas, U.S. Bureau of Refugees, Freedmen, and Abandoned Lands, 1865–1869, RG 105, National Archives.

160. Reprinted in John Townsend, *The Doom of Slavery in the Union: Its Safety Out of It* (Charleston: Evans and Cogswell, 1860), 34.

161. Reprinted in Townsend, *The Doom of Slavery in the Union,* 35–36.

162. Frederick Law Olmsted, "A Tour in the Southwest," in *The Papers of Frederick Law Olmsted,* ed. Charles Capen McLaughlin, associate editor Charles E. Beveridge (Baltimore: Johns Hopkins University Press, 1977), 2:304. Historians have concurred with Olmsted. "In Texas, Arkansas, and Louisiana," remarks Genovese, "slaveholders had to exercise vig-

ilance, for many slaves went over the Mexican border or escaped to friendly Indians" (*Roll, Jordan, Roll,* 648).

163. Olmsted, *A Journey through Texas,* 123.

Chapter 4. "Hung Sure as Hell": White-on-White Mob Violence in Central Texas

1. The seven men were identified as Daniel Sessions, Isaac Ellington, Bernard Maye, George Shackleford, and three men named Schoonover. "Register of Felonies Committed in Texas, 1866–1868, Department of Texas and the 5th Military District," pt. 1, 4853, entry nos. 1682–88 and 1155–61, RG 393, U.S. Department of War, National Archives 1 (hereafter NA); "Record of Criminal Offenses Committed in the State of Texas," Records of the Assistant Commissioner for the State of Texas, Bureau of Refugees, Freedmen, and Abandoned Lands (hereafter BRFAL), 1865–69, film 5853, reel 32, entry nos. 1682–88, RG 105, U.S. Department of War, NA.

2. Some studies of lynching appropriately survey the lynching of whites, but the subject deserves more attention. It is especially surprising that historians have focused so little attention on white-on-white lynching in Texas. Scholars, for example, claim that Texas in general and central Texas in particular were especially prone to white-on-white mob violence. Richard Maxwell Brown, one of the most accomplished historians of vigilantism in America, has written that Texas surpassed all other states for its history of mob violence. Brown has particularly focused on central Texas. "No region," he noted in 1975, "has surpassed the acute, long-term violence of central Texas." Other sources seem to confirm that exceptional history. According to the records of Tuskegee University, lynch mobs executed more whites in Texas than in any other state.

The degree to which Texas was uniquely violent, however, remains controversial, and the evidence needed to prove conclusively Brown's assertion remains only partially collected. The relevant surviving primary documents—thousands of nineteenth-century county newspapers—are so extensive that they could never be collected and analyzed by any one scholar. The case of central Texas is illustrative. Two of the most comprehensive studies of mob violence conducted at the national level are Brown's examination of American vigilante organizations and the lynching records collected by Daniel Williams and the staff of the Tuskegee University Archives. Brown's research notes five vigilante movements in the seven central Texas counties studied in this chapter. Brown, however, is only able to list thirteen of the victims executed by these groups between 1860 and 1894. The lynching inventory compiled by Tuskegee covers only the period after 1882 and includes just eleven whites lynched in those seven counties. Even taken together, they fail to identify the vast majority of victims of mob violence in the seven central Texas counties.

Without doubt, similar extensive county-by-county research in other parts of the United States would greatly add to current estimates of those killed by extralegal violence. Definitive conclusions about the relative violence of Texas compared to that of other states must await future research. Given the intractability of proving or disproving claims for the uniqueness of Texas violence, this study confines itself to the more modest but perhaps more important task of explaining why so many Anglos died at the hands of vigilante mobs in central Texas. Richard Maxwell Brown, *Strains of Violence: Historical Stud-*

ies of American Violence and Vigilantism (New York: Oxford University Press, 1975), 237; Richard Maxwell Brown, "The American Vigilante Tradition," in *Violence in America: Historical and Comparative Perspectives*, ed. Hugh Davis Graham and Ted Robert Gurr (Washington: Government Printing Office, 1969), 1:178–80; Daniel T. Williams, comp., "Amid the Gathering Multitude: The Story of Lynching in America, a Classified Listing," Lynching Files, Tuskegee University Archives, Tuskegee University, Tuskegee, Ala.

3. The seven counties studied include Bell, Bosque, Coryell, Falls, Hill, Limestone, and McLennan. Details of the sixty-seven Anglos lynched in central Texas can be found in Appendix A, "Victims of Mob Violence in Central Texas, 1860–1922."

4. Interview with Leroy Dean, Folklore Project, WPA Federal Writers' Project, Manuscript Division, Library of Congress, Washington (hereafter MFWP)

5. James K. Greer, ed., *Buck Barry: Texas Ranger and Frontiersman* (Waco: Moody Texas Ranger Library, 1978), 121–22; "Reminiscences," James Buckner Barry Papers, 1847–1917, Center for American History, University of Texas at Austin.

6. Greer, ed., *Buck Barry*, 123.

7. Ibid., 123.

8. Ibid., 120–23. There are, of course, other explanations for the rise of white lynching in central Texas. It must be remembered that the lynching of whites was only new to central Texas. Whites had been killed by mobs long before 1860 in other parts of the United States, particularly in the South and West.

9. William W. Starm to J. W. Throckmorton, 17 Aug. 1865, in *Texas Indian Papers, 1825–1916*, ed. James Day and Dorman Winfrey, 4 vols. (Austin: Texas State Library, 1959–61), 4:105.

10. Charles B. Pearre to J. W. Throckmorton, Dec. 1866, Office of the Governor, Records of A. J. Hamilton, RG 301, Archives and Information Services Division, Texas State Library and Archives Commission, Austin (hereafter Texas State Archives).

11. William Baker to Mary Baker, 14 Oct. 1866, uncatalogued, William Baker Papers, South Caroliniana Library, University of South Carolina, Columbia.

12. For an important article outlining the theoretical issues in "whiteness" scholarship, see George Lipsitz, "The Possessive Investment in Whiteness: Racialized Social Democracy and the 'White' Problem in American Studies," *American Quarterly* 47 (1995): 369–87. Examples of the rich scholarship on whiteness include David Roediger, *Wages of Whiteness: Race and the Making of the American Working Class* (New York: Verso, 1991); Eric Lott, *Love and Theft: Blackface Minstrelsy and the American Working Class* (New York: Oxford University Press, 1993); Neil Foley, *The White Scourge: Mexicans, Blacks, and Poor Whites in Texas Cotton Culture* (Berkeley: University of California Press, 1997); and Grace Elizabeth Hale, *The Making of Whiteness: The Culture of Segregation, 1890–1930* (New York: Pantheon Books, 1997).

13. Interview with Mrs. George Fowler, MFWP.

14. *Bellville Countryman*, 31 May 1862.

15. *Galveston Daily News*, 15 April 1866.

16. *San Antonio Express*, 6 June 1874; Bertha Atkinson, "History of Bell County," master's thesis, University of Texas at Austin, 1929, 132; Bill O'Neal, "The Mass Lynching at Belton," *Real West* 28 (June 1985): 25; George W. Tyler, *The History of Bell County* (San Antonio: Naylor, 1936), 302–3.

17. Interview with Emma Falconer, MFWP.

18. Interview with John H. Roberston, MFWP.

19. Interview with Leroy Dean, MFWP.

20. *Texas State Gazette* (Austin), 3 Aug. 1861, quoted in Zelma Scott, *A History of Coryell County, Texas* (Austin: Texas State Historical Association, 1965), 60.

21. Atkinson, "History of Bell County," 132.

22. *Corpus Christi Daily Gazette*, 25 Aug. 1876.

23. Appendix A, "Victims of Mob Violence."

24. *San Antonio Express*, 28 July 1877.

25. Excerpted in the *Galveston News*, 21 May 1875.

26. Interview with Leroy Dean, MFWP.

27. Texas State Constitution of 1845 in *Documents of Texas History*, ed. Ernest Wallace and David M. Vigness (Austin: Steck, 1963), 150.

28. Jacob de Cordova, "Texas: Her Resources and Her Public Men" (Philadelphia: E. Crozet, 1858), 351.

29. H. P. N. Gammel, comp., *The Laws of Texas, 1822–1897* (Austin: Gammel Book Co., 1898), 1:1069–85.

30. Two important essays on this topic are Walter L. Buenger, "Texas and the Riddle of Secession," *Southwestern Historical Quarterly* 87 (Oct. 1983): 151–82; and Charles William Ramsdell, "The Frontier and Secession" in *Studies in Southern History and Politics* (Port Washington: Kennikat Press, 1914), 63–79. For information on relations between planters and yeomen in Texas, see Randolph B. Campbell and Richard G. Lowe, *Wealth and Power in Antebellum Texas* (Dallas: Southern Methodist University Press, 1987); and Vista Kay McCroskey, "Plain Folk in Texas, 1821–1860," Ph.D. diss., Texas Christian University, 1990.

31. For an extended discussion (and specific evidence) of the reasons that most non-slaveholders supported planters and slavery in central Texas, see William D. Carrigan, "Between South and West: Race, Violence, and Power in Central Texas, 1836–1916," Ph.D. diss., Emory University, 1999, 104–34.

32. *Texas State Gazette* (Austin), 8 Dec. 1860.

33. "Memoir of Rev. Thaddeus McRae," unpublished typescript, 23–24, Rev. Thaddeus McRae Collection, Archives and Special Collections, J. D. Williams Library, University of Mississippi.

34. Wallace E. Oakes to Edward Clark, 17 April 1861, Office of the Governor, Records of Edward Clark, RG 301, Texas State Archives.

35. The ineffectiveness of the courts is revealed by the number of indictments brought in 1861 and 1862. All three central Texas counties surveyed recorded a relatively small number of indictments during the Civil War, especially in 1861 and 1862. Bosque County Civil and Criminal Minute Books, vol. A; Falls County Civil and Criminal Minute Books, vol. B; and McLennan County Civil and Criminal Minute Books, vol. D, Texas County Records, Texas Collection, Baylor University, Waco, Tex.

36. *State of Texas v. Charles Warren*, case no. 295 (fall 1861), McLennan County Case File and Civil and Criminal Minute Books, vol. D, 18, 28–30, McLennan County Archives, Waco, Tex.

37. *State of Texas v. Charles Warren; Waco Daily Examiner,* 12 and 20 May 1885.

38. The following are all in the McLennan County Civil and Criminal Minute Books, vol. D, McLennan County Archives, Waco, Tex.; *State of Texas v. Eli Ensor,* case no. 301 (fall 1861), *State of Texas v. Demetrius Hays,* case no. 302 (fall 1861), *State of Texas v. William R. Johnson,* case no. 310 (spring 1862–fall 1864), and *State of Texas v. William R. Johnson, Thompson Newby, Andrew Evans, Lankford Cassady, John Blankinship, Lewis Blankinship, Elisha Sanderfer, and T. M. Holt,* case no. 313 (spring 1862–spring 1866); see also *William R. Johnson v. State of Texas,* case no. 2011, Appeal from McLennan County, case no. 310, 10 Jan. 1865, M 4391, Appeals Case Files, Texas State Archives.

39. "Minutes of the Bosque County Committee of Safety," 17 March 1862, excerpted in "Early History of Bosque County," Bosque County Collection, Meridian, Tex.

40. Jasper Starr to E. M. Pease, 21 Oct. 1867, Office of the Governor, Records of Elisha Pease, RG 301, Texas State Archives.

41. *Bellville Countryman,* 31 May 1862.

42. John D. Johnson, McLennan County Dictation, P-024, Bancroft Library, University of California, Berkeley.

43. Jeffrey Kent Lucas, "Hill County History: Early Settlement through Congressional Reconstruction," master's thesis, Baylor University, 1993, 63.

44. George E. Burney to Pendleton Murrah, 14 Jan. 1863, Office of the Governor, Records of Pendleton Murrah, RG 301, Texas State Archives; see also George Erath to Pendleton Murrah, 20 March 1864, and P. Gathings to Pendleton Murrah, 12 April 1864.

45. H. L. Helton et al. to Pendleton Murrah, 11 Jan. 1864, Office of the Governor, Records of Pendleton Murrah, RG 301, Texas State Archives. Other letters emphasizing the "destitute and helpless condition" of the homefront include E. M. Wilder et al. to Pendleton Murrah, 30 Jan. 1864; John S. Scofield to Pendleton Murrah, 30 Jan. 1864; and D. G. Chamberlain to Pendleton Murrah, 16 April 1864.

46. Robert L. Kerby, *Kirby Smith's Confederacy: The Trans-Mississippi South, 1863–1865* (New York: Columbia University Press, 1972), 94.

47. Allan Coleman Ashcraft, "Texas: 1860–1866, the Lone Star State in the Civil War," Ph.D. diss., Columbia University, 1960, 240.

48. Greer, ed., *Buck Barry,* 172.

49. H. E. McCulloch to Samuel Boyer Davis, 25 March 1862, in *War of the Rebellion: A Compilation of the Official Records of the Union and Confederate Armies,* comp. Robert N. Scott, ser. 1 (Washington: Government Printing Office, 1883), 9:704. For additional information on Confederate concerns with Unionists and deserters, see David Paul Smith, "The Limits of Dissent and Loyalty in Texas," in *Guerrillas, Unionists, and Violence on the Confederate Homefront,* ed. Daniel E. Sutherland (Fayetteville: University of Arkansas Press, 1999), 133–49; James Marten, *Texas Divided: Loyalty and Dissent in the Lone Star State, 1856–1874* (Lexington: University Press of Kentucky, 1990); and Georgia Lee Tatum, *Disloyalty in the Confederacy* (Chapel Hill: University of North Carolina Press, 1934), esp. 44–53.

50. "Memoir of Rev. Thaddeus McRae," 26.

51. C. B. H. Blood to W. H. Seward, 23 May 1862, in *War of the Rebellion,* comp. Scott, ser. 1, 9:685–86.

52. The best discussion of the Gainesville lynching is Richard B. McCaslin, *Tainted Breeze: The Great Hanging at Gainesville, Texas, 1862* (Baton Rouge: Louisiana State University Press, 1994).

53. E. A. Limmer Jr. et al., Bell County Historical Commission, *Story of Bell County, Texas* (Austin: Eakin Press, 1988), 1:50–61; C. L. Sonnichsen, *Ten Texas Feuds* (Albuquerque: University of New Mexico Press, 1957), 68–69.

54. D. R. Wallace to Rufus Burleson, President of Waco University, 21 Sept. 1864, Rufus Columbus Burleson Papers, Texas Collection, Baylor University, Waco, Tex.

55. James Smallwood, "When the Klan Rode: White Terror in Reconstruction Texas," *Journal of the West* 25 (1986): 4. A number of historians have explored violence in the South in the late 1860s. Violence, Dan T. Carter wrote, "affected every aspect of the lives and thinking of southerners—rich and poor, black and white." Dan T. Carter, *When the War Was Over: The Failure of Self-Reconstruction in the South, 1865–1867* (Baton Rouge: Louisiana State University Press, 1985), 11. Important monographs that explore violence in the postbellum period include Lou Falkner Williams, *The Great South Carolina Ku Klux Klan Trials of 1871–1872* (Athens: University of Georgia Press, 1996); Allen W. Trelease, *White Terror: The Ku Klux Klan Conspiracy and Southern Reconstruction* (New York: Harper and Row, 1971); George C. Rable, *But There Was No Peace: The Role of Violence in the Politics of Reconstruction* (Athens: University of Georgia Press, 1984); Leon L. Litwack, *Been in the Storm So Long: The Aftermath of Slavery* (New York: Knopf, 1979), and Edward L. Ayers, *Vengeance and Justice: Crime and Punishment in the Nineteenth-Century American South* (New York: Oxford University Press, 1984). These explorations of postbellum violence should be read alongside the impressive studies of southern violence during the antebellum period. Dickson D. Bruce Jr., *Violence and Culture in the Antebellum South* (Austin: University of Texas Press, 1979); Bertram Wyatt-Brown, *Southern Honor: Ethics and Behavior in the Old South* (New York: Oxford University Press, 1982); and Jack K. Williams, *Dueling in the Old South: Vignettes of Social History* (College Station: Texas A&M University Press, 1980). Only a few historians have given detailed attention to violence in Texas during Reconstruction. James M. Smallwood explored white-on-black violence in *Time of Hope, Time of Despair: Black Texans during Reconstruction* (Port Washington: Kennikat Press, 1981), and Barry A. Crouch has produced an important article on violence in Texas from the records of the Freedmen's Bureau in "A Spirit of Lawlessness: White Violence, Texas Blacks, 1865–1868," *Journal of Social History* 18 (1984): 217–32. Gregg Cantrell emphasizes the psychological ramifications of the political atmosphere of 1867 and 1868 in the rise of violence during the period in "Racial Violence and Reconstruction Politics in Texas, 1867–68," *Southwestern Historical Quarterly* 93 (1990): 333–55. In contrast to these historians, William L. Richter, *The Army in Texas during Reconstruction, 1865–1870* (College Station: Texas A&M University Press, 1987), downplays the importance of violence in the period and focuses on the role of the U.S. Army in provoking white resistance. One attempt to explain violence at the local level is Randolph B. Campbell, *Grass-Roots Reconstruction in Texas, 1865–1880* (Baton Rouge: Louisiana State University Press, 1997). These works have been able to suggest a number of important conclusions about violence in Texas during the period. This book, a local study, builds on their work by placing Reconstruction violence at the center of a much longer historical pattern of violence in Texas.

56. "Reports of Field Agents, June 1865–Dec. 1868," entry nos. 1–2305, BRFAL, 1865–69,

RG 105, NA; "Records of Murders and Assaults, 1867–1868," entry nos. 401–1000, Ledger of the Records of the Texas State Police, Texas State Archives (hereafter RTSP).

57. The population of Texas in 1870 was 818,579; the population of the four counties of the Upper Brazos River valley was 35,785. U.S. Bureau of the Census, *The Statistical Population of the United States: Compiled from the Original Returns of the Ninth Census (June 1, 1870)* (Washington: Government Printing Office, 1872). Although statistics for such a small population can only be suggestive and not definitive, it may be useful to point out the murder rate in central Texas from 1865 to 1870 would be calculated at 56.4 per 100,000 inhabitants.

58. Barry Crouch found 939 murders in Texas between 1865 and 1868 ("A Spirit of Lawlessness," 217–32). According to my research in the Freedmen's Bureau Papers and the Texas State Archives, ninety-three men and one woman were murdered in central Texas during that same period. "Reports of Field Agents, June 1865–Dec. 1868," entry nos. 1–2305, BRFAL, 1865–69, RG 105, NA; "Records of Murders and Assaults, 1867–1868," entry nos. 401–1000, Texas State Archives.

59. Between January 1866 and April 1870, 221 crimes were reported in McLennan County, the most of any county in the state during the period. Richter, *The Army in Texas during Reconstruction,* 152. There are several possible explanations for this high level of violence: a combination of intense partisan conflict, heightened murder and mob violence, and scrupulous reporting by area officials.

60. Matthew Young to Kirkman, (early July), 1867, "Letters Sent, Bell County, Texas," entry no. 3663, BRFAL, 1865–69, RG 105, NA.

61. A. W. Evans, Sub-Assistant Commissioner, Waco, Tex., "Statement of Murders, Felonies & c., committed in the District of Waco, Texas, since December 31, 1866," in "Record of Criminal Offenses Committed in the State of Texas," BRFAL, 1865–59, RG 105, NA.

62. Register of Felonies Committed in Texas, 1866–1868, Department of Texas and the 5th Military District, RG 393, pt. 1, 4853, entry numbers 936, 938, NA; "Record of Criminal Offenses Committed in the State of Texas," entry no. 1109, BRFAL, 1865–69, RG 105, NA; and "Records of Murders and Assaults, 1867–1868," Hill County, entry no. 862, Ledger Book (401–1000), RTSP; "Record of Criminal Offenses Committed in the State of Texas," entry no. 785, BRFAL, 1865–69, RG 105, NA.

63. "Record of Criminal Offenses Committed in the State of Texas," BRFAL, 1865–1869, entry no. 2123, RG 105, NA.

64. A. W. Evans to Adjutant, 2 April 1867, Office of the Governor, Records of J. W. Throckmorton, RG 301, Texas State Archives.

65. Matthew Young to Edward Miller, 20 July 1867, "Letters Sent, Bell County, Texas," entry no. 3663, BRFAL, 1865–69, RG 105, NA.

66. "Record of Criminal Offenses Committed in the State of Texas," entry no. 782, BRFAL, 1865–69, RG 105, NA.

67. "Record of Criminal Offenses Committed in the State of Texas," entry no. 2226, BRFAL, 1865–69, RG 105, NA.

68. Lucas, "Hill County History," 105–6.

69. F. B. Sturgis to Henry Ellis, 27 Dec. 1867, "Letters Sent, Falls County, Texas," entry no. 3739, BRFAL, 1865–69, RG 105, NA.

70. *San Antonio Daily Express,* 2 July 1874.

71. Charles Stiles to J. P. Richardson, 12 Nov. 1867, "Letters Sent, Bell County, Texas," entry no. 3739, BRFAL, 1865–69, RG 105, NA.

72. *Galveston Daily News,* 28 June, 25 and 31 July 1866, and 7 April 1867; "Southern Justice," *Harper's Weekly,* 23 March 1867, 184–85; Sonnichsen, *Ten Texas Feuds,* 72–74.

73. Edward and Kate Sturm McCall Rotan Papers, Texas Collection, Baylor University, Waco, Tex.

74. William Markham Sleeper Papers, Texas Collection, Baylor University, Waco, Tex.

75. "Record of Criminal Offenses Committed in the State of Texas," entry no. 695, BRFAL, 1865–69, RG 105, NA.

76. Lucas, "Hill County History," 105.

77. Edward and Kate Sturm McCall Rotan Papers, Texas Collection, Baylor University, Waco, Tex.

78. Tax Rolls, Bosque, Falls, Hill, and McLennan Counties, 1855–73, Texas Collection, Baylor University, Waco, Tex. The 1873 data for Bosque County were missing, and 1874 data have been substituted. Data for 1873 were missing for Hill County. I have substituted 1874 data. Complete tables containing this data can be found in Carrigan, "Between South and West," 169–79.

79. *Brownsville Daily Ranchero,* 20 Jan. 1867, entry no. 696, BRFAL, 1865–69, RG 105, NA.

80. John Martin Parks to (Pres?), McLennan County, Texas, 15 April 1869, Goodwin-Morriss Papers no. 3252, Southern Historical Collection, Wilson Library, University of North Carolina at Chapel Hill.

81. F. B. Sturgis, 3 Jan. 1867, "Letters Sent, Falls County, Texas," entry no. 3739, BRFAL, 1865–69, RG 105, NA.

82. Testimony of Samuel Pointer in *Testimony Taken by the Joint Select Committee to Inquire into the Condition of Affairs in the Late Insurrectionary States, South Carolina,* 3 vols. (Washington: Government Printing Office, 1872), 1:27. Thanks to Hyman Rubin for this reference.

83. I have taken my sample of the 1860 manuscript census and traced all males eight years of age or older forward in time to 1870. For 1870 I have used John M. Usry, comp., *Index to 1870 U.S. Census, McLennan County* (Waco: Central Texas Genealogical Society, 1976) and the various indexes at the Genealogical Archives of the Texas State Library in Austin.

84. I have used the following criteria to verify individuals between 1860 and 1870: same last name, same first name or initial, same middle initial, approximately ten years older in 1870 than in 1860, and same wife or domestic partners. Anyone who works long in the census will realize that the spelling of names is inconsistent from census year to census year. I have tried to take that into account as best I could. When I was unsure that an 1870 listing referred to the same individual listed in the 1860 sample, I included them in the statistics. Despite the fact that omitting them would enhance my argument, to include questionable cases corrects to a certain degree for individuals who lived in Texas but have escaped my attempts to ferret them out. One problem with this technique is that some (but not all) of the indexes I used listed only heads of household, ignoring many male non-heads of household. Fortunately, Usry's index of McLennan County did list all males twenty-one or older and male non-heads of households when their last name was not the same as the head of household.

85. Quoted in Campbell, *Grass-Roots Reconstruction in Texas,* 177.

86. Edward King, *Texas: 1874: An Eyewitness Account of Conditions in Post-Reconstruction Texas* (Houston: Cordovan Press, 1974), 74.

87. James Jay Emerson to J. T. Kirkman, 31 Aug. 1867, "Letters Sent, McLennan County, Texas," no entry no., BRFAL, 1865–69, RG 105, NA.

88. Report of D. F. Stiles, 17 Jan. 1868, "Letters Sent, McLennan County, Texas," entry no. 3781, BRFAL, 1865–69, RG 105, NA.

89. Interview with Edwin Punchard, MFWP.

90. For evidence of Oliver's devoted Republicanism see J. W. Oliver to J. P. Newcomb, 15 Aug. 1870, 2F105, folder 5, and J. W. Oliver to J. P. Newcomb, 26 July 1873, 2F107, folder 4, Newcomb Papers, General Correspondence, Center for American History, University of Texas at Austin. The clash between Oliver and local whites is described in numerous sources; see Edward and Kate Sturm McCall Rotan Papers, Texas Collection, Baylor University, Waco, Tex.; William M. Sleeper and Allan D. Sanford, *Waco Bar and Incidents of Waco History* (Waco: Hill Printing, 1941), 36–38; Campbell, *Grass-Roots Reconstruction in Texas, 1865–1880*, 184–85; and Tony E. Duty, "The Home Front: McLennan County in the Civil War," *Texana* 12 (1974): 223–24.

91. A. J. Evans to E. M. Pease, 9 March 1867, Office of the Governor, Records of E. M. Pease, RG 301, Texas State Archives.

92. James Jay Emerson to J. T. Kirkman, 31 Aug. 1867, "Letters Sent, McLennan County, Texas," entry no. 3781, BRFAL, 1865–69, RG 105, NA.

93. Thomas Harrison to A. J. Hamilton, 22 Jan. 1866, Office of the Governor, Records of A. J. Hamilton, RG 301, Texas State Archives.

94. "Historical Sketch of Waco," 3.

95. William C. Nunn, *Texas under the Carpetbaggers* (Austin: University of Texas Press, 1962), 247–53.

96. For a similar argument regarding taxpayer's conventions in South Carolina, see Williams, *The Great South Carolina Ku Klux Klan Trials.*

97. *Waco Register,* quoted in *Daily State Journal* (Austin), 1 Dec. 1870.

98. For example, see *Report of the Superintendent of the Bureau of Immigration of the State of Texas* (Austin: J. G. Tracy, 1871).

99. D. F. Davis to E. J. Davis, 22 March 1870, Office of the Governor, Records of E. J. Davis, RG 301, Texas State Archives.

100. Ida Leggett Hall, "History of the Negro in Waco, Texas," *Waco Heritage and History* 14 (1984): 11.

101. Homer Lee Kerr, "Migration into Texas, 1860–1880," *Southwestern Historical Quarterly* 70 (1966): 184–216. Although it might have been useful to separate black from white immigrants, Kerr's published statistics reflect the movement of all Texans.

102. Interview with George Ogden, MFWP.

103. Edward and Kate Sturm McCall Rotan Papers, Texas Collection, Baylor University, Waco, Tex.

104. Lucy E. Parsons, ed., *Life of Albert Parsons* (Chicago: Lucy E. Parsons Publisher, 1889), 6–9; David Roediger and Franklin Rosemont, eds., *Haymarket Scrapbook* (Chicago: Charles H. Kerr Publishing, 1986), 13–14, 27, 93; Carolyn Ashbaugh, *Lucy Parsons: American Revolutionary* (Chicago: Charles H. Kerr Publishing, 1976), 13–14.

105. *Belton Journal* quoted in the *Waco Day,* 19 Nov. 1887.

106. Parsons, ed., *Life of Albert Parsons*, 6–9; Roediger and Rosemont, eds., *Haymarket Scrapbook*, 13–14, 27, 93; Ashbaugh, *Lucy Parsons*, 13–14.

107. Roediger and Rosemont, eds., *Haymarket Scrapbook*, 27.

108. "Murders Clipping File," Bosque County Collection, Bosque County Historical Society, Meridian, Tex.; *Daily Democratic Statesman* (Austin), 31 July 1875.

109. Walter Baker, "Political History of McLennan County," master's thesis, Baylor University, 1936, 190 (quotation), 191.

110. The historical markers detailing the founding of these groups can be found under "Old Settlers and Veterans Association of Falls County" and "Confederate Veterans and Old Settlers Reunion Grounds" at the Texas Historic Sites Atlas, a Web site maintained by the Texas State Historical Commission at http://atlas.thc.state.tx.us/ (accessed 20 Jan. 2003).

111. The Confederate Research Center is in the Harold B. Simpson History Center of Hill College in Hillsboro, Texas.

112. Interview with Leroy Dean, MFWP. On William C. Quantrill in Texas, see McCaslin, *Tainted Breeze*, 134, 166.

113. Another central Texas historical marker honors Richard Love of Limestone County, one of the "armed" men who forced Republican governor E. J. Davis to relinquish the government to Democrat Richard Coke. "Moffat" and "Richard Love" at the Texas Historic Sites Atlas, accessed on 20 Jan. 2003.

114. Interview with Sarah Ann Ross Pringle, MFWP.

115. Interview with Mrs. George Fowler, MFWP.

116. See, for example, Sleeper and Sanford, *Waco Bar and Incidents of Waco History*, 36–38.

117. Interview with Edwin Punchard, MFWP. Edward Rotan's memoirs also recall the conflict with Oliver as "the most interesting incident" of Reconstruction. Edward and Kate Strum McCall Rotan Papers, Texas Collection, Baylor University, Waco, Tex.

118. Patricia Ward Wallace, *Waco: Texas Crossroads* (Woodland Hills: Donning, 1983), 31.

119. *Waco Day*, 6 May 1886.

120. The following interviews with central Texans contain references to white-on-white mob violence: John H. Robertson, Dave May, Edwin Punchard, Belle Little, Mrs. George Fowler, Emma Falconer, William Monroe Graves, and Leroy Dean, all MFWP. Local histories that refer to white-on-white mob violence include William Curry, *A History of Waco with Allusions to Six-Shooter Junction* (Waco: Texian Press, 1968), 90–91; Wallace, *Waco: Texas Crossroads*, 59; and George W. Tyler, *The History of Bell County* (San Antonio: Naylor, 1936), 302–3.

121. "Bell County Jail, Early," Texas Historic Sites Atlas (accessed 20 Jan. 2003).

122. Tables and a name-by-name list of victims of mob violence in central Texas appear in Appendixes A and B.

123. Interview with William Monroe Graves, MFWP.

124. Justifications for lynching outside the South can be found in many places, including *Wilmington Every Evening* (Delaware), 26 June 1903; John Eagle to his wife Margaret, Gold Hill, California, 12 Sept. 1853, Huntington Library, San Marino, California. My thanks to Janice Barrow for the reference to the Delaware newspaper.

125. A discussion of the research methods adopted in the analysis of central Texas's court records appears in Appendix C, "Terms, Sources, and Methods."

126. *State of Texas v. Ed Busby,* cases no. 3846 and 4821, Case Files of the Nineteenth District Court, McLennan County Archives, Waco, Tex.

127. The three cases involving men sentenced to life in prison for sexual assault were: *State of Texas v. Lee Robinson,* case no. 2743, *State of Texas v. Dave Robenson,* case no. 2838, *State of Texas v. Tom Quarles,* case no. 4118, Case Files of the Fifty-fourth District Court, McLennan County Archives, Waco, Tex.

128. Statistical Records of the Texas State Penitentiary, Texas State Archives.

129. *Waco Evening News,* 11, 12 April 1894.

130. *Waco Times Herald,* 14 Dec. 1921.

131. *Waco Times Herald,* 14 Dec. 1921, 7 Jan. 1922; *Chicago Defender,* 31 Dec. 1921; *Corpus Christi Caller,* 14 Dec. 1921.

132. *Waco Times Herald,* 14 Dec. 1921.

133. At least forty-three men were indicted for rape or assault to rape in McLennan County between 1867 and 1916. For a number of reasons including periodic incomplete or illegible records, a more likely estimate for the total number of rape and sexual assault cases during these years in McLennan County would double that figure.

134. *Waco Tribune,* 23 June 1895; *State of Texas v. H. S. Morris,* case no. 1165, Fifty-fourth District Court, Case File, McLennan County Archives, Waco, Tex.

135. *State of Texas v. A. F. Gazley,* case no. 4889, 19th District Court, fall term 1885, Case File, McLennan County Archives, Waco, Tex.

136. *Waco Times Herald,* 15, 18, 22, and 28 Dec. 1921, 3 and 7 Jan. 1922.

Chapter 5. "No Justice in It": Racial Violence and Reconstruction

1. Freedmen's Bureau agent Charles Haughn listed the names of only four of the "desperados," but it is probable that the mob was much larger. Report of Charles Haughn, 30 Sept. 1868, "Record of Criminal Offenses Committed in the State of Texas," Records of the Assistant Commissioner for the State of Texas, U.S. Bureau of Refugees, Freedmen, and Abandoned Lands (hereafter BRFAL), 1865–69, entry nos. 2073–85, RG 105, U.S. Department of War, National Archives (hereafter NA). I examined these records both on-site at the National Archives and on microform through Inter-Library Loan. To the above should be added the following microform edition information: film 5853, reel 32. The date of 26 September and the statement that as many as twenty black women were assaulted comes from the account of the episode in Carolyn Ashbaugh, *Lucy Parsons: American Revolutionary* (Chicago: Charles H. Kerr Publishing, 1976), 14–15.

2. Although lynching patterns varied from place to place and over time, this turn-of-the-century decline in lynching departed from the general pattern of continued racial violence throughout the South. This unusual pattern will be explained in chapter 7.

3. To a certain extent the growing size of lynch mobs in the twentieth century is a function of the region's growing population. It was not possible to have a mob of fifteen thousand in Waco in 1860, yet the increase in mob size is out of proportion to the rate of population growth. Mobs attending the lynching of blacks were growing in relative size as well as absolute size.

4. My emphasis on the continuity of white-on-black violence (rather than a set of changes that account for the racialization of lynching in the late nineteenth century) draws on the work of George C. Wright, *Racial Violence in Kentucky, 1865–1940: Lynch-*

ings, Mob Rule, and *"Legal Lynchings"* (Baton Rouge: Louisiana State University Press, 1990); W. Fitzhugh Brundage, *Lynching in the New South: Georgia and Virginia, 1880–1930* (Urbana: University of Illinois Press, 1993); and Christopher Waldrep, *The Many Faces of Judge Lynch: Extralegal Violence and Punishment in America* (New York: Palgrave, 2002).

5. At least six slaves were hanged by vigilance committees in Texas in 1860, but the numbers may have been much larger. One report noted that fifty blacks had been executed in one month in one county alone. Wendell G. Addington, "Slave Insurrections in Texas," *Journal of Negro History* 35 (1950): 408–34. For the account of the slave lynched in Cameron, see "Diary, 13 July 1860," James Buckner Barry Papers, 1847–1917, Center for American History, University of Texas at Austin.

6. Clear and specific evidence does not exist for the lynching of an African American in central Texas before 1865. Circumstantial evidence is strong, however, that vigilantes targeted slaves they suspected of plotting insurrection. Fear of a slave rebellion in central Texas existed throughout the Civil War but probably peaked in 1865. Dan T. Carter, "The Anatomy of Fear: The Christmas Day Insurrection Scare of 1865," *Journal of Southern History* 42 (Aug. 1976): 345–64; interview with William P. Jones, Manuscripts from the Federal Writers' Project, American Memory Digital Collection, Library of Congress (hereafter MFWP).

7. "Reports of Field Agents, June 1865–Dec. 1868," entry nos. 1–2305, esp. 68, 69, 662, 1009, 1578, 1946, 2032, 2034–2036, 2042, 2125, 2126, 2225, BRFAL, 1865–69, RG 105, NA; "Records of Murders and Assaults, 1867–1868," Ledger of the Records of the Texas State Police (hereafter RTSP), Archives and Information Services Division, Texas State Library and Archives Commission, Austin (hereafter Texas State Archives).

8. "Reports of Field Agents, June 1865–Dec. 1868," entry nos. 1–2305, BRFAL, 1865–69, RG 105, NA; "Records of Murders and Assaults, 1867–1868," RTSP.

9. The murder rate for blacks during those five years is an astounding 86.4 per 100,000. By comparison, the annual murder rate of African Americans in the United States in 1996 was approximately 27.5 per 100,000 inhabitants. That figure is based on the number of blacks murdered in the United States in 1996, which have been projected to be 9,626.5 (or 49 percent of all murders). The African American population of the United States in 1996 has been estimated at approximately thirty-five million. For 1996 statistics see *Uniform Crime Reports* (Washington: Government Printing Office, 1997), 14, 397.

10. In 1996, 93 percent of black murder victims were killed by African Americans. *Uniform Crime Reports*, 14, 397.

11. Between 1865 and 1868, Barry Crouch found, 373 African Americans were murdered by whites in Texas. According to my research in the Freedmen's Bureau Papers and the Texas State Archives, forty-two black men were murdered in central Texas during the same period. Crouch, "A Spirit of Lawlessness: White Violence, Texas Blacks, 1865–1868," *Journal of Social History* 18 (1984): 217–32; see also "Record of Criminal Offenses Committed in the State of Texas," BRFAL, 1865–69, RG 105, NA, and "Records of Murders and Assaults, 1867–1868," RTSP.

12. Randolph B. Campbell, *Grass-Roots Reconstruction in Texas 1865–1880* (Baton Rouge: Louisiana State University Press, 1997), 178, 176.

13. Calvin Kennard in *The American Slave: A Composite Autobiography: Supplement, Series 2*, ed. George P. Rawick (Westport: Greenwood Press, 1979), 6:2179.

14. Allan Coleman Ashcraft, "Texas, 1860–66: The Lone Star State in the Civil War," Ph.D. diss., Columbia University, 1960, 260.

15. Annie Whitley Ware in *The American Slave: Supplement, Series 2*, ed. Rawick, 10:3963.

16. Thomas Ford, Philip Howard, and S. S. Nichols to A. J. Hamilton, 6 Sept. 1865, Office of the Governor, Records of A. J. Hamilton, RG 301, Texas State Archives. William Richard's name was added to the list of slave buyers in Philip Howard, Sub-Assistant Commissioner, Meridian, Tex., to L. K. Morton, 25 Sept. 1866, "Miscellaneous Records Relating to Murders and Other Criminal Offenses Committed in Texas, 1865–68," BRFAL, 1865–69, RG 105, NA. For additional references to blacks being held in bondage after the Civil War, see F. B. Sturgis to Henry Ellis, 27 Dec. 1866, "Letters Sent, Marlin, Texas," entry no. 3739, Philip Howard to Robert Pool, 13 Aug. 1867, and Philip Howard to Isaac Malone, 28 Oct. 1867, Meridian, Tex., entry no. 3748, all in "Letters Sent, Records of the Subassistant Commissioners for the BRFAL," RG 105, NA; *Frank Briggs v. Herman Ward, Joe Grover v. Rev. William Beaver, Maria Madison v. Tom Waller, Caroline Green v. Captain William Beck*, "Register of Complaints, Belton, Texas," entry no. 3665, BRFAL, 1865–69, RG 105, NA.

17. Philip Howard, Sub-Assistant Commissioner, Meridian, Tex., to L. K. Morton, 25 Sept. 1866, BRFAL, 1865–69, RG 105, NA.

18. Neither the Minute Books nor the existing case files regularly identify the race of the individual indicted. Five of the defendants listed in Table 8 are clearly identified as "freedmen," but circumstantial evidence suggests that most, if not all, were once enslaved.

19. *State of Texas v. Jack Harris*, case no. 521, and *State of Texas v. Eli Bradly*, case no. 525, both in McLennan County Civil and Criminal Minute Books, vol. D, McLennan County Archives, Waco, Tex. Attention to context helps to assess the significance of these harsh sentences. In their first fifteen years of operation, the courts of Bosque, Falls, Hill, and McLennan counties rendered only six guilty verdicts for theft, burglary, or robbery. In the eight years following the end of the Civil War, those same courts handed down at least thirty guilty verdicts, often to black defendants. Furthermore, the severity of the punishments increased as well. Before 1865 five of the six men found guilty of theft were fined, whipped, or sentenced to less than a year in prison. A man convicted of horse theft earned the most severe penalty, five years in prison. After the Civil War, more than half of those convicted for theft received sentences of five years or more in prison. The legal system in central Texas, for both whites and blacks, was fundamentally transformed and enlarged by emancipation.

20. For example, Gen. J. J. Reynolds, commander of the Fifth Military District, issued Special Order Number 206. That order removed Judge Thomas Harrison and District Attorney C. B. Pearre and replaced them with Unionists and Republicans. A. J. Evans became judge of the Eleventh Judicial District, and J. J. Vardeman became district attorney. McLennan County Civil and Criminal Minute Books, vol. E, fall 1867, McLennan County Archives, Waco, Tex.

21. On the flight of refugees in Texas, see Randolph B. Campbell, *An Empire for Slavery: The Peculiar Institution in Texas* (Baton Rouge: Louisiana State University Press, 1989), 243–46; and Mary Elizabeth Massey, *Refugee Life in the Confederacy* (Baton Rouge: Louisiana State University Press, 1964), esp. 90–93, 119, 123–24.

22. Calvin Kennard in *The American Slave: Supplement, Series 2*, ed. Rawick, 6:2179.

23. William Moore in *The American Slave: Supplement, Series 2*, ed. Rawick, 7:2767–68.

24. S. L. Love of Milam County, Tex., to Mrs. S. V. Young of Concord, N.C., 27 Dec. 1869, in the Burton and Young Papers and Books no. 111, Southern Historical Collection, Wilson Library, University of North Carolina at Chapel Hill.

25. Aaron Ray in *The American Slave: Supplement, Series 2,* ed. Rawick, 8:3256.

26. Diary Pages, 1838–94, undated, Billingsley Papers, Center for American History, University of Texas at Austin. Other examples of sharecropping arrangements in central Texas can be found in the "Diary of Henrietta Hardin Carter Harrison," Carter-Harrison Family Papers, Texas Collection, Baylor University, Waco, Tex.; and the slave narratives of the Works Progress Administration. See, for example, Sarah Wilson in *The American Slave: Supplement, Series 2,* ed. Rawick, 10:4221–22.

27. Janey Landrum in *The American Slave: Supplement, Series 2,* ed. Rawick, 6:2270–71.

28. Ellen Kelly in *The American Slave: Supplement, Series 2,* ed. Rawick, 6:2172.

29. Sam Forge in *The American Slave: Supplement, Series 2,* ed. Rawick, 4:1370–71.

30. Thomas Ford, Philip Howard, and S. S. Nichols to A. J. Hamilton, 6 Sept. 1865, Office of the Governor, Records of A. J. Hamilton, RG 301, Texas State Archives.

31. Entry no. 78, BRFAL, 1865–69, RG 105, NA.

32. Entry no. 2032, BRFAL, 1865–69, RG 105, NA.

33. Entry no. 1843, BRFAL, 1865–69, RG 105, NA.

34. Entry no. 2087, BRFAL, 1865–69, RG 105, NA.

35. Entry no. 2043, BRFAL, 1865–69, RG 105, NA.

36. F. B. Sturgis to Charles Griffin, 2 May 1867, "Letters Sent, Marlin, Texas," entry no. 3739, BRFAL, 1865–69, RG 105, NA.

37. Entry no. 2124, BRFAL, 1865–69, RG 105, NA.

38. "Reports of Field Agents, June 1865–Dec. 1868," entry nos. 1–2305, BRFAL, 1865–69, RG 105, NA.

39. Sam Forge in *The American Slave: Supplement, Series 2,* ed. Rawick, 4:1370–71.

40. Anderson Jones in *The American Slave: Supplement, Series 2,* ed. Rawick, 6:2066.

41. Sam Forge in *The American Slave: Supplement, Series 2,* ed. Rawick, 4:1370–71.

42. Entry no. 91, BRFAL, RG 105, NA.

43. Entry no. 2045, BRFAL, RG 105, NA.

44. Entry no. 2044, BRFAL, RG 105, NA.

45. Entry no. 1574, BRFAL, RG 105, NA.

46. B. G. Shields, Carolina, Falls County, to E. M. Pease, Austin, Texas, 14 June 1868, film 5853, reel 32, target 5: "Miscellaneous Records Relating to Murders and other Criminal Offenses Committed in Texas, 1865–1868," BFRAL, RG 105, NA.

47. Entry no. 65, BRFAL, RG 105, NA.

48. "Reports of Field Agents, June 1865–Dec. 1868," entry nos. 1–2305, BRFAL, RG 105, NA; "Records of Murders and Assaults, 1867–1868," RTSP.

49. On the roles of black women before and after the Civil War, see Jacqueline Jones, *Labor of Love, Labor of Sorrows: Black Women, Work, and the Family from Slavery to the Present* (New York: Vintage, 1985).

50. "Reports of Field Agents, June 1865–Dec. 1868," entry nos. 1–2305, BRFAL, RG 105, NA; "Records of Murders and Assaults, 1867–1868," RTSP.

51. Entry no. 19, BRFAL, RG 105, NA.

52. *New York Times,* 31 Aug. 1868; "Record of Criminal Offenses Committed in the State

of Texas," entry no. 1938, BRFAL, RG 105, NA. Mrs. Wilson's first name is, unfortunately, not given in the reports.

53. For additional references to the rape of black women in central Texas during Reconstruction (all in RG 105, NA), see Testimony of T. N. Barton, Complaints of Freedmen to F. B. Sturgis, Register of Complaints, Marlin, Tex. (entry no. 3740); *Emily Reed v. E. A. Bingham*, Register of Complaints Recorded by Charles Rand, Marlin, Tex. (entry no. 3742); *Louis Jones v. W. A. Carter*, Register of Complaints, Belton, Tex. (entry no. 3665); and *Freedmen's Bureau v. John Driver*, case no. 151, Register of Complaints, Meridian, Tex. (entry no. 3749).

54. Entry no. 70, BRFAL, RG 105, NA.

55. Entry no. 90, BRFAL, RG 105, NA.

56. Entry no. 1185, BRFAL, RG 105, NA.

57. B. G. Shields, Carolina, Falls County, to E. M. Pease, Austin, Texas, 14 June 1868, BRFAL, RG 105, NA.

58. T. Lindsay Baker and Julie Baker, eds., *The WPA Oklahoma Slave Narratives* (Norman: University of Oklahoma Press, 1996), 284.

59. Walter F. Cotton, *History of Negroes in Limestone County* (Mexia, Tex.: J. A. Chatman and S. M. Merriwether, 1939), 18; James M. Smallwood, Barry A. Crouch, and Larry Peacock, *Murder and Mayhem: The War of Reconstruction in Texas* (College Station: Texas A&M University Press, 2003), 121–24.

60. Smallwood, Crouch, and Peacock, *Murder and Mayhem*, 121–24; Cotton, *History of Negroes in Limestone County*, 18–19.

61. Ida Leggett Hall, "History of the Negro in Waco, Texas," *Waco Heritage and History* 14 (1984): 9. Hall's essay was originally written in 1928 for a sociology class at Baylor University. The activities of the Fishbackers are also discussed in the William Markham Sleeper Papers, Texas Collection, Baylor University, Waco, Tex.

62. Hattie Gates in *The American Slave: Supplement, Series 2*, ed. Rawick, 5:1458–66.

63. Joe Oliver in *The American Slave: Supplement, Series 2*, ed. Rawick, 8:2981–82.

64. *The New Era* (Washington), 30 March 1871.

65. Hall, "History of the Negro in Waco, Texas," 14.

66. Quoted in *The New Era* (Washington), 23 June 1870.

67. Matthew Young to J. T. Kirkman, 13 July 1867, "Letters Sent, Belton, Texas," entry no. 3663, BRFAL, RG 105, NA.

68. Quoted in Campbell, *Grass-Roots Reconstruction in Texas*, 177.

69. *The Freedmen's Press* (Austin, Texas), 15 Aug. 1868.

70. Report of Charles Haughn, 1 Aug. 1868, entry numbers 1945 and 1390, Register of Felonies Committed in Texas, 1866–1868 (4853), Department of Texas and the 5th Military District, RG 393.

71. *The New Era* (Washington), 28 Sept. 1871.

72. D. F. Davis to E. J. Davis, 12 Jan. 1870, Office of the Governor, Records of E. J. Davis, RG 301, Texas State Archives.

73. *Flake's Bulletin* (Galveston), 22 May 1867, 4; Carl H. Moneyhon, *Republicanism in Reconstruction Texas* (Austin: University of Texas Press, 1980).

74. Campbell, *Grass-Roots Reconstruction in Texas*, 173. Few central Texans could match the devotion to black political organizing displayed by Albert Parsons. Parsons wrote that

he "supported the thirteenth, fourteenth, and fifteenth constitutional amendments and the reconstruction measures securing the political rights of the colored people." Moreover, Parsons translated his beliefs into actions as he "took the stump to vindicate my convictions." Parsons, ed., *Life of Albert Parsons*, 9; A. R. Parsons to J. P. Newcomb, 9 Sept. 1870, Newcomb Papers, General Correspondence, Center for American History, University of Texas at Austin.

75. D. F. Davis to E. J. Davis, 12 Jan. 1870, Office of the Governor, Records of E. J. Davis, RG 301, Texas State Archives; Campbell, *Grass-Roots Reconstruction in Texas*, 181.

76. Campbell, *Grass-Roots Reconstruction in Texas*, 175–80.

77. *The New Era* (Washington), 16 June 1870.

78. Cotton, *History of Negroes in Limestone County*, 11; *New Era* (Washington), 16 June 1870; Campbell, *Grass-Roots Reconstruction in Texas*, 180; Merline Pitre, *Through Many Dangers, Toils and Snares: The Black Leadership of Texas, 1868–1900* (Austin: Eakin Press, 1985), 24, 28.

79. Smith-Cobb Family Papers, Texas Collection, Baylor University, Waco, Tex.; Pitre, *Through Many Dangers, Toils and Snares*, 9; Smallwood, *Time of Hope, Time of Despair*, 136–40.

80. Pitre, *Through Many Dangers, Toils and Snares*, 86.

81. Ibid., 27.

82. Campbell, *Grass-Roots Reconstruction in Texas*, 172, 174.

83. *Waco Semi-Weekly Examiner*, 5 Dec. 1871; Alwyn Barr and Robert A. Calvert, eds., *Black Leaders: Texans for Their Time* (Austin: Texas State Historical Association, 1981).

84. William Blocker, Shad Willis, and L. Graves, Freedmen, to E. J. Davis, 15 Oct. 1870, Officer of the Governor, Records of E. J. Davis, RG 301, Texas State Archives.

85. *The New Era* (Washington), 21 Dec. 1871.

86. Pitre, *Through Many Dangers, Toils and Snares*, 32.

87. "An Act to Incorporate the Howard Institute of Waco, Texas," in *The Laws of Texas, 1822–1897*, comp. H. P. N. Gammel (Austin: Gammel Book Co., 1898), 6:335–37. African Methodist Episcopal church leaders A. W. Jones and Nannie T. Jones were the school's first teachers. Garry H. Radford, Sr., *The History of the Black Man in Waco, Texas, June 10, 1866–January 1, 1984: Life Stories of Those Who Believed They Could Overcome Impediments* (Austin: Nortex, 1985), 67–98. Mullens later bought a town lot adjacent to the school. Smith-Cobb Family Papers, Texas Collection, Baylor University, Waco, Tex.

88. John Gordon, "The Negro in McLennan County," master's thesis, Baylor University, 1931, 67–70.

89. "Report of the Secretary of War," *House Executive Documents*, 40th Cong., 3d sess., ser. 1367, doc. no. 1, pt. 1, 1053.

90. Naomi R. Cobb, comp., "New Hope Eighty-Six Years Ago," New Hope Baptist Church Records (Waco), Texas Collection, Baylor University, Waco, Tex.

91. *State of Texas v. James Reagan and Robb Blocker*, case no. 653; *State of Texas v. Burrell Duncan and John Thompson*, case no. 656, McLennan County Civil and Criminal Minute Books, vol. E, McLennnan County Archives, Waco, Texas; *State of Texas v. W. P. Cunningham*, case no. 519; *State of Texas v. Dick Ables*, case no. 607; *State of Texas v. Lucious Roach*, case no. 614; *State of Texas v. George Porter*, case no. 675; *State of Texas v. Jonas DeArnand*, case no. 676; *State of Texas v. Dick Ables*, case no. 819; *State of Texas v. W. Roy,*

case no. 875; and *State of Texas v. Elijah Coleman*, case no. 957, all in Hill County Civil and Criminal Minute Books, vol. A, Texas Collection, Baylor University, Waco, Tex.

92. William Moore in *The American Slave: Supplement, Series 2*, ed. Rawick, 7:2773.

93. Ruthe Winegarten, *Black Texas Women: 150 Years of Trial and Triumph* (Austin: University of Texas at Austin Press, 1995), 88.

94. Report of Charles Haughn, 31 Oct. 1868, entry numbers 1194–96, Register of Felonies Committed in Texas, 1866–1868 (4853), Department of Texas and the 5th Military District, RG 393; *The New Era* (Washington), 28 Sept. 1871.

95. Alton Hornsby Jr., "The Freedmen's Bureau Schools in Texas, 1865–1870," *Southwestern Historical Quarterly* 76 (1973): 408.

96. Edward and Kate Sturm McCall Rotan Papers, Texas Collection, Baylor University, Waco, Tex.

97. "D. C. Giddings v. W. T. Clark," *House Reports* (Serial 1528), 42d Cong., 2d sess., report no. 65, 7.

98. Cotton, *History of Negroes in Limestone County*, 12.

99. *Galveston News*, 28 May 1875.

100. Interview with Mrs. George Fowler, MFWP.

101. Cotton, *History of Negroes in Limestone County*, 12; Smallwood, Crouch, and Peacock, *Murder and Mayhem*, 124.

102. Report of Special Committee on Lawlessness and Violence in Texas, 8 July 1868, Senate Miscellaneous Document, 40th Cong., 2d sess., 3, 5, Texas Collection, Baylor University, Waco, Tex.

103. *Message of Governor Edmund J. Davis to Twelfth Legislature, April 28, 1870* (Austin: Tracy, Siemering, 1870).

104. James Alex Baggett, "The Rise and Fall of the Texas Radicals, 1867–1883," Ph.D. diss., North Texas State University, 1972, 157.

105. *Crockett Herald* quoted in *Dallas Herald*, Sept. 23, 1871.

106. Aurelia Effie Cockrell Gray to Sarah (Horton) Cockrell, 13 Oct. 1871, Sarah (Horton) Cockrell Papers, Rare Book, Manuscript, and Special Collections Library, Duke University, Durham, N.C.

107. *Flake's Bulletin* (Galveston), 14 Aug. 1870, 5, and 25 Aug. 1870, 3.; Campbell, *Grass-Roots Reconstruction*, 185–86.

108. Wallace, *Waco: Texas Crossroads*, 31.

109. Campbell, *Grass-Roots Reconstruction*, 185–86.

110. Interview with Mrs. George Fowler, MFWP; Ricky Floyd Dobbs, "'A Slow Civil War': Resistance to the Davis Administration in Hill and Walker Counties, 1871," master's thesis, Baylor University, 1989, 56–79; Otis A. Singletary, "The Texas Militia during Reconstruction," *Southwestern Historical Quarterly* 60 (1956): 30.

111. Moneyhon, *Republicanism in Reconstruction Texas*, 191.

112. Richard Coke was the first to sign (and probably the principal author of) the McLennan County petition that urged the legislature to take special measures to suppress alleged abolitionist activities. Richard Coke et al. to the Legislature of the State of Texas (no date), Petition, Texas State Archives. For other details on Coke's life, see Richard Coke Papers, Texas Collection, Baylor University, Waco, Tex.

113. Parsons's fate is detailed in the *Waco Day*, 6 May 1886. The ongoing political or-

ganizing of David F. Davis and Stephen Cobb is mentioned in the *Waco Daily Examiner*, 13 Oct. and 14 Nov. 1878.

Chapter 6. *"A New Crime": The Changing Character of Mob Violence in the Late Nineteenth Century*

1. *San Antonio Daily Express*, 2 and 11 July 1874. A full listing of mob violence victims from 1874 appears in Appendixes A and B.

2. *Austin Daily Statesman*, 28 Aug. 1897. A full list of mob violence victims from 1897 appears in Appendix A.

3. In addition to the black and white victims, there was one additional victim, a Mexican man hanged in 1872. His case is discussed in the following chapter.

4. Central Texans routinely defended the importance of law and order even while simultaneously justifying lynchings. They did not see the two as fundamentally opposed. Both mob violence and the legal system were imperfect. They were subject to abuse and also potentially useful for enforcing justice and punishing criminals. Central Texans routinely saw no great conflict between the two systems of justice and no contradiction in supporting both modes of punishment. At the same time, many viewed mob violence as a necessary evil that could be abandoned if problems of the legal system were remedied. Characteristic defenses of mob law and the legal system can be found in the following local sources: *Waco Day*, 4 Aug. 1886; *Waco Weekly Stock and Farm News*, 19 July 1889; *Waco Weekly News*, 19 July 1889; and interviews with William Monroe Graves, Leroy Dean, Dave May, John H. Robertson, George Ogden, and Mrs. George Fowler, all Folklore Project, WPA Federal Writers' Project, Manuscript Division, Library of Congress, Washington (hereafter MFWP). Additional details about the beliefs of central Texans toward mob law in the late nineteenth century are explored throughout this chapter.

5. *Waco Daily Examiner*, 19 July 1885.

6. *Waco Daily Examiner*, 2 June 1883. Additional reports of authorities discovering the corpses of African Americans can be found in the *Waco Morning News*, 12 June 1895, 21 Jan. 1896, and the *Waco Times-Herald*, 8 Oct. 1901 and 28 Dec. 1904. One of the most intriguing of these underreported murders was that of a fifty-year-old African American named Sam Henderson, who was found in 1906 near the Cotton Belt bridge, his neck and shoulder broken. *Waco Times-Herald*, 19 March 1906.

7. *Waco Daily Examiner*, 1 Nov. 1878.

8. Most scholars have relied on records collected by the *Chicago Tribune*, Tuskegee University, the Association of Southern Women for the Prevention of Lynching, and the National Association for the Advancement of Colored People. There are several problems with these sources. First, as Christopher Waldrep has pointed out, reporting and collecting lynching statistics was always heavily influenced by political pressures. As a result, the definition of lynching changed over time to suit the perceived needs and goals of each group. Christopher Waldrep, "Word and Deed: The Language of Lynching, 1820–1953," in *Lethal Imagination: Violence and Brutality in American History*, ed. Michael Bellesiles (New York: New York University Press, 1999), 229–30. Second, lynching inventories do not become anything close to reliable until the last decade of the nineteenth century. Even then scholars such as Stewart Tolnay and E. M. Beck in *A Festival of Violence: An Analy-*

sis of Southern Lynchings, 1882–1930 (Urbana: University of Illinois Press, 1995) have found them plagued with numerous errors. Tolnay and Beck have, rightly, been very critical of lynching inventories. They did not, however, conduct a thorough search through local newspapers for additional lynchings unreported in these inventories. Thus, the net result of Tolnay and Beck's research was to eliminate reports that had been mis-reported as lynchings without adding hardly any newly discovered lynchings to their totals.

To be fair, the type of research that needs to be done requires the efforts of numerous scholars and could not have been completed by Tolnay and Beck alone. When it is completed, however, scholars will find that the years between the end of Reconstruction and the beginning of the systematic compilation of lynching data in the 1890s hold numerous previously unknown stories of lynching throughout Texas and the South. Some of this research has already begun. Several historians other than Tolnay and Beck have conducted their own research into the local newspaper records, including George C. Wright, *Racial Violence in Kentucky, 1865–1940: Lynchings, Mob Rule, and "Legal Lynchings"* (Baton Rouge: Louisiana State University Press, 1990); W. Fitzhugh Brundage, *Lynching in the New South: Georgia and Virginia* (Urbana: University of Illinois Press, 1993); Terrence Finnegan, "'At the Hands of Parties Unknown': Lynching in Mississippi and South Carolina, 1881–1940," Ph.D. diss., University of Illinois, 1993; Michael Pfeifer, "Lynching and Criminal Justice in Regional Context: Iowa, Wyoming, and Louisiana, 1878–1946," Ph.D. diss., University of Iowa, 1998; Marilyn Kaye Howard, "Black Lynching in the Promised Land: Mob Violence in Ohio, 1876–1916," Ph.D. diss., Ohio State University, 1999; and Richard Allan Buckelew, "Racial Violence in Arkansas: Lynchings and Mob Rule, 1860–1930," Ph.D. diss, University of Arkansas, 1999.

9. Gebe Austin and Bob Hall were only two of the many unconfirmed cases of mob violence in central Texas. Vague references in oral interviews, brief stories in newspapers, and sketchy details from government reports all suggest that acts of vigilantism and lynching were probably far more common than traditional lynching inventories would indicate. A list of more than sixty unconfirmed cases of mob violence in central Texas appears in Appendix B.

10. F. B. Williams, who thrashed his young black servant for carelessness in 1877, provides one example (*Waco Daily Examiner,* 4 Feb. 1877). Many additional examples can be found in the indictments contained in McLennan County Civil and Criminal Minute Books, vols. G–X, McLennan County Archives, Waco, Tex.

11. In 1896 a group of whites robbed "an industrious colored man" of $13 in cash that he had just obtained from the sale of a bale of cotton (*Waco Tribune,* 17 Oct. 1896). Many additional examples can be found in the indictments contained in the McLennan County Civil and Criminal Minute Books, vols. G–X, McLennan County Archives, Waco, Tex.

12. *Waco Times Herald,* 18 Feb. 1898.

13. Ida Leggett Hall, "History of the Negro in Waco, Texas," *Waco Heritage and History* 14 (1984): 14.

14. Quoted in Wayne Gard, *Frontier Justice* (Norman: University of Oklahoma Press, 1949), 109.

15. *Waco Times Herald,* 29 Jan. 1898.

16. Quoted in Gard, *Frontier Justice,* 201.

17. *Waco Times Herald,* 23 Sept. 1898.

18. *Waco Times Herald*, 17 Feb. 1898.

19. *The Iconoclast* 5 (Feb. 1895): 9–10.

20. Interview with John T. Cox, MFWP.

21. *Galveston News*, 28 May 1875.

22. Edmund J. Davis to Attorney General Alonzo Taft, 9 Sept. 1876, U.S. House of Representatives, *House Executive Documents*, 44th Cong., 2d sess., 1876 (serial 1755), no. 30, 143. These reported deaths have not been added to my statistics for mob violence in central Texas because I lack additional specific details.

23. *Waco Times Herald*, 1–13 Sept. 1898, favorably quoting the *Sherman Register*.

24. *Waco Times Herald*, 1 Sept. 1898. The three farmers did not indicate how much they were willing to pay these potential black workers, but one can presume that the wages they had in mind would have been lower than the amount desired by either the blacks or the whitecappers.

25. *Waco Daily Examiner*, 27 Oct. 1876.

26. *Waco Daily Examiner*, 18 Dec. 1877.

27. *State of Texas v. Andrew McCarty*, case no. 2946, Case Files of Nineteenth District Court, McLennan County Archives, Waco, Tex.; *Waco Daily Examiner*, 18 Sept. 1877. Brinkley's death so outraged local whites that they prosecuted one of the white men involved. They found him guilty but only of second-degree murder because he was "under the influence of liquor."

28. Full details on this data can be found in Appendix A. Using the definition of lynching adopted by the National Association for the Advancement of Colored People, my research indicates that mobs killed at least thirty-six blacks and at least twenty-seven whites in Bell, Bosque, Coryell, Falls, Hill, Limestone, and McLennan counties between the end of Reconstruction and the turn of the century. That is a significant increase over the number of central Texas lynching victims reported by both the NAACP (twenty-three) and Tuskegee (thirty-three). Other such intense local studies in Texas and other lynch-prone states would net similar gains in the number of victims of mob violence. Moreover, I have not uncovered anything close to the actual record of mob violence in late-nineteenth-century central Texas.

29. *Waco Examiner and Patron*, 30 July 1875.

30. *Waco Daily Advance*, 22 Jan. 1874.

31. *Waco Daily Advance*, 14 Jan. 1874.

32. Interviews with Emma Falconer (first quotation), Mrs. George Fowler (second quotation), and William Monroe Graves (third quotation), all MFWP.

33. "Brief Biographies of Eminent Texians," John Henry Brown Family Papers, Center for American History, University of Texas, Austin, Texas.

34. *Waco Daily Examiner*, 29 Aug. 1873.

35. "The Lynching at Giddings," U.S. House of Representatives, *House Executive Documents*, 44th Cong., 2d sess., 1876 (serial 1755), doc. no. 30, 136.

36. *Waco Daily Advance*, 27 Jan. 1874.

37. Interview with Sarah Ann Ross Pringle, MFWP.

38. *Waco Daily Advance*, 25 Aug. 1874.

39. Christopher Waldrep, *Roots of Disorder: Race and Criminal Justice in the American South, 1817–1880* (Urbana: University of Illinois Press, 1998), 1–5, 27–29. In his study of

Warren County, Mississippi, Waldrep found that dueling (a form of extralegal violence between white men) declined while lynching and racial violence were on the rise.

40. Examples of the rich literature on racial violence in the United States include Tolnay and Beck, *A Festival of Violence;* Brundage, *Lynching in the New South;* Wright, *Racial Violence in Kentucky;* Edward L. Ayers, *Vengeance and Justice: Crime and Punishment in the Nineteenth-Century American South* (New York: Oxford University Press, 1984); Joel Williamson, *The Crucible of Race: Black-White Relations in the American South Since Emancipation* (New York: Oxford University Press, 1984); Jacquelyn Dowd Hall, *Jessie Daniel Ames and the Southern Women's Campaign against Lynchings* (New York: Oxford University Press, 1979); Elliott M. Rudwick, *Race Riot at East St. Louis* (Carbondale: Southern Illinois University Press, 1964); Arthur R. Raper, *The Tragedy of Lynching* (Chapel Hill: University of North Carolina, 1933); and Walter White, *Rope and Faggot: A Biography of Judge Lynch* (New York: Knopf, 1929).

41. *Waco Day,* 4 Aug. 1886.

42. *Waco Weekly News,* 19 July 1889.

43. *Waco Daily Examiner,* 19 May 1876.

44. *Waco Daily Examiner,* 4 Nov. 1877.

45. *Waco Daily Examiner,* 16 July 1885.

46. *Waco Daily Examiner,* 17 July 1885.

47. Ibid.

48. *Waco Daily Examiner,* 25 Oct. 1885.

49. Quoted in *San Antonio Herald,* 18 Sept. 1857. James McGovern has also pointed to the importance of the public reaction in the history of lynching (*Anatomy of a Lynching: The Killing of Claude Neal* [Baton Rouge: Louisiana State University Press, 1982]).

50. *Waco Weekly News,* 24 Feb. 1893.

51. Among the rich literature on planter persistence, Michael Wayne's study of the Natchez district deserves special mention for its careful explanation of how planters remained economically powerful and dominant while simultaneously being transformed by the developments of emancipation and Reconstruction. Michael Wayne, *The Reshaping of Plantation Society: The Natchez District, 1860–1880* (Baton Rouge: Louisiana State University Press, 1983), 203.

52. "Brief Biographies of Eminent Texians," John Henry Brown Family Papers, Center for American History, University of Texas, Austin; unpublished finding aid, Richard Coke Papers, Texas Collection, Baylor University, Waco, Tex. Coke was not the only former Confederate to attain political power in the wake of the Republican collapse. Gen. Lawrence "Sul" Ross became sheriff in McLennan County in 1874. At the same time, former slaveholder Davis Gurley moved into the district clerk's office. Richard Henry Harrison, son of the famous slaveholder and Confederate Gen. James E. Harrison, became an influential lawyer in Waco and was elected to the Texas state senate for McLennan and Falls counties. A staunch defender of the former Confederacy, Harrison used his position to urge passage of bills to fund a home for disabled and Confederate veterans. *Waco Daily Advance,* 14 Jan. 1874; *Waco Daily Times Herald,* 16 Jan. 1898.

53. Randolph B. Campbell, *Grass-Roots Reconstruction in Texas, 1865–1880* (Baton Rouge: Louisiana State University Press, 1997), 188–90. See also Campbell's important work on the question of persistence in *A Southern Community in Crisis: Harrison County,*

Texas, 1850–1880 (Austin: Texas State Historical Association, 1983). The life of W. A. Fort illustrates the ability of the economic elite to bridge the Old and the New South. Fort was born in Alabama in 1826, but he moved to Texas in 1854 and settled south of Waco on the Brazos River, where he became a planter. After the close of the Civil War, Fort sensed the difficulties that would attend the transition to free labor and left planting for the life of a merchant. In 1869 he opened a banking institution with a partner named George W. Jackson. "No safer or more reliable institution," wrote the *Waco Examiner*, "has ever existed in our country than this." Continuing his successful adjustment to the new era, Fort became involved in leading three other prominent Waco businesses—the Suspension Bridge Company, the Street Railway Company, and the Cotton Exchange. *Waco Examiner*, 30 Aug. 1878.

54. Historical attention to the Reconstruction-era intimidation of black voters has largely concentrated on the 1875–76 elections in Louisiana, Mississippi, and South Carolina. Eric Foner, *Reconstruction: America's Unfinished Revolution* (New York: Harper and Row, 1988), 569–70.

55. Hall, "History of the Negro in Waco, Texas," 11.

56. C. M. Thompson of Waco, Texas, to Gen. U. S. Grant, Washington, D.C., 16 Nov. 1876, U.S. House of Representatives, *House Executive Documents*, 44th Cong., 2d sess. (serial 1755), no. 30, 144.

57. *Waco Daily Examiner*, 11 Jan. 1876.

58. Loren Schweninger, *Black Property Owners in the South, 1790–1915* (Urbana: University of Illinois Press, 1990), 148.

59. Jonathan M. Wiener, *Social Origins of the New South: Alabama, 1860–1885* (Baton Rouge: Louisiana State University Press, 1978); Jay R. Mandle, *The Roots of Black Poverty: The Southern Plantation Economy after the Civil War* (Durham: Duke University Press, 1978); Dwight B. Billings, *Planters and the Making of a "New South": Class, Politics, and Development in North Carolina, 1865–1900* (Chapel Hill: University of North Carolina Press, 1979). One historian of black agricultual laborers in Texas has concurred with these assessments, writing that Texas "landowners, wanting Negroes to remain in their former inferior position in society, devised numerous methods to re-enslave black agricultural workers." Keith Krawczynski, "Agricultural Labor of Black Texans," master's thesis, Baylor University, 1989, 77. The cycle of debt bondage can be seen in the account books of the James B. Billingsley Plantation Records, Center for American History, University of Texas at Austin.

60. Campbell, *Grass-Roots Reconstruction in Texas*, 188–90.

61. Wright, *Racial Violence in Kentucky*, 127–54; Ayers, *Vengeance and Justice*, 260–64.

62. James Smallwood wrote that most rural blacks were denied the chance to become landowners by "the discriminatory homestead law, by Anglos who refused to sell them land, and by inability to secure credit." Smallwood, *Time of Hope, Time of Despair: Black Texans during Reconstruction* (Port Washington: Kennikat Press, 1981), 67.

63. Schweninger, *Black Property Owners in the South*, 162.

64. Lawrence D. Rice, *The Negro in Texas, 1874–1900* (Baton Rouge: Louisiana State University Press, 1971), 178.

65. John Ramsey Gordon, "The Negro in McLennan County, Texas," master's thesis, Baylor University, 1932, 30; Krawczynski, "Agricultural Labor of Black Texans," 84–87. The

economic regression of central Texas blacks was probably somewhat unusual in the post-bellum South. Loren Schweninger found that the total number of black property owners were increasing in both the South and in Texas from 1870 to 1910. Yet there is reason to suspect that opportunities for entering the landowning class were diminishing for blacks in Texas as the century drew to a close. The percentage rate of increase, for example, dipped dramatically during the same period. Between 1870 and 1890 black property ownership increased more than 1,000 percent in Texas. From 1890 to 1900 the percentage increase dropped to 61 percent; between 1900 and 1910 it slowed to 5 percent. Schweninger, *Black Property Owners in the South,* 164. Robert Kenzer has concurred with Schweninger that the postbellum period witnessed a slow economic advance for blacks in North Carolina. Robert C. Kenzer, *Enterprising Southerners: Black Economic Success in North Carolina, 1865–1915* (Charlottesville: University of Virginia Press, 1997).

66. Rice, *The Negro in Texas,* 185–95.

67. Jingjing Xie, "The Black Community in Waco, Texas: 1880–1900," master's thesis, Baylor University, 1988, 65.

68. Oliver and other Republican-appointed judges clearly sought to provide freedmen with fair trials in central Texas. In 1867 newly appointed Judge A. J. Evans sustained a motion for a new trial for John Bedwell, who had been sentenced to four years and six months in prison for burglary. The jury in the new trial found him not guilty. *State of Texas v. John Bedwell,* case no. 519, McLennan County Civil and Criminal Minute Books, vols. D and E, McLennan County Archives, Waco, Tex.

69. The first case to consider blacks for a jury occurred in 1900, although none were selected until the next year. *Waco Weekly Tribune,* 29 Dec. 1900; *Waco Weekly Tribune,* 9 March 1901.

70. Matthew J. Mancini, *One Dies, Get Another: Convict Leasing in the American South, 1866–1928* (Columbia: University of South Carolina Press, 1996), 1–2. Edward Ayers argues (*Vengeance and Justice,* 185–86) that the end of slavery and the appearance of thousands of suddenly unaccounted-for blacks, united with a need for cheap labor demanded by emerging capitalists, initiated and maintained the convict lease system across the South.

71. Thomas Michael Parrish, "'This Species of Slave Labor': The Convict Lease System in Texas, 1871–1914," master's thesis, Baylor University, 1976, 16.

72. Mancini, *One Dies, Get Another,* 176.

73. *Waco Daily Examiner,* 3 Dec. 1885.

74. *Waco Day,* 31 Jan. 1888.

75. *Waco Daily Examiner,* 2 Dec. 1876.

76. *Waco Times-Herald,* 20 Sept. 1906.

77. For a discussion of "legal lynchings," see Wright, *Racial Violence in Kentucky.*

78. There are many accounts of Davis's execution, which probably was the first legal hanging to occur in Waco. *Waco Daily Examiner,* 7 Feb., 23 Aug., 28 Aug., and 31 Aug. 1877; see also the recollections of Jake Compton in *The American Slave: A Composite Autobiography, Supplement, Series 2,* ed. George P. Rawick (Westport: Greenwood Press, 1979), 3:902–7.

79. Reprinted in *Waco Daily Examiner,* 28 Aug. 1877.

80. *Waco Day,* 13 Dec. 1887. Other examples of "legal lynchings" include the execution

of Silas Wood in November of 1876 and the sentencing of John Rome in July 1901. *Waco Daily Examiner,* 11 Nov. 1876; *Waco Weekly Tribune,* 13 July 1901.

81. *State of Texas v. Conrad Jackson,* case no. 5596, Case Files of the Nineteenth District Court, McLennan County Archives, Waco, Tex.; *Waco Evening News,* 16 July 1888.

82. *State of Texas v. Lee Robinson,* case no. 2743, Case Files of the Fifty-fourth District Court, McLennan County Archives, Waco, Tex.; *Waco Weekly Tribune,* 17 June 1905.

83. Parrish, "'This Species of Slave Labor,'" 20–21.

84. "Record of Criminal Offenses Committed in the State of Texas," Records of the Assistant Commissioner for the State of Texas, U.S. Bureau of Refugees, Freedmen, and Abandoned Lands, 1865–1869, film 853, reel 32, RG 105, U.S. Department of War, National Archives.

85. The struggle over gender, race, and sexuality in the transition from slavery to freedom is discussed in Leslie A. Schwalm, *A Hard Fight for We: Women's Transition from Slavery to Freedom in South Carolina* (Urbana: University of Illinois Press, 1997); and Laura F. Edwards, "Sexual Violence, Gender, Reconstruction, and the Extension of Patriarchy in Granville, North Carolina," *North Carolina Historical Review* 68 (1991): 237–60.

86. *Waco Examiner and Patron,* 10 Sept. 1875.

87. *State of Texas v. Willis Oakes,* case no. 700, McLennan County Civil and Criminal Minute Books, vol. E, McLennan County Archives, Waco, Tex.; *State of Texas v. Morgan Bond,* case no. 342, Hill County Civil and Criminal Minute Books, vol. A, Texas Collection, Baylor University, Waco, Tex.

88. *State of Texas v. Lee Robinson,* case no. 2743, Case Files of the Fifty-fourth District Court, McLennan County Archives, Waco, Tex.

89. Martha Hodes, *White Women, Black Men: Illicit Sex in the Nineteenth-Century South* (New Haven: Yale University Press, 1997).

90. *Waco Daily Examiner,* 12 June 1877.

91. Clipping in the Laura L. Perry Papers, Texas Collection, Baylor University, Waco, Tex.

92. *Whitney Messenger,* 27 June 1884, emphasis added.

93. *Waco Daily Examiner,* 20 May 1884.

94. *Waco Daily Examiner,* 27 March 1886.

95. *State of Texas v. Thomas Burney,* case no. 5093, Case Files of the Nineteenth District Court and Civil and Criminal Minute Books, vol. N, McLennan County Archives, Waco, Tex.

96. *Waco Day,* 4 Aug. 1886. Although Harris's hanging was attended by hundreds and reported in the local press, the lynching was not reported in the inventories compiled by the NAACP or Tuskegee Institute.

97. According to the *Waco Weekly News* (14 Nov. 1890), a black man who entered a house and asked a white woman for a glass of water could be considered to be committing sexual assault.

98. *Waco Stock and Farm News,* 19 July 1889. Henry Davis is sometimes also referred to as "William Davis."

99. *Waco Day,* 2 Aug. 1886. The mob, of course, followed the newspaper's instructions by lynching Bill Harris the next day.

100. *Waco Evening News,* 18 Aug. 1888.

101. *Waco Weekly News,* 22 April 1892.

102. *Waco Weekly News,* 3 March 1893.

103. *Waco Times-Herald,* 17 Feb. 1898.

104. *Waco Weekly News,* 24 June 1892.

105. *State of Texas v. William Holmes,* case no. 1027, Case Files of the Fifty-fourth District Court, Civil and Criminal Minute Books, vol. 1 (p. 349), McLennan County Archives, Waco, Tex.

106. John W. Stevens, *Reminiscences of the Civil War* (Hillsboro: Hillsboro Mirror Print, 1902), 206–7, 209–10. Thanks to T. Michael Parrish for a photocopy of this document.

107. The best historiographic discussion of the "causes" of lynching can be found in the introduction to Brundage, *Lynching in the New South.*

108. Leon Litwack, in a widely read and highly publicized work, observed that "instances of organized black resistance to white controls" were few in the late nineteenth and early twentieth centuries. Litwack disagreed with black leaders such as Frederick Douglass and Walter White who believed that lynching in the South reflected the continuing resistance of blacks to white authority, dismissing such opinions as "bold talk in the face of harsh realities." Leon Litwack, *Trouble in Mind: Black Southerners in the Age of Jim Crow* (New York: Alfred A. Knopf, 1998), 324, 320.

109. Litwack, *Trouble in Mind,* 322.

110. For example, see Hall, *Jessie Daniel Ames;* Gail Beederman, "'Civilization,' the Decline of Middle-Class Manliness, and Ida B. Wells' Anti-Lynching Campaign," *Radical History Review* 52 (Winter 1992): 5–30; Brundage, *Lynching in the New South;* and Robert L. Zangrando, *The NAACP Crusade against Lynching* (Philadelphia: Temple University Press, 1980).

111. A few scholars have begun to probe the dimensions of grassroots resistance to white power during the era of Jim Crow. Robin D. G. Kelly, for example, has insisted that "hidden transcripts" exist that historians have heretofore ignored. Robin D. G. Kelley, *Race Rebels: Culture, Politics, and the Black Working Class* (New York: Free Press, 1994). W. Fitzhugh Brundage has written an important but all-too-brief essay on black resistance to mob violence at the grassroots level: "The Roar on the Other Side of Silence: Black Resistance and White Violence in the American South, 1880–1940," in *Under Sentence of Death: Lynching in the South,* ed. W. Fitzhugh Brundage (Chapel Hill: University of North Carolina Press, 1997). Despite these efforts, however, the story of organized local black resistance to white violence, especially in the late-nineteenth-century South, has largely escaped historians' attention.

112. For example, see Tolnay and Beck, *A Festival of Violence.*

113. *Waco Daily Examiner,* 2 Aug. 1877.

114. *Waco Stock and Farm News,* 6, 12 July 1889.

115. *Waco Stock and Farm News,* 6 July 1889; *Waco Weekly Tribune,* 8 Nov. 1902.

116. Living under segregation drove some blacks in central Texas to leave and others to fight. Those who remained often chose their battles wisely, accommodating to white desires at certain times and resisting white domination at others. Maintaining the proper balance was difficult if not impossible. Those who resisted subordination at every turn, like the men and women who resisted slavery at every turn, often earned a quick death at the hands of a white mob. Those who spent most of their lives accommodating to white whims

risked internalizing white attitudes and beliefs. Some black men and women cracked under the pressures of this relentless balancing act. In 1877 a local black woman named Eliza Jackson attempted to take her life by swallowing morphine. A year later another black woman attempted to drown herself in the Brazos River, and a black prisoner due to be sent to the penitentiary for a second time attempted to take his life by swallowing oxolic acid. In 1888 a black mother sought to save her newborn baby from the travails of life by killing the child. Suicide among African Americans was not new and not linked solely to the troubles brought about by being black in segregated central Texas. Nevertheless, the threat of racial violence, either to oneself or to a member of one's family, exacted a psychic toll on black central Texans. *Waco Daily Examiner*, 8 and 27 Aug. 1877, and 3 Dec. 1878; *Waco Evening News*, 18 Aug. 1888.

117. James Smallwood, for example, wrote that as "a result of continuing violence and hostility, many freedmen completely withdrew from politics after 1875, striving neither for civil nor political rights." Smallwood, *Time of Hope, Time of Despair*, 157.

118. *Waco Daily Advance*, 16 July 1874.

119. For evidence of the continued participation of black voters even in the midst of many electoral defeats, see *Waco Daily Examiner*, 25 Oct. 1885; For examples of the many Republican rallies that were held over this period, see *Waco Daily Examiner*, 15 Oct. 1878; *Waco Weekly News*, 30 Sept. 1892.

120. According to one estimate, black Greenbackers outnumbered white Greenbackers five to one. Examples of the harassment of Greenbackers included use of a steam engine to drown out speakers at Greenback rallies, arrest of the black chair of the Greenback Central Committee on the charge of "allowing gambling to be carried on in his house," and disallowance of black voters who could not prove their residence in the county to the satisfaction of the Democratic registrars. *Waco Daily Examiner*, 18 and 20 Aug., 13 and 17 Oct., and 6 Nov. 1878.

121. *Waco Daily Examiner*, 2 Aug. 1885.

122. First mention of the Farmer's Alliance in a local paper was the *Waco Daily Examiner*, 19 Oct. 1877. Discussion of the all-white membership of the McLennan County alliance can be found in the *Waco Day*, 10 Jan. 1888.

123. Douglass Geraldyne Perry, "Black Populism: The Negro in the People's Party in Texas," master's thesis, Prairie View University, 1945, 45 and map.

124. *Waco Weekly News*, 30 Sept. 1892.

125. Many black Republicans, dissatisfied with their party's endorsement of Clark, voted for Hogg on the basis of his record against mob violence. Political analysts of the time concluded that the black vote provided the margin of victory for Hogg's reelection in 1892. *Dallas Morning News*, 14 Nov. 1892, quoted in Duane Ginn, "Racial Violence in Texas, 1884–1900," master's thesis, University of Houston, 1974.

126. *Waco Weekly Tribune*, 22 Sept. 1900.

127. *Waco Weekly Tribune*, 22 Aug. 1903.

128. *Waco Daily Advance*, 7 July 1874.

129. Ruthe Winegarten, *Black Texas Women: 150 Years of Trial and Triumph* (Austin: University of Texas at Austin Press, 1995), 75.

130. *Dallas Morning News*, 9 Aug. 1905.

131. *Waco Day*, 18 Jan. 1888. The protests of other black leaders also found their way into

the white press from time to time. See, for example, *Waco Daily Examiner,* 13 June 1877, and *Waco Tribune,* 13 May 1899.

132. *Waco Day,* 21 Jan. 1888.

133. *Waco Daily Examiner,* 22 Sept. 1878.

134. *Waco Daily Examiner,* 7 Oct. 1885.

135. *Waco Times-Herald,* 22 Feb. 1898.

136. *Waco Times-Herald,* 11 Jan. 1898. Apparently, Roden Long was not convicted, but his ultimate fate remains unknown. Neither the original case file nor the Falls County Criminal Minutes for 1898 have survived.

137. *Waco Weekly News,* 19 July 1889.

138. *Waco Daily News,* 5 Jan. 1891.

139. *Waco Daily News,* 6 Jan. 1891.

140. *Waco Daily News,* 5 Jan. 1891.

141. *Waco Daily News,* 5–6 Jan. 1891.

142. *Waco Daily News,* 5 Jan. 1891.

143. *Waco Daily News,* 6 and 21 Jan. 1891.

144. *Waco Daily News,* 21 Jan. 1891.

145. Ginn, "Racial Violence in Texas," 78; *Waco Post,* 25 July 1895; *Dallas Morning News,* 21 July 1895; "Lynchings in Texas, 1882–1942," unpublished inventory list, Lynching Files, Tuskegee University Archives, Tuskegee, Ala. Unfortunately, central Texas newspapers from the period have not survived (with the exception of the German-language *Waco Post*), and thus little is known of local reaction to the murder of the Phillips family.

146. *Waco Post,* 25 July 1895. "Die furchtbare Explosion soll sogar verschiedene Vögel in der Nähe getodtet haben." The *Post* made little editorial comment on the incident but noted that the "cause is said to be an old quarrel between whites and blacks" (Die Ursache soll ein alter Streit zwischen Weisse und Schwarze sein). My thanks to Kent Keeth of the Texas Collection at Baylor University for his help with these translations.

147. Ginn, "Racial Violence in Texas," 79.

Chapter 7. "A Damnable Outrage": Mob Violence in Twentieth-Century Central Texas

1. *State of Texas v. Sank Majors,* case no. 8827, Case Files of the Nineteenth District Court, McLennan County Archives, Waco, Tex.

2. *Waco Weekly Tribune* 12 Aug. 1905; *State of Texas v. Sank Majors,* case no. 8827, Case Files of the Nineteenth District Court, McLennan County Archives, Waco, Tex.

3. *Waco Times-Herald,* 8 Aug. 1905; Rogers M. Smith, "The Waco Lynching of 1916: Perspective and Analysis," master's thesis, Baylor University, 1971, 33.

4. *Dallas Morning News,* 9 Aug. 1905.

5. *Waco Times-Herald,* 8 Aug. 1905.

6. Ibid.; *Dallas Morning News,* 9 Aug. 1905.

7. "Lynchings in Texas, 1882–1942," unpublished inventory list, Lynching Files, Tuskegee University Archives, Tuskegee, Ala.

8. *Waco Weekly Tribune* 22 Aug. 1896.

9. *Waco Tribune,* 12 Sept. 1896.

10. *State of Texas v. Bruce Kendrick, Will Rogers, Lee Kelly, Charles Stephonson, Bill Brian, Henry Downing, Rugus Evans, Bob Hobbs, Walker Hall, and Floyd Miller,* case no. 1485, Case Files of the Fifty-fourth District Court, McLennan County Archives, Waco, Tex.

11. *Waco Weekly Tribune,* 12 Nov. 1904.

12. For information on Sparks, see *Waco Weekly Tribune,* 29 Jan. 1900.

13. *African Methodist Episcopal Church Review* 17 (April 1901): 396–97.

14. *State of Texas v. Will King,* case no. 2041, Case Files of the Fifty-fourth District Court, McLennan County Archives, Waco, Tex.

15. *State of Texas v. Will King,* case no. 1969, Case Files of the Fifty-fourth District Court, McLennan County Archives, Waco, Tex.

16. *Waco Weekly Tribune,* 17 Nov. 1900.

17. *State of Texas v. Will King,* case no. 2026, Case Files of the Fifty-fourth District Court, McLennan County Archives, Waco, Tex.

18. *Waco Weekly Tribune,* 29 Dec. 1900.

19. *Waco Weekly Tribune,* 26 Jan. 1901.

20. *Waco Weekly Tribune,* 2 Feb. 1901; *State of Texas v. Will King,* case no. 2026, Case Files of the Fifty-fourth District Court, McLennan County Archives, Waco, Tex.

21. *Waco Weekly Tribune,* 2 Feb. 1901.

22. *Waco Weekly Tribune,* 9 Feb. 1901.

23. Ibid.

24. *Waco Weekly Tribune,* 20 April 1901.

25. *State of Texas v. Will King,* cases no. 1969 and no. 2026, Case Files of the Fifty-fourth District Court, McLennan County Archives, Waco, Tex.

26. *Waco Weekly Tribune,* 20 April 1901.

27. *Waco Weekly Tribune,* 27 April and 4 May 1901; *State of Texas v. Will King,* cases no. 1969, no. 2026, no. 2041, Case Files of the Fifty-fourth District Court, McLennan County Archives, Waco, Tex.

28. *Waco Weekly Tribune,* 26 Oct. 1901.

29. *Waco Weekly Tribune,* 9 March 1901.

30. *African Methodist Episcopal Church Review* 17 (April 1901): 396–97. The *Review* cited a story from an African American newspaper, the *Houston Independent,* as its source.

31. *Dallas Morning News,* 9 Aug. 1905.

32. *Waco Weekly Tribune,* 12 Aug. 1905.

33. Ibid.

34. *Waco Times-Herald,* 8 Aug. 1905.

35. *Dallas Morning News,* 25 April 1906, cited in David William Livingston, "The Lynching of Negroes in Texas, 1900–1925," master's thesis, East Texas State University, 1972, 51.

36. *Dallas Morning News,* 16 Sept. 1906.

37. Livingston, "The Lynching of Negroes in Texas," 42.

38. *Waco Times-Herald,* 16 Sept. 1906.

39. *Waco Semi-Weekly Tribune,* 22 Dec. 1909.

40. *Report on Population of the United States at the Eleventh Census: 1890,* pt. 1 (Washington: Government Printing Office, 1895); *Fourteenth Census of the United States, State Compendium, Texas* (Washington: Government Printing Office, 1925).

41. *Dallas Morning News,* 9 Aug. 1905.

42. *Dallas Morning News*, 10 Aug. 1905.

43. *Waco Daily Examiner*, 2 Aug. 1877.

44. *Waco Weekly Tribune*, 8 Nov. 1902.

45. *Waco Semi-Weekly Tribune*, 30 June 1917.

46. *Waco Weekly Tribune*, 22 Aug. 1903.

47. *Waco Semi-Weekly Tribune*, 30 June 1917.

48. *Waco Times-Herald*, 10 Sept. 1906. Jones is also referred to as "Jesse Washington," a name he apparently held before coming to Waco. In order not to confuse the reader with another young black of the same name mentioned later, I refer to the young black man who died in 1906 solely as Jesse Jones.

49. *Waco Times-Herald*, 25 Sept. 1906; *State of Texas v. Jesse Jones*, case no. 2818, Case Files of the Fifty-fourth District Court, McLennan County Archives, Waco, Tex.

50. *Waco Times-Herald*, 25 Sept., 30 Nov. 1906; *State of Texas v. Jesse Jones*, case no. 2818, Case Files of the Fifty-fourth District Court, McLennan County Archives, Waco, Tex.

51. George C. Wright, *Racial Violence in Kentucky* (Baton Rouge: Louisiana State University Press, 1990), 223–44, 251–305. George Wright has argued that during the early twentieth century the court system began to take on the role of the mob by applying swift justice to black criminals.

52. John Ramsey Gordon, "The Negro in McLennan County, Texas," master's thesis, Baylor University, 1932, 37. Gordon, conducting his research during the 1930s, had access to a more complete set of records than I did. Nevertheless, my research on nearly two hundred McLennan County murder cases confirms the general pattern that Gordon documented.

53. *State of Texas v. W. E. Ratliff*, case no. 7625, Case Files of the Fifty-fourth District Court, McLennan County Archives, Waco, Tex.; *Waco Times-Herald*, 14 Jan. 1927, 9–11 April 1928; Ida Leggett Hall, "History of the Negro in Waco, Texas," *Waco Heritage and History* 14 (1984): 32–33. Robert Lloyd Smith was an important business leader in black central Texas. Although he had been born and educated in South Carolina and Georgia, Smith rose to local fame after he came to Texas in 1885. Smith began his public education in the public schools of Charleston. After finishing secondary work at a black private school, he attended the University of South Carolina before the state legislature closed it to blacks in 1877. He then transferred to Atlanta University and graduated in 1879. When Smith first came to Texas, he settled in Oakland, a small village of three hundred people in Colorado County, and set to work organizing a Village Improvement Society to help rid the black community of Oakland of poverty and lawlessness. After a flourish of success with the society, he changed the organization's name to the "Farmers' Improvement Society" and broadened his goals to include the problems of black farmers throughout Texas. For his efforts, Smith was elected to the state legislature in 1894 from a majority white district. During the early twentieth century he moved to Waco, where he devoted the rest of his life to the Farmers' Improvement Society and eventually oversaw the establishment of central Texas's only black-owned bank. In 1911 Smith's friend and ally Booker T. Washington said that Smith and his wife were "helping the Negro in Texas to get homes, become farmers, save their money and lead useful lives." Farmers' Improvement Society Papers, Manuscripts Division, Texas Collection, Baylor University, Waco, Tex.; "An Account of Washington's Tour of Texas," 7 Oct. 1911, in *The Booker T. Washington Papers*, ed. Louis R. Harlan (Urbana: University of Illinois Press, 1972–89), 11:325.

54. *Waco News Tribune,* 8 Sept. 1925.

55. Lorenzo J. Greene, *Selling Black History for Carter G. Woodson: A Diary, 1930–33* (Columbia: University of Missouri Press, 1996). Thanks to Clive Webb for this reference.

56. "Investigation of Mexican Affairs," *Senate Documents,* 66th Cong., 2d sess., serial no. 7665–666, vol. 9–10, 2160 (quotation), 2148, 2157.

57. Samuel Bryan, "Mexican Immigrants in the United States," *The Survey,* 7 Sept. 1912, 726–30; Max Sylvius Handman, "Economic Reasons for the Coming of the Mexican Immigrant," *American Journal of Sociology* 35 (1930): 601–11.

58. *La Prensa* (San Antonio), 20, 27 Nov. 1913; *Waco News Tribune,* 6 Jan. 1923.

59. Among the many works on anti-Mexican violence in the Southwest borderlands, see F. Arturo Rosales, *¡Pobre Raza! Violence, Justice, and Mobilization among México Lindo Immigrants, 1900–1936* (Austin: University of Texas Press, 1999). Rosales's chapter 6, "Civilian Violence against Mexican Immigrants," is a complete and sophisticated discussion of anti-Mexican violence in the early twentieth century. Additional works that discuss violence against Mexicans include Carey McWilliams, *North from Mexico: The Spanish-Speaking People of the United States* (New York: Greenwood Press, 1968); Americo Paredes, *With His Pistol in His Hand: A Border Ballad and Its Hero* (Austin: University of Texas Press, 1958); Robert J. Rosenbaum, *Mexicano Resistance in the Southwest: "The Sacred Right of Self-Preservation"* (Austin: University of Texas Press, 1981); Arnoldo De León, *They Called Them Greasers: Anglo Attitudes toward Mexicans in Texas, 1821–1900* (Austin: University of Texas Press, 1983); David Montejano, *Anglos and Mexicans in the Making of Texas, 1836–1986* (Austin: University of Texas Press, 1987); Alfredo Mirande, *Gringo Justice* (Notre Dame: University of Notre Dame Press, 1987); Rodolfo Acuna, *Occupied America: A History of Chicanos,* 3d ed. (New York: HarperCollins, 1988); James A. Sandos, *Rebellion in the Borderlands: Anarchism and the Plan of San Diego, 1904–1923* (Norman: University of Oklahoma Press, 1992); Oscar J. Martinez, ed., *U.S.–Mexico Borderlands: Historical and Contemporary Perspectives* (Wilmington: Scholarly Resources, 1996); Richard Griswold del Castillo and Arnoldo De León, *North to Aztlan: A History of Mexican Americans in the United States* (New York: Twayne Publishers, 1996); Neil Foley, *The White Scourge: Mexicans, Blacks, and Poor Whites in Texas Cotton Culture* (Berkeley: University of California Press, 1997); and Manuel G. Gonzalez, *Mexicanos: A History of Mexicans in the United States* (Bloomington: University of Indiana Press, 1999).

60. *La Crónica* (Laredo), 29 June 1911; Arnoldo De León, *Mexican Americans in Texas: A Brief History* (Arlington Heights: H. Davidson, 1933), 50; *New York Times,* 26 June 1911.

61. "Proceedings of the Joint Commission of the Senate and the House in the Investigation of the Texas Ranger Force," Thirty-sixth Legislature, Regular Session, Legislative Papers, Archives and Information Services Division, Texas State Library and Archives Commission, Austin (hereafter Texas State Archives); *Brownsville Herald,* 28 Dec. 1917. Mexican reaction to the Porvenir massacre can be found in *La Prensa* (San Antonio), 28 Dec. 1917. For two historical examinations of the Porvenir massacre, see Douglas V. Meed, *Bloody Border: Riots, Battles, and Adventures along the Turbulent U.S.–Mexican Borderlands* (Tucson: Westernlore Press, 1992), and Glenn Justice, *Revolution on the Rio Grande: Mexican Raids and Army Pursuits, 1916–1919* (El Paso: University of Texas at El Paso Press, 1992).

62. *San Antonio Express,* 11 Sept. 1915.

63. For some of the many accounts of Mexicans being removed from jail or the au-

thorities and lynched, see "Proceedings of the Joint Commission of the Senate and the House in the Investigation of the Texas Ranger Force," Thirty-sixth Legislature, Regular Session, Legislative Papers, Texas State Archives; Frank Pierce, "Partial List of Mexicans Killed in the Valley since July 1, 1915," Records of the Department of State Relating to the Internal Affairs of Mexico, 1910–1929, Microfilm Publication M274, vol. 51, file 812/17186, National Archives; *Brownsville Herald,* 19 Aug. and 15, 21 Sept. 1915; *San Antonio Express,* 15 Sept. 1915; James A. Sandos, *Rebellion in the Borderlands: Anarchism and the Plan of San Diego, 1904–1923* (Norman: University of Oklahoma Press, 1992), 87; Meed, *Bloody Border,* 128; and Evan Anders, *Boss Rule in South Texas: The Progressive Era* (Austin: University of Texas Press, 1982).

64. Virgil Lott, "The Rio Grande Valley," unpublished manuscript, Center for American History, University of Texas at Austin. Accounts of violence against Mexicans in south Texas can be found throughout the English-language and Spanish-language newspapers between 1915 and 1917. See, for example, *Brownsville Herald,* 7, 9, 13, 19, 23, 27, and 30 Aug. 1915, 1, 3, 10, 15, 16, and 25 Sept. 1915, and 26 Dec. 1917; and *La Prensa* (San Antonio), 20 Aug. 1915 and 27, 28 Dec. 1917.

65. *Waco Weekly Tribune,* 22 Sept. 1900.

66. Salvador Guerrero, *Memorias: A West Texas Life* (Lubbock: Texas Tech Press, 1991), 9.

67. *Waco News Tribune,* 17 Sept. 1925.

68. *Waco News Tribune,* 8 Sept. 1925.

69. *McKinney Messenger,* 9 Nov. 1872.

70. *Waco Evening News,* 19 May 1894; *Waco Weekly Tribune,* 20 Nov. 1897; *Waco Times-Herald,* 30 Nov. 1904.

71. Court records indicate that Mexicans in central Texas committed crimes that might have merited lynching in south Texas. There are many instances of Mexicans being convicted of horse theft, a crime for which they were often lynched in south Texas. Central Texas came close to lynching a Mexican in 1921, when three men, including Pedro Sanchez and José Flores, killed Deputy Sheriff Oscar B. Sharp of Falls County. Instead of being lynched, however, the three men were tried, convicted, and sentenced to death. "Legal Hangings in Falls County, 1860–1921," index to Criminal Minutes, vol. B, Falls County Courthouse, Marlin, Tex.

72. Oral memoirs of Ernest Calderon, Texas Collection, Baylor University, Waco, Tex., 19.

73. Oral memoirs of Tomas Arroyo, Texas Collection, Baylor University, Waco, Tex., 5.

74. *La Prensa* (San Antonio), 12 Jan. 1915.

75. For specific cases involving Mexicans and the central Texas court system, see *State of Texas v. Jose Costio,* case no. 1104, *State of Texas v. Cornitious Marques,* case no. 1758, *State of Texas v. Juan Thomas and Juan Martinez,* case no. 1759, *State of Texas v. Santa Anna alias Juan Martinez,* case no. 1767, *State of Texas v. John Lopez,* case no. 1816, and *State of Texas v. Albert Velasco,* case no. 1838, all in Case Files of the Fifty-fourth District Court, McLennan County Archives, Waco, Tex.; see also *State of Texas v. Jesus Aura,* case no. 4938, McLennan County Civil and Criminal Minute Books, vol. N, McLennan County Archives, Waco, Tex.

76. *State of Texas v. John Anderson,* case no. 3250, and *State of Texas v. Grover Ross,* case no. 4148, both in Case Files of the Fifty-fourth District Court, McLennan County Archives, Waco, Tex.; *Waco Semi-Weekly Tribune,* 13 April 1912.

77. Oral memoirs of Julia Duran, Texas Collection, Baylor University, Waco, Tex., 5.

78. Neil Foley, *The White Scourge: Mexicans, Blacks, and Poor Whites in Texas Cotton Culture* (Berkeley: University of California Press, 1997), 41.

79. As C. Vann Woodward brilliantly documented, the segregated South did not emerge fully developed after the collapse of Reconstruction. Edward Ayers, among others, has emphasized the importance of the changing generations of the New South. C. Vann Woodward, *The Strange Career of Jim Crow,* 2d rev. ed. (New York: Oxford University Press, 1966); Edward Ayers, *Vengeance and Justice: Crime and Punishment in the Nineteenth-Century American South* (New York: Oxford University Press, 1984).

80. Hall, "History of the Negro in Waco, Texas," 24–25.

81. *Waco Evening News,* 14 Jan. 1889.

82. *Waco Times-Herald,* 11 Dec. 1898.

83. Quoted in *Waco Weekly News,* 11 March 1905.

84. *Waco Day,* 24 Oct. 1889.

85. *Waco Weekly News,* 22 Nov. 1889.

86. *Waco Times-Herald,* 6 March 1898.

87. The story of the formation of the Committee of Six and the Good Government Club and the subsequent city election can be found in the *Waco Times-Herald* between 19 March 1898 and 22 Sept. 1898.

88. *Waco Times-Herald,* 28 July 1900.

89. Lamar L. Kirven, "A Century of Warfare: Black Texans," Ph.D. diss., Indiana University, 1974, 87–89.

90. *Waco Messenger,* 13 Oct. 1933.

91. For a fuller discussion of the changing black community of central Texas, particularly the rise of a black professional class in Waco, see William D. Carrigan, "Between South and West: Race, Violence, and Power in Central Texas, 1836–1916," Ph.D. diss., Emory University, 1999, 251–57.

92. Marlin, Mart, Temple, Waco, Branch Files, National Association for the Advancement of Colored People Archives, Manuscript Division, Library of Congress, Washington (hereafter NAACP Papers).

93. *Waco Daily Examiner,* 20 June 1876.

94. *Waco Daily Examiner,* 20 June 1877.

95. *Waco Daily Examiner,* 20 June 1886.

96. *Waco Weekly Tribune,* 22 June 1901.

97. *Waco Weekly Tribune,* 24 June 1904.

98. *Waco Times-Herald,* 20 June 1927.

99. *Waco Evening News,* 9 Aug. 1888.

100. *Waco Evening News,* 19 Jan. 1889.

101. *Waco Weekly Tribune,* 9 June 1900.

102. Ibid.

103. Stephenson's book was favorably reviewed in the *Waco Weekly News,* 11 March 1905.

104. The most powerful argument that "consumer culture created spectacle lynchings" is found in Grace Elizabeth Hale, *Making Whiteness: The Culture of Segregation in the South, 1890–1940* (New York: Pantheon Books, 1998), 199–239 (quotation on 205). James Allen discusses the importance of lynching photography in twentieth-century racial violence. James

Allen et al., *Without Sanctuary: Lynching Photography in America* (Santa Fe: Twin Palms, 2000), 166–205.

105. Leon Litwack, *Trouble in Mind: Black Southerners in the Age of Jim Crow* (New York: Alfred A. Knopf, 1998), 285.

106. Newsclipping of the *Montgomery Advertiser*, 23 July 1910, box 1, Lynching Records, Tuskegee University Archives, Tuskegee, Ala.

107. Quoted in *Story of Bell County, Texas*, ed. E. A. Limmer et al., Bell County Historical Association (Austin: Eakin Press, 1987), 1:54–55.

108. Newsclipping of the *Atlanta Constitution*, 31 July 1915, box 2, Lynching Records, Tuskegee University Archives, Tuskegee, Ala.

109. One of the reasons that Stanley's guilt is in doubt is that a ring stolen from the Grimes family was found in the ashes of the fire. A complete physical examination of Stanley before his death had not turned up the ring, so authorities concluded that it was placed in the fire after Stanley's lynching. Stanley had been identified as a suspect because he wore a pair of trousers that carried the name "Mr. Grimes" but claimed that two other black men had given him the trousers. No additional investigation into the Grimes's killing took place. *Waco Morning News*, 31 July 1915; Limmer, ed., *Story of Bell County*, 55–56.

110. *Dallas Morning News*, 21 Jan. 1919; G. N. T. Gray, "The Burning of Bragg Williams, a Report on the Hillsboro, Texas Horror and other Materials Relating to the Lynching of Bragg Williams," pt. 1, NAACP Papers.

111. Allen et al., *Without Sanctuary*, plates 25 and 26.

112. *Waco Morning News*, 1 Aug. 1915.

113. Gray, "The Burning of Bragg Williams," 3.

Epilogue

1. *Waco Semi-Weekly Tribune*, 17 May 1916.

2. London *Times*, 17 May 1916. Numerous clippings from newspapers published in the United States can be found in Lynching Files, Tuskegee University Archives, Tuskegee, Ala.

3. *New York Age*, 25 May 1916.

4. *Chicago Defender*, 20 May 1916.

5. Untitled newsclipping from Harrisburg, Pa., 16 May 1916; *New Bedford Standard*, 22 May 1916; *Battle Creek News*, 16 May 1916; "Lynchings—1916 Discussions," Lynching Files, Tuskegee University Archives, Tuskegee, Ala.

6. *Montgomery Advertiser*, 16 May 1916; *Birmingham Christian Advocate*, 18 May 1916; Newsclippings, "Lynchings—1916 Discussions," Lynching Files, Tuskegee University Archives, Tuskegee, Ala.

7. *Houston Chronicle*, editorial, 16 May 1916. For numerous other instances of rebuke from newspapers see James M. SoRelle, "The 'Waco Horror': The Lynching of Jesse Washington," *Southwestern Historical Quarterly* 86 (1983): 517–36; and Rogers M. Smith, "The Waco Lynching of 1916: Perspective and Analysis," master's thesis, Baylor University, 1971.

8. "The Waco Horror," special supplement, and W. E. B. Du Bois, "Lynching," both in *The Crisis* 12 (1916): 1–8 and 135.

9. Joel E. Spingarn to Philip G. Peabody, 4 Aug. 1916, National Association for the Advancement of Colored People Archives, Manuscript Division, Library of Congress, Washington (hereafter NAACP Papers).

10. "A Practical Way to Cut Down Lynching," *The Survey*, 20 Jan. 1917, 461.

11. *The Nation*, 18 May 1916, 530–31.

12. "Moving against Lynching," *The Nation*, 3 Aug. 1916, 101.

13. John L. Kessler, "In Justice to Waco," *The Nation*, 28 Dec. 1916, 609.

14. Reprinted in *W. E. B. Du Bois: A Reader*, ed. David Levering Lewis (New York: Henry Holt, 1995), 495–502.

15. Samuel Eliot Morison, *The Oxford History of the American People* (New York: Oxford University Press, 1965), 794.

16. Among the many sources that could be cited with regard to Waco's reputation for racism, one of the most influential was Frank Tannenbaum, *Darker Phases of the South* (New York: G. P. Putnam, 1924), 158–60. Jesse Washington's lynching was also featured in John C. Van Deusen, *The Black Man in White America* (Washington: Associated Publishers, 1938), 58. In Frank Shay, *Judge Lynch: His First Hundred Years* (New York: Ives Washburn, 1938), the author devotes more attention to Jesse Washington than any other lynching in Texas. In 1998 several newspapers picked up an Associated Press story on the 1916 lynching (*Daily Texan*, 2 June 1998).

17. Bragg Williams Newsclippings, Subject File: Lynching Records, Administrative Files, NAACP Papers.

18. For a thorough discussion of the important Kirven case, see Monte Akers, *Flames after Midnight: Murder, Vengeance, and the Desolation of a Texas Community* (Austin: University of Texas Press, 1999).

19. The remarkable persistence of Jesse Thomas's murder, especially among black Wacoans, will be discussed in detail later in the Epilogue.

20. Oral memoir of Oscar Emil Hessdoerfer, Texas Collection, Baylor University, Waco, Tex., 91.

21. Kessler, "In Justice to Waco," 609.

22. Elisabeth Freeman wrote to Roy Nash: "I have not found a Christian minister who has protested against the action of the white folk" (Freeman to Nash, 21 May 1916, NAACP Papers). That soon changed. After the wave of criticism against Waco, several religious groups and institutions published condemnations of the mob violence that claimed Jesse Washington. The faculty of Baylor University and the Waco Baptist Pastors Association both published resolutions in late May censuring the racial violence. These leaders genuinely detested the actions of the mob, but their commitment stopped short of pursuing a case against its leaders.

23. Elisabeth Freeman, "The Waco Lynching," NAACP Papers.

24. William Curry, *A History of Early Waco with Allusions to Six-Shooter Junction* (Waco: Texian Press, 1968), 88–90.

25. Patricia Ward Wallace, *Waco; Texas Crossroads* (Woodland Hills: Windsor Publications, 1983), 59. Wallace's number is incorrect. A photograph of the 1916 lynching that appears in Curry's book and the reports of the NAACP is packed with more than a thousand spectators. Furthermore, it is clear that more people are beyond the range of the photograph. Not all historians writing in Waco, however, minimize the number of participants and witnesses to Jesse Washington's lynching. Both Smith ("The Waco Lynching of 1916") and SoRelle ("The 'Waco Horror'") document the figure of fifteen thousand. Both of these scholarly works, however, received little attention from a Waco public that was never their audience.

26. Lewis S. Delony, *Forty Years a Peace Officer: A True Story of Lawlessness and Adventure in the Early Days of Southwest Texas* (n.p., n.d.), 60–61. Delony's memoir can be found in the Texas Collection of Baylor University.

27. Delony, *Forty Years a Peace Officer,* 60–61.

28. Elisabeth Freeman to Roy Nash, Wednesday, 23 May(?), 1916, 3, NAACP Papers.

29. Roger Norman Conger, telephone interview with author, Waco, Tex., Oct. 1992; Roger Norman Conger, *Highlights of Waco History* (Waco: Texian Press, 1945); Roger Conger, *Pictorial History of Waco* (Waco: Texian Press, 1964); Roger Conger, *Waco: A Basic History* (Waco: Texian Press, 1984); Roger Conger, "Waco: Cotton and Culture on the Brazos," *Southwestern Historical Quarterly* 75 (1972): 54–60.

30. Oral memoir of Harold Lester Goodman, Texas Collection, Baylor University, Waco, Tex., 33.

31. Ibid.

32. Madison Alexander Cooper Jr. Papers, Texas Collection, Baylor University, Waco, Tex. (hereafter Cooper Papers).

33. Madison Alexander Cooper Jr. to Bowers, Clipping Service Correspondence, Cooper Papers.

34. Madison A. Cooper, *Sironia, Texas* (Cambridge: Riverside Press, 1951), 1459–81; Miscellaneous Notes, "Character Development," Cooper Papers.

35. Cooper, *Sironia,* 301.

36. Miscellaneous Notes, "Plot, Polishing," Cooper Papers.

37. *Waco Semi-Weekly Tribune,* 27, 30 June and 17 July 1917; *State of Texas v. Oliver Courtrade,* case no. 4476, Case Files of the Fifty-fourth District Court, McLennan County Archives, Waco, Tex.

38. Newsclipping of *Waco Times-Herald,* 25 Jan., 12 April 1919, "1919—Assaults without Lynchings," Lynching Files, Tuskegee University Archives, Tuskegee, Ala.

39. *Waco Times-Herald,* 16–17 March, 1, 9, 30 April, and 17 May 1929; *State of Texas v. Jordan Scott,* cases no. 8094 and 8095, Case Files of the Fifty-fourth District Court, McLennan County Archives, Waco, Tex.

40. Newsclipping of *Wichita Falls Times,* 7 Feb. 1923, Lynching Files, Tuskegee University Archives, Tuskegee, Ala.

41. Newsclipping of *Houston Post,* 18 Jan. 1922, Lynching Files, Tuskegee University Archives, Tuskegee Ala.

42. *Waco Times-Herald,* 14 May 1930.

43. *Waco Messenger,* 28 May 1937. A nearly complete run of the *Waco Messenger* from 1933 to the 1980s can be found at the Archives of Paul Quinn College in Dallas, Tex.

44. Oral memoir of Garry Hamilton Radford, Texas Collection, Baylor University, Waco, Tex., 203–4.

45. Additional evidence of the motivations and fears of the business leadership in central Texas during the civil rights movement can be found in Robin Carlysle Bean, "The Role of the Commercial-Civic Elite in the Desegregation of Public Facilities in Waco, Texas," master's thesis, Baylor University, 1990.

46. Bean, "The Role of the Commercial-Civic Elite."

47. *Houston Informer,* 27 Jan. (quotations) and 20 Jan. 1923.

48. *Waco Times-Herald,* 26 May 1922. The name of the female companion, Maggie Hays, was never mentioned in the newspapers but is identified by Rogers Smith in his mas-

ter's thesis, "The Waco Lynching of 1916." Hays's name was confirmed in an interview with Willie Long Smith on 23 Oct. 1992. Smith was born in 1890 and remembered the incident and Hays; she worked all of her life as a domestic servant for the same white family in Waco. Smith maintained that her information regarding the lynching of Jesse Thomas came from talking with another domestic servant, one who worked at the Harris home.

The Waco police's widespread search of Waco's black community was reported to me by Hayward Weaver, whose uncle, Loy Manos, was picked up but not jailed. I interviewed Weaver on 22 October 1992 in his home in Waco. Weaver, the first black to work at the Waco Post Office, has lived in the city all his life and is descended from the slaves of the family for which McLennan County is named. Tape for interviews with Smith and Weaver are in my possession, as are all subsequent personal interviews on audiotape unless otherwise noted.

49. *Waco Times-Herald,* 26 May 1922.

50. *Waco Times-Herald,* 27 May 1922.

51. Ibid.

52. Author interview with Willie Long Smith, Waco, Tex., 23 Oct. 1992. Although she mentioned the crowd outside the jail, Sank Johnson, and details of the lynching that followed, Smith confused a number of the factual details of the event. Her general rendering of the incident, however, was independently repeated by a longtime Jewish resident of Waco: "They took him [Thomas] in to see this girl that—the victim of the rape, and of course, she was in a state of terror anyway; and when they took the Negro in—any Negro they would have taken in she just screamed with fright and they assumed that that was enough." See the oral memoirs of Harold Lester Goodman, Texas Collection, Baylor University, Waco, Tex., 26–27.

53. Interview with Willie Long Smith; *Waco Times-Herald,* 27 May 1922; author interview with Kneeland Clemons, Waco, Tex., 12 Nov. 1992. Clemons said that his mother, who was pregnant with Kneeland, as well as other blacks, hid in their houses in fear of violence as the body was dragged through town. Clemons, the son of a pharmacist, grew up in North Waco with Hayward Weaver in the early twentieth century.

54. *Waco Times-Herald,* 30 July 1923, 28 May 1922; *Austin Statesman,* 28 May 1922; William S. Foster, *Observations* (Waco, 1976), 92.

55. Oral memoir of Harold Lester Goodman, Texas Collection, Baylor University, Waco, Tex., 30.

56. Oral memoir of Joseph M. Dawson, Texas Collection, Baylor University, Waco, Tex., 54; *Waco Times-Herald,* 29, 30 May 1922; *Austin Statesman,* 28 May 1922.

57. Evidence that white Wacoans remembered more about Washington than about Thomas comes from several sources. When local histories did mention the lynchings, such as William Curry's *A History of Waco with Allusions to Six-Shooter Junction,* they mentioned the lynching of Jesse Washington but failed to discuss the murder of Thomas, instead talking about the legal hanging of Roy Mitchell. Other factors that suggest white Wacoans remember more of Washington comes from the nature of the two acts of violence. Washington's murder had been anticipated for weeks and a larger crowd attended. They left with pictures taken by a photographer who had been apprised of the preparations for the burning. Thomas's murder, on the other hand, caught many Wacoans off

guard and it was not until later that the mob coalesced and paraded the body around the streets of Waco.

58. Oral memoirs of Clemmie Holloway Long and Willie Long Smith, Texas Collection, Baylor University, Waco, Tex., 131.

59. Oral memoirs of Marcus Langley Cooper Jr., Texas Collection, Baylor University, Waco, Tex., 125.

60. Author interviews with Willie Long Smith and Kneeland Clemons.

61. Of the people interviewed, only Willie Long Smith distinguished between the two lynchings; the others, being too young to remember the incidents firsthand, generally told me of only one. In their descriptions of the lynching, few remembered the names of those involved, but the narratives they recount coincide more closely to Jesse Thomas's murder than that of Jesse Washington.

62. In 1905 a black man had decried the lynching of Sank Majors in Waco. He was later visited by a "vigilance committee" and given 150 lashes with a whip for his comments. According to the *Waco Times-Herald* articled entitled "Negro Whipped by Vigilance Committee" (10 Aug. 1905), one terrorist said, "There is not much danger of any of the Negroes who attend to their own business and keep their mouths shut being disturbed, . . but there are some who must be checked by some means or other."

63. *George Fryer v. Paul Quinn College,* case no. 1194, Case Files of the Seventy-fourth Judicial District Court, McLennan County Archives, Waco, Tex. My thanks to Katherine Walters to alerting me to this document. On Smith's legal woes, see Mrs. A. T. Smith to Roy Nash, 9 Aug. 1916, Memorandum from Roy Nash to Joel Spingarn, 11 Aug. 1916, NAACP Papers. My thanks to James SoRelle for providing me with this reference. SoRelle, "The 'Waco Horror,'" 531n.

64. Cited in Lawrence Levine, *Black Culture and Black Consciousness: Afro-American Folk Thought from Slavery to Freedom* (New York: Oxford University Press, 1977), 206.

65. The oral memoir of Marcus Langley Cooper most clearly indicates the blurring of the two lynchings. Cooper explained that the lynching victim was innocent (as was Thomas) and that he was retarded (something alleged of Jesse Washington but never of Jesse Thomas). Oral memoirs of Marcus Langley Cooper Jr., Texas Collection, Baylor University, Waco, Tex., 126. In addition to blurring the two lynchings together, African American remembrances of the lynching often added details that clearly had not occurred in the early twentieth century. Baylor professor Vivian Malone Mayes, for example, cited her father and maintained that one of the lynching victims (probably Jesse Thomas because she recalls that their parents said the man was innocent but did not mention him by name) had been tarred and feathered. Mayes provided her recollection of the lynching as the interviewer in the oral memoirs of Kneeland H. Clemons, Texas Collection, Baylor University, Waco, Tex., 7.

66. Author interview with Mary Denkins, Waco, Texas, 11 Jan. 1994.

67. Oral memoirs of Maggie Langham Washington, Texas Collection, Baylor University, Waco, Tex., 51. One of the most interesting things about this interview is that Washington elaborated on the connection with the lynchings when asked about the 1953 tornado. Her local white interviewers displayed no knowledge of the story of the tornado's wrath.

68. Author interview with Mary Denkins. Denkins was born in 1941 in a small rural community only a few miles from Waco. She moved to the city while a young girl and has spent the rest of her life there. She owns her own catering business.

69. Ibid.

70. Ibid.

71. Oral memoirs of Maggie Langham Washington, Texas Collection, Baylor University, Waco, Tex., 51.

72. W. E. B. Du Bois, *Black Reconstruction in America: An Essay toward a History of the Part which Black Folk Played in the Attempt to Reconstruct Democracy in America, 1860–1880* (New York: Harcourt, Brace, 1935), 124.

73. Interview with Johnetta Ray in *Drylongso: A Self-Portrait of Black America,* ed. John Langston Gwaltney (New York: New Press, 1993), 227–29.

74. Hudie Ledbetter, "The Titanic," History in Song Web site at <http://www.fortunecity .com/tinpan/parton/2/> (accessed 21 Mar. 2004).

75. Jeff Place, "Supplemental Notes on the Selections," in *A Booklet of Essays, Appreciations, and Annotations Pertaining to the Anthology of American Folk Music Edited by Harry Smith* (Washington: Smithsonian Folkways Recordings, 1997), 46–47.

76. For discussions of the use of religion by African Americans to protect themselves and attack others in the postbellum period, see Robin D. G. Kelley, "'We Are Not What We Seem': Black Working Class Opposition in the Jim Crow South," *Journal of American History* 80 (1993): 88–89. For the theory and background of African American Christianity as a tool of resistance (and as a tool of accommodation), see Gayraud S. Wilmore, *Black Religion and Black Radicalism; An Interpretation of the Religious History of Afro-American People,* 2d ed. (Maryknoll: Obris Books, 1983); Lawrence Levine, *Black Culture and Black Consciousness* (New York: Oxford University Press, 1977); Vincent Harding, "Religion and Resistance among Antebellum Negroes, 1800–1860," in *The Making of Black America,* ed. August Meier and Elliot Rudwick (New York: Atheneum, 1969), 1:179–97; Albert J. Raboteau, *Slave Religion: The "Invisible Institution" in the Antebellum South* (New York: Oxford University Press, 1978); Eugene D. Genovese, *Roll, Jordan, Roll: The World the Slaves Made* (New York: Vintage Books, 1972), 159–285; Evelyn Brooks Higginbotham, *Righteous Discontent: The Women's Movement in the Black Baptist Church, 1880–1920* (Cambridge: Harvard University Press, 1993); and William E. Montgomery, *Under Their Own Vine and Fig Tree: The African American Church in the South, 1865–1900* (Baton Rouge: Louisiana State University Press, 1993).

77. Author interview with the Rev. Eric Hooker, Waco, Tex., 7 Jan. 1994. Hooker grew up in Waco, and after serving as pastor in other parts of the state and region, he has returned to pastor Second Baptist Church, one of the oldest and largest churches in black Waco.

78. On the struggle to overturn the white primary, see Katherine K. K. Walters, "The Great War in Waco, Texas: African Americans, Race Relations, and the White Primary, 1916–1922," master's thesis, Southwest Texas State University, 2000. On the NAACP in early-twentieth-century Texas, see Steve Reich, "Soldiers of Democracy: Black Texans and the Fight for Citizenship, 1917–1921," *Journal of American History* 82 (1996): 1478. On the activities of the NAACP in central Texas after World War I, see Branch Files, boxes G-204, G-205, C-193, C-196, C-197, C-199, C-200, C-201, C-202, E-95, E-96, C-147, C-149, C-151,

C-152, C-153, and E-16, NAACP Papers. Information on black activism in central Texas during the 1940s and 1950s can be found in Charles H. Martin, "The Civil Rights Congress and Southern Black Defendants," *Georgia Historical Quarterly* 71 (Spring 1987): 25–52, esp. 32. On the civil rights movement in central Texas, see Bean, "The Role of the Commercial-Civic Elite." For biographical information on Oscar DuCongé, mayor of Waco, see the inventory to the DuCongé Papers, the Texas Collection, Baylor University, Waco, Tex.

79. This line of argument appears in W. Fitzhugh Brundage, *Lynching in the New South: Georgia and Virginia, 1880–1930* (Urbana: University of Illinois Press, 1993), and Stewart E. Tolnay and E. M. Beck, *A Festival of Violence: An Analysis of Southern Lynchings, 1882–1930* (Urbana: University of Illinois Press, 1995).

80. For a discussion of black resistance to lynching and racial violence, see W. Fitzhugh Brundage, "The Roar on the Other Side of Silence: Black Resistance and White Violence in the American South, 1880–1940," in *Under Sentence of Death: Lynching in the South,* ed. W. Fitzhugh Brundage (Chapel Hill: University of North Carolina Press, 1997), 271–91.

81. Author interview with Mary Denkins; author interview with James Leeper, Waco, Texas, summer 1993. I talked casually with Leeper while he was working. The tale of the tornado emerged during the majority of interviews I conducted. Six of the fifteen black Wacoans with whom I conducted interviews mentioned the tornado tale without being asked about stories of racial violence in the city, and four more mentioned it when I asked for stories about mob violence. Without any prior knowledge, interviewers for Baylor University's Institute for Oral History also uncovered the tale of the tornado.

82. Tolnay and Beck make the most persuasive case for black flight as a form of resistance to lynching. Tolnay and Beck, *A Festival of Violence,* 202–38.

83. Harold Lester Goodman and Marcus Langley Cooper Jr. recalled that blacks left Waco after its early-twentieth-century racial violence. Oral memoirs of Harold Lester Goodman and Marcus Langley Cooper Jr., both in Texas Collection, Baylor University, Waco, Tex., 29, 127. According to U.S. Census data, the black population of Waco underwent a net out-migration of 553 during the first decade after the start of the city's racial violence.

84. This quotation was taken from a sociological report compiled by a Baylor student in 1927. Selese Hunter, "A Study of the Negroes Engaged in the Professions and Business Activities in Waco, Texas," unpublished report, 1927, Texas Collection, Baylor University, Waco, Tex.

85. *Daily Texan* (Austin), 2 June 1998.

86. *Houston Chronicle,* 30 June 2002.

87. Scott Ellsworth, *Death in a Promised Land* (Baton Rouge: Louisiana State University Press, 1982).

Appendix C: Terms, Sources, and Methods

1. W. Fitzhugh Brundage, "Lynching," in *Violence in America: An Encyclopedia,* ed. Ronald Gottsman (New York: Charles Scribner's Sons, 1999), 297–303, quotation on 297.

2. The 1940 NAACP definition of lynching is discussed in Christopher Waldrep, "War of Words: The Controversy over the Definition of Lynching, 1899–1940," *Journal of Southern History* 66 (2000): 75–100; and W. Fitzhugh Brundage, *Lynching in the New South:*

Georgia and Virginia, 1880–1930 (Urbana: University of Illinois Press, 1993), 291–92, quotation on 291. In order to eliminate repetition and improve this text, I employ the term *mob violence*. That term encompasses all lynchings but includes other forms of mob action, especially nonlethal ones, as well. This study also employs the terms *vigilantism* and *vigilantes*. These terms are not synonyms for lynching but indicate a particular form of it. Like "lynching," the term is not precise, but vigilante-led lynch mobs tend to be more deliberate and careful, sometimes to the point of orchestrating entire mock trials and appointing a "defense" for the victim. They typically justify their actions as necessary because of the undeveloped or ineffectual state of the legal system and enjoy widespread— if not universal—community support. As with mob violence, however, the use of the term *vigilante* does not necessarily indicate that a victim was killed.

APPENDIX A

Victims of Mob Violence in Central Texas, 1860–1922

Name	Race	County, Area	Date	Crime	Size and Action of Mob (if Known)	Source(s)
—Covington	W	Bosque	June 1860	Horse theft	Hanged by vigilance committee	Greer, ed., *Buck Barry*, 121–23[a]
—Tucker	W	Bosque	Early Aug. 1860	Horse theft	Hanged by mob of over 100 people	Greer, ed., *Buck Barry*, 121–23
John Garner	W	McLennan	Sept. 1860	Murder	Hanged by vigilance committee	Greer, ed., *Buck Barry*, 121–23
Unknown	W	Central Texas	April 1861	Murder and cattle theft	Hanged by mob from Coryell, Hamilton, Bosque, Comanche, and McLennan counties	Scott, *Coryell County*, 60[b]
Unknown	W	Central Texas	April 1861	Murder and cattle theft	Hanged by mob from Coryell, Hamilton, Bosque, Comanche, and McLennan counties	Scott, *Coryell County*, 60
Unknown	W	Central Texas	April 1861	Murder and cattle theft	Hanged by mob from Coryell, Hamilton, Bosque, Comanche, and McLennan counties	Scott, *Coryell County*, 60
Demetrius Hays	W	McLennan	Dec. 1861	Harboring a fugitive slave	Murdered by mob of men led by William Johnson	McLennon Co. Criminal Minute Book
Eli Ensor	W	McLennan	Dec. 1861	Fornication with a person of color	Murdered by a mob of men led by William Johnson	McLennan Co. Criminal Minute Book
—Thompson	W	McLennan	ca. 1 May 1862	Horse theft	Hanged by parties unknown	*Bellville Countrymen*, 31 May 1862
—Thompson	W	McLennan	ca. 1 May 1862	Horse theft	Hanged by parties unknown	*Bellville Countrymen*, 31 May 1862

Name	Race	County, Area	Date	Crime	Size and Action of Mob (if Known)	Source(s)
— Wood	W	McLennan	20 May 1862	Being a Yankee abolitionist	Hanged by mob of 8 men	*Belleville Countrymen,* 31 May 1862
J. T. Russell	W	McLennan	23 May 1862	Murder (of Wood)	Shot by "enraged citizenry"	*Belleville Countrymen,* 31 May 1862
Henry Russell	W	McLennan	23 May 1862	Murder (of Wood)	Shot by "enraged citizenry"	*Belleville Countrymen,* 31 May 1862
C. T. Tinsley	W	McLennan	23 May 1862	Murder (of Wood)	Shot by "enraged citizenry"	*Belleville Countrymen,* 31 May 1862
Unknown	W	Bell	Early 1865	Desertion	Hanged by unknown members of the Home Guard and Confederate army	Sonnichsen, *Ten Texas Feuds,* 69c
Unknown	W	Bell	Early 1865	Desertion	Hanged by unknown members of the Home Guard and Confederate army	Sonnichsen, *Ten Texas Feuds,* 69
Unknown	W	Bell	Early 1865	Desertion	Hanged by unknown members of the Home Guard and Confederate army	Sonnichsen, *Ten Texas Feuds,* 69
— Shakelford	W	Bell	March 1866	Horse theft	Killed by unknown men	*Galveston Daily News,* 15 April 1866
— Park	W	Bell	7 April 1866	Horse theft	Hanged by unknown vigilantes	*Galveston Daily News,* 15 April 1866
Jasper Lindley	W	Bell	Body found ca. 12 June 1866	Horse theft	Shot by unknown vigilantes	*Galveston Daily News,* 28 June 1866
Sam Miller	W	Bell	Body found ca. 12 June 1866	Horse theft	Shot by unknown vigilantes	*Galveston Daily News,* 28 June 1866

Name	Race	County, Area	Date	Crime	Size and Action of Mob (if Known)	Source(s)
Thomas Duncan	W	Bell	July 1866	Murder	Shot by posse of 17 men	*Galveston Daily News*, 25 July 1866
Daw	W	Bell	July 1866	Murder	Shot by posse of 17 men	*Galveston Daily News*, 25 July 1866
Unknown	B	Bosque	22 Aug. 1866	Unknown	Hanged by parties unknown	"Record of Criminal Offenses Committed in Texas, 1865–1869," RG 105, entry 68
Unknown	B	Bosque	22 Aug. 1866	Unknown	Hanged by parties unknown	"Record of Criminal Offenses Committed in Texas, 1865–1869," RG 105, entry 69
Jonathan Lindley	W	Bell	Dec. 1866	Murder	Shot by vigilantes while in jail	*Galveston Daily News*, 31 July 1866; *Harper's Weekly*, 23 Mar. 1867, 184–85
Newton, Lindley	W	Bell	Dec. 1866	Murder	Shot by vigilantes while in jail	*Galveston Daily News*, 31 July 1866; *Harper's Weekly*, 23 Mar. 1867, 184–85
Unknown	B	McLennan	Mar. 1867	Unknown	"Brutal murder" by Tuck Decker and others	"Record of Criminal Offenses Committed in Texas, 1865–1869," RG 105, entry 662
George Gray	B	Falls	3 Aug. 1867	Unknown	Shot from thicket by persons unknown	"Record of Criminal Offenses, Committed in Texas, 1865–1869," RG 105, entry 1009

Name	Race	County, Area	Date	Crime	Size and Action of Mob (if Known)	Source(s)
Joe Pitts	B	McLennan	4 April 1868	Unknown	Shot in the head by parties unknown	"Record of Criminal Offenses Committed in Texas, 1865–1869," RG 105, entry 1578
— Schoonover	W	Corner of McLennan, Coryell, and Bell counties	5 May 1868	Unionist outlaw	Killed by "a mob of Texans" alleged to be part of the KKK	"Record of Criminal Offenses Committed in Texas, 1865–1869," RG 105, entry 1682
— Schoonover	W	Corner of McLennan, Coryell, and Bell counties	5 May 1868	Unionist outlaw	Killed by "a mob of Texans" alleged to be part of the KKK	"Record of Criminal Offenses Committed in Texas, 1865–1869," RG 105, entry 1683
— Schoonover	W	Corner of McLennan, Coryell, and Bell counties	5 May 1868	Unionist outlaw	Killed by "a mob of Texans" alleged to be part of the KKK	"Record of Criminal Offenses Committed in Texas, 1865–1869," RG 105, entry 1684
George Shackleford	W	Corner of McLennan, Coryell, and Bell counties	5 May 1868	Unionist outlaw	Killed by "a mob of Texans" alleged to be part of the KKK	"Record of Criminal Offenses Committed in Texas, 1865–1869," RG 105, entry 1685
Isaac Ellington	W	Corner of McLennan, Coryell, and Bell counties	5 May 1868	Unionist outlaw	Killed by "a mob of Texans" alleged to be part of the KKK	"Record of Criminal Offenses Committed in Texas, 1865–1869," RG 105, entry 1686
Daniel Sessions	W	Corner of McLennan, Coryell, and Bell counties	5 May 1868	Unionist outlaw	Killed by "a mob of Texans" alleged to be part of the KKK	"Record of Criminal Offenses Committed in Texas, 1865–1869," RG 105, entry 1687

Name	Race	County, Area	Date	Crime	Size and Action of Mob (if Known)	Source(s)
Bernard Maye	W	Corner of McLennan, Coryell, and Bell counties	5 May 1868	Unionist outlaw	Killed by "a mob of Texans" alleged to be part of the KKK	"Record of Criminal Offenses Committed in Texas, 1865–1869," RG 105, entry 1688
Unknown	W	McLennan	5 May 1868	Murder	Unknown, "a Union Boy"	"Record of Criminal Offenses Committed in Texas, 1865–1869," RG 105, entry 1693
Unknown	W	Bosque	3 June 1868	Unknown	Hanged by Vigilance Committee	"Record of Criminal Offenses Committed in Texas, 1865–1869," RG 105, entry 1782
Unknown	W	Bosque	3 June 1868	Unknown	Hanged by Vigilance Committee	"Record of Criminal Offenses Committed in Texas, 1865–1869," RG 105, entry 1783
Unknown	W	Bosque	3 June 1868	Unknown	Hanged by Vigilance Committee	"Record of Criminal Offenses Committed in Texas, 1865–1869," RG 105, entry 1783
Unknown	W	Bosque	3 June 1868	Unknown	Hanged by Vigilance Committee	"Record of Criminal Offenses Committed in Texas, 1865–1869," RG 105, entry 1784
Caleb	B	McLennan	1 Aug. 1868	Murder	Unknown	"Record of Criminal Offenses Committed in Texas, 1865–1869," RG 105, entry 1946

Name	Race	County, Area	Date	Crime	Size and Action of Mob (if Known)	Source(s)
Unknown	B	Falls	31 Aug. 1868	Unknown	Found hanging in the woods	"Record of Criminal Offenses Committed in Texas, 1865–1869," RG 105, entry 2034
Unknown	B	Falls	31 Aug. 1868	Unknown	Found hanging in the woods	"Record of Criminal Offenses Committed in Texas, 1865–1869," RG 105 entry 2035
Unknown	B	Falls	31 Aug. 1868	Unknown	Found hanging in the woods	"Record of Criminal Offenses Committed in Texas, 1865–1869," RG 105 entry 2036
Unknown	B	McLennan	5 Sept. 1868	Looking for work/ disobeying white man's orders	Unknown	"Record of Criminal Offenses Committed in Texas, 1865–1869," RG 105 entry 2032
Turner Norwood	B	McLennan	5 Sept. 1868	Unknown	Shot in own door by parties unknown	"Record of Criminal Offenses Committed in Texas, 1865–1869," RG 105, entry 2042
William H. Addams	W	McLennan	30 Sept. 1868	Being a Yankee and refusing to leave county	Unknown	"Record of Criminal Offenses Committed in Texas, 1865–1869," RG 105, entry 2123
Aleck (Albert) Bennett	B	McLennan	31 Oct. 1868	Unknown	Shot by 30 masked men	"Record of Criminal Offenses Committed in Texas, 1865–1869," RG 105 entry 2125

Name	Race	County, Area	Date	Crime	Size and Action of Mob (if Known)	Source(s)
Henry Killum	B	McLennan	31 Oct. 1868	Unknown	Shot by 30 masked men	"Record of Criminal Offenses Committed in Texas, 1865–1869," RG 105 entry 2126
Unknown	B	Falls	3 Nov. 1868	"Trying to escape"	Shot by posse of 5 after being captured	"Record of Criminal Offenses Committed in Texas, 1865–1869," RG 105 entry 2225
Spears	B	Limestone	Mar. 1869	Robbing a black man in Springfield	Killed by a group of blacks	"Abstract of Crimes Committed in Texas, 1869–1870," RG 393, pt.1, entry 4855, vol. 1, March 1869
Jeff Puckett	B	Limestone	27 Dec. 1869	Unknown	Murdered by 3 white men	"Abstract of Crimes Committed in Texas, 1869–1870," RG 393, pt.1, entry 4855, vol. 1, March 1869
Elijah	B	McLennan	27 Dec. 1869	Unknown	Murdered by 3 white men	"Abstract of Crimes Committed in Texas, 1869–1870," RG 393, pt. 1, entry 4855, vol. 1, March 1869
—Thornton	B	McLennan	29 Jan. 1870	Unknown	Unknown	"Abstracts of Crimes Committed in Texas, 1869–1879," RG 393, pt. 1 entry 4855, vol. 2

Name	Race	County, Area	Date	Crime	Size and Action of Mob (if Known)	Source(s)
—Frank	B	McLennan	29 Jan. 1870	Unknown	Unknown	"Abstracts of Crimes Committed in Texas, 1869–1870," RG 393, pt. 1 entry 4855, vol. 2
Jerry Lindsay	W	McLennan	10 July 1870	Cattle theft	Shot by a "large group of disguised men"	Texas State Police Records, entry 1099
Unknown Mexican	M	Limestone	9 Nov. 1872	Theft	Hanged by party of 8–9 men	*McKinney Messenger*, 9 Nov. 1872
John Alexander	W	Bell	24 May 1874	Horse theft	Shot by 20–50 men	*San Antonio Express*, 6 June 1874; Atkinson "History of Bell County," 132–33[d]
William Henry Grumbles	W	Bell	24 May 1874	Horse theft	Shot by 20–50 men	Atkinson, "History of Bell County," 132–33
William S. Smith	W	Bell	24 May 1874	Horse theft	Shot by 20–50 men	Atkinson, "History of Bell County," 132–33
J. S. McDonald	W	Bell	24 May 1874	Horse theft	Shot by 20–50 men	Atkinson, "History of Bell County," 132–33
Marion McDonald	W	Bell	24 May 1874	Horse theft	Shot by 20–50 men	Atkinson, "History of Bell County," 132–33
—Wingfield	W	Bell	24 May 1874	Horse theft	Shot by 20–50 men	Atkinson, "History of Bell County," 132–33
—Buckneal	W	Bell	24 May 1874	Horse theft	Shot by 20–50 men	Atkinson, "History of Bell County," 132–33
—Crow	W	Bell	24 May 1874	Horse theft	Shot by 20–50 men	Atkinson, "History of Bell County," 132–33
Lloyd Coleman	W	Bell	24 May 1874	Horse theft	Shot by 20–50 men	Atkinson, "History of Bell County," 132–33

Name	Race	County, Area	Date	Crime	Size and Action of Mob (if Known)	Source(s)
Unknown	B	Coryell	15 June 1874	Horse theft	Unknown	*San Antonio Daily Express*, 2 July 1874
Unknown	B	Coryell	15 June 1874	Horse theft	Unknown	*San Antonio Daily Express*, 2 July 1874
Nathaniel Burges	B	Limestone	July 1874	"No Provocation"	5	*San Antonio Daily Express*, 11 July 1874
Mrs. Burges	B	Limestone	July 1874	"No Provocation"	5	*San Antonio Daily Express*, 11 July 1874
Unknown	B	Limestone	22 May 1875	Unknown	Taken from jail and shot by a mob of men	*Galveston News*, 28 May 1875
Unknown	B	Bosque	26 July 1875	Murder	30	*Austin Daily Democratic Statesman*, 31 July 1875; *Iredell Times*, 5 March 1976
Ledwell	W	Bosque	26 July 1875	Murder	Hanged by mob of 30 men	*Austin Daily Democratic Statesman*, 31 July 1875; *Iredell Times*, 5 March 1976
— Wood	W	Bosque	26 July 1875	Murder	Hanged by mob of 30 men	*Austin Daily Democratic Statesman*, 31 July 1875; *Iredell Times*, 5 March 1976
James McCann	B	McLennan	31 Sept. 1876	Threatening to murder	Hanged and tortured by several men	*State of Texas v. Dublin, Cleaver, et al.*, case 2746, 19th District Court Case Files
Allen Bowen	W	Coryell	20 July 1877	Testifying against a white man	Unknown (found hanging from a tree)	*San Antonio Daily Express*, 28 July 1877

Name	Race	County, Area	Date	Crime	Size and Action of Mob (if Known)	Source(s)
Mart Horrell	W	Bosque	15 Dec. 1878	Murder and robbery	Shot by 100–300	*Galveston News*, 17 Dec. 1878
Tom Horrell	W	Bosque	15 Dec. 1878	Murder and robbery	Shot by 100–300	*Galveston News*, 17 Dec. 1878
Chaney	W	Coryell	15 Apr. 1883	Unknown	Unknown	Tuskegee Lynching Files
John O'Conner	W	Coryell	15 Apr. 1883	Unknown	Unknown	Tuskegee Lynching Files
Thomas Woods	W	Coryell	28 July 1883	Horse theft	Unknown	Tuskegee Lynching Files
Isaac (Zeke) Lady	B	Hill	24 June 1884	Rape	Taken from jail and hanged by mob of 300	*Whitney Messenger*, 27 June 1884
John Howard	W	Coryell	23 Aug. 1884	Arson	Unknown	Tuskegee Lynching Files
Sim Woods	B	McLennan	16 July 1885	Resisting arrest	Shot by posse of 3 men	*Waco Daily Examiner*, 16 July 1885
T. O. Polk	W	Coryell	15 Mar. 1886	Horse theft	Unknown	Tuskegee Lynching Files
Sidney Davis	B	Bosque	10 July 1886	Rape	Unknown	Tuskegee Lynching Files
Bill Harris	B	McLennan	4 Aug. 1886	Rape	Hanged by mob of hundreds	*Waco Day*, 4 Aug. 1886
William (Henry) Davis	B	McLennan	13 July 1889	Attempted rape	Hanged by mob of 100 men	*Waco Weekly Stock and Farm News*, 19 July 1889
Unknown	W	Hill	14 Dec. 1889	Murder and theft	Unknown	Tuskegee Lynching Files
Unknown	W	Hill	14 Dec. 1889	Murder and theft	Unknown	Tuskegee Lynching Files
Williams	B	Limestone	5 Apr. 1890	Rape	Taken from police, hung, and shot by a mob	*Waco Daily News*, 5 Apr. 1890
Unknown	B	Limestone	5 Apr. 1890	Rape	Unknown	Tuskegee Lynching Files
Unknown	B	Limestone	14 Aug. 1890	Rape	Unknown	Tuskegee Lynching Files
Unknown	B	Limestone	14 Aug. 1890	Rape	Unknown	Tuskegee Lynching Files
George Taylor	W	Falls	4 Jan. 1891	Murder	Unknown	*Waco Daily News*, 6 Jan. 1891
Charles Beall	B	Falls	2 Jan. 1891	Attempted murder	Hanged by a mob of 200	*Waco Weekly News*, 9 Jan. 1891

Name	Race	County, Area	Date	Crime	Size and Action of Mob (if Known)	Source(s)
Jasper Williams	W	Coryell	27 Feb. 1891	Unknown	Unknown	Tuskegee Lynching Files
Unknown	W	Coryell	27 Feb. 1891	Unknown	Unknown	Tuskegee Lynching Files
Unknown	W	Coryell	27 Feb. 1891	Unknown	Unknown	Tuskegee Lynching Files
Sheppard Monroe	W	Bell	28 May 1891	Unknown	Unknown	Tuskegee Lynching Files
Unknown	B	McLennan	26 Apr. 1892	Murder	Unknown	Tuskegee Lynching Files
George Williams	B	McLennan	14 June 1893	Rape	Possibly lynched by a black mob for rape of a young black girl	Dallas Morning News, 14 June 1893
Edward Cash	W	Coryell	11 Apr. 1894	Fence cutting	Hanged by 10	Waco Evening News, 11 Apr. 1894
Alfred Bren	B	Coryell	14 Apr. 1894	Unknown	Unknown	Tuskegee Lynching Files
Mary Phillips	B	Falls	20 July 1895	Murder	Murdered by group of men who exploded house with a bomb	Waco Post, 25 July 1895; Dallas Morning News, 21 July 1895
Hannah Phillips	B	Falls	20 July 1895	Murder	Murdered by group of men who exploded house with a bomb	Waco Post, 25 July 1895; Dallas Morning News, 21 July 1895
Abe Phillips Jr.	B	Falls	20 July 1895	Murder	Murdered by group of men who exploded house with a bomb	Waco Post, 25 July 1895; Dallas Morning News, 21 July 1895
Edward Phillips	B	Falls	20 July 1895	Murder	Murdered by group of men who exploded house with a bomb	Waco Post, 25 July 1895; Dallas Morning News, 21 July 1895
Benjamin Johnson a.k.a. Benjamin Harrison	B	Falls	20 July 1895	Murder	Murdered by group of men who exploded house with a bomb	Waco Post, 25 July 1895; Dallas Morning News, 21 July 1895
K. D. ("Kid") Taylor	B	Falls	20 July 1895	Murder	Murdered by group of men who exploded house with a bomb	Waco Post, 25 July 1895; Dallas Morning News, 21 July 1895

Name	Race	County, Area	Date	Crime	Size and Action of Mob (if Known)	Source(s)
Unknown	B	Falls	20 July 1895	Murder	Murdered by group of men who exploded house with a bomb	*Waco Post*, 25 July 1895; *Dallas Morning News*, 21 July 1895
Anderson Vaughn	B	McLennan	21 Aug. 1896	Competing against whites (whitecapping)	Shot by a "band of men" while asleep in house. Ten men indicted in 54th District Court	*Waco Weekly Tribune*, 22 Aug. 1896
Dave Cotton	B	Falls	13 May 1897	Rape	Taken from officers of the law and hanged by a mob of more than 100, some of whom were masked	*Dallas Morning News*, 16 May 1897
Berry Williams	B	Falls	13 May 1897	Rape	Taken from officers of the law and hanged by a mob of more than 100, some of whom were masked	*Dallas Morning News*, 16 May 1897
Sabe Stewart	B	Falls	13 May 1897	Rape	Taken from officers of the law and hanged by a mob of more than 100, some of whom were masked	*Dallas Morning News*, 16 May 1897
Wesley Johnson	B	Falls	27 Aug. 1897	Rape	Unknown	*Austin Daily Statesman*, 28 Aug. 1897
Sank Majors	B	McLennan	7 Aug. 1905	Rape	Hanged by a mob of 400	*Waco Weekly Tribune*, 12 Aug. 1905
Mitchell Frazier	B	Falls	15 Sept. 1906	Murder	Hanged by a group of white men	*Waco Weekly Tribune*, 19 Sept.1906; *Dallas Morning News*, 16 Sept. 1906
Lincoln Porter	B	Limestone	24 Apr. 1906	Entering room of white woman	Posse found Porter in a field and shot him	*Waco Semi-Weekly Tribune*, 28 Apr. 1906
Will Parker	B	Limestone	7 Jan. 1909	Assault	Unknown	Tuskegee Lynching Files
Coke Mills	B	Falls	20 Dec. 1909	Murder (city marshal presumed at time to have suffered mortal wound)	Taken from jail and hanged by a mob of 50	*Waco Semi-Weekly Tribune*, 22 Dec. 1909; *New York Age*, 3 Jan. 1910

Name	Race	County, Area	Date	Crime	Size and Action of Mob (if Known)	Source(s)
Henry Gentry	B	Bell	12 Jan. 1910	Murder and rape	Burned in downtown Belton by the posse that apprehended him	Montgomery Advertiser, 23 July 1910; Story of Bell County, 54–55[c]
Will Stanley	B	Bell	30 July 1915	Murder	Burned by mob estimated at 5,000	Waco Morning News, 31 July 1915
Jesse Washington	B	McLennan	15 May 1916	Murder	Burned and mutilated by mob of 15,000	SoRelle, "The 'Waco Horror,'"[f]
Elijah Hayes	B	McLennan	23 June 1917	Assault	Beaten to death with pieces of cordwood by dozens of men; 5 arrested	Waco Semi-Weekly Tribune, 27, 30 June, 17 July 1917
Robert Jefferson	B	Bell	29 June 1917	"No offense"	Unknown	Tuskegee Lynching Files
Gene Brown	B	Limestone	27 July 1918	Attempted rape	Hanged by mob of 150	Waco Times-Herald, 28 July 1918
Bragg Williams	B	Hill	30 Jan. 1919	Murder	Burned by mob numbering in the hundreds	Dallas Morning News, 21 Jan. 1919
Curley Hackney	W	McLennan	13 Jan. 1921	Rape	Hanged by 300	Waco Times-Herald, 14 Dec. 1921
Alexander Winn	B	Limestone	15 Aug. 1921	Rape	Unknown	Montgomery Advertiser, 17 Aug. 1921
Jesse Thomas	B	McLennan	26 May 1922	Murder and rape	Shot after capture by small posse, then burned by thousands	Waco Times-Herald, 26, 27 May 1922

Sources: a. James K. Green, ed., Buck Barry: Texas Ranger and Frontierman (Waco: Moody Texas Ranger Library, 1978).
b. Zelma Scott, A History of Coryell County, Texas (Austin: Texas State Historical Association, 1965).
c. C. L. Sonnichsen, Ten Texas Feuds (Albuquerque: University of New Mexico Press, 1957).
d. Bertha Atkinson, "History of Bell County," master's thesis, University of Texas at Austin, 1929.
e. E. A. Limmer Jr. et al., Bell County Historical Commission, Story of Bell County, Texas (Austin: Eakin Press, 1988).
f. James M. SoRelle, "'The Waco Horror': The Lynching of Jesse Washington," Southwestern Historical Quarterly 86 (1983): 517–36.

APPENDIX B

Unconfirmed Cases of Mob Violence in Central Texas, 1835–1922

Name	Race	County	Date	Crime	Size and Action of Mob	Source(s)
Unknown Tawakoni mother	IN	On Brazos River, central Tex.	July 1835	Resisting capture	Decapitated by posse of 18 men	Jenkins, *Recollections,* 24–26[a]
Unknown	IN	Central Tex.	Ca. 1836	Horse theft	Killed by posse of "10 to 12 whites"	Erath Papers[b]
Unknown	IN	Central Tex.	Ca. 1844	Horse theft	Killed by posse of "10 to 12 whites"	Erath Papers
Unknown	IN	Central Tex.	Ca. 1844	Horse theft	Killed by posse of "10 to 12 whites"	Erath Papers
Unknown	IN	Central Tex.	Ca. 1844	Horse theft	Killed by posse of "10 to 12 whites"	Erath Papers
Unknown	IN	Central Tex.	Early 1850s	Horse theft	Shot by a posse of ca. 29 men	*Story of Bell County,* 17–19[c]
Elderly Waco	IN	Brazos Reserve	April 1859	Resisting capture	Shot and scalped by white vigilantes	*Waco Southerner,* 8 June 1858; *Dallas Weekly Herald,* 1 June 1859
Unknown	W	Central Tex.	July 1860	Plotting slave rebellion	Hanged by parties unknown	Barry Papers,[d] 13, 23–25 July 1860
Unknown	W	Central Tex.	July 1860	Plotting slave rebellion	Hanged by parties unknown	Barry, 13, 23–25 July 1860
Unknown	W	McLennan	1865	Unknown	"Lynched in Waco"	*Dallas Morning News,* 9 Aug. 1905
Unknown	W	McLennan	1865	Unknown	"Lynched in Waco"	*Dallas Morning News,* 9 Aug. 1905
John Slimp	W	Bell	"Just after the Civil War"	Horse theft	Hanged by vigilance committee of 50 men	Smith, "Hanging of John Slimp"[e]
Unknown	IN	Coryell	1866	Attempted murder	Shot and scalped by mob of 30–40 men	Wilbarger, *Indian Depredations*[f]
Unknown	IN	Coryell	1866	Attempted murder	Shot and scalped by a mob of 30–40 men	Wilbarger, *Indian Depredations*

Name	Race	County	Date	Crime	Size and Action of Mob	Source(s)
Unknown	IN	Coryell	1866	Attempted murder	Shot and scalped by a mob of 30–40 men	Wilbarger, *Indian Depredations*
Unknown	IN	Coryell	1866	Attempted murder	Shot and scalped by a mob of 30–40 men	Wilbarger, *Indian Depredations*
Unknown	IN	Coryell	1866	Attempted murder	Shot and scalped by a mob of 30–40 men	Wilbarger, *Indian Depredations*
Unknown	IN	Coryell	1866	Attempted murder	Shot and scalped by a mob of 30–40 men	Wilbarger, *Indian Depredations*
Luke Adams	B	Bosque	1866	Unknown	Whipped to death	"Record of Criminal Offenses Committed in Texas, 1865–1869," RG 105, entry 66[g]
Henry Harding	B	Bosque	1866	Unknown	Whipped to death	"Record of Criminal Offenses Committed in Texas, 1865–1869," RG 105, entry 66
Unknown	W	Bell	3 Dec. 1866	Unknown	Shot by mob while lodged in Belton jail	*Harper's Weekly*, 23 May 1867, 184–85
Lewis Abby	B	Bosque	June 1867	Suing a white man	Called out of his house and shot by by 2. Four men led by E. J. Talley suspected.	Howard to Emerson[h]
Unknown	B	McLennan	Feb. 1868	Unknown	Shot. Four men led by E. J. Tally suspected.	Stiles to Richardson[i]
"Wild Bill" Miller	W	Coryell	2 Feb. 1869	Unknown	Killed by parties unknown	"Abstracts of Crimes Committed in Texas, 1869–1870," RG 393, pt. 1, entry 4855[j]

Name	Race	County	Date	Crime	Size and Action of Mob	Source(s)
John Calvin	B	McLennan	4 Feb. 1869	Unknown	Murdered by parties unknown	"Abstracts of Crimes Committed in Texas, 1869–1870," RG 393, pt. 1, entry 4855
Unknown	B	McLennan	15 Mar. 1869	Unknown	Murdered by unknown group of white men	"Abstracts of Crimes Committed in Texas, 1869–1870," RG 383 pt. 1, entry 4855
Unknown	B	McLennan	15 Mar. 1869	Unknown	Murdered by unknown group of white men	"Abstracts of Crimes Committed in Texas, 1869–1870," RG 393, pt. 1, entry 4855
Unknown	W	Missouri	July 1868	Being a Unionist	Tracked by group of men from Bell County and murdered	Galveston News, 10 July 1868
— Grundy	W	Falls	Late 1860s	Cattle theft	Hanged by vigilantes	Interview with J. H. Robertson[k]
— Heaton	W	Falls	Late 1860s	Dispute over purchase of cattle	Murdered by group of vigilantes led by Abner Walker	Interviews with Dean and Fowler[l]
John George	W	Northern Tex. (Denton County)	1869	Unknown	Hanged by band of at least 7 "desperate characters" from Hill County	Tex. State Police Records, Hill Co., entry 871[m]
William George	W	Northern Tex. (Denton County)	1869	Unknown	Hanged by band of at least 7 "desperate characters" from Hill County	Tex. State Police Records, Hill Co., entry 871
Unknown	IN	Bosque	1869	Trespassing and being a "marauder"	Killed by a "crowd of citizens"	Greer, ed., Buck Barry, 208–9[n]
Unknown	IN	Bosque	1869	Trespassing and being a "marauder"	Killed by a "crowd of citizens"	Greer, ed., Buck Barry, 208–9
Unknown	IN	Bosque	1869	Trespassing and being a "marauder"	Killed by a "crowd of citizens"	Greer, ed., Buck Barry, 208–9

Name	Race	County	Date	Crime	Size and Action of Mob	Source(s)
Unknown	IN	Bosque	1869	Trespassing and being a "marauder"	Killed by a "crowd of citizens"	Greer, ed., *Buck Barry*, 208–9
Unknown	IN	Bosque	1869	Trespassing and being a "marauder"	Killed by a "crowd of citizens"	Greer, ed., *Buck Barry*, 208–9
Unknown	IN	Bosque	1869	Trespassing and being a "marauder"	Killed by a "crowd of citizens"	Greer, ed., *Buck Barry*, 208–9
Milt Brothers	W	Central Tex., possibly McLennan Co.	late 19th cent. (1870s?)	Cattle theft	Hanged by vigilantes	Interview with Fowler[o]
Dickson	W	Banks of Brazos River	Aug. 1876	Inappropriate behavior toward a white woman	Hanged and tortured by 2 men	*Corpus Christi Daily Gazette*, 29 Aug. 1876
Unknown	W	Bell	Late 1870s	Unknown	Taken from jail, hanged	Atkinson, "History of Bell County," 133[p]
Unknown	B	Bell	Late 1870s	Unknown	Taken from jail, hanged	Atkinson, "History of Bell County," 133
Unknown	W	McLennan	ca. 1882	Horse theft	Hanged by parties unknown	Interview with May[q]
Unknown	B	McLennan	2 June 1883	Unknown	Strangled and shot by parties unknown	*Waco Daily Examiner*, 2 June 1883
Bob Hall	B	McLennan	July 1885	Attempting to escape	Shot; body never found	*Waco Daily Examiner*, 19 July 1885
Jim Kriner	B	McLennan	12 Sept. 1890	Threatening white man	Tenant farmer shot in dispute with landlord and landlord's son	*Waco Weekly Weekly Examiner*, 12 June 1895
Unknown 20-year-old	B	McLennan	12 June 1895	Unknown	Found dead near M.K.&T. depot	*Waco Morning News*, 12 June 1895
Unknown 15-year-old	B	McLennan	21 Jan. 1896	Unknown	Found dead on M.K.&T. tracks	*Waco Morning News*, Jan. 1896
Judge Triggs	B	McLennan	8 Oct. 1901	Unknown	Found dead on M.K.&T. tracks	*Waco Times-Herald*, 8 Oct. 1901

Unknown 45-year-old	B	McLennan	28 Dec. 1904	Unknown	Found dead "in the calaboose"	*Waco Times-Herald,* 28 Dec. 1904
Unknown	M	McLennan	30 Nov. 1904	Unknown	Found dead on the Texas Central railroad tracks	*Waco Times-Herald,* 30 Nov. 1904
Sam Henderson Henderson	B	McLennan	19 Mar. 1906	Unknown	Found dead near Cotton Bell Bridge, neck and shoulder broken	*Waco Times-Herald,* 19 Mar. 1906

Sources: a. John Holland Jenkins, *Recollections of Early Texas: The Memoirs of John Holland Jenkins,* ed. John Holmes Jenkins (Austin: University of Texas Press, 1958).

b. George Bernard Erath Papers, Center for American History, University of Texas at Austin.

c. E. A. Limmer Jr. et al., eds., *The Story of Bell County, Texas* (Austin: Eakin Press, 1988).

d. James Buckner Barry Papers, 1847–1917, Center for American History, University of Texas at Austin.

e. D. B. Smith, "The Hanging of John Slimp," *Frontier Times* (Aug. 1926): 36–38.

f. J. W. Wilbarger, *Indian Depredations in Texas* (Austin: Hutchings Printing House, 1889).

g. "Record of Criminal Offenses Committed in the State of Texas," Records of the Assistant Commissioner for the State of Texas, U.S. Bureau of Refugees, Freedmen, and Abandoned Lands, 1865–1860, National Archives (hereafter BRFAL).

h. "Letters Sent, Bosque County, Texas," RG 105, entry 3748, BRFAL.

i. "Letters Sent, McLennan County, Texas," RG 105, ledger 3781, BRFAL.

j. "Abstract of Crimes Committed in Counties of Texas and the Ninth Military District, 1865–1870," Office of Civil Affairs, Record of U.S. Army Continental Command, 1821–1920, RG 393, NA.

k. Interview with John H. Robertson, Manuscripts of the Federal Writer's Project, Manuscript Division, Library of Congress (MFWP).

l. Interviews with Leroy Dean and Mrs. George W. Fowler, MFWP.

m. Records of the Texas State Police, Archives Division, Texas State Library, Austin.

n. James K. Greer, ed., *Buck Barry: Texas Ranger and Frontiersman* (Waco: Moody Texas Ranger Library, 1978).

o. Interview with Mrs. George W. Fowler, MFWP.

p. Bertha Atkinson, "History of Bell County," master's thesis, University of Texas at Austin, 1929.

q. Interview with Dave May, MFWP.

Terms, Sources, and Methods

Lynching is understood as broad term "applied to various forms of summary punishment inflicted by self-appointed groups without regard to established legal procedures." The use of the word throughout American history has "been neither precise nor stable." By the 1830s lynching had "become synonymous with death at the hands of a mob."[1] The meaning of lynching, nevertheless, continued to fluctuate over the next century. Most important, the justifications used to defend lynching also shifted and vacillated over time. As this study demonstrates, these changes mattered. The frequency of lynching episodes, the chosen forms of execution, and the ethnic and racial character of lynching victims did not remain static.

This study attempts to chart these changes in lynching over an eighty-year period. Charting these transformations was helped, however, by classifying extralegal violence according to a single standard definition. This study employs the definition of lynching most commonly used by scholars and agreed upon by antilynching advocates in 1940. According to that definition, the following must occur for an episode to be classified as a lynching: there must be evidence that the victim died and that the victim died illegally at the hands of a group acting under the "pretext of service to justice, race, or tradition."[2]

Using the most frequently employed definition has not eliminated the difficulty of classifying lynching episodes. I have enumerated more than 180 possible lynching cases in seven central Texas counties. Distinguishing which cases merited inclusion on my list of lynching victims and which did not has caused me considerable angst. For a variety of reasons, I decided not to include more than sixty cases on the main list of victims found in Appendix A. I have excluded, for example, episodes involving Native Americans be-

cause of the military and wartime context that dominated Anglo-Indian relations in Texas. In other cases, specific details such as month and year, name
of victim, and place of execution remained too vague for me to include the
episode on the final list. These "unconfirmed" cases appear in Appendix B.
By including those victims who did not make the list, I hope to encourage
others to make their own determinations about what should and should not
be included. Undoubtedly, some will think that I should have moved some
of the victims from Appendix B to Appendix A. Others will think just the op-
posite. To facilitate future research, I have included the key source docu-
menting each lynching episode directly into the tables.

Scholarly examinations of lynching and racial violence often divide into
either state level surveys or individual case studies. I seek to chart the middle ground and examine lynching in a specific region within a state. The benefits of that approach include the ability to examine a larger time frame than
most lynching studies. This book traces the history of mob violence for more
than eighty years, whereas most works on lynching concentrate on a single
episode or the period from 1880 to 1920. The expanded time period was especially important in tracing the development of historical memory in central Texas, a process that occurs over generations. An additional advantage
of the region-within-a-state approach is immersion in the abundant primary
sources available at the county level. These rich sources allowed me to discover many more cases of lynching than traditional inventories had reported
earlier. More important, the wealth of primary sources allowed me better to
grasp how both local and national forces intersected patterns of mob violence.

The most important sources for this study are contemporary newspapers.
The strengths of newspaper records have been documented, but they are still
underused in studying nineteenth- and early-twentieth-century America. During this period, offices in the seven counties of central Texas routinely published dozens of daily and weekly newspapers. Most were printed in English,
but German- and Spanish-language newspapers also appeared. African Americans in central Texas published their own newspapers as well. Many local
county and town newspapers have disappeared, but scattered issues can still
be found and read profitably. To the best of my knowledge, I have read widely
in central Texas newspapers from the earliest surviving ones of the 1850s
through the 1920s. During this period, but especially before the 1870s when
surviving central Texas newspapers are scarce, I also read better-preserved
newspapers in Texas cities such as Austin, Dallas, and Galveston. For the years
after 1872, it becomes easier to focus on central Texas because of extant daily
newspapers published in Waco. For the era after 1930 and through the 1970s,
I read selectively and focused particularly on an African American weekly, the

Waco Messenger. Like all sources, newspaper records are flawed and must be used cautiously in conjunction with other documents; most reflect the racial views and perspectives of their Anglo owners and editors.

I have also emphasized oral interviews as a means of balancing these limitations. Although oral interviews are notoriously unreliable for specific dates and facts, they are one of the few alternatives available at many times for the voices of the poor and disenfranchised. Moreover, they are superb for analyzing historical memory and its impact on society. This study uses several different types of oral sources. First, I rely extensively on the irreplaceable oral interviews conducted by the Federal Writers' Project under the Works Progress Administration during the 1930s, when government agents interviewed hundreds of central Texans about their lives in the nineteenth century.

Texas is especially well represented in interviews conducted with former slaves. Although only one of more than a dozen states where interviews were conducted, Texas narratives fill eleven of the thirty-nine total volumes compiled by George P. Rawick. Equally important to the interviews with former slaves are interviews conducted with central Texas Anglos under the subject of "Pioneer Reminiscences." Although not compiled in bound volumes, the Manuscript Division of the Library of Congress holds 445 interviews conducted in Texas. Second, I have also read dozens and dozens of interviews with central Texans conducted by officials at Baylor University. The earliest of these interviews took place around 1920, but most date from the birth of Baylor's nationally renowned Institute for Oral History in the 1970s. Finally, I have conducted a dozen interviews myself for material primarily included in the Epilogue.

Local government records are a critical third category of sources. I consulted city directories, tax rolls, and probate minutes, but the most important documents were those associated with the central Texas court system. Beginning in 1851 when McLennan County was founded, court records provide an irreplaceable window onto violence and punishment in the region. Criminal minute books—simple chronological listings of court activities—are extant from this earliest period, but the corresponding case files—which contain rich materials such as grand jury indictments, depositions, testimonies, and motions by defense and prosecution—are less likely to have survived. Using both the minute books and case files, I have compiled a database of more than two thousand cases. For the period before 1875, I surveyed records in four counties: Bosque, Falls, Hill, and McLennan. Of those four, McLennan County was the only that preserved case files. For the period between 1875 and 1916, I restricted my research to a sampling of criminal court records preserved in McLennan County Archives in Waco, Texas. The records of the Nineteenth District Court, the Fifty-fourth District Court, and the Seventy-

fourth District Court primarily concern McLennan County, although juris-
dictions changed slightly over the forty-year period.

Documents from state and national government agencies also proved important. Appeals from central Texas courts to the Texas Court of Criminal
Appeals and the Texas State Supreme Court, for example, often contained useful information. Manuscript census returns, both those collected by the state
of Texas before annexation and those compiled by the Bureau of the U.S. Census from 1850 to 1930, provided valuable social, economic, and demographic
data. The records of the Texas State Police and the Bureau of Refugees, Freedmen, and Abandoned Lands were absolutely critical for the turbulent era of
the Civil War and Reconstruction. The reports filed by the local agents for the
Freedmen's Bureau were especially revealing of the period's lawlessness and
violence. Correspondence and petitions to the Office of the Governor were
yet another significant source of information about central Texas. These documents were especially helpful before the 1870s, an era from which there are
few extant local newspapers.

Finally, archival manuscript sources were consulted. Given the relatively
limited geographic area of the study, such sources proved elusive. The two
best places to find collections of letters, diaries, and other unpublished records
about central Texas are the Texas Collection of Baylor University in Waco and
the Texas State Library and Archives in Austin. The archival holdings of the
Center for American History at the University of Texas at Austin were also
very constructive. Some of the most important archival holdings, however,
are located outside Texas entirely. Two depositories hold essential materials
on lynching: the Papers of the National Association for the Advancement of
Colored People at the Library of Congress in Washington, D.C., and the lynching files of the Tuskegee University Archives in Tuskegee, Alabama. In addition, I have found that numerous archives throughout the South—especially
the Southern Historical Collection at the University of North Carolina, the
Special Collections of Duke University, and the South Caroliniana Library
of the University of South Carolina—hold correspondence from men and
women in Texas writing to relatives in the southeastern states. The Bancroft
Library of the University of California is also an untapped resource for regional history. Men selling the historical works of Hubert Howe Bancroft interviewed the hundreds of individuals throughout the United States who purchased Bancroft's books. The transcriptions of these life history "dictations"
are arranged by state and county and preserved in Berkeley, California. For
a more comprehensive listing of works consulted, see the bibliography to my
dissertation "Between South and West: Race, Class, and Power in Central
Texas, 1836–1916," Emory University, 1999.

A final word about sources and geography. Central Texas, as defined in the introduction, can be found north of Austin, south of Dallas, and stretching from east to west from the Trinity River to the edge of the Plains. This study emphasizes particular parts of that expansive territory. In order to maintain focus and limit the amount of research, I focus on seven counties at the heart of the region: Bell, Bosque, Coryell, Falls, Hill, Limestone and McLennan. At times, the focus narrows to Bosque, Falls, Hill, and McLennan counties. At other times, attention shifts solely to McLennan County and the city of Waco. This narrowing of focus, which occurs increasingly throughout the course of the text, is a function of surviving sources and shifting population. McLennan County and the city of Waco become increasingly populous and therefore important in central Texas during the eighty years of this study. McLennan County also possesses the most complete set of newspapers and government records of any central Texas county. Finally, it is a diverse place, which, if forced to choose, mirrors greater central Texas better than any other single county in the region.

Index

Abrams, Seymour, 123
Adams, Luke, murder of, 122
Adam, William H., disappearance of, 94
African Americans: memories by, of racial violence, 14; restrictions of, under Texas law, 21–22; among first American settlers in Texas, 34, 47, 49–50, 66; in the Panic of 1860, 49, 79–80; as runaway slaves, 51–61, 226n; relationship with Native Americans, 57–61, 74–75, 227n–29n; as alleged rapists or would-be-rapists, 75, 78, 147–48; as victims of rape, 112; as victims of robbery and property destruction, 112, 134; as victims of racial violence, 112–15, 120–23, 132, 135–37, 141, 150, 170, 184–87, 196, 198–200; reasons for violence against, during Reconstruction, 116, 121, 124–25; and Juneteenth, 117, 182; and voting, 124–26, 130, 138–39, 143–44; and ideology of self-help, 127; and schools during Reconstruction, 127–28; and churches during Reconstruction, 127–28; participation in the Texas State Police, 129, 144; changing attitudes toward, 133, 181–83; as victims of white-capping, 134, 164–65; changes in life of, during late nineteenth century, 142–48; as landowners, 144–45; and central Texas judicial system, 146–48, 166–68; and self-defense, 154–60; out-migration from central Texas, 170–74; compared with Mexicans in central Texas, 177–79; residential segregation of, 179–80; disfranchisement of, 180–

81; and the growth of black community in Waco, 181; and the historical memory of Jesse Washington, 198–206; and the historical memory of Jesse Thomas, 198–206; and Waco tornado, 202–6; importance of religion for, 203–4; and the psychological toll of living under Jim Crow, 259n–60n. *See also* emancipation; labor disputes; National Association for the Advancement of Colored People; rebellions, slave; resistance; sharecropping; slavery; women
Alamo, the, 21, 23, 29, 74
Alcantra, Ramon, murder of, 177
annexation of Texas, 17, 22–23; as desired by Americans, 19, 214n; and stereotyping of Mexicans, 27–28; impact of, on Anglo-Indian conflict, 40–41; population growth and, 50, 66; and abolitionist movement, 71
Austin, Gebe, murder of, 133
Austin, Moses, 18
Austin, Stephen F., 18, 20–21, 33, 74
Austin, Texas, 26; and forced expulsion of Mexicans, 29; public meeting regarding Mexicans and slaves, 73; in Panic of 1860, 77

Barnard, George, 55–56, 66–67, 227n
Barry, James Buckner ("Buck"): and memoir, 45; historical marker, 46; and fugitive slave named Peter, 67; and Panic of 1860, 78; and first lynchings of Anglos in central Texas, 82–83
Beall, Charles, 158–59

Bell County: groups of Indian fighters in, 36; Bird Creek Battlefield marker in, 46; and Panic of 1860, 78; lynchings in, 84–85, 92, 94–95; violence against Unionists in, 92–95; and Albert Parsons, 101–2; historical marker in, 105. *See also* Belton; Temple

Belton: and *Belton Independent*, 42; 1874 lynching at town jail, 84–85; 1866 lynching at the town jail, 94–95; historical marker in, 105; intimidation of black voters in, 124; mob violence against Mexican in, 177; and lynching of Henry Gentry, 184–85; mentioned, 9

Bennett, J. N., 142, 153

Bishop, James, murder of, 94

Bolton, Harrell, murder of, 198

Bosque County: petition for protection against Indians, 41; and James Buckner Barry, 45, 67; criminal court in, 69; murder of Unionists in, 78; lynching of Covington in, 82; murder and violence in, 85, 95, 121–22; suspension of courts in, during Civil War, 90; vigilance committee established in, 90; lynchings in, 102–3; resistance to emancipation in, 117; and Mexican immigrants, 174

Brann, William Cowper, 135

Brazos Indian reservation: creation of, 41; as source of frustration for white settlers, 41–42; attack by white settlers, 42; closed down, 43; importance of, for history of mob violence in Texas, 43, and Alison Nelson, 46

Brinkley, Asa, murder of, 136, 254n

Brothers, Milt, lynching of, 104

Brown, John: influence in Texas of Harpers Ferry raid, 48, 88

Brown, Richard Maxwell, 236n

Burney, Harris, 136

Burney, Tom, 151

Burton, John, murder of, 89, 91

Butts, Miles, killing of, 141

Caballo, Juan, 72

Caddos, 33, 37, 42

Calhoun, John C., 27

California Gold Rush: as influence on Texan attitudes toward mob violence, 24, 28; participation in, by central Texans, 215n

Callahan, James, 72, 231n, 233n–234n

"Camp Safety," 92

"Cart War," 29

Cash, Edward, lynching of, 108

Cazneua, Jane McManus Storm, 212n, 216n

central Texas: reasons for study of, 7; definition of, 8, 299; early Mexican settlers in, 28–30; as home to taverns, brothels, and gambling houses, 35; as home to historical markers celebrating Indian fighting, 46; population increase before Civil War, 50, 66; characteristics of, enhancing slave flight, 59–61; first lynchings of Anglos in, 82–83; collapse of local economy in, after Civil War, 95–96; persistence rate of population from 1860 to 1870, 96–97; as scene of excessive violence during Reconstruction, 116; compared to other parts of South after Civil War, 123; struggle for political control over, during Reconstruction, 125; occupied by U.S. Army, 128; changing character of mob violence in, 132–33; support for lynching blacks in, 133, 140, 150–53; racial violence in, during late nineteenth century, 134–37, 141–42, 151–52, 158–60; out-migration of African Americans from, 170–74; in-migration of Mexicans to, 174–79; growth of virulent anti-black prejudice in, 181–83; in relation to rest of South and the United States, 187; attitudes toward extralegal violence and the law, 252n

Cherokees, 33, 37, 56, 58

children: endangered by Native Americans, 33, 40, 44, 83, 91; of slaves separated from parents, 52; endangered by rebellious slaves and abolitionists, 78–79; as participants in mob violence, 79; mob violence against, 122, 128, 135, 160; education for, of African Americans, opposed, 127–28; murder of, 185

Christian, James, murder of, 94

civic leader opposition to lynching: in Waco, 13–14, 196–98. *See also* legal prosecution of lynchers

Coacoochee (Wild Cat), 72

Cobb, Stephen, 126–27, 131

Coke, Richard: and the Panic of 1860, 77; election as governor, 105, 131; and "Redemption" of Texas, 131; in historical memory, 137–39; as example of postwar persistence of elite, 143; and George Clark, 156; and Pat Neff, 196

Cole, W. F., 183

Colorado County: forced explusion of Mexicans in, 29, 73; and slave plot of 1856, 75

Comanches, 33, 37, 58
Confederate Army: volunteers for, 89; soldiers from, and escape of Charles Warren, 89; man forced to join, 91; deserters from, 91–92; and lynching of deserters, 92
Confederate States of America: disloyalty toward, as a justification for mob violence, 82, 86, 89–92; Texas and, 88; problems with criminal court system under, 89–91; opposition to, during Civil War, 91–92; confiscation of property of, 99
Cooper, Madison, 194–95
Coryell County: and hanging of Allen Bowen, 85; and secession crisis, 88; and lynching of Edward Cash, 108; mob violence in, 132
Cotton, Giles, 65, 126
criminal courts, central Texas. *See* judicial system
Crunk, Wendall, 207–8
Covington, —, lynching of, 82–83

Daura, Minnie, 110
Davis, David F., 100, 125, 131, 155
Davis, E. J., 97, 99, 125, 129, 131
Davis, Henry, lynching of, 141, 152, 158
Davis, Perry, hanging of, 147
de Cordova, Jacob, 86
Delony, Lewis, 193–94
Denkins, Mary, 202–3, 206
Democratic Party: as the party of white conservatives in postbellum central Texas, 82, 105; and "Redemption" of Texas, 131; African American participation in, 156
desertion: from Confederate Army, 91–92
Dickson, —, murder of, 85
Dixon, Simpson ("Dixie"), 123
Douglass, Frederick, 71, 259n
Doyle, J. W. P., murder of, 96
Du Bois, W. E. B. (William Edward Burghardt), 191, 204, 208

Escott, Paul, 52, 62
Emancipation: and "Juneteenth," 117; resistance to, by slaveholders, 117; actions of freedpeople after learning of, 119–20
Ensor, Eli, murder of, 90

Falls County: early Mexican pioneers in, 28; as home of John Marlin, 46; and fugitive slaves, 55, 62, 67; criminal court in, 69–71; violence against Unionists in, 94; migra-

tion of outlaws to, 96; formation of Civil War veteran's society in, 103; sharecropping in, 119–20; mob violence in, 123, 158–60, 170; whitecappers in, 134, 158; black self-defense in, 158; and Mexican immigrants, 174. *See also* Marlin, Texas
Farmer's Improvement Bank, 173–74
"Fishbackers" (gang), 123
Ford, J. O., 157
Frazier, Mitchell, lynching of, 170
Freeman, Elisabeth, 191, 193–94
frontier, role of: in encouraging mob violence, 12, 183, 187; and the Panic of 1860, 48, 79; influence on slave flight and resistance, 50–61; influence on slave-master relations, 64–66; and the defense of white-on-white lynching, 82, 106–7; definition of, 223n; mentioned, 7
Fryer, Lucy, murder of, 1, 201

Garner, John, lynching of, 82–83
Gentry, Henry, lynching of, 184–85
Gibson, Lester, 207–8
Gildersleeve, Fred, photographs of, 2, 6
Goliad, 29, 74
Gomez, Antonio, lynching of, 175
Grant, U.S., 144
Greenback Party, 155
Groesbeck, 129, 135, 170
"G.T.T." (gone to Texas), 25, 215n
Guerra, Juan Chapa, lynching of, 29

Hackney, Curley, lynching of, 108–11
Hadley, Zeke, lynching of, 151
Hall, Bob, disappearance of, 133
Hall, Ida Leggett, 123
Hamilton, A. J., 125
Harris, Bill, lynching of, 141, 152
Hayes, Rutherford B. 144
Hays, Demetrius, murder of, 90
Hays, Elijah, lynching of, 196
Heaton, —, murder of, 104
Hill County: settlement stymied by Native Americans, 37; slavery in, 65; violence against Unionists in, 94, 96; outlaws in, 95; formation of Civil War veteran's society in, 103; and Reconstruction, 130; whitecappers in, 135; lynchings in, 151, 185. *See also* Hillsboro
Hillsboro, 1, 9, 103, 124, 151, 187
Horse, John. *See* Caballo, Juan
Houston, Sam, 21, 37, 39

interracial unions: between Native American man and black woman, 58; between Mexican man and black woman, 71; between white man and black woman; 90; between white woman and black man, 150. *See also* Parsons, Albert
Ish, William, 142

Jackson, Conrad, hanging of, 147
Jackson, John, murder of, 136
Johnson, Lawrence, 207–8
Johnson, Wesley, lynching of, 132, 163
Johnson, William R., and indictment for murder, 90
Jones, Churchill, 61–62, 64
Jones, Jesse, hanging of, 172–73
judicial system in central Texas: influenced by mob violence, 13, influence on mob violence, 14; criminal court of McLennan County, 35, 69, 71, 89–90; and slavery, 68–71; inability of, to prosecute for extralegal violence, 42–43, 82, 129; opposed by elites during Reconstruction, 97–102; increasing efficiency of, 106–8, 247n; expanded role in punishing blacks after Civil War, 118, 247n; black participation in, during Reconstruction, 126; influence on historical memory of mob violence, 139–42; and African Americans, 146–48, 157, 166–68, 172–74; changing treatment of sexual assault, 150; anger with treatment of African American criminals by, 167–69; mistreatment of Mexicans by, 178. *See also* legal prosecution of lynchers; local authorities

Karankawas, 33
Kealing, H. T., 157
King, Will, 166–69
Ku Klux Klan, 96, 124–25, 138–39, 142, 194, 197

labor disputes: during Reconstruction, 120–21; during late nineteenth century, 156–57, 160, 164–65
Lamar, Mirabeau B., 38
Ledwell, — , lynching of, 102
"legal lynchings," 147, 172–73, 257n–58n
legal prosecution of lynchers: in case of Demetrius Hays, 90; in case of Eli Ensor, 90; in case of Edward Cash, 108; in case of Curley Hackney, 109–11; in case of Anderson Vaughn, 164–65; in case of Elijah Hays, 196

Limestone County: Anglo-Indian violence in, 38; plot involving fugitive slaves in, 73, 76; intimidation of black voters in, 128–29; shooting of black soldier in, 130; mob violence in, 132, 135, 170, 177; historical marker in, 244n. *See also* Cotton, Giles; Trammell, Meritt
Lincoln, Abraham, 79, 88–90
Lindley, Jasper, murder of, 94
Lindley, Jonathan and Newton, lynchings of, 94–95
local authorities: tolerance of lynching, 13–14, 42–43, 97–102; opposition to lynching, 14, 163–64; opposition to white-on-white lynching, 105–11. *See also* judicial system in central Texas
Long, Roden, 158
lynching: new approaches to the study of, 7–8; definition of, 10, 31–32, 295–96; as reinforced in central Texas by Anglo-Indian conflict, 32–33, 44; and Panic of 1860, 48, 78; reasons for, of Anglos, 81–82; reasons given for, by mobs killing Anglos, 84–85, 106–7, 132–33; difficulty of compiling statistics on, 85, 133–34, 210n, 252n–54n; and secession, 88; and Civil War, 88–92; and Reconstruction, 92–102; decline of, of whites, 106–11, 132; of blacks in central Texas, 113–15, 132, 136–37, 141, 150, 170, 184–87, 196, 198–200; 254n; as public "spectacle," 113–14, 184; comparison of patterns of, between whites and blacks, 114–15; chronology of, 115; changing patterns of, in central Texas, 132–33, 139–40, 142–43, 160–61; reasons for, during late nineteenth century, 137–61; decline of, in central Texas, 163–64, 189–98; threats to commit, 167; of Mexicans in central Texas, 177–78; influence of national and regional stories on, in central Texas, 183–84; influence of technological change on, 184; cases of, averted, 196. *See also* vigilance committees; vigilantism; whitecapping

"manifest destiny," 27, 32, 40, 45, 219n
Marlin, James, 37
Marlin, John, 35, 38, 46
Marlin, Texas, 85, 94, 151, 158
masculinity: and the protection of women and children, 27, 33, 40, 44, 75, 78–79, 83, 91, 108–10, 148–49, 160–61; and lynching, 142, 168

Mason, William, 129–30
Matthews, John, 158
McCarty, Andrew: and killing of Asa Brinkley, 136; conviction of, 254n
McCormick, John, murder of, 93
McLennan County: lynchings in, 1–7, 84, 90–91, 108–11, 141, 152, 162–63, 192, 198–99; criminal court in, 35, 69, 71, 89–90, 107–8, 118, 146–48, 173; and fugitive slaves, 55; and free persons of color, 68; and Panic of 1860, 77; violence against Unionists in, 81, 94; crime in, 93; persistence rate of population, 1860–70, 96–97; and violence during Reconstruction, 112, 116, 120–21, 123, 128; success of Republican Party in, 125; African American participation in county government, 126; establishment of black churches and schools, 127–28; racial violence in, 133–37; whitecappers in, 134, 164–65; postwar persistence of elite in, 143, 255n–56n; black landownership patterns in, 145; third parties in, 155–56; resistance to mob violence by blacks in, 158; and the Will King case, 165–68; mural in county courthouse, 207; reasons for focus on, 209n, 299. *See also* Waco
McRae, Thaddeus, 88
Majors, Sank, lynching of, 162–63, 168–69, 171, 271n
Medlock, David, 126
Meinig, D. W., 8
memory, cultural, 12
memory, historical: as an explanation for central Texas's culture of violence, 7–8; definition and discussion of, 10–12; overview of, 14–15; of early Texas history, 17–18, 30, 219n; of violence against Native Americans, 31; of Indian fighters, 44–47, 222n; and slave resistance, 73–74; and white-on-white vigilantism, 82, 103–5; role of, in racial violence of Reconstruction, 113, 131; of Richard Coke, 137–39; importance of, in return of racial violence, 169; and Mexicans in central Texas, 177–78; and central Texas's culture of violence, 187; of Jesse Washington, 189–206; of Jesse Thomas, 198–206; of Waco tornado, 202–6; and place of Mexicans in central Texas history, 207; and place of Native Americans in central Texas history, 208. *See also* memory, cultural
Mexia, 132

Mexican army: entry into Texas, 21; victory at Alamo, 21; defeat at Battle of San Jacinto, 21; in U.S.-Mexican War, 23; Anglo attitudes toward soldiers in, 27; runaway slaves and, 53–54
Mexicans: as allies of Anglos in Texas independence movement, 21; ethnic and racial stereotyping of, 21, 23, 26–29, 177; abandoning central Texas, 28–30; forced removal from Texas communities, 29, 73, 75; mob violence against, 29, 175–77; blame for slave resistance, 49, 73–74; as victims of whitecapping, 135; migration to central Texas, 174–75; mob violence in south Texas and, 175–76; labor of, desired by central Texans, 176–77; treatment of, in central Texas, 177–79; compared to African Americans, 177–79; as abettors to fugitive slaves, 226n, 234n; mentioned, 8, 13, 14, 19, 99, 148, 207. *See also* Mexico
Mexico: independence from Spain, 18; tensions with American colonists in Texas, 19–24; as destination for fugitive slaves, 52–57; illegal crossings into, to capture fugitive slaves, 72–73; mentioned 14, 94. *See also* Mexican army; Mexicans
Milam, Benjamin, 34, 53
Miller, Sam, murder of, 94
Mills, Coke, lynching of, 170
Mitchell, William, killing of, 166
mob violence. *See* vigilantism
Moffat, historical marker in, 103–4
Montejano, David, 210n
Mullens, Shepard, 126–27
murder: as justification for lynching, 85; frequency of, during Reconstruction, 116; punishment of, by central Texas courts, 173. *See also* lynching; vigilantism

National Association for the Advancement of Colored People (NAACP), 14; investigations of Jesse Washington lynching, 6, 191, 193–94; and anti-lynching campaign, 154; growth of branches in central Texas, 181; and investigation into Bragg Williams lynching, 187; and Waco branch, 204–5
Native Americans: in early central Texas, 32–33; resistance of, to American settlers, 34, 36–37; treaty negotiations with, 37–40; germ warfare used against, 38; rights to land disputed, 39–40; ethnic and racial stereotyping of, 40, 219n; and fugitive

slaves, 56–61, 74–75, 227n–29n; and "bad
white men," 83; mentioned, 7, 8, 13, 14, 22,
148, 149, 207, 295–96. *See also* Caddos; Comanches; Karankawas; Tonkawas; Wichitas
Neff, Pat, 196
Neighbors, Robert, murder of, 43

Oliver, John W., 97–98, 104–5, 146
Olmsted, Frederick Law, 25–26, 29, 54–55, 73,
79–80
O'Sullivan, John, 17, 212n

Panic of 1860, 48–49, 76–80; historiography
of, 222n–23n
Parsons, Albert: joins Confederacy, 101; as
Radical Republican, 101; attempted lynch-
ing of, 102; marriage to Lucy Gathings,
102; historical memory of, in central
Texas, 104; move to Chicago, 105; execu-
tion of, 105; reaction to collapse of
Reconstruction, 131
Parsons, William H.: and Panic of 1860,
77–78; and Albert Parsons, 101
Phillips, Abe, 160
Phillips, Mary, lynching of, 160, 165
Phillips, Wesley, 160
Polk, James K., 23
Populist Party, 155–56
Porter, Lincoln, lynching of, 170
Porvenir massacre, 176
Prohibition Party, 155

Quantrill, William C., 103

racial stereotypes. *See* subheadings under
African Americans; Mexicans; Native
Americans
Radford, Garry Hamilton, 197
Rangel, Jesús M., 175
Ranke, Leopold von, 11
rape: alleged danger of, by Mexican soldiers,
27, 148; alleged danger of, by Native
Americans, 33, 40, 44, 83, 91, 148–49;
alleged danger of, by African Americans,
75, 78–79, 113–14, 149; as cause for lynching whites, 85, 109, 153; punishment for by
courts before 1890, 107; punishment for
after 1890, 108; role of class and status of
alleged rapist in punishment, 109–10; role
of class and status of alleged victim in
punishment, 110; of black women, 112,
122; as cause for lynching blacks, 114,

149–53, 162, 168, 198–99; punishment by
castration, 122; punishment by whipping,
122; changing attitudes toward, 147–53,
160–61; importance of, as justification for
lynching, 168
rebellions, slave: evidence for and against,
48–49; worries over by Texans, 53, 74–80;
plots of 1856, 75–76
refugee slaveholders, 118–19
Republican Party: fear of victory by, in 1860,
79, 88; opposed with violence, 81, 93–97,
124–25; policies of, that angered central
Texans, 98–102; historical memory of,
104; success of, in central Texas, 125; fall
from power, 131; black participation in,
after Reconstruction, 155
resistance to white majority: by racial, ethnic, and political minorities, 13; by Native
Americans, 34, 36–37; by slaves, 49–62; by
Unionists, 88–102; by African Americans
after Reconstruction, 153–60, 164; histori-
ography of, by African Americans after
Reconstruction, 154, 259n; as spur to
twentieth-century racial violence, 169;
historiography of, by slaves, 224n; defini-
tion of, by slaves, 225n
Rhodes, Norville, 123
Robinson, Lee, 147–48, 168
Roediger, David, 102
Rose, Jesse, murder of, 94
Rose, Willie Lee, 63
Ross, Lawrence Sullivan, 103
Ross, Shapley P., 36, 47; memoir of, 45
Russell, Henry, lynching of, 91
Russell, J. T., lynching of, 91

San Antonio 8–9, 22
Sanchez, Luis, 30
San Jacinto, Battle of, 21
Santa Anna, Gen. Antonio, 20–21, 53,
213n–14n
Santayana, George, 11
Scott, Judge Samuel R., 164–68
sexual assault. *See* rape
sharecropping, 119–20, 144–45
slave patrols, 13, 24; establishment of in Falls
County, 67; establishment of in Waco, 67
slavery: role in encouraging mob violence,
12–13, 49; early development in Texas,
19–22, 49–50, 213n; and problem of runaway slaves, 51–61; and punishment of
slaves, 62–64; and paternalism, 63–66,

116–17; 229n–231n; intellectual defense of, 63; regulation of, by Texas law, 68–71; extralegal actions in defense of, 72–79; support of, by nonslaveholders, 86–88. *See also* Panic of 1860; rebellions, slave; refugee slaveholders; resistance to white majority; slave patrols
Smith, A. T., 201
Smith, Robert Lloyd, 173–74, 263n
Smithwick, Noah, 56–57
Smith, Willie Long, 199–201
Spain, 18; slavery in American colonies of, 19; and the "Black Legend," 26
Stanley, Will, lynching of, 185–87
Stephenson, John C., 183
Stevens, John, 153
Sublett, L. M., 156

Taylor, George, murder of, 159
Teixeria, Antonia, 109–10
Temple, 9, 185–87
Texas: independence from Mexico, 7, 20–21, 217n; American colonization of, 18–21; perceptions of, 24–26, 123; population increase before Civil War, 50; study of vigilantism and lynching in, by scholars, 236n, 240n
Texas army: victory at San Jacinto, 21; size increase by Mirabeau B. Lamar, 38
Texas Cotton Palace (Waco), 46
Texas Rangers, 23–24, 26; authorization to patrol central Texas, 37; Hall of Fame Museum in Waco, 46; and Mexicans, 175–76
Texas State Police: establishment of, 129; as source of frustration for white majority, 129; and "Waco Riot," 129–30; attacks upon, 130
Texas Troubles. *See* Panic of 1860
theft, livestock: as justification for lynching whites, 84–85; as justification for lynching blacks, 114
Thelen, David, 11
Thomas, Jesse, murder of, 192, 198–206
Thompson, C. M., 144
Throckmorton, J. W., 83
Tinsley, C. J.: as witness for Charles Warren, 89; and lynching of Wood, 91; lynching of, 91
Tonkawas, 32–33
tornado, Waco, 202–6
Tornel y Mendívil, José María, 17
Trammell, Meritt, 104, 128–29

Travis, William, 20, 23
Tucker, — , lynching of, 82–83
Turner, Frederick Jackson, 12

United States Magazine and Democratic Review, 17, 27. *See also* Cazneua, Jane McManus Storm; O'Sullivan, John
Upper Brazos river valley. *See* central Texas
U.S. Army: welcome by Texans, 22, 41; Anglo Texans and, 23; victory in U.S.-Mexican War, 23; Tejanos in, 30; role of, in conquest of central Texas, 36; and defense of Brazos Indian Reservation, 42; importance of, during Reconstruction, 92–94, 118, 128; killing of soldiers and former soldiers from, 94, 103–4, 130; and Lindley case, 94–95; reports of, regarding violence in central Texas, 116; in "Waco Riot," 130; and capture of Jesús M. Rangel, 175
U.S.-Mexican War, 1846–48, 23, 29

Vaughn, Anderson, murder of, 164–65
vigilance committees, 29; and Panic of 1860, 48–49; and slave plots in Texas, 74–80; and lynching whites, 82–83; and secession, 88; during Civil War, 88–92; and Reconstruction, 120–21
vigilantism: impact on historical memory, 7, 30; in vernacular of central Texans, 10; attitudes toward, prior to settlement in Texas, 24–26; perceived need for, in Texas, 26; and Mexicans, 29; and Anglo-Indian conflict in central Texas, 32–33, 36, 44; and Brazos Indian reserve, 41–43; against Native Americans, 42–43; and Panic of 1860, 48–49, 78; reasons for, against Anglos, 81–82; reasons for, according to vigilantes, 84–85, 106–7, 132–33; difficulty of distinguishing from murder, 85; and secession, 88; and Civil War, 88–92; and Reconstruction, 92–102; decline of, against whites, 106–11, 133; against blacks in central Texas after Civil War, 113–14, 120–23, 132, 135, 164–65, 198–200. *See also* Austin, Texas; Colorado County; lynching; vigilance committees; whitecapping
voting and politics, 87, 124–26, 130, 138–39, 143–44, 154–56. *See also* African Americans; Texas

Waco: lynchings in, 1–7, 108–11, 162–63, 192, 198–99; importance of, 9, 66–67, 299; as

Indian village, 33–34, 37; escape of fugitive slaves from, 55; slave patrol in, 67; in Panic of 1860, 77–78; reputation for lawlessness, 95; conditions of, after Civil War, 95; killing of African Americans in, 121, 135, 141–42; and "Waco Riot," 129–30; conditions for African Americans in, 145–46; praise for treatment of African Americans, 168; population growth of, 170; out-migration of African Americans from, 170–74; in-migration of Mexicans to, 174–79; growth of residential segregation in, 179–80; disfranchisement movements in, 180–81; growth of black community in, 181; reaction to Jesse Washington lynching in, 189–206
Waldrep, Christopher, 10, 252n
Warren, Charles, 89, 91
Washington, Jesse, lynching of, 1–7; photographs of, 2–5; place of lynching, in history of racial violence, 6; residents of central Texas and event, 6–7; as turning point in central Texas race relations, 14, 115, 189; as climactic moment in history of lynching in central Texas, 140, 163, 185; historical memory of, by whites, 189–98; historical memory of, by blacks, 198–206
Watkins, Matt, 135

Weatherford, W. D., 31
whitecapping, 10; distinguished from lynching, 134; victims of, 135, 164–65; causes of, 135–36. *See also* lynching; vigilantism
"whiteness," 83
Wichitas: Kichais, 32; Taovayas, 32; Tawakonis, 32–34, 37–38; Wacos, 32–34, 37, 46; Wichita proper, 32
Wigfall, Louis T., 35
Wild Cat. *See* Coacoochee
"Wilkerson's Valley Raid," 31
Williams, Bragg, lynching of, 185, 192
Wilson, James, murder of, 135
Wilson, Thomas, murder of, 122
women: opinions of, on life in Texas, 25, 64, 84, 104; endangered by kidnappers and rapists, 27, 33, 40, 44, 75, 78–79, 83, 91, 108–10; as victims of mob violence, 38, 95, 112, 128, 132, 135, 137, 160, 165; as fugitive slaves, 53; and Panic of 1860, 78–79; and Reconstruction, 112, 121–22; of African descent and the "double burden," 122; changing attitudes toward sexual assault against, 148–53. *See also* rape
Wood, — , lynching of, 90–91
Wood, — , lynching of, 102
Woods, Sim, killing of, 141–42, 157
Wright, George C., 147

WILLIAM D. CARRIGAN, born and raised in Texas, holds a Ph.D. in history from Emory University and now lives in New Jersey, where he is an assistant professor of history at Rowan University. He continues to be drawn to the study of mob violence and is collaborating with Clive Webb of the University of Sussex on a history of extralegal violence and Mexicans in the United States.

The University of Illinois Press
is a founding member of the
Association of American University Presses.

University of Illinois Press
1325 South Oak Street
Champaign, IL 61820-6903
www.press.uillinois.edu